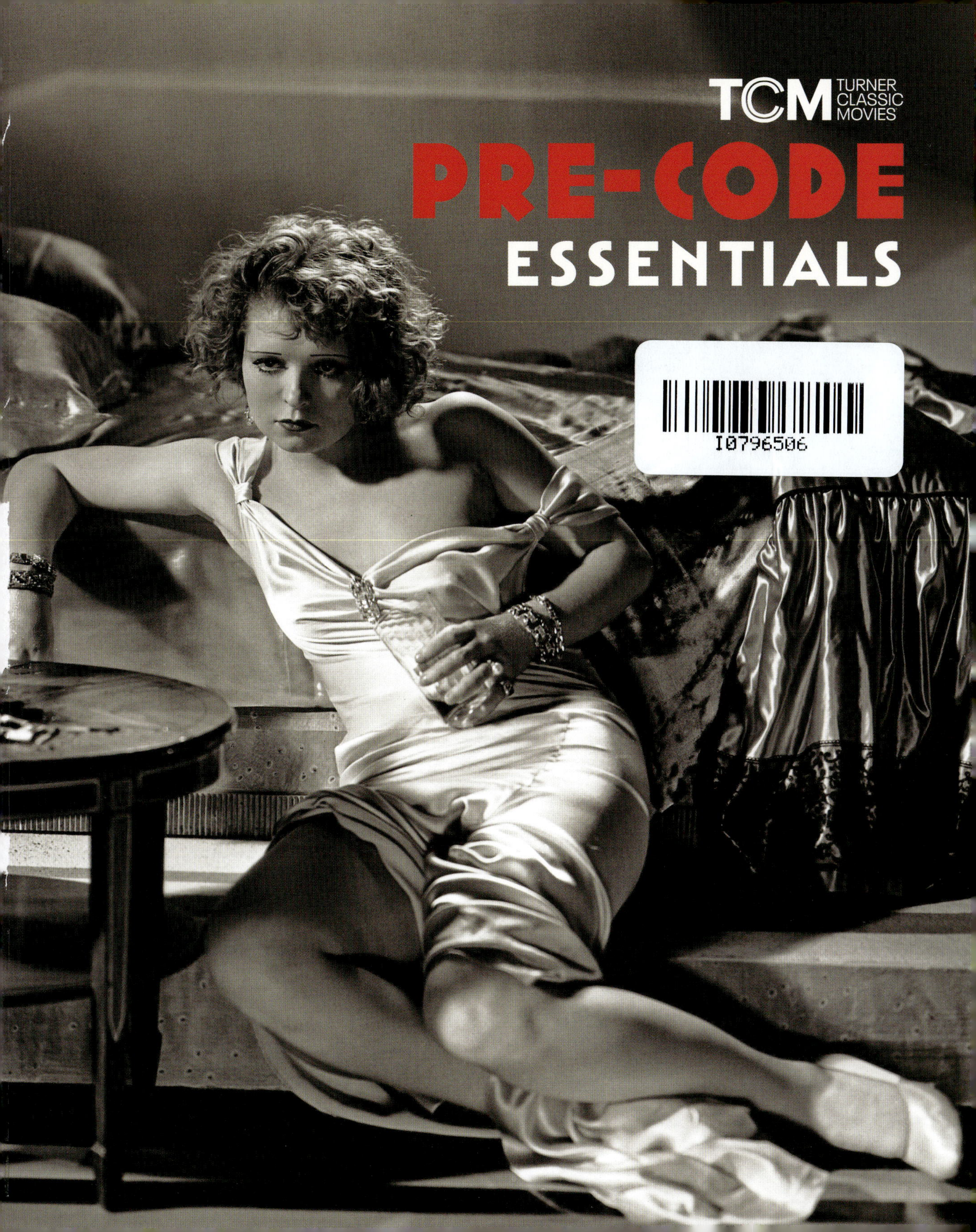
TCM TURNER CLASSIC MOVIES
PRE-CODE
ESSENTIALS
I0796506

TCM TURNER CLASSIC MOVIES

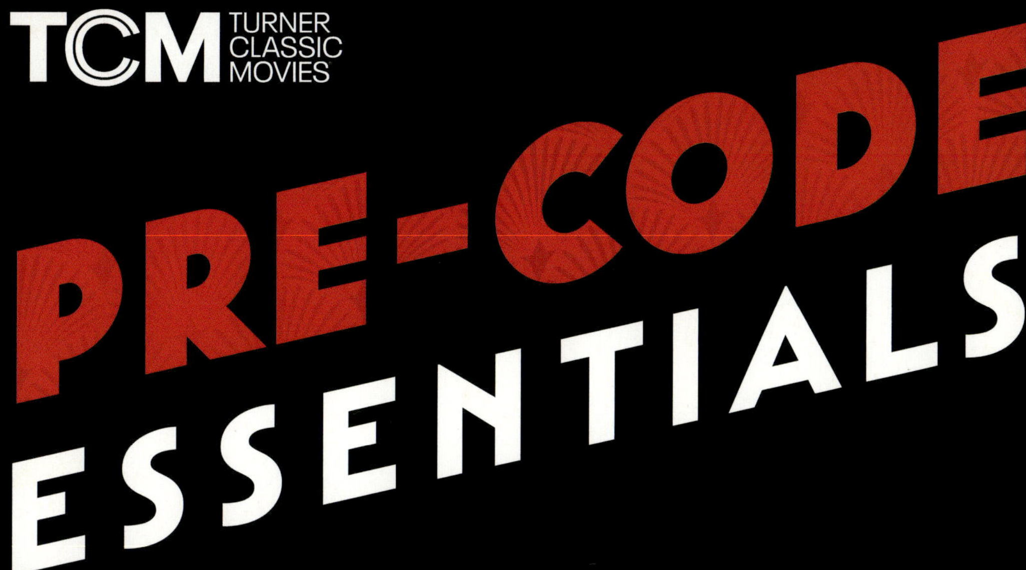

PRE-CODE ESSENTIALS

MUST-SEE CINEMA

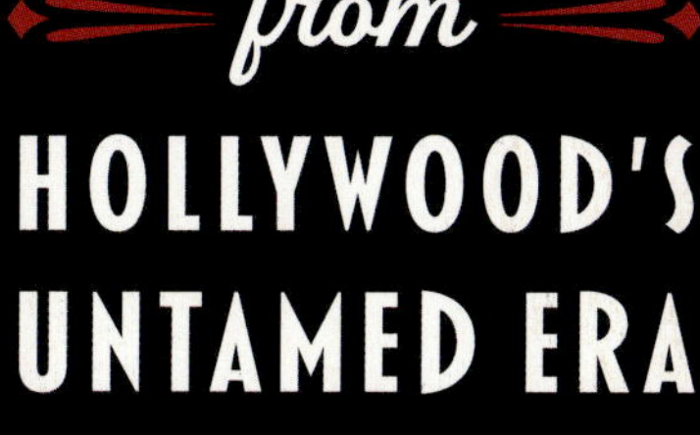

from HOLLYWOOD'S UNTAMED ERA 1930-1934

KIM LUPERI and DANNY REID

RUNNING PRESS
PHILADELPHIA

Page i: Clara Bow experiences the highs, lows, and everything in between in *Call Her Savage*.

Page v: Barbara Stanwyck could play it all—and in this early 1930s photo, she's leaning sweet.

Running Press
Hachette Book Group
1290 Avenue of the Americas, New York, NY 10104
www.runningpress.com
@Running_Press

First Edition: October 2025

Published by Running Press, an imprint of Hachette Book Group, Inc. The Running Press name and logo are trademarks of Hachette Book Group, Inc.

The Hachette Speakers Bureau provides a wide range of authors for speaking events. To find out more, go to www.hachettespeakersbureau.com or email HachetteSpeakers@hbgusa.com.

Running Press books may be purchased in bulk for business, educational, or promotional use. For more information, please contact your local bookseller or the Hachette Book Group Special Markets Department at Special.Markets@hbgusa.com.

Image credits: Pages xiv, 51 (bottom), 64, 99 (bottom), 203, and 204: Authors' collection. Pages 4, 16 (top right), 48, 49 (top left), 56, 84, 112, 137, 145, 200, and 205: Association of Motion Picture and Television Producers (AMPTP) records, Margaret Herrick Library, Academy of Motion Picture Arts and Sciences. Pages 81, 180, and 198: Courtesy of the Academy Film Archive. Pages 86, 87 (top right), 127 (top left), 132, and 155: Courtesy of Darin Barnes. All other photography courtesy Turner Classic Movies, Inc.

Print book cover and interior design by Susan Van Horn and Sheryl Kober

Library of Congress Cataloging-in-Publication Data
Names: Luperi, Kim, author. | Reid, Danny, author.
Title: Pre-code essentials : must-see cinema from Hollywood's untamed era, 1930-1934 / Kim Luperi and Danny Reid.
Description: First edition. | Philadelphia : Running Press, 2025. | Includes bibliographical references and index.
Identifiers: LCCN 2025005172 (print) | LCCN 2025005173 (ebook) | ISBN 9798894140551 (paperback) | ISBN 9798894140575 (ebook)
Subjects: LCSH: Motion pictures—United States—History—20th century. | Nineteen thirties.
Classification: LCC PN1993.5.U6 L87 2025 (print) | LCC PN1993.5.U6 (ebook) | DDC 791.43/75097309043—dc23/eng/20250403
LC record available at https://lccn.loc.gov/2025005172
LC ebook record available at https://lccn.loc.gov/2025005173

ISBNs: 979-8-89414-055-1 (paperback), 979-8-89414-057-5 (ebook)

Printed in Malaysia

PCF

10 9 8 7 6 5 4 3 2 1

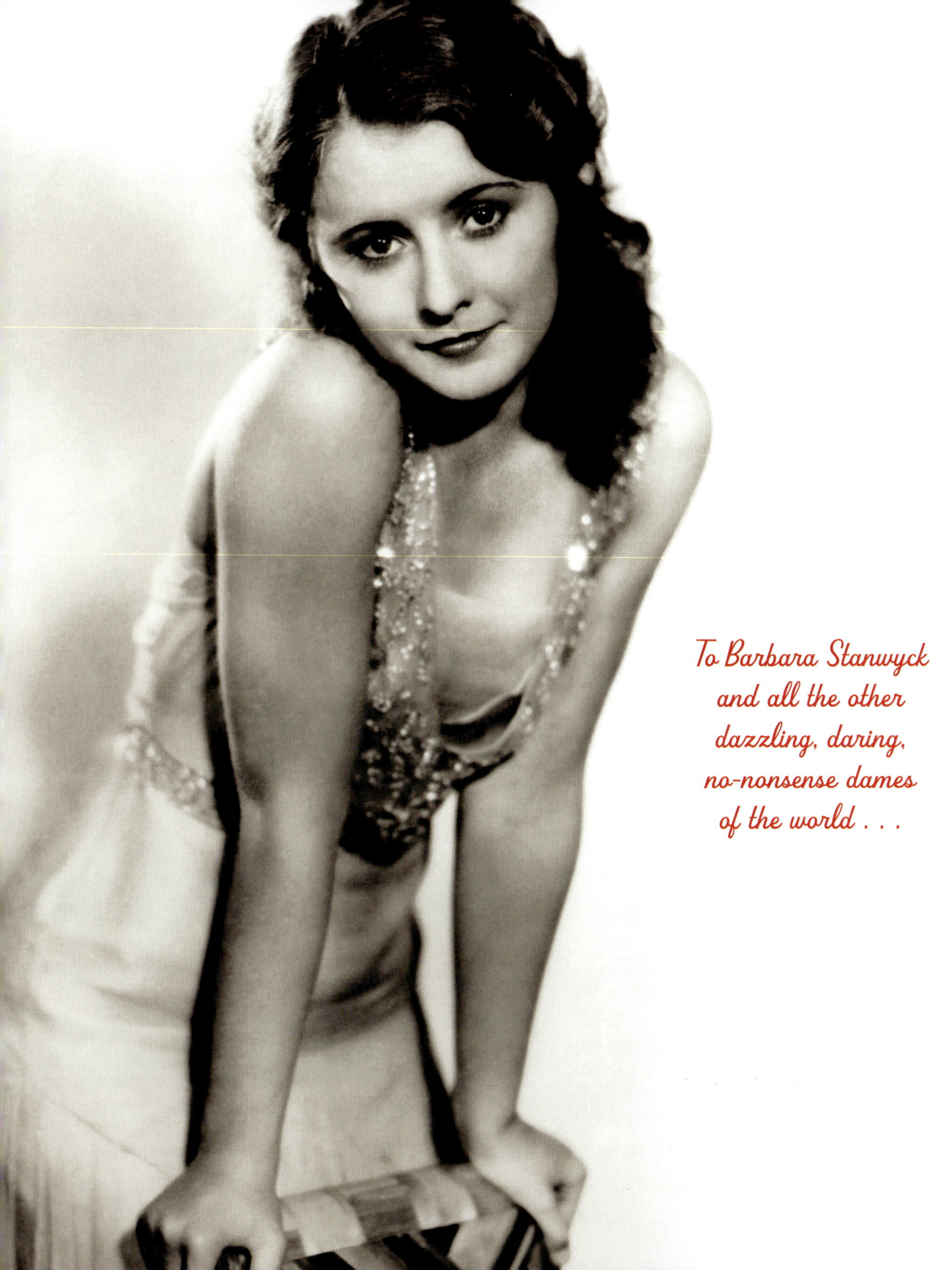

*To Barbara Stanwyck
and all the other
dazzling, daring,
no-nonsense dames
of the world . . .*

Contents

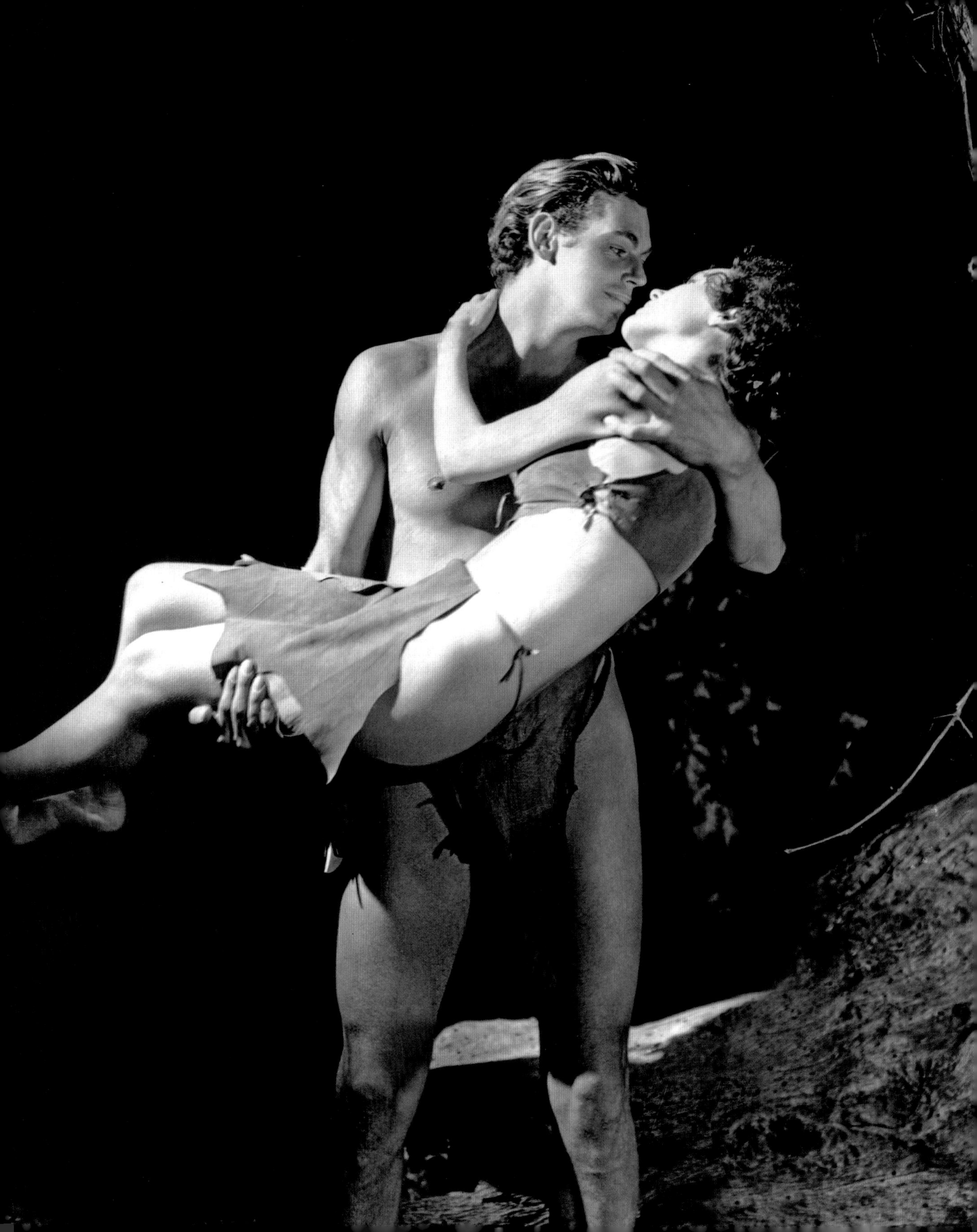

What Is Pre-Code?

"WAIT, TARZAN!"

With those famous last words from Jane, Tarzan rips off her evening gown and throws her in the lagoon. What follows is a delicate dance beneath the water as Tarzan's chiseled body swirls gracefully around Jane's nude figure. The sequence lasts over a minute, features full-frontal nudity, and doesn't deny the nature of Tarzan and Jane's erotic, unmarried relationship.

The year is 1934, and Hollywood has gone off the rails. The signs are everywhere—every boundary that the film industry could push was being shoved, gleefully so, leading to vociferous public outcry and threats of harsh censorship from the federal government. The problem's not just the nudity in *Tarzan and His Mate*, nor is it in *Queen Christina* (1933), where queen-of-the-box-office Greta Garbo kisses a woman on the mouth and bemoans the end of their love affair. It's not when Gertrude Michael swoons a song about "Sweet Marijuana" to a chorus of half-naked women in *Murder at the Vanities* (1934). Nor is it even when Ann in *Ann Vickers* (1933) mourns her abortion after a doomed love affair and reflects solemnly on the decision.

No, these moments aren't isolated incidents, but a culmination of Hollywood's most desperate and daring period of filmmaking, the pre-Code era. Limits—political, social, ethical—were getting tested further with each movie released as the studios' debts piled up and the country's unemployment numbers skyrocketed. Desperation is the mother of creativity, and the films of this time are bolder, more exciting, and more dynamic than what would come before or after.

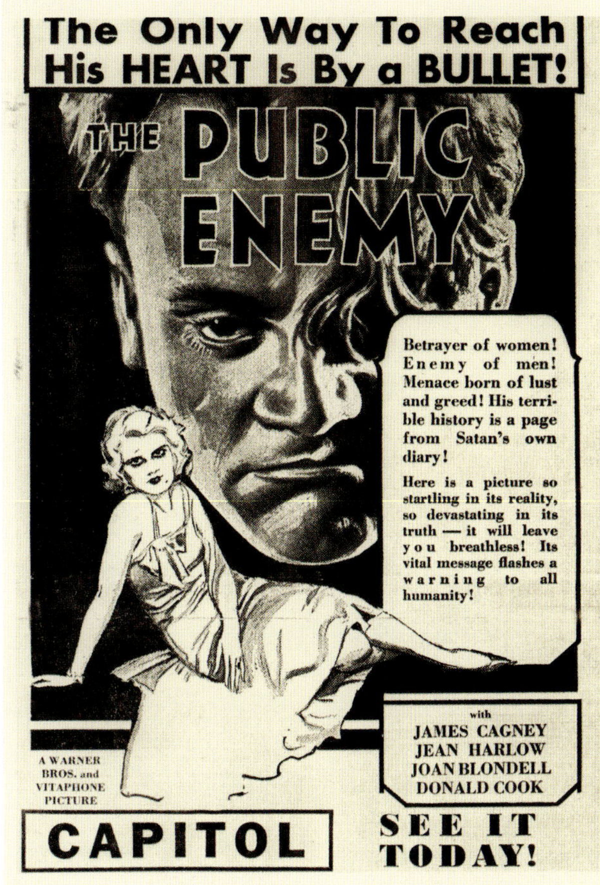

ABOVE: What a tagline! **OPPOSITE:** Johnny Weissmuller and Maureen O'Sullivan play jungle lovers in *Tarzan and His Mate* (1934) who have little need for societal norms like clothing or marriage.

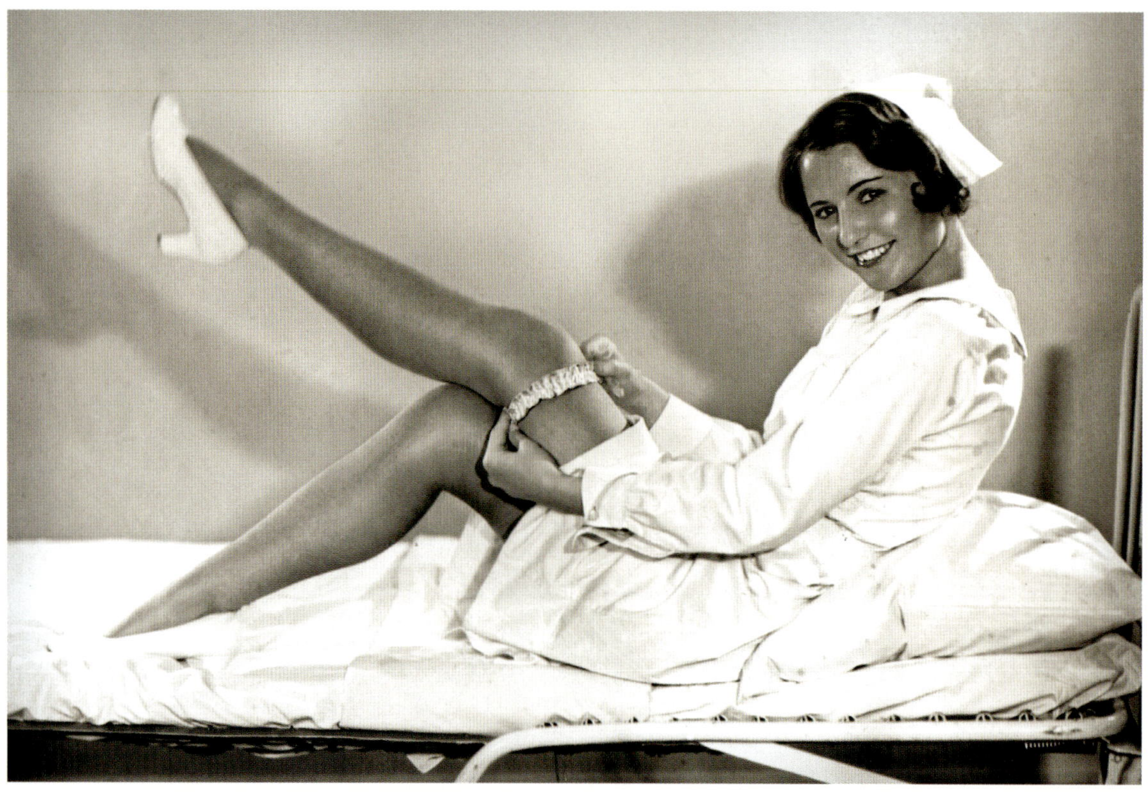

Night Nurse (1931) shows as much skin as it does nursing, which Barbara Stanwyck displays here.

Some aspects of pre-Code cinema are easy to define. First, the dates: While some scholars place the era's origins around 1927 (when sound debuted) or 1929 (when sound had been largely accepted by the industry), our book starts with the adoption of the Motion Picture Production Code on March 31, 1930, and lasts through the full enforcement of the Code in early July 1934. (This is awkward, but we have to get it over with: "Pre-Code" is actually a misnomer, as it is *after* the Code is adopted but *before* it is strictly enforced. Don't worry, there are no quizzes at the end of this book.)

The next piece of the puzzle is the social context. As you might recall from your history classes, during the early 1930s, the world was on fire. The Great Depression turned everything upside down at the end of 1929 and its effects reverberated through the decade; unemployment topped 25 percent in 1932. Frustrated and unpaid veterans marched on Washington and were brutally dispersed by the military. Charles Lindbergh's baby son was kidnapped and found murdered. And, all the while, the bloody rise of fascism in Germany and Italy was noted by some Americans with reverent awe and glee.

Both the country and Hollywood woke up every day with a sword over their heads, and for the latter, empty theaters to fill. Exhibitors needed product. Audiences needed escapism. How would they provide?

The eight major studios that ran Hollywood in 1930 had seen the explosion of the talkies in 1927—a major investment of money not just in equipment but also the theaters they owned—and now their bottom lines were threatened. All the studios struggled with finances, with only Metro-Goldwyn-Mayer (MGM) remaining in the black through the decade. While going to the movies was extremely popular in the 1930s—adult women were the biggest purveyors—the Depression created a scarcity. The studios had to work to get their audience in, and they would try anything. Well, sex sells, after all. We know it now, and Hollywood knew it in the 1930s. Nudity would pop up in movies, sometimes subtly—watch the locker room behind John Wayne in *Arizona* (1931) or Genevieve Tobin gleefully taking a bath in front of her cuckolded husband in *Easy to Love* (1934). Or even the musical extravaganza from *Meet the Baron* (1933), "Wearing a Great Big Smile," where a room full of showering chorines were wearing nothing but.

But beyond just nudity, movies were *about* sex and love in ways that they hadn't been before, and they posed real questions about relationships, lust, and meaning. If your family is starving, how much are you willing to sell to keep them afloat, asks *The Easiest Way* (1931)? How would a glamorous female CEO handle dating, as seen in *Female* (1933)?

Moving on from sex, how about controversy? Two men sit under a bridge in the pouring rain in *Heroes for Sale* (1933), wondering if they're witnessing the end of America. (Not yet, it seemed.) A conservative missionary's eyes are opened as she falls in love with a man of another race—gasp!—in *The Bitter Tea of General Yen* (1933). After *I Am a Fugitive from a Chain Gang* (1932) brutally depicted how the state of Georgia treats its inmates, the government threatened to kill the director and stars if they ever dare to step foot in their state.

Many films of this period took hard, nuanced looks at modern society—a society that had barely pulled itself out of the trenches, literally and figuratively, after the Great War, only to be pummeled by the Great Depression—and the ways these events affected everyday people.

Thus, we reach pre-Code cinema. Not just based on the date—because there are movies like *Little Women* (1933) from this time that are as clean as the morning dew—but rather on their content and intent. Overarching everything else, we define pre-Code as more of a spirit, or a vibe, if you will. In this period there existed a freedom and willingness—and in some ways, pressure—to tackle "risky" subjects and present them through a lens that made these pictures more honest, relatable, and yes, even more fun, than audiences had seen before. We used the word *pressure* because the risk of failure, namely bankruptcy to the studios, was greater than censorship . . . for a time.

And it took an alliance between politicians, producers, the Catholic Church, and thousands mobilized around the nation to put an end to the "pre-Code" era. Moral groups, crusading in the early twentieth century on issues ranging from winning (most) women the right to vote to the prohibition of alcohol, found fertile ground to fight against the movie business. But their objections were nothing new. In 1915, the Supreme Court proclaimed that motion pictures were not protected by the First Amendment. This set off a chain of events, as at least seven states (Pennsylvania, New York, Ohio, Massachusetts, Maryland, Kansas, and Virginia, for starters) and hundreds of cities like Chicago began creating their own censor boards to regulate what could or couldn't be shown. Some states were strict, while others often accepted what the studios offered with few modifications. The cuts these boards demanded could change a film's story trajectory or even render a movie entirely unintelligible.

And Hollywood managed to do itself no favors. Scandal after scandal rocked the motion picture community throughout the 1920s, lending newspapers fodder for big headlines and bigger profits. The still-unsolved murder of William Desmond Taylor included scintillating details of Tinseltown drug usage. The trial of Fatty Arbuckle was front-page news as the comedian was accused of raping and essentially "crushing" a woman to death under his girth. Moral crusaders and yellow newspapers made these scandals into a national reckoning and sketched out dark paths for strict federal controls of the motion picture industry.

Of course, the very last thing Hollywood wanted was federal censorship. They needed to act—or at least make it *look* like they were. And so, in 1922 the industry set up a trade organization, the Motion Picture Producers and Distributors of America (MPPDA), and installed former Postmaster General Will H. Hays as its head. Hays initiated self-regulation plans for Hollywood, including the inconspicuously titled "Don'ts and Be Carefuls" in 1927, and established the Studio Relations Committee (SRC) to administer the directives. As they did during the late 1920s and after the adoption of the 1930 Code, the SRC reviewed scripts and finished films, doling out recommendations to studios on what material they believed censor boards were apt to cut. But there was nothing forcing studios to listen to the SRC's suggestions or make changes—and many didn't.

The censor battles take months and years across cities and states until things come to a head in the spring of 1934. That April, the Catholic Legion of Decency rounded up millions of signatures from devoted followers pledging to condemn distasteful, immoral movies. In May, a cardinal in Philadelphia took to the pulpit in church and directed attendees to boycott all films; box office numbers in the city fell 40 percent. The potential loss of millions of Catholic moviegoers was cataclysmic—and word on the street was that other religious groups were ready to join the fray.

As the crusade ramped up, the studios, absolutely terrified, turned to Joseph Breen. Finally, in July 1934, America's taming of Hollywood was sealed with the enforcement of a modified version of the 1930 Production Code. No more unwed mothers on the movie screens, and perhaps couples should stick to separate beds going forward. No longer will the villain get away at the end of the picture, nor will the criminals wink at the camera as they drive off with the girl, their pockets overflowing with illegal cash. And gone were movies that challenged the American establishment, as skewering the religious, the rich, and the political class became taboo.

But, before those changes ushered in decades of tamer cinema (with the occasional flashes of brilliance—we're not here to knock 1942's *Casablanca* for Christ's sake), there was an era where you could witness a movie shake the nation's foundation. Take the woman sitting on a cat and demanding to know what's under her, with W. C. Fields chortling back, "Ah, it's a pussy!" That would be *International House* (1933)—and that's not even the craziest moment in that picture.

No matter where we are in life, there are pre-Codes that find sympathy for all the disasters of

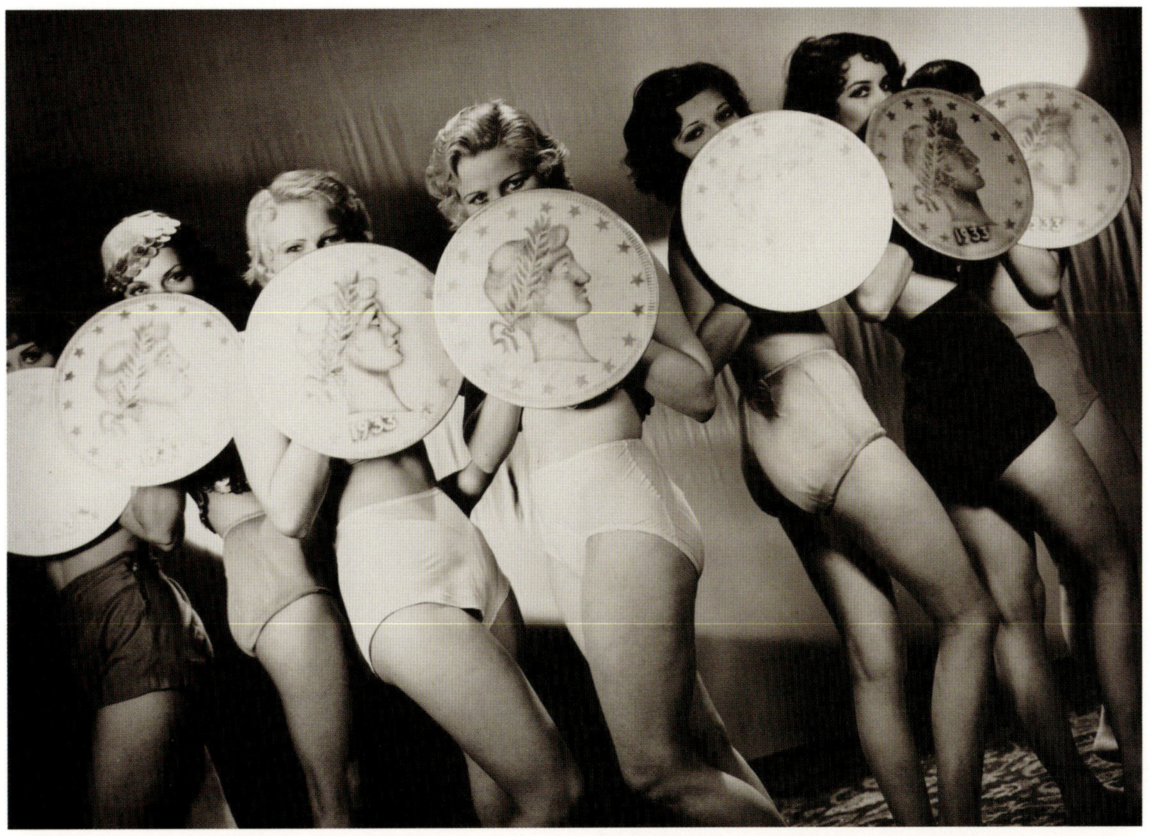

You're not just in the money in *Gold Diggers of 1933*, you're wearing the money!

modern society. Marriage and infidelity, economic depression and hopelessness, gender and racial inequality, and so many more topics are open for surprisingly nuanced and daring exploration. Some readers might also find how remarkably relevant these subjects remain over ninety years later. From the politics of *Gabriel Over the White House* (1933) and the religious hypocrisy of *Rain* (1932) to the proud single motherhood of *Only Yesterday* (1933), the frank authenticity many movies of this era imparted makes them relatable decades later, oftentimes shockingly so. Watching characters face some of the same problems we continue to battle a century later makes one realize how close we are to the past—and how little we've learned from it.

This book is written for both pre-Code novices and aficionados. We've gathered together fifty of the most representative and notable films of the early 1930s for you to peruse. In addition to summaries and background information, you can also revel in detailed information from each film's censorship file, if available, from the Production Code Administration (PCA) records housed at the Academy of Motion Picture Arts and Sciences' Margaret Herrick Library. This inside look at

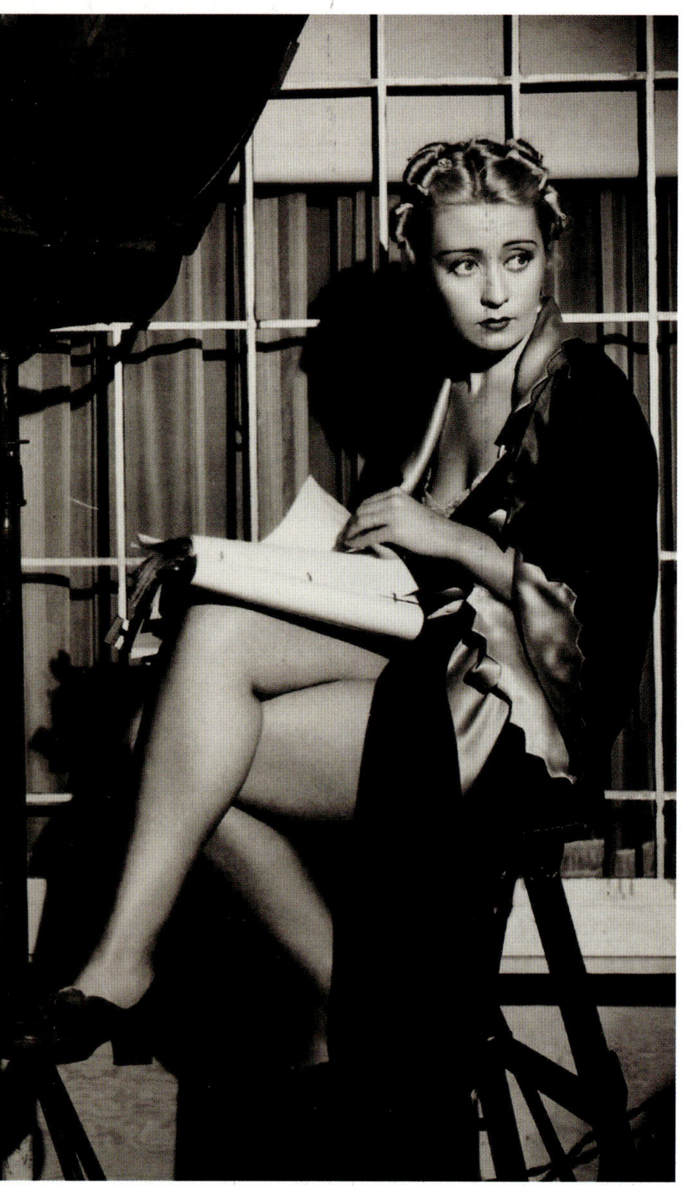

Joan Blondell, who appeared in over thirty features during the pre-Code era, taking a quick break on the set of *Footlight Parade* (1933).

correspondence between the studios and SRC, including meticulous notes of material cut by local censor boards, provides fascinating context to the period. You'll start to see the same censor entities mentioned over and over—those in the US and abroad—which represent the surviving documentation. (Other censor boards did exist, but the edits they made to films were either not reported to the SRC or have not survived in the PCA files.) Not only do these documents open our eyes to the daily, monthly, and yearly struggles Hollywood faced at this time—they also reveal some ways in which the public responded. From serious to funny, confusing to surprising, enlightening to frustrating, the files are vital historical artifacts, and we are proud to share so much content from them with you.

We also make it a point to show how relevant elements of these pre-Code pictures remain. Strikingly brazen, authentic stories of sexuality, female agency, class, politics, and beyond were told during this period, a reflection of the reality of the Depression and its effect on Hollywood and America as a whole. The parallels that can be drawn between these tales from the early 1930s and cinema nearly a century later are sometimes as stark and eye-opening as the pictures themselves.

Assembling this list was never easy or even wholly agreed upon at times, and what follows may not be the *best* movies of the pre-Code era, but they are certainly some of the most emblematic. If you want a taste of the era or a way to prove your bona fides, this is the perfect place to start. And maybe never stop.

—Danny & Kim

GLOSSARY

MOTION PICTURE PRODUCERS AND DISTRIBUTORS OF AMERICA (MPPDA)

Incorporated in March 1922 in New York City, the MPPDA united American movie studios and put at its head Will H. Hays. Hays pushed for self-censorship at the studios and would advocate for "morality" on the screen and help promote the idea of cleaned-up pictures. The MPPDA would be colloquially known as "The Hays Office."

STUDIO RELATIONS COMMITTEE (SRC)

The SRC was founded in 1927 as the censoring arm of the MPPDA, the intermediary between studios and censor boards tasked with enforcing the Production Code in 1930. Headed by Jason Joy and four colleagues, the SRC responded to scripts with suggestions and comments and previewed prints so they could make further recommendations before films were sent out for exhibition. In the early 1930s, only about 20 percent of movies were being viewed by the SRC. Script comments, often based on feedback they received from local censor boards, were routinely ignored by the studios. The SRC had little influence on the filmmaking process and instead had to spend much of the time trying to help studios avert scandals with their releases, working with censor boards, and advocating for films they had little power to change.

THE MOTION PICTURE PRODUCTION CODE OF 1930

Written in 1930 by Jesuit priest Daniel A. Lord and Catholic layman Martin Quigley, the Production Code (or the "Hays Code") was a guiding document created as a philosophical treatise to rationalize film censorship. It laid out what could and could not be shown in movies produced in the United States, including sections banning depictions of nudity, sex, miscegenation, profanity, and insults to other countries or races, among other things.

THE CATHOLIC LEGION OF DECENCY

Founded in 1934, the Catholic Legion of Decency was formed primarily to counter "the brazen indecency of [American] cinema." The Legion would make use of highly publicized boycotts, spread through Sunday sermons at local churches, to pinpoint films that were scandalous or immoral. They would also publish ratings of films, with C being the dreaded "condemned" that could lead local churches to stage protests and picket showings.

PRODUCTION CODE ADMINISTRATION (PCA)

In 1934, with the rise of the Legion and the continued threats of local censor boards, Hays created a new department of the MPPDA, the PCA. Starting in early July 1934, all films had to go through the PCA, from getting script approval to final edits, even for rereleases (the only way for studios to make money on old movies until television became commonplace in the 1950s). Producers who attempted to bypass the PCA were fined and would meet serious problems in the press.

Under the PCA, American films would simplify. Sex would get heavily coded, almost to the point of absurdity, while violence flourished. The attitudes and tastes of Joseph Breen alone shaped the next twenty years of American motion pictures, creating a Hollywood that was often infantilizing. Under Breen's and Hays's watch, anti-Nazi sentiment was policed away, and socially conscious filmmaking was forced to the margins.

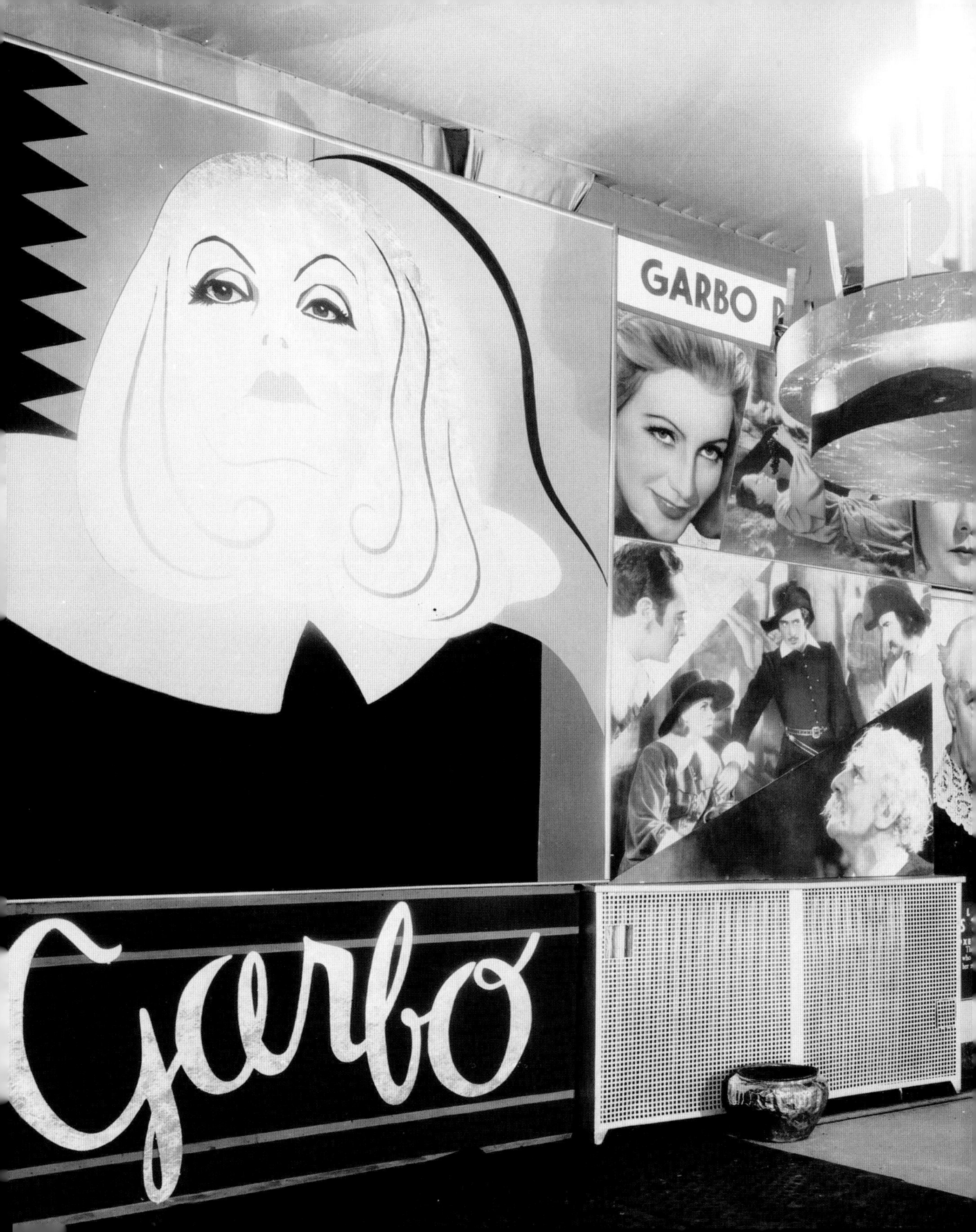

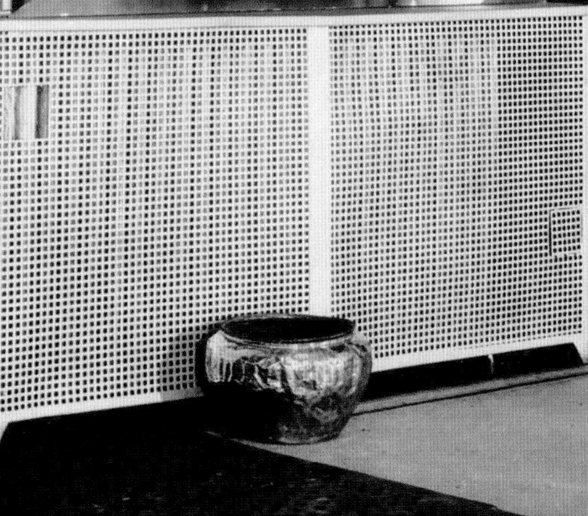
GARBO
Garbo

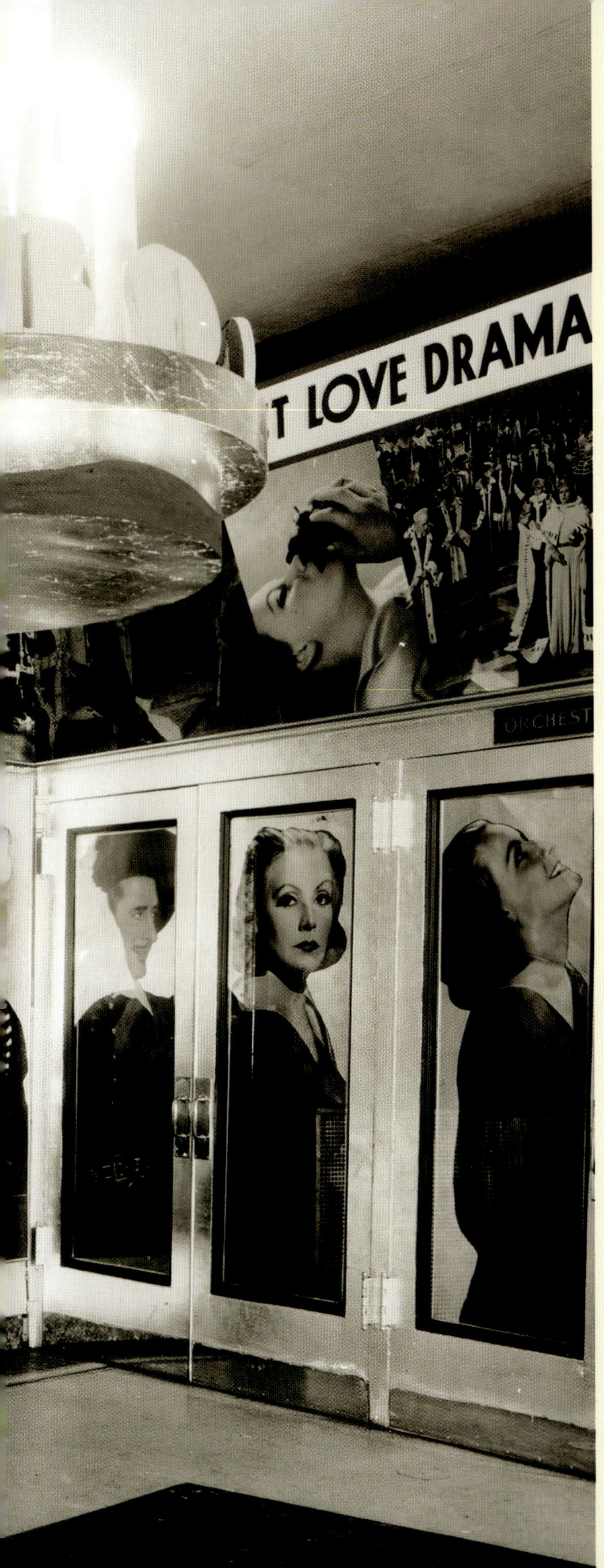

CAST OF CHARACTERS

Will H. Hays: Indiana-born Hays was revered for his folksy charm. He gained regard as the US postmaster general under Warren G. Harding and chaired the Republican National Committee. Taking over as the head of the MPPDA in 1922, he worked to limit the tension between studios and state censorship boards.

Colonel Jason Joy: A former Red Cross secretary, Joy headed the SRC through the fall of 1932, when he left for an executive position at Fox. A few years later, he became director of the studio's public relations department.

Dr. James Wingate: A former New York state censor, Wingate served as Joy's replacement. His tenure saw the SRC's lack of ability to enforce the Production Code come to a head.

Joseph Breen: After working for the SRC through the early 1930s, Breen saw the organization as weak-willed and impotent to stop Hollywood's excess. Coordinating with the Catholic Legion of Decency and other censorship organizations, he would force the studios to run all the films they produced from July 1934 to 1954 through the new PCA—and by him as the PCA's head.

MGM knew how to market their stars. This display is for *Queen Christina* (1933).

A Note About the Selected Films

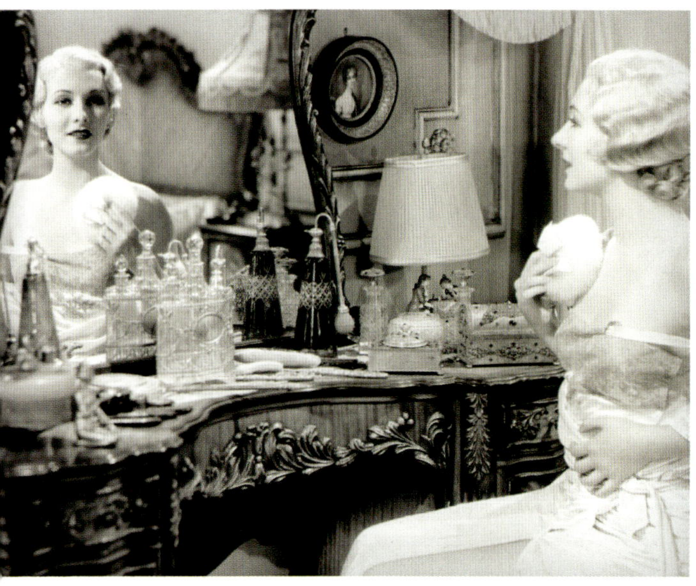

Karen Morley is dolled up and ready to go in *Scarface* (1932). Are you ready? Time to enter the world of pre-Code Hollywood!

THE AVAILABILITY AND UNAVAILABILITY OF movies throughout the last century has shaped what is commonly referred to as film history, altering perceptions of importance and keeping many cinematic gems buried. Some of the films included in this book are classics and widely remembered. Others, at the behest of censors, were locked in studio vaults for decades. Other films still were cut to pieces, only restored recently where possible—and for some of these pictures, it is looking more and more likely that we will never see complete prints of them as originally shown. (The most famous missing film of the time is 1933's *Convention City*, a box office hit that hasn't been seen in public in eight decades. For you completionists, we highly suggest you take up the search for it.)

At the time film histories and canons were written in the 1960s and '70s, many of the pre-Codes featured here were in incomplete states or unavailable to view. Through the tireless work of archivists, preservationists, programmers, and authors, the genre of pre-Code cinema emerged from the ashes of the past, and, thanks to home video and their own unabashed and unforgettable attitude, they have finally entered common film lexicon with other era-specific "genres" like film noir or New Hollywood.

With that said, of the roughly 1,500 American feature films released between March 1930 and July 1934, hundreds are unavailable for an average viewer to watch, especially legally. The list in this book is not definitive but represents the most famous and the favorites of two die-hard lovers of this era of cinema. We wanted to offer commentary and background on the full process of how these pictures were made and perceived, and how these films, released nearly a century ago, still have things to say that modern movies don't—or won't.

THE DIVORCEE

STARRING
Norma Shearer, Chester Morris, Conrad Nagel, and Robert Montgomery

DIRECTED BY
Robert Z. Leonard

RELEASED BY
MGM, April 1930

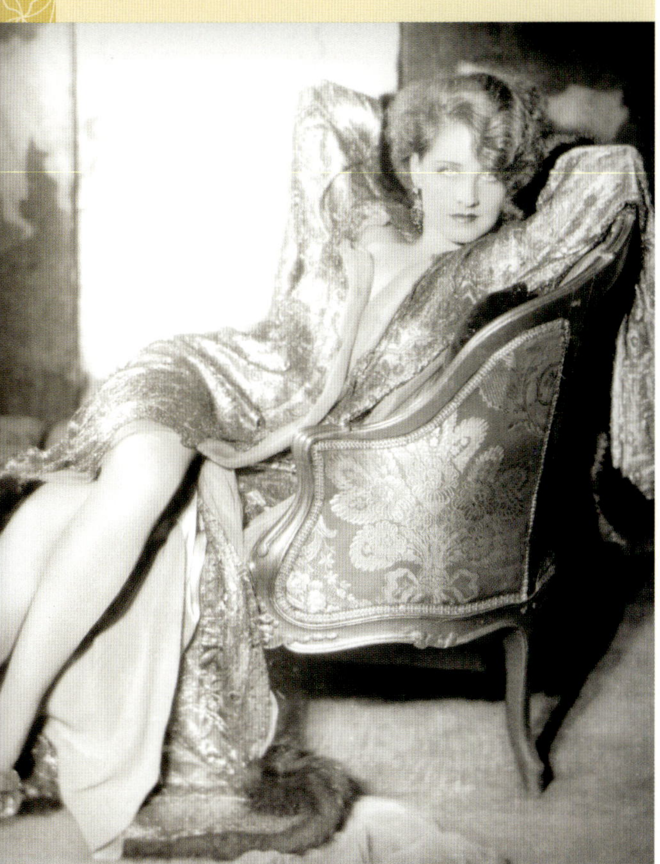

Photographed by George Hurrell, Norma Shearer understood the assignment.

Emerging from the bon vivant morality of the 1920s Jazz Age, *The Divorcee* became the first talkie to capture the energy of the era and carry it to its logical end. Showcasing the controversial concept of divorce, the film blasted onto the screen the life of a woman freed of marriage and taking on all the affairs she can handle with decadence and glee. Norma Shearer's central performance delivers an electric thrill that pointed toward the wild ride of the pre-Code years soon to come.

The Divorcee introduces Jerry (Shearer) and Ted (Chester Morris), rapturously in love. A sharp-dressing woman with a career of her own, Jerry lives in bliss with Ted until the night of their third anniversary, when she walks in on Ted embracing Janice (Mary Doran) at a party in their own home. Shattered, Jerry ends up evening the score later that night with the accommodating Don (Robert Montgomery). Realizing the deep, emotional consequences of her actions, she bluntly informs Ted that she's "balanced our accounts." Though Ted often professed a belief in gender equality, he becomes churlish as Jerry takes a stand for her choices and her future. She divorces him and embarks on a series of flings, exploring the world of a wealthy divorcée as she figures out where her personal happiness lies.

No doubt about it, Jerry put the double standard on blast in *The Divorcee*, most famously in her explosive speech to Ted after a failed attempt at reconciliation. Almost a century later, the conviction with which she launches her vindication garners nods of acknowledgment and exuberant applause. The woman knows her worth, and she's not taking her husband back until he knows it, too—and doesn't forget it. It remains incredibly empowering to witness a woman boldly making her own decisions about her relationships, her standards, and her body; Jerry leverages her agency to do what's right for her in the moment, a pivotal nod to women's autonomy that's just as timely a century later.

Based on the novel *Ex-Wife* by Ursula Parrott, which was so controversial it was originally published anonymously, *The Divorcee*'s journey to the big screen also proved contentious. In fact, the novel gained such notoriety that the SRC mandated against using *Ex-Wife* as the title; heck, they wouldn't even allow the name of the source novel in the credits! (MGM skirted that order with the phrasing, *Based on a novel by Ursula Parrott.*) Though Parrott's second book, which led to the future Shearer vehicle *Strangers May Kiss* (1931), was published right before *The Divorcee* debuted, audiences would have clearly known which novel the credit referred to.

Casting the lead role turned out to be a battle, too. Shearer had to fight to play the part, originally assigned to Joan Crawford. Despite a decade's worth of star power behind Shearer, her husband, MGM production chief Irving Thalberg, initially balked at her request to take on the role. Seeking to convince him that she could be the sexy and alluring Jerry, Shearer enlisted the aid of photographer George Hurrell. The resulting series of steamy photos proved to Thalberg that she could transform into an uninhibited woman with glamour and sex appeal.

Considering the notoriety of *Ex-Wife*, which the SRC deemed "wholly unsuitable for picturization," a close watch was kept on the movie from a censorship angle. MGM promised they'd position Jerry as a woman of high moral character who is in love with her husband and has *only* one affair, but that's not what they delivered, which frustrated some in the SRC. However, the script found an ardent supporter in reviewer W. F. Willis. "I want to declare at the very outset, for myself, that I think it is a great story—an important story—one which *should* be told—one which should be received seriously as a sincere contribution to our mass of moral thought," he proclaimed. Based on the office's knowledge of what censor boards were apt to cut, Willis meticulously noted several pages' worth of lines and situations to alter so as to not unnecessarily "jolt" the censors. Suggestions included toning down the drinking, reframing Jerry's declaration to Ted that he's the only man her door is closed to, and deleting the line, "We want to live together! Then why don't we?"

"So look for me in the future where the primroses grow. And pack your man's pride with the rest. And from now on, you're the only man in the world that my door is closed to!"

—Jerry, the titular divorcée, opting to take the dramatic route out of her marriage

The Divorcee premiered in April 1930, mere weeks after Hollywood adopted the Production Code. The MPPDA's Maurice McKenzie expressed his confidence to the Dallas Film Board of Trade

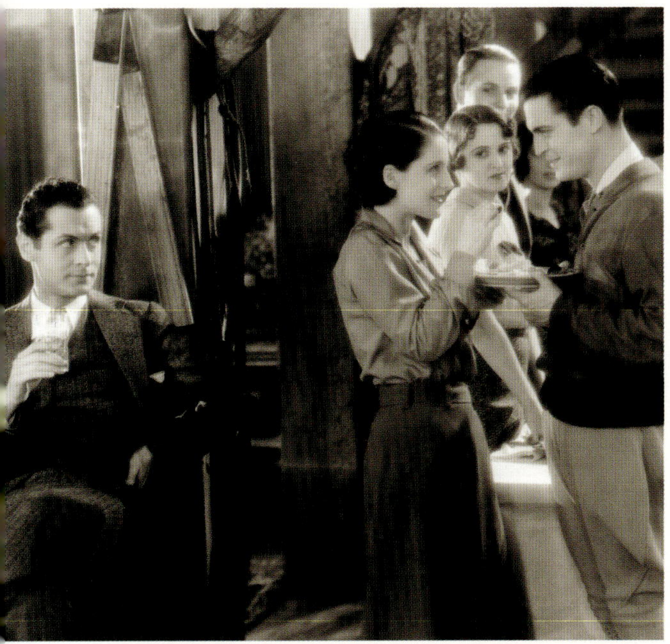

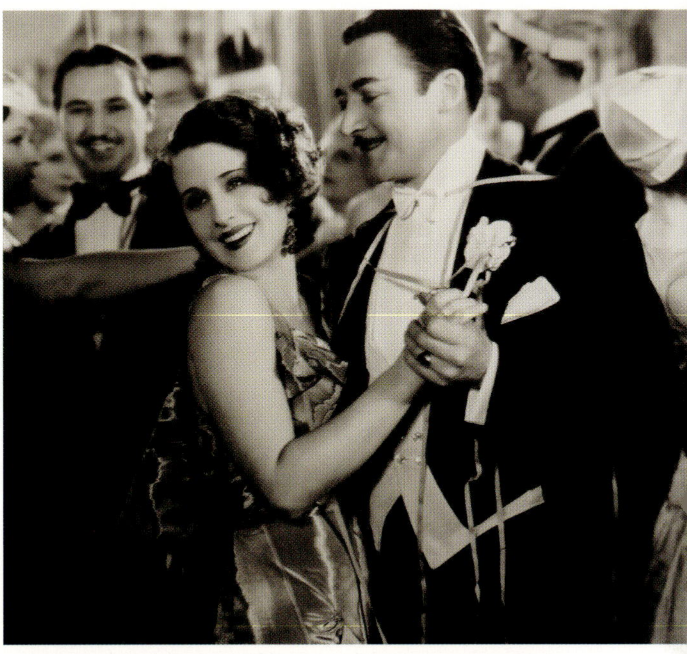

FROM LEFT: Norma Shearer and Chester Morris are still in the honeymoon phase, which is why everyone, including Robert Montgomery, is jealous of them. • Party, drink, dance, repeat.

that the Code would have "proper effect," but *The Divorcee* demonstrated the opposite right off the bat. By September, the *N.Y. Telegraph* pondered what happened to the Code, commenting that studios promised to abide by the document and "then along came Metro with 'Divorcee,' the picture version of 'Ex-Wife,' and knocked the code for a row of big figures. Now every picture concern is trying for something sensational and startling." With its bold, modern story and strong, independent female lead, *The Divorcee* certainly started a trend—and for four years, there was no looking back.

In 1940, writer/producer Val Lewton queried the PCA about revisiting *The Divorcee*. Joseph Breen shut that down fast, reporting that "this office was deluged with protests" when the film debuted and it was "cut into shreds" by censor boards in New York, Pennsylvania, Ohio, and Maryland. While reports from the last three boards are curiously missing from the movie's PCA file, New York excised about a dozen lines, including a sizable portion of Jerry's damning "Loose women, great—but not in the home, eh, Ted?" speech. Elsewhere, reaction was mixed; Virginia recorded only one cut, while Alberta and British Columbia rejected the film (though the latter eventually reversed its decision).

Filmed over twenty-two days, *The Divorcee* was a huge commercial success. While the direction and editing highlighted some of the faults in early-talkie filmmaking, a dynamic, thought-provoking treatment by Zelda Sears and Nick

Grinde (with dialogue credited to John Meehan) and Shearer's dedication to getting the picture right proved to be an explosive combination. Not to mention, the star won the Best Actress Oscar for her performance, and the film was nominated for Outstanding Production.

The door to the pre-Code period was officially opened—and Jerry ran right through. *The Divorcee*'s success showed Hollywood the power of both women-led pictures and controversy at the box office, which, for the most part, would turn into a recipe for success over the next few years. This, as the reality of the Depression began to sink in across the nation, found the industry at one of its most crucial moments. A wave of imitators would follow *The Divorcee*, each pushing the boundary of accepted morality further and further until it became unrecognizable. For what was sinful and decadent in 1930 would look like child's play by 1934.

Less than four months after the adoption of the Production Code, problems are already brewing, as SRC head Jason Joy bemoans to colleague (and future Oscar-winning screenwriter) Lamar Trotti.

June 21, 1930

Mr. Lamar Trotti
469 Fifth Avenue
New York City

Dear Lamar:

We are struggling mightily with a cycle of sophistication which the success of "DIVORCEE" induced. The difficulty is to find delicate treatments and people who are able to develop delicate treatments for every situation and we have an out-crop of that kind of theme in every studio. I already know that some of them are going to get into trouble and the producers and public will fail to realize that it was lack of ability rather than because of the theme which caused the trouble. Whenever you see anything wrong in any picture or even verging on the border, I wish you would let me know.

Jason S. Joy

ALL QUIET ON THE WESTERN FRONT

STARRING
Lew Ayres and Louis Wolheim

DIRECTED BY
Lewis Milestone

RELEASED BY
Universal, August 1930

More than a dozen years after the end of World War I, the cost of more than eight million dead and twenty million injured still lingered. As much as daily reminders of crippled veterans and lost loved ones reverberated, these sights belied a world that overwhelmingly saw the war as a contest of egos between the masters of Europe that slovenly and eagerly killed their subjects. Many Americans witnessed their soldiers head "over there" in patriotic glory and return, shell-shocked, to a country that had filled their jobs and moved on. With the silent era producing masterpieces like *The Big Parade* (1925) and *Wings* (1927), the early sound era, too, saw a slate of strongly pacifist productions that played to audiences' disgust and frustrations.

The best of these anti-war films was *All Quiet on the Western Front*. The movie was based on Erich Maria Remarque's 1928 semi-autobiographical novel of the same name, which was a massive bestseller, moving two and a half million copies within its first eighteen months of publication. The adaptation became a passion project for Carl Laemmle Jr., the production head of Universal Studios. Otherwise known as Junior Laemmle, he had been given the job by his father at the tender age of twenty-one just as sound movies were making their inroads. But rather than sticking with the Western and family fare that had governed Universal's output to that point, Junior pushed the studio into taking big budget risks. *All Quiet* was the one that paid off.

The story follows Paul (Lew Ayres), a callow German youth who is enticed to enlist by cheering teachers and big parades. But once Paul reaches the front, his world shrinks into a dirty, rat-infested bunker, where he's constantly bombarded and forced into untenable battles. Only the guidance of the gruff but experienced Katczinsky (Louis Wolheim) helps Paul and his fellow soldiers retain their dignity. Brief moments of joy, such as spending the night with a beautiful woman while on leave, are countered by the endless days of watching comrades being slowly picked off as the war grinds on.

Returning home after years on the front, Paul voices his frustrations at his old schoolmaster who had so enthralled him, only to be called an unpatriotic coward by the teacher's newest pupils. After Katczinsky is killed, Paul is devastated and broken as the war slogs slowly to an end—but not before it claims his life.

"We live in the trenches out there. We fight. We try not to be killed; sometimes we are. That's all."

—Paul, speaking to a class of students on the glamorous life of a soldier

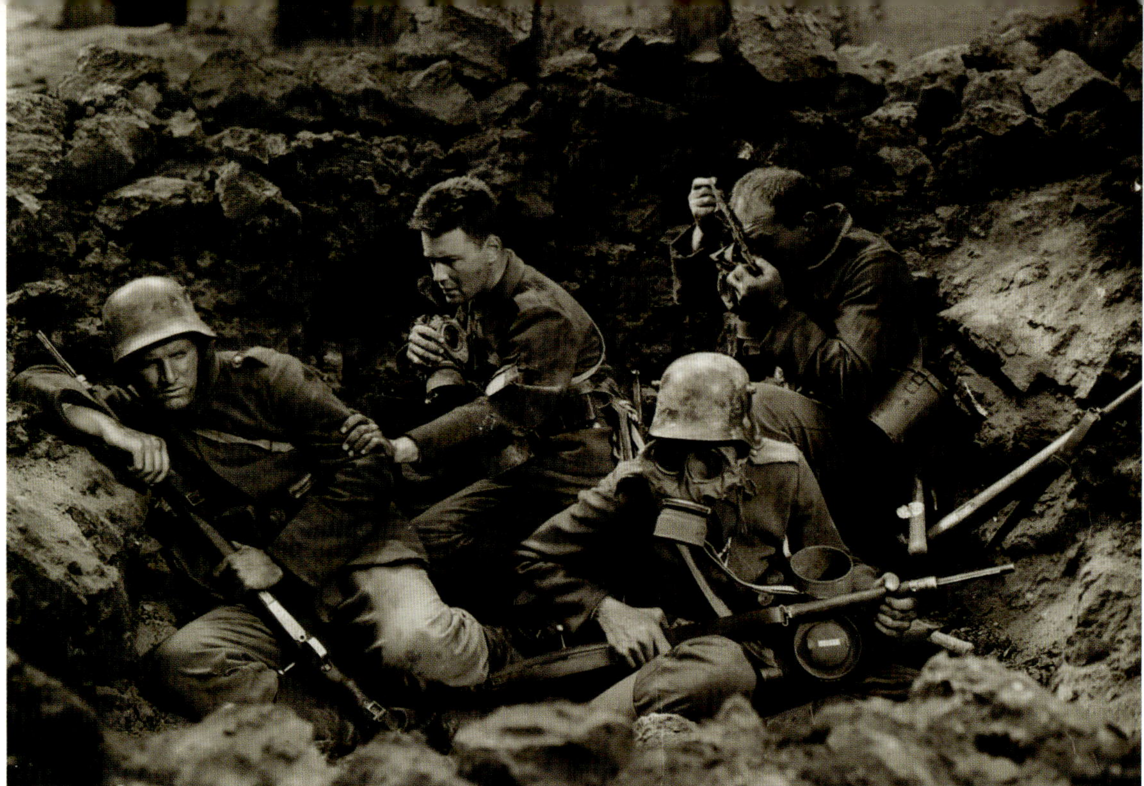

All Quiet on the Western Front pulled no punches showing war is hell.

All Quiet on the Western Front was director Lewis Milestone's second sound feature, and one of the most expansive for the time. It was shot simultaneously as a silent and sound version to accommodate theaters that had yet to make the full conversion to talkies. The sound film stands as the first major picture to capture the inhumane horrors of war—stark, violent, and unremitting, refusing to spare the audience any relief from the grim reality of trench warfare. That was a revelation to viewers: They may have *seen* harrowing combat scenes before, but they had never *heard* it. The explosions, the shots, the clamor, the cries, the distress—these auditory notes dispense the movie's message of universal human suffering like a punch to the gut. Universal utilized nearly two thousand extras in the battle scenes, many of them Great War veterans, including Germans; the actors reported strong camaraderie between the combatants as well as a deadly serious atmosphere that emerged when the mock combat reached full pitch.

The film's final shot, with Paul's hand reaching toward a butterfly on the scarred battlefield, was unscripted. The book concludes with Paul in a state of turmoil as the war ends; while the screenwriters attempted to affix a noble death to the character, it didn't feel right to Laemmle Jr. or Milestone. Cinematographer Karl Freund suggested the moment of reaching for the butterfly to tie into the film's sense of hope being just out of reach, becoming one of the most iconic endings in cinema history in a silent, futile instant.

With a big price tag attached, Universal had a lot to lose if the film didn't meet the satisfaction of the SRC. Thankfully, Jason Joy not only approved

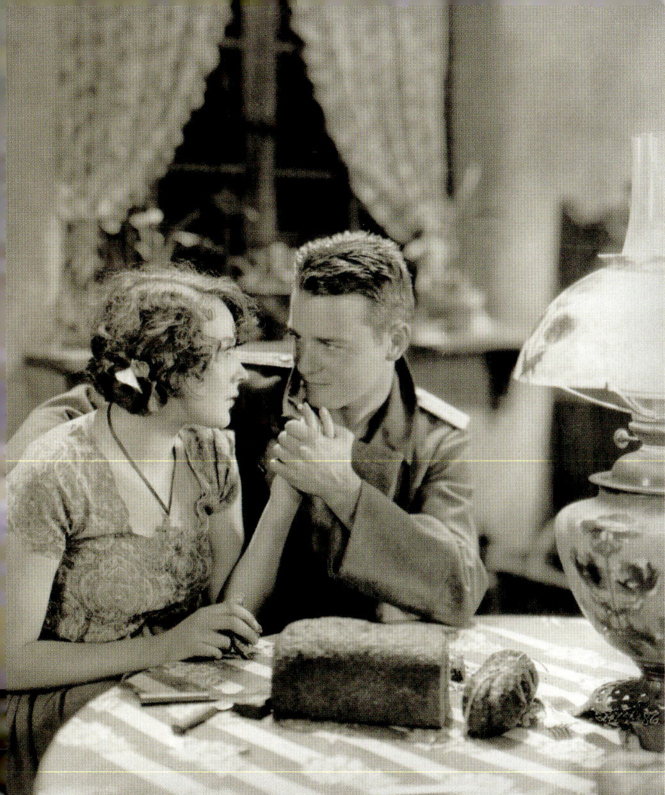

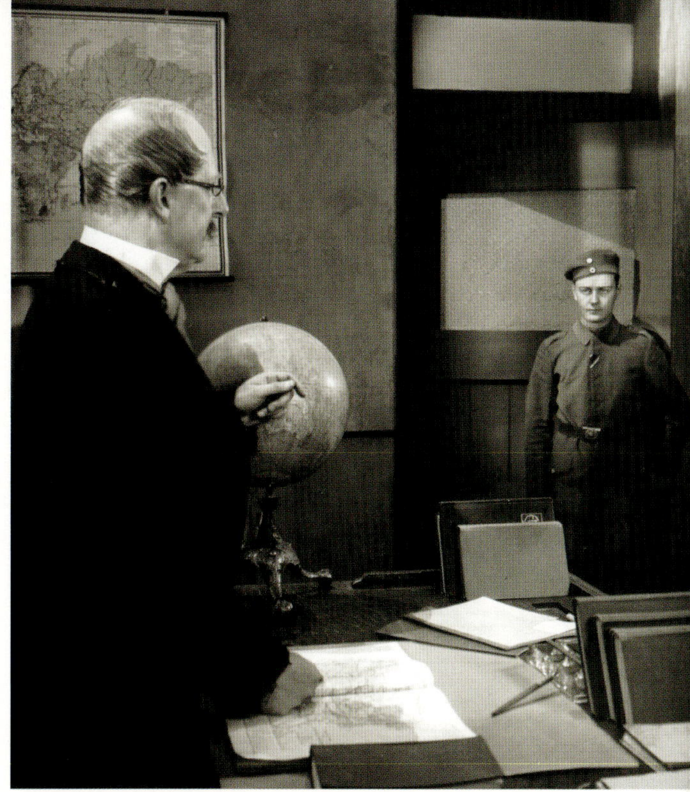

FROM LEFT: Finally, some action the soldiers can get behind. • Lew Ayres has some feedback for the teacher who persuaded his class to go to war. And it's not positive.

of the movie, he also attempted to head off any bad publicity by promoting it through a number of civics groups at home and abroad. He wasn't always successful; for one, the American Legion threatened to picket the picture because of the way it sympathized with Germans.

Most domestic censor objections focused on nudity and implied sexuality. Select local boards derided the scene of Paul and other soldiers swimming in the raw for "unduly exposing themselves." Censors in Ohio, Pennsylvania, Massachusetts, and New York also trimmed parts of the sequence where Paul spends the night with a French woman; imagery of their shadows on the wall proved a favorite target. Internationally, Poland outright banned the movie for being too kind to their former occupiers. It was barred in Italy until 1956, France until 1963, and Austria until 1980, fifty years after its release.

Though many of these nations leveled accusations of the film being too sympathetic to the Germans, it was the Nazi Party in Germany that reacted with the most vitriol. Members saw the novel and the movie as an insult to their national honor. Some party members set rats loose in theaters to scare patrons out. Where this didn't succeed, Nazis picketed the film and started riots inside movie houses at the behest of future Nazi propaganda minister Joseph Goebbels.

Despite cuts and bans, the movie brought back nearly three times its cost for Universal and became the first talkie to win the Best Picture

Oscar (called Outstanding Production until 1942). The film would be remade twice, in 1979 and 2022, neither time maintaining the same stoic spirit of the original, though the latter picked up four Academy Awards, including Best International Feature and a nomination for Best Picture, proving once again how relatable and relevant the story remains.

Unfortunately, the movie suffered over the intervening decades as foreign politics and domestic moralities dictated its fate. *All Quiet* was first reissued in the US in 1934, in a version trimmed down from 135 minutes to 90. When Universal wanted to rerelease the film in 1938, the PCA required the studio to delete the majority of the scene in which Paul and the French woman spend the night together. In 1939, after the outbreak of World War II in Europe, another change was made: Newsreel footage was inserted at the beginning and end with a narrator expressing sympathy for the German people and lambasting Nazism. By then, the addition wouldn't lose Universal any sway with Hitler's government, which had banned the film in 1933. It wouldn't be shown again in Germany until 1952.

Almost six decades after its original release, *All Quiet on the Western Front* was returned to its former glory with the censored footage restored in 1998; that same year, *Saving Private Ryan* hit theaters, a modern-day classic that director Steven Spielberg claimed was heavily influenced by Milestone's epic. Nearly a century later, *All Quiet on the Western Front* remains one of the quintessential American war movies. Brooding and empathetic, it asks the audience to see themselves in their enemies, to look at the ways they are lied to by those in power, and to gaze at the devastation from which there is no salvation.

The emotional stages one goes through when they attack the enemy, watch him die, and have to hide with the body in the trenches for hours.

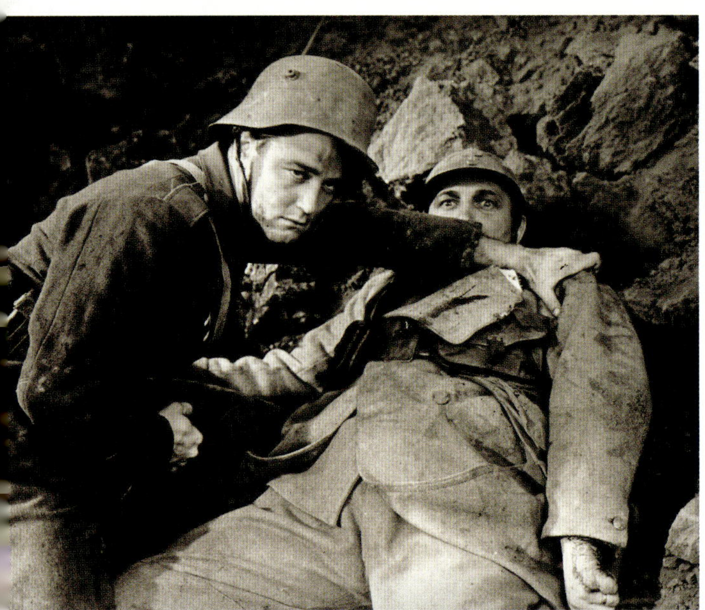

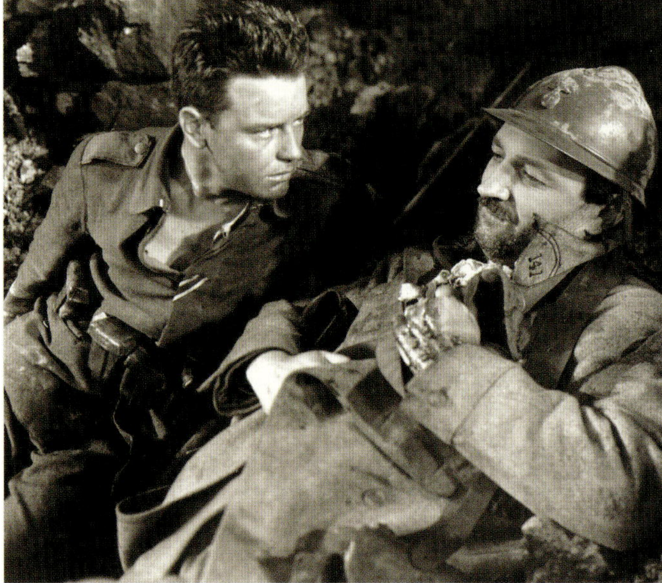

MADAM SATAN

STARRING
Kay Johnson, Reginald Denny, Lillian Roth, and Roland Young

DIRECTED BY
Cecil B. DeMille

RELEASED BY
Paramount, September 1930

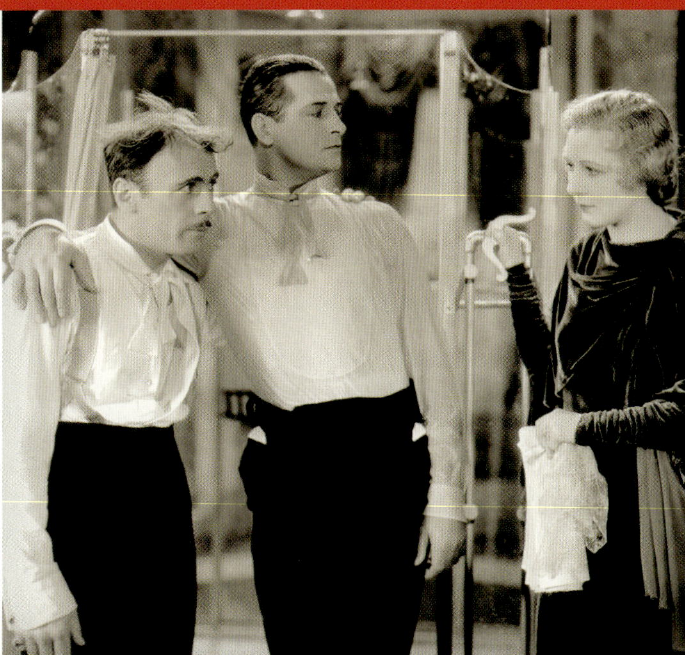

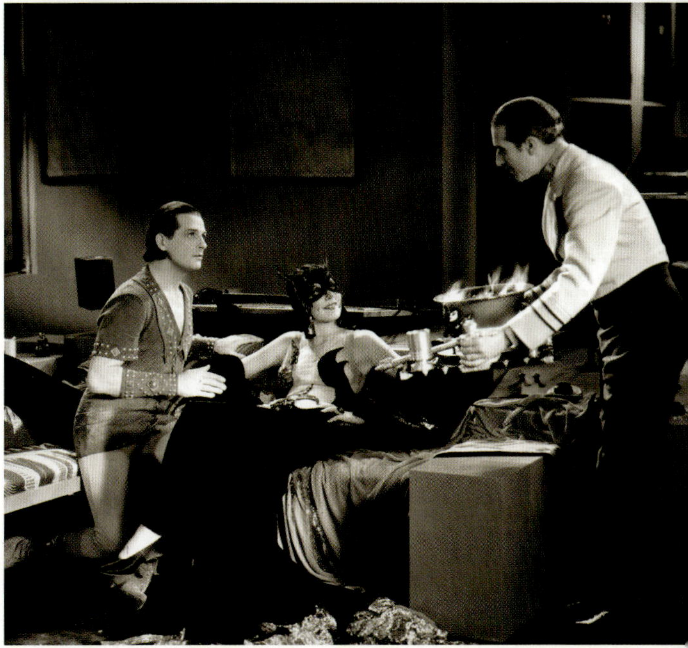

Money, sex, decadence: *Madam Satan* has it all in spades. Cecil B. DeMille's first (and only) musical unfolds almost as two separate movies: the first, a slow boudoir romantic comedy, and the second, an exorbitantly surreal musical aboard a zeppelin that ends in disaster. Nonetheless, *Madam Satan* remains a bewildering picture that takes delight in serving up wildly pre-Code sequences that astonish.

Madam Satan begins on a low note: Refined Angela (Kay Johnson) discovers her husband, Bob (Reginald Denny), and his friend Jimmy (Roland Young) stumbling home from a wild night out; soon thereafter, she suspects Bob is stepping out on her with Trixie (Lillian Roth). Angela protests that all her rival has is her body, and when confronting her, Trixie wholeheartedly agrees. "You made him sick of virtue, I'll make him so sick of vice he'll scream for decency," Angela fires back.

And what better way to commence the honorable woman versus gold digger competition than

FROM TOP: Kay Johnson goes from cold . . . •
. . . to hot as Madam Satan.

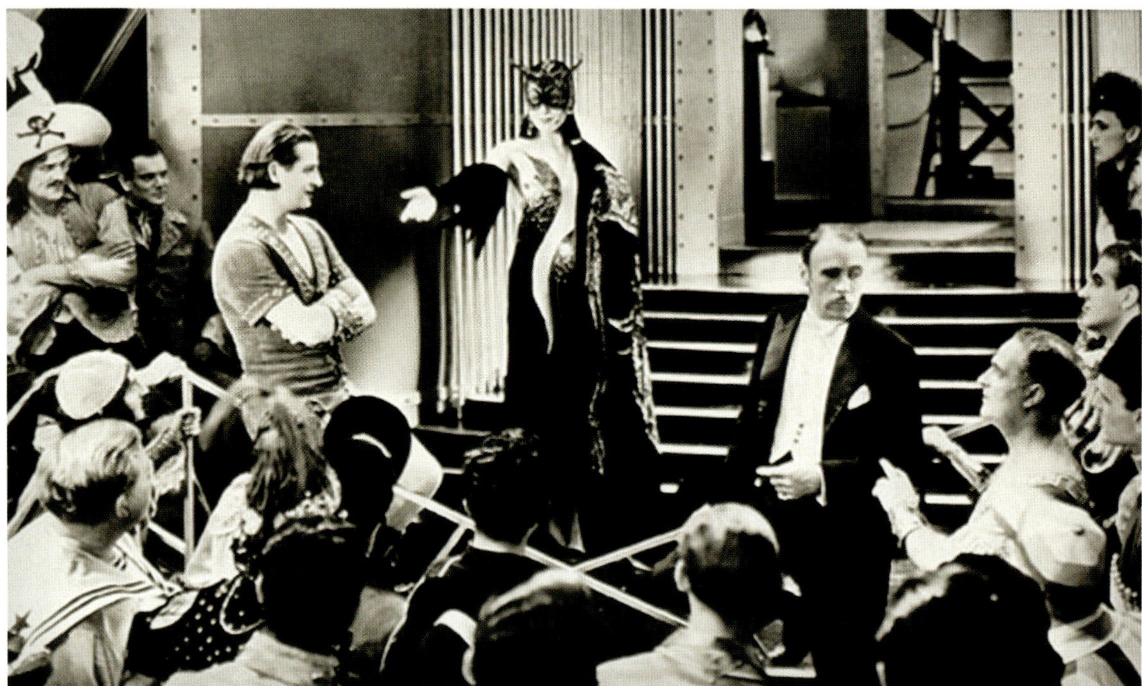

Kay Johnson giving a master class on how to captivate a crowd as Madam Satan.

at a masquerade ball inside a zeppelin? Scantily clad revelers, bizarre dances, an auction for the most beautiful woman—it all goes down at this bawdy soiree. To add to the chaos, a mystery woman emerges to ensnare everyone's attention. Bob races over to the enigmatic Madam Satan, without recognizing his own wife, and wins her. But sparks also fly outside, as lightning strikes the airship, forcing partygoers into parachutes before the whole thing crashes and burns.

The product of three female screenwriters, Jeanie Macpherson, Gladys Unger, and Elsie Janis, *Madam Satan* did not shy away from taking jabs at the precarity of some male egos. For starters, the film lampoons Bob's and Jimmy's inability to control their childish impulses toward women. Both men gleefully jump at the chance to "go to hell with Madam Satan"—as most of the guys at the party do—while Bob ends up dumping Trixie for the mysterious Madam like a child entranced by a shiny new toy.

From beginning to end, the picture also offers commentary on the sexual double standards women can face in marriage. Bob decries his wife's lack of sex appeal right from the start; according to him, Angela's traditional demeanor propelled him directly into Trixie's tantalizing arms. So when Angela takes a page from her rival's book and sexes

"Who wants to go to hell with Madam Satan?"

—the titular Madam Satan, at a party on a blimp, apparently having a friggin' blast

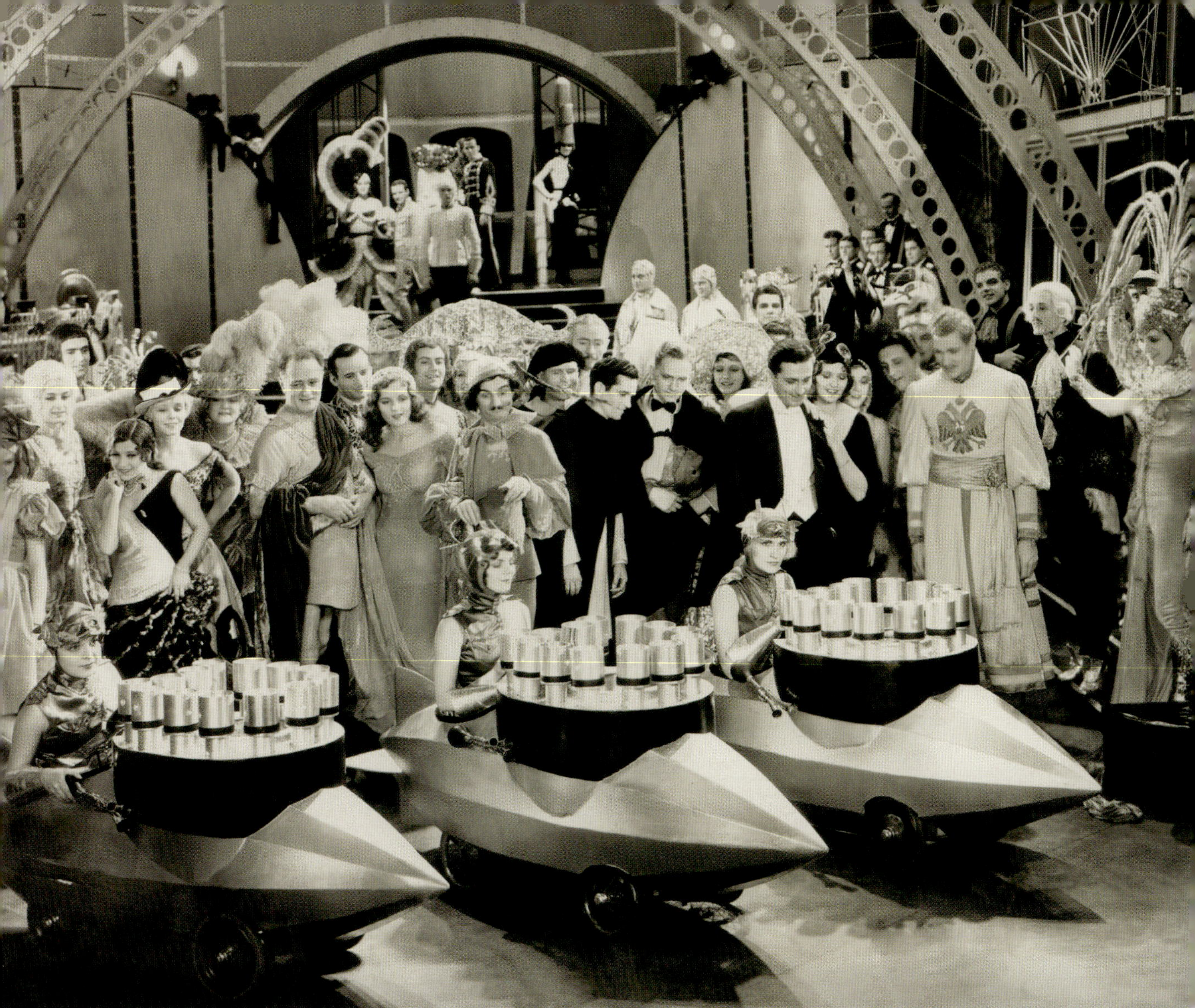

Cecil B. DeMille spared no expense making this zeppelin party as outlandish as possible.

herself up as the alluring Madam Satan, how does Bob react when he finds out he's been seducing his own wife in disguise? He huffily resents her for becoming an unrepentant sexpot. Only after Trixie agrees to give Bob up (in exchange for Angela's parachute) does Bob return home for good—to the same wife who's got some new tricks up her sleeve. (As a sign of the times, however, it's worth noting that while Trixie may lose Bob at the end, there's no shortage of men for her to tackle next and no punishment for her wicked ways outside of a perilous parachute jump.)

Double standards aside, *Madam Satan* tackles several themes that remain pertinent. Taking the central marriage subject and examining how important it is to strike a balance between being

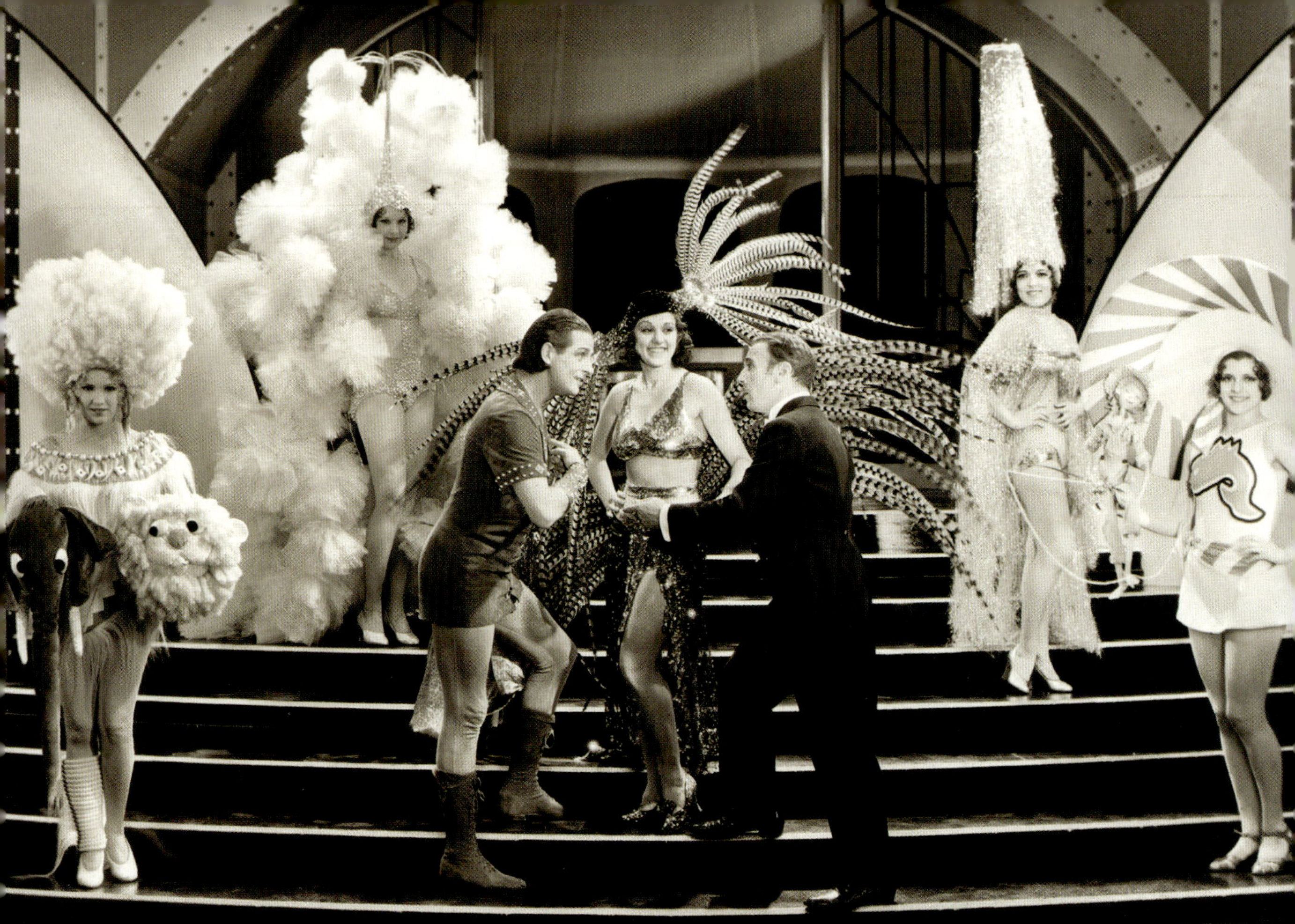

Which is the most outrageous costume in *Madam Satan*? That's for you to decide.

friends and lovers remains timeless. And the idea that we all wear different masks for different people (hello, social media) continues to be relevant, even if few of our masks are quite as extraordinary as Madam Satan's.

The picture's most ridiculous plotline, the calamitous finale aboard the blimp, was inspired by a newspaper headline. During the last days of the roaring twenties, chartering zeppelins for the purposes of partying was cool for a certain subset of wealthy American youths. Such an odd exploit stuck with DeMille, who conceived the air machine's destruction as a farewell to the Jazz Age and all the pretense, debauchery, and rebellion that came with it.

While the party provides a fantastical setting for Angela to assume the Madam Satan persona, it mainly exists as a magnificent pre-Code indulgence of outré costumes and ribald language. Ironically, *Madam Satan*'s creation coincides with the debut of the official 1930 Production Code, as the film began production in March 1930, the month the Code was formally adopted. "The Code, after all, is a human document, and nothing human is perfect," DeMille affirmed at the time, acknowledging that even people who shared the same beliefs differed in how they felt the principles should be applied.

Madam Satan's tumultuous censorship journey is a prime example of that. When consulted in December 1929 on titling the film *Madam Satan*, Jason Joy didn't foresee any issue with it. Presumably, that statement applied *only* to the title. "It is my opinion that the censors will frown upon the theme of the story unless it appears to them to be so fantastic and amusing as to have 'no moral value,'" Joy wrote DeMille. "By this I mean that the censors will probably desire to protect the young women of the country from the idea that they must employ 'passion and deceit' in order to live successfully with their husbands." In ten-plus pages, Joy thoroughly detailed individual lines and visuals that would have to go, including this snippet of one of Trixie's initial blasts: "I give him something to work for! Soft arms around his neck. Warm lips to his—white shoulder to kiss—perfumed hair! I make him thrill—I make him laugh—I 'jazz' all the dullness out of his life for him! I give him what he needs the most—a home from home!"

Following a meeting with the SRC, DeMille "agreed to change the philosophy of the story so as to indicate the wife's acceptance of the gold digger's method by declaring war against her and fighting a successful battle." Apparently, a seduction battle would be more desirable to censors—just as long as the wife won out.

Many American censor boards interpreted *Madam Satan* as a farce and, as a result, graded it lightly. Chicago only had one request, to remove a quip a man aims at Trixie: "I know you by your appendix scar." Massachusetts agreed, and also threw out a scene where Trixie parachutes into a Turkish bath and an exchange in which she decries: "Is a body made out of flesh and blood—is that what you mean? Well, I'm not ashamed of it—it got me where I am today."

Foreign boards proved tougher to crack. Several Canadian territories initially rejected the picture, only to eventually pass it through an appeal process, while the British censors excised three pages' worth of content, including most of Trixie and Angela's contest and lines like, "Oh, she hasn't been a maiden for a long time."

Madam Satan's production mirrored the opulence on-screen; with an original budget of $1.3 million and a production schedule of seventy days, DeMille crossed the finish line after only fifty-nine days and just under a million spent. Unfortunately, by the time filming wrapped in May 1930, the popularity of musicals had diminished at the box office; audience reception to early sound extravaganzas cooled almost as quickly in 1930 as it had heated up the year prior. By the picture's September debut, all the bells and whistles DeMille heaved on the movie just made for a greater dud. Had the film been released either half a year earlier or two short years later, it is unlikely to have suffered from this fatigue.

Admittedly, *Madam Satan* isn't DeMille's greatest contribution to cinema, but the film earns its spot in this book because it embraces its ludicrous plot with a sense of flamboyance, bawdiness, and glee emulated in later pre-Codes. Similar to *The Divorcee*, the protagonist in *Madam Satan* doesn't just let her husband get away with his dalliances—she gets even to own the situation, using her wits and body to do so. And because this is DeMille, she claps back in the most overdramatic, resplendent way possible. Despite its flaws, *Madam Satan* remains a nonsensical film one must see to fully believe.

THE PUBLIC ENEMY

STARRING
James Cagney, Jean Harlow, and Edward Woods

DIRECTED BY
William A. Wellman

RELEASED BY
Warner Bros., May 1931

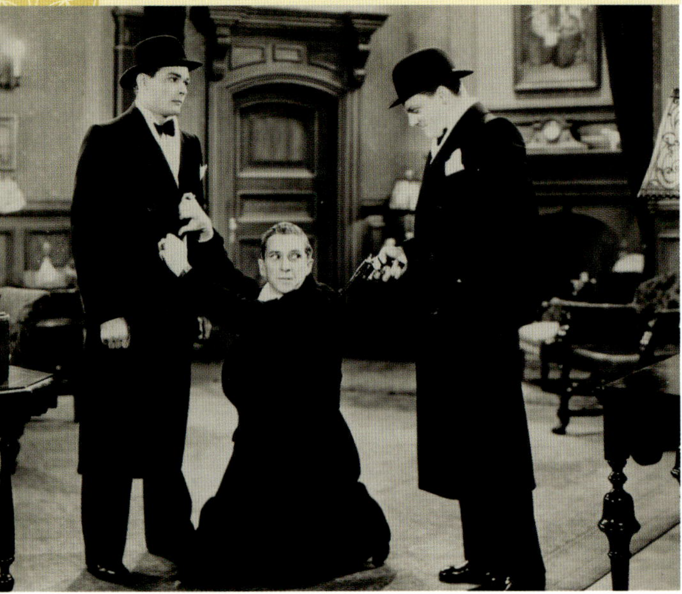

James Cagney shows little mercy in *The Public Enemy*.

While films about organized crime had been produced for at least two decades, the genre exploded in popularity with the advent of talking pictures. Inspired by real-life gangsters and bootleggers who regularly humiliated the law, Warner Bros. found great success with *Little Caesar* (1931) and opted to follow up with another ripped-from-the-headlines epic of crime and lust. *The Public Enemy* added vigorous doses of violence and sex and made stars out of James Cagney, Mae Clarke, and Joan Blondell. It also heated up national worries about filmed depictions of violence and the very real hoodlums who ran amok in America at the time.

In *The Public Enemy*, Tom Powers (Cagney) can't help but get himself into trouble. He joins a gang at a young age and soon moves up from petty theft to armed robbery. When Prohibition starts, Tom and his best friend, Matt (Edward Woods), begin robbing alcohol shipments and make names for themselves among the bootleggers. While Tom's influence, wealth, and power grow, his mother (Beryl Mercer) remains devoted to her other son, the generous Mike (Donald Cook), leaving Tom inflamed and pushing him deeper into the world of crime and "dames."

After a fling with dancer Kitty (Clarke), Tom falls hard for society girl Gwen (Jean Harlow). But as he spirals deeper into crime, Tom gets cocky and sloppy, which leads to Matt's untimely death. He enacts a revenge killing on a rival mobster, signing his proverbial death warrant and resulting in Tom's bandaged body being returned to his childhood home, left as a warning for his family.

The Public Enemy was a passion project for producer Darryl F. Zanuck. He demanded that director William A. Wellman avoid sentimentality, and despite the overtures of family and respectability at the end, the last scene's sudden impact turned any sense of treacly redemption into a cruel joke.

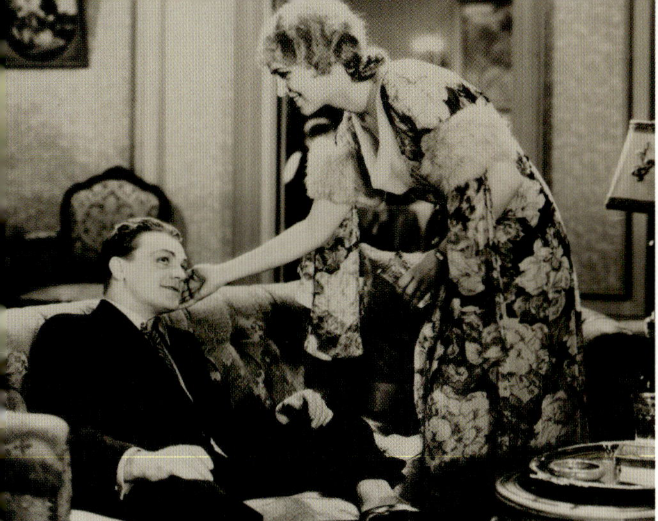

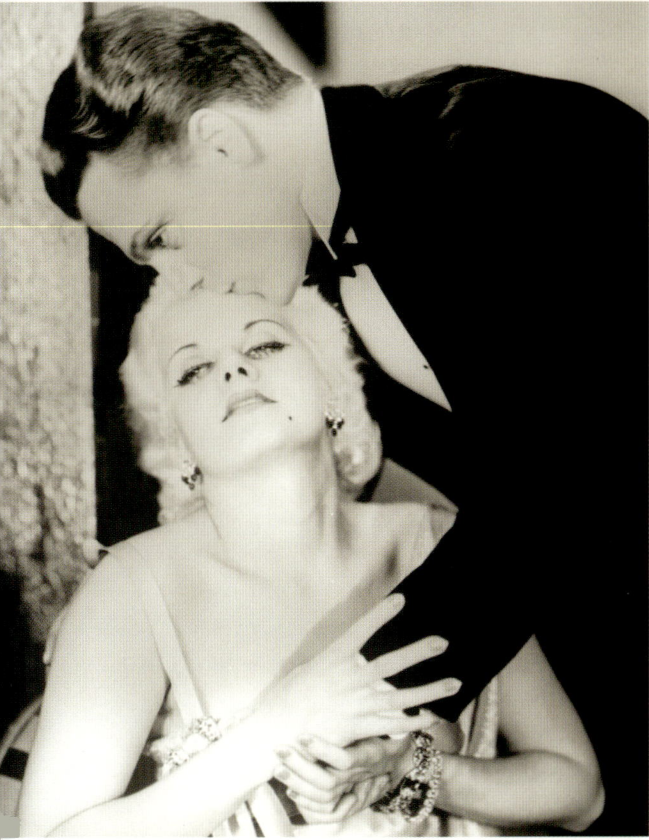

FROM TOP: It's not just the women who get taken advantage of in pre-Codes. • James Cagney couldn't resist Jean Harlow. And soon audiences couldn't, either.

"You are different, Tommy. Very different. And I've discovered it isn't only a difference in manner and outward appearances. It's a difference in basic character."

—Gwen, a society girl who has fallen for the thuggish Tommy and notices that his way of doing things arouses her interest

The film succeeds on the merit of the irrepressible Cagney, who almost wasn't the star. Originally Woods, who plays Matt, was set as the lead until Wellman recognized Cagney's energy and switched the two parts. Cagney had a rough-and-tumble time on set; during one fight scene, he was punched in the face and had a tooth chipped by Woods. Not to mention the machine gunner who attacks Tom late in the movie used real bullets, almost pulverizing the actor.

The film's infamous grapefruit scene is probably one of the most memorable from the era, and its origins have just as much controversy. Cagney wrote that the scene was based on a real incident of a Chicago gangster who rubbed his moll's face in an omelet, with a substitution made to make the scene more cinematic. Clarke later insisted that Cagney came up with the idea on set. She felt cornered into filming it and was still bitter about it decades later when it seemed to be the only thing that dominated her legacy. This scene was cut in Ohio and Maryland, though violence wasn't the issue; with Tom and Kitty in their pajamas, it's hard for audiences not to pick up on the fact that the two unmarried characters spent the night together.

January 6, 1931.

Col Jason S. Joy
5504 Hollywood Boulevard
Hollywood, California

Dear Col Joy:

I want to check up with you and make sure that you are received all of our new manuscripts. Have you received the scripts on THE DEVIL WAS SICK and RULING PASSION yet? SVENGALI, MALTESE FALCON and THE PUBLIC ENEMY will soon be completed. THE PUBLIC ENEMY is the sequel to THE DOORWAY TO HELL, and we are up against a tough proposition, as this story is the biography of a couple of young gentleman from Chicago. However, as you know better than I, DOORWAY TO HELL is not being cut by the censor boards, other than ONE or TWO small eliminations, and I believe this is because they realize that the picture has a strong moral tone, and that is, THE FUTILITY OF CRIME AS A BUSINESS OR AS A PROFIT. This theme in DOORWAY TO HELL is emphasized by the last title in the picture and I believe this is why the picture has not been mutilated by the censors. In PUBLIC ENEMY, we also have a very strong moral theme, to-wit: If there is PLEASURE and PROFIT in CRIME, or the violation of the 18th Amendment, THAT pleasure and THAT profit can only be momentary, as the basic foundation of law violation, ultimately ends in disaster to the participants.

Also, a SECONDARY THEME, which is that - PROHIBITION is not the cause of the present CRIME WAIVE - mobs and gangs have existed for years and years - BECAUSE of ENVIRONMENT, and the only thing that PROHIBITION has done, is to bring these unlawful organizations more noticeably before the eye of the public. The REPEAL of the 18th Amendment could not possibly stop CRIME or GANG WARFARE. The only thing that can STOP Same, is the betterment of ENVIRONMENT and living conditions in the lawer regions. In other words, PUBLIC ENEMY is the story of two boys who know nothing but CRIME, STEALING, CHEATING and KILLING, and they both come to their death in the picture because of their activities, despite the fact that one of the boys has definitely reformed and on his way to a straight life when he meets his end.

Our picture is going to be a biography more than a plot. There can not possibly be any violation of the Code in same. However, there can be criticism of certain episodes and incidents which we must use to forcibly illustrate our theme. I feel that if we can sell the idea that CRIME is not profitable - IT ends in disgrace of disaster - AND THAT only by the betterment of ENVIRONMENT and EDUCATION for the masses can we overcome the widespread tendency toward LAW BREAKING - we have then punched over a moral that should do a lot toward protecting us, as I feel we have been protected in "DOORWAY TO HELL".

Sincerely yours,

(Signed) Darryl Zanuck

Original letter in "Beauty and The Boss" file.

FROM TOP: Darryl F. Zanuck wanted to make it clear that the theme of *The Public Enemy* was that violence does not pay. But also, one has to show the violence before proving it does not pay. • William A. Wellman and a lion cub, of like minds.

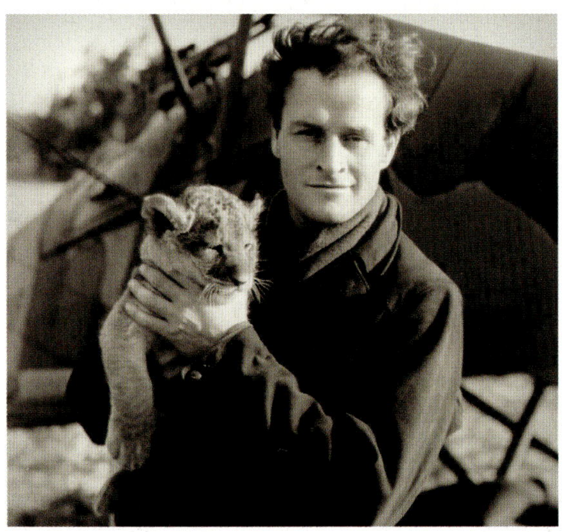

But the grapefruit moment ties into the movie's deeper attempts to grapple with modern masculinity. Tom spends much of the movie stuck on his genuine inability to win his mother's love. In what could be easily read as an oedipal fixation, he instead seeks out power through violence and sex. Tom's inability to be satisfied here only further humiliates him, as late in the film he is assaulted by a gangster's moll, a rare case of female-on-male sexual violence portrayed on-screen, and his wounded ego pushes him closer to his eventual fate. His incapacity to reexamine his circumstances or break out of the cycle of retribution ultimately dooms him.

Shot in twenty-six days on a budget of $151,000, *The Public Enemy* raked in a million dollars at the box office, making it one of the highest-grossing pictures of the year. But, while much of the film feels very snappy for 1931, one element stands out: a national sensation after *Hell's Angels*

(1930), Jean Harlow's performance as the society sexpot who drives Tom out of his mind is a struggle. With training and work, she would polish her craft and become one of the biggest stars of the decade before her untimely death in 1937.

Several episodes made *The Public Enemy* controversial; shoving that grapefruit in Kitty's face, spitting beer into a speakeasy owner's mug, Tom's rape, his demise—all these scenes showcase Wellman's proclivity to push the envelope in distressing, yet surprising, ways. Another provocative scene involves a tailor smiling broadly at Tom's biceps and making suggestive comments, one of many "pansy" scenes that were common in the early thirties and set the censors ablaze. In spite of this, Jason Joy labeled the film "entirely satisfactory," believing the movie a good portrayal of the natural consequences a gangster faced.

Besides the mentioned controversies over the grapefruit scene, New York excised chunks of the film, eliminating a warehouse robbery, the scene of Tom killing gangster Putty Nose, and much of Tom's implied rape. Fearing the influence these pictures made on impressionable minds, Joseph Breen would ban *The Public Enemy* from being reissued to theaters until 1953, effectively banishing the film to Warner's vaults, where it languished for over twenty years.

Audiences were reportedly spellbound by *The Public Enemy*, and it's not hard to understand why. Cagney's magnetic performance, plus the way Wellman couches the film in melodramatic language with violent, heated flare-ups, still gives an adrenaline jolt. For all the warnings pasted onto the picture and for all the pain Tom endures in his quest for money and power, Cagney's charisma gives it a completely different energy: that of sly smarts and gleeful recklessness. Cagney's macho performance changed the way men appeared in the movies during the pre-Code period and kickstarted one of the longest and most fascinating film careers of Hollywood's Golden Age.

William A. Wellman

Born the scion of a wealthy Bostonian family, William A. Wellman never took kindly to authority and sought to make his mark on the world. At twenty-one, he ran away to join the French Lafayette Escadrille—a group of American pilots who fought for France before America entered World War I. He was awarded a medal for confirmed kills and was shot down in combat. He turned his experiences overseas into a book, which led him to Hollywood. After a brief stint working as an actor, he would go on to direct dozens of films, his first great achievement helming the first movie to win Best Picture at the Academy Awards, *Wings*.

Wellman's crisp and no-nonsense style and willingness to tackle thorny pictures about both men and women was perfectly matched with the Warner Bros. milieu of the early 1930s. *The Public Enemy* made James Cagney into a star and created hundreds of imitators. Other pre-Codes Wellman directed, like *Night Nurse* (1931), *Safe in Hell* (1931), *Heroes for Sale* (1933), and *Wild Boys of the Road* (1933), are covered in this book and only comprise about a quarter of his output at the time. Some of Wellman's other great pre-Code pictures include *Female* (1933), *Midnight Mary* (1933), and *So Big!* (1932).

NIGHT NURSE

STARRING
Barbara Stanwyck, Ben Lyon, Joan Blondell, and Clark Gable

DIRECTED BY
William A. Wellman

RELEASED BY
Warner Bros./First National, August 1931

Tough-as-nails nurses and grinning bootleggers team up to take on an unrepentant would-be child murderer in *Night Nurse,* one of the great romps of pre-Code Hollywood. Filled with a truly gratuitous number of scenes where the leading ladies strip down to their underwear, *Night Nurse* aims for and achieves a raucous, callous kind of fun, establishing a direct line to 1970s nurse exploitation movies while not shying away from social consciousness in the process.

The film opens with Lora Hart (Barbara Stanwyck) landing a job as a nurse trainee in a city hospital. She's put under the tutelage of Joan Blondell's Maloney, who, in one of the movie's many great lines, sneers, "I was afraid the hospital would burn down before I could get into it. Now I have to watch myself with matches." In addition to her time working in the ward, Lora spends her training period getting into extracurricular hijinks with Maloney, one episode of which involves fixing up and then covering up handsome bootlegger Mortie's (Ben Lyon) gunshot wound.

After graduating, Lora becomes the titular night nurse, watching over wealthy Mrs. Ritchey's (Charlotte Merriam) two young daughters who show signs of severe malnutrition. No one seems to care, though, from the consulting doctor on the case (also insinuated to be a drug addict) to the family's blackhearted chauffeur, Nick, played by a young and smoldering Clark Gable. Lora finally figures out that she's stumbled upon a scheme to kill the girls for their inheritance, and, with Mortie's aid, she must save the children before they starve to death.

Night Nurse may be the most carefree ode to mischief among Warner's early-1930s output. Set in the world of bootleggers and easy-flowing gin, the movie showcases a general cold malaise that's common throughout pre-Code films. Government action here, until goaded, is inept or riddled in red tape. Survival comes in the form of luck and kindness, while Nick and his cronies posit a parallel world of truly cruel crimes, ones that even casual criminals like Mortie are revulsed by. Heck, these issues still frustrate people. With a message that it's okay to bend the rules—legal or otherwise—to make sure justice is served, *Night Nurse* is an elegy to following your instincts and speaking up for what's right even in the face of substantial forces.

"Oh, ethics, ethics, ethics! . . . Isn't there any ethics about letting poor little babies be murdered?"

—Lora Hart, dedicated nurse and, in this film, a rare stalwart against a plot to kill kids for their inheritance (you read that right)

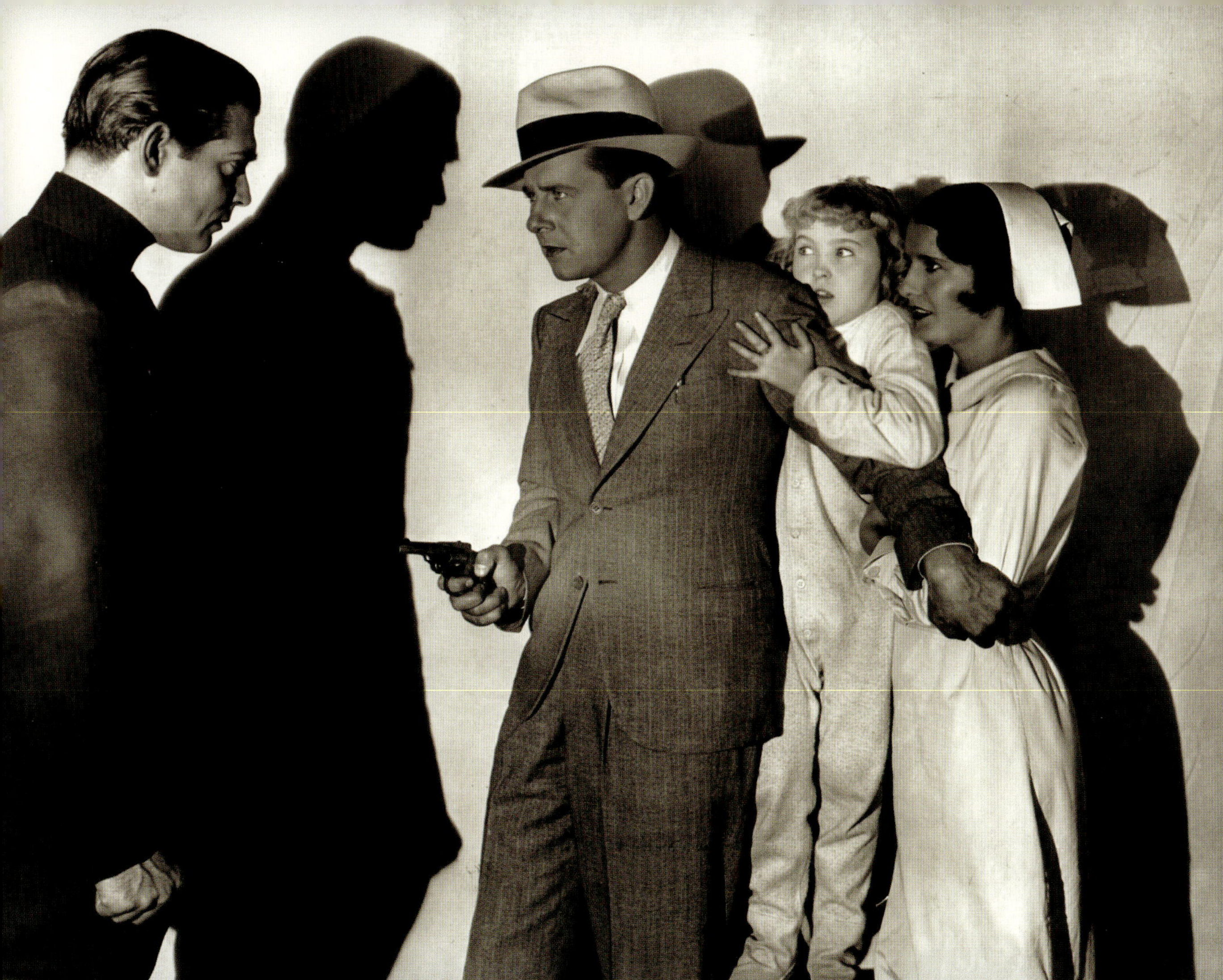

Teaming up with bootlegger Ben Lyon to save innocent children (this one is Betty Jane Graham) from malevolent chauffeur Clark Gable: all in a day's work for nurse Barbara Stanwyck.

Barbara Stanwyck, who shot to stardom in 1930 with Frank Capra's *Ladies of Leisure*, fits perfectly in the Warner Bros. repertoire of tough dames. While early in the film she conveys the naivete of a bright-eyed newbie, her dedication to the profession and staunch belief in helping the needy give the film real power and push. When Lora lays out one drunken lout with a single punch in the middle of the picture, it's hard not to stand up and cheer.

This is the first of five collaborations between director William A. Wellman and Stanwyck, which would include 1943's rowdy *Lady of Burlesque*, wherein Stanwyck does a cartwheel in high heels, among other improbable feats. Wellman's tough, brisk attitude meshes perfectly with Stanwyck's thorny and mushy sides, giving him the perfect muse for an openhearted but deeply cautious view on a perilous world.

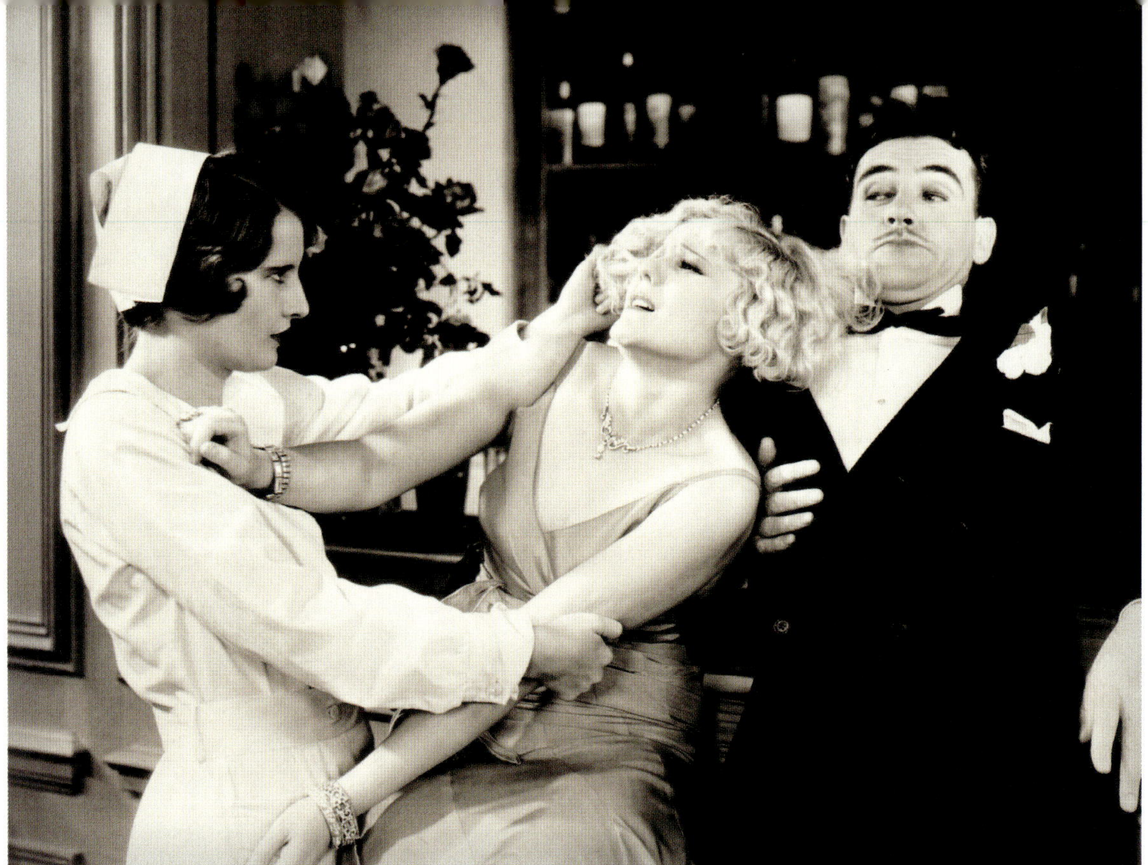

Barbara Stanwyck trying to smack some motherly instinct into Charlotte Merriam.

Night Nurse features plum roles for Gable and Blondell, both also at the start of long, storied careers. While Gable played the heavy in this film and 1931's *A Free Soul* (where his gangster's pining for Norma Shearer leads to severe consequences), MGM recognized his bad boy persona could be turned into a perfect romantic lead. Blondell, meanwhile, is one of the true queens of the pre-Code era, with her wisecracks and a seen-it-all attitude that helps deflate any lofty pretentions these workmanlike films could be accused of.

Originally, *Night Nurse* was *a lot* more anarchic and depraved—if you can imagine that. The SRC read Dora Macy's book, in which Mrs. Ritchey, juggling both Nick and her brother-in-law as lovers, had another child, Juanita, a teenage daughter she also ignored. Upon arriving home from boarding school, Juanita is raped and impregnated by Nick. Meanwhile, Lora is implored not to press charges against Nick for his horrid actions; she ultimately does—and she loses her reputation. All this despicable material, and the SRC's final judgment? "It is not a particularly pleasant story, but I think it will cause no great concern."

Warner Bros. eventually toned down the tale, but issues persisted, particularly in portraying the bootlegger as a hero, showing Mrs. Ritchey as perpetually drunk, and suggesting the ethics of the medical profession could stand above justice. Jason Joy consulted a physician and a nurse, both movie fans, who provided their feedback. Meanwhile, the studio hired gossip columnist Louella

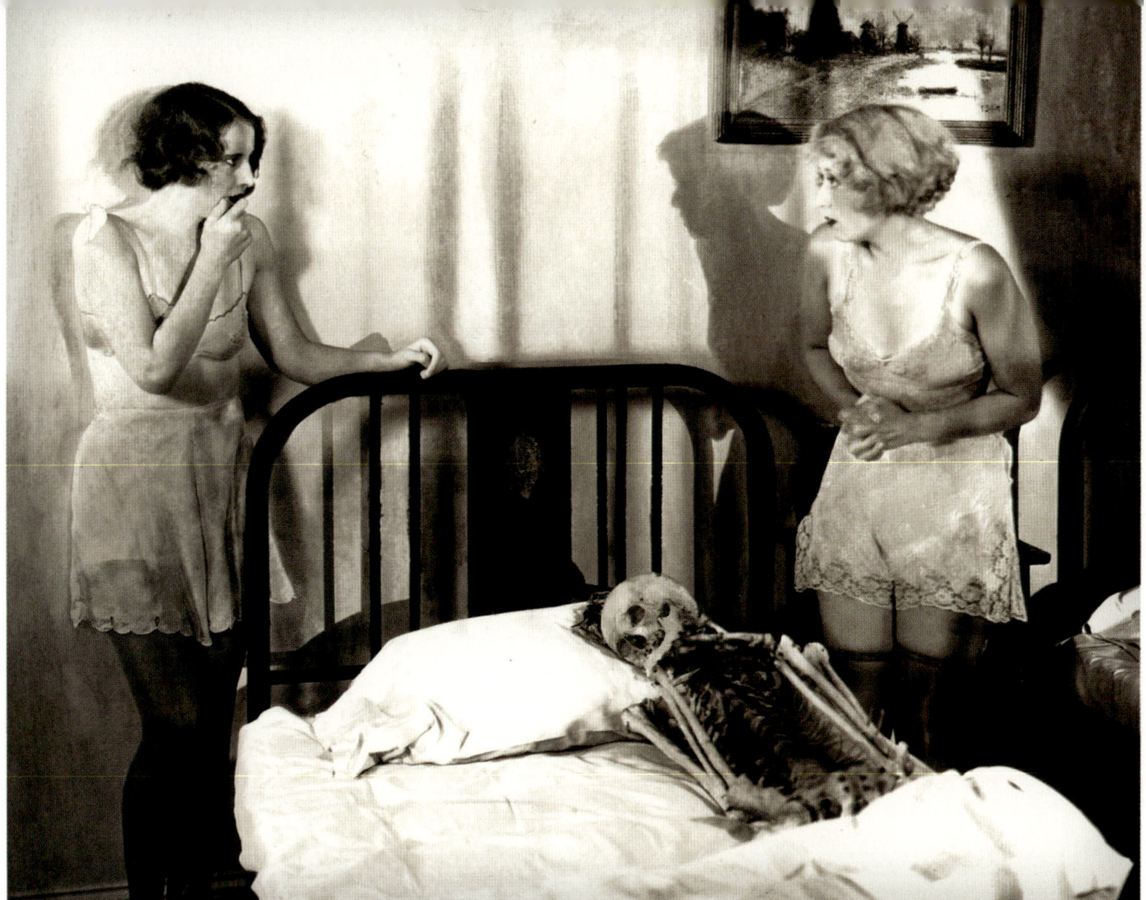

That skeleton scared Barbara Stanwyck's and Joan Blondell's clothes off!

Parsons's husband, Dr. Henry Watson Martin, as a technical advisor—and he took none of the advice imparted by Joy's contacts. Joy's worry that the picture would offend some in the medical industry rang true; one doctor wrote Will H. Hays challenging the doctors and nurses' connections with the underworld, a twitching doctor clearly under the influence, and the nurses' frequent undressing, among other things.

Local censor boards found a variety of items to cut. Frequent offenders included dialogue from disrobing scenes like "You can't show me a thing, I just came from the delivery room" and "Everybody here's seen more than you've got," scenes of excessive drunkenness, and a quip about washing bedpans. Miraculously, the movie endured only a few edits in 1936 to clinch a Production Code seal for rerelease, including excising the word *nut* (which some regions found offensive) and shortening scenes showing the nurses undressing. Through it all, the child murder plot escaped scrutiny—somehow.

There are a lot of great elements to *Night Nurse*, from its day-in-the-life look at working in the ward to the sheer power exuded by Stanwyck to the jaw-dropping ending. The gleeful immorality and irreverent tone make it one of the most enjoyable films of the era on a base level, but the convergence of a bevy of great stars and Wellman's truly go-for-broke pace cinch *Night Nurse* as fresh and exciting even a century later.

SAFE IN HELL

STARRING
Dorothy Mackaill, Donald Cook, and Ralf Harolde

DIRECTED BY
William A. Wellman

RELEASED BY
Warner Bros./First National, August 1931

"The only time you'll ever touch me is when you tie that rope around my neck!"

—Gilda, who is a bit touchy after years of bad business

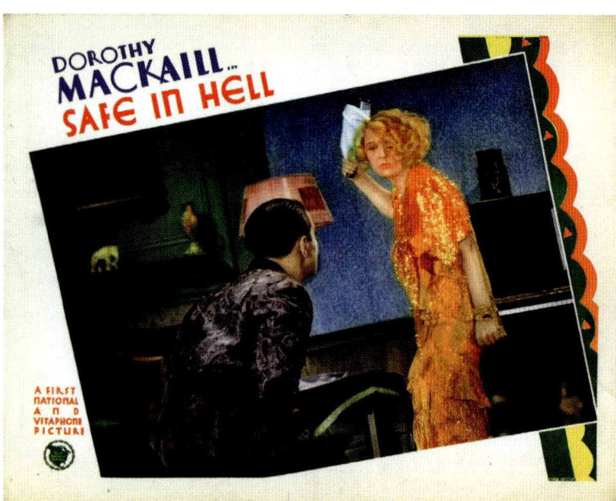

There was at least one publicity tale told from the bottle's perspective (which gets broken by Dorothy Mackaill momentarily). True story!

Charming, isn't it? That's Gilda (Dorothy Mackaill) for you. Such sentiment sums up the futility of Gilda's situation and the despicable environment she's dropped into in *Safe in Hell.* In fact, the mere act of viewing this picture makes one feel dirty, the film's plot radiating a putrid stench and oppressive heat that seems to emanate directly from the screen. With its constant provocation, *Safe in Hell* easily earns its place among the bleakest, feistiest pictures of the era.

The paradox of the film's title wasn't lost on director William A. Wellman, nor is it lost on modern viewers. As her attitude attests, Gilda isn't really protected anywhere. The hazards of simply saying no, like she did, can lead to devastating consequences, something we continue to witness a century later, as an inability to accept rejection can lead to violent retaliation. Gilda's circumstances ruefully prove how dangerous the world can be for women.

Safe in Hell opens in New Orleans, where prostitute Gilda encounters Piet (Ralf Harolde), a man she used to work for . . . until he raped her. Rejecting his renewed advances, Gilda knocks Piet out as a fire engulfs the room—and Piet. Needing to skip town, Gilda is whisked away by her lover, the seafaring Carl (Donald Cook), to a remote island with no extradition law. Unfortunately, the island's sole hotel, managed by Leonie (Nina Mae McKinney), hosts a cadre of desperate male fugitives who repulsively anticipate Gilda's appearance downstairs each day. Gilda promises to remain true to Carl but is left adrift among the jackals—until Piet shows up, very much alive.

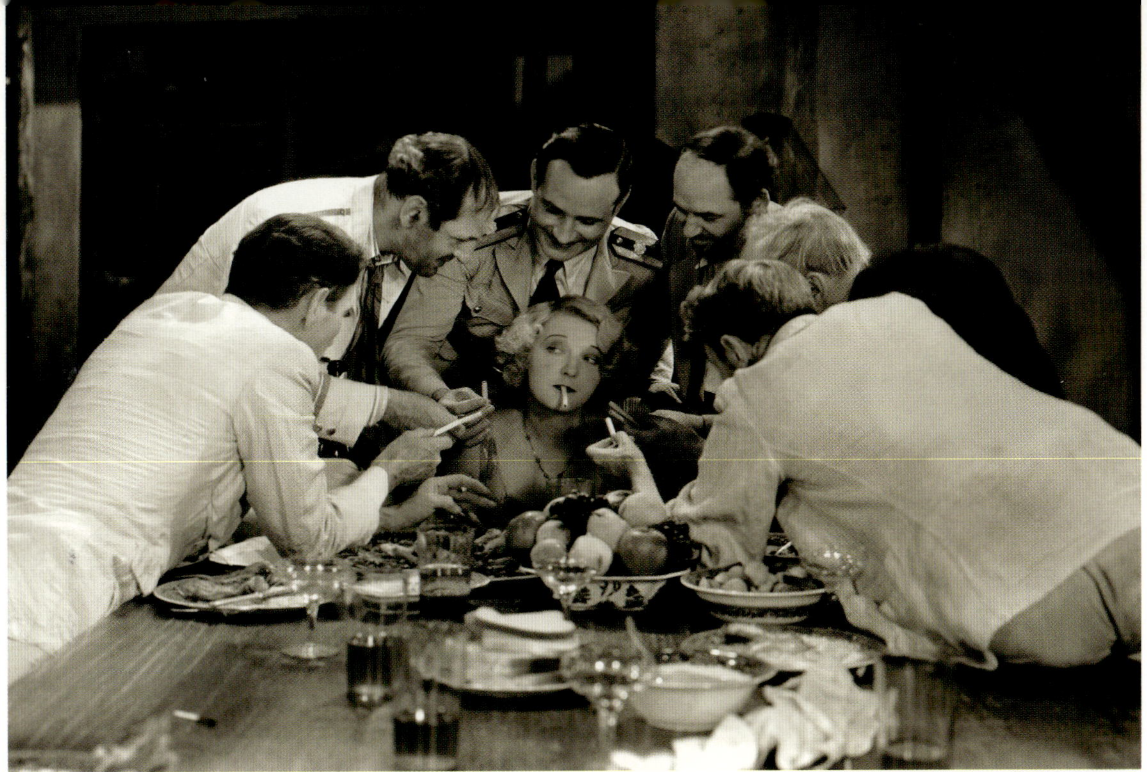

If you can't get them to stop salivating over you every morning, join them.

When the island's domineering warden, Mr. Bruno (Morgan Wallace), loans Gilda a gun, a weapon illegal to possess, she uses it to protect herself from Piet. To her horror, she learns the price of her actions is becoming Bruno's mistress for life. Rather than face that hell, Gilda confesses to murder and is sentenced to death.

For a time, it seemed that backstage studio and casting antics threatened to rival the drama *Safe in Hell* delivered on-screen. Not only did the picture straddle a shutdown and summer layoff period Warner Bros. was struggling through, it originally had a completely different star. After signing a three-year deal with Warners, Barbara Stanwyck was cast as Gilda—but she didn't stay, because Columbia Pictures claimed she owed them one more movie on her contract and filed an injunction.

The studio started production with Lilian Bond as Gilda and several other original cast members, including Boris Karloff as Bobo, eventually played by Noble Johnson, and Spencer Williams in the role of Newcastle, completed by Clarence Muse. But production head Darryl F. Zanuck disliked what he saw so much that he fired Bond and replaced then-director Michael Curtiz with Wellman. (The studio shutdown may have resulted in the other roles being recast.) Warner Bros. then plucked Dorothy Mackaill from a Hawaiian vacation to star, but kept Stanwyck around, paying her until the studio knew for certain whether she would appear in the picture. Two sets of costumes were ready to go as lawyers battled it out, with Mackaill officially stepping into hers once the ruling came down.

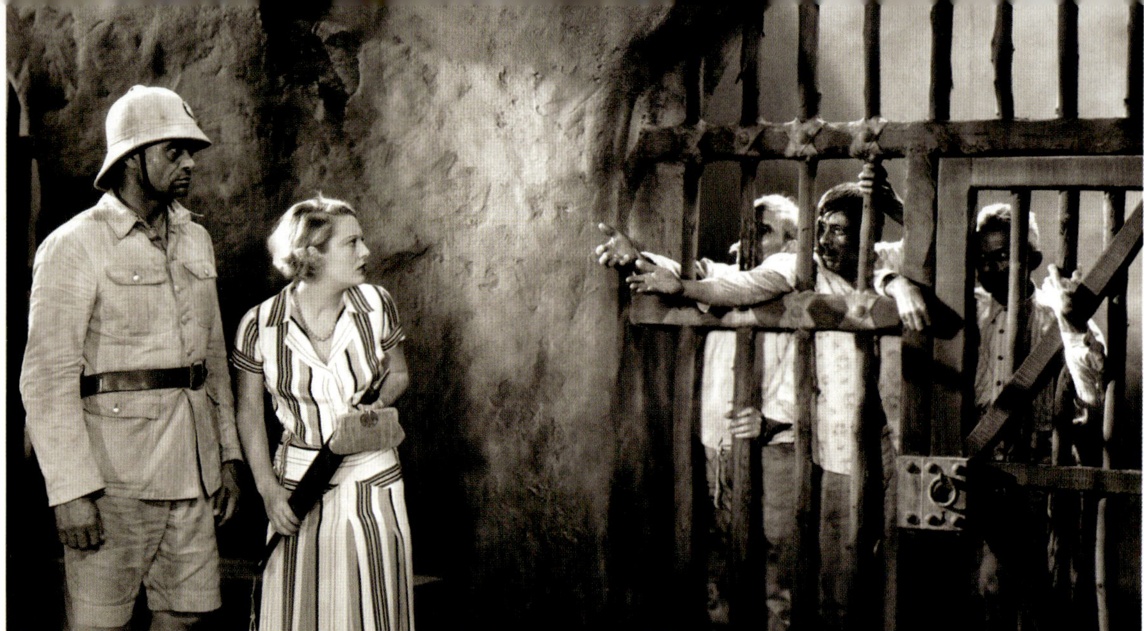

Dorothy Mackaill is *truly* not safe anywhere.

As far as most critics were concerned, the uncertainty that reigned over production seeped into the finished film. Though praise was heaped upon Wellman's strong direction, Mackaill's hard-boiled turn as a woman "more sinned against than sinning," and McKinney's inspired performance, several outlets objected to the movie's overstated degeneracy and implausible plot turns, including *Variety*, which lamented the "constantly depressing air of evil which prevails throughout the picture." In fact, *Safe in Hell* pushes the moral iniquity to the point where many reviewers pondered what type of entertainment the film provided, if any.

Viewing the movie decades later, it's tiring watching Gilda constantly rebuff the steady stream of repugnant males vying for her attention, but at the same time, her durability compels, and the fact that she wins the cons' friendship without succumbing to their badgering adds a certain level of esteem to all those involved. Except Piet and Bruno. They're certifiably the worst.

Enjoyable or not, the picture lured audiences in; Zanuck reported that *Safe in Hell* made a substantial amount for the studio, second that year only to the virtuous *The Man Who Played God* (1932). (Yes, you can laugh at the irony of that.) No doubt a publicity campaign teeming with sordid material helped. *Variety* noted the film's "'Not for Children' slogan . . . gets equal billing in marquee lights with the title." To that effect, pressbook pages offered assorted images of Mackaill poised in a dramatic face-off with a man or gazing into the distance with a hardened stare and a cigarette dangling from her lips. Her sexuality roared across gripping taglines such as "With lips tempting many—She took men for bad or for worse!" What the film lost in lackluster reviews, it made up for with high-octane marketing, which certainly raised eyebrows—and most likely the ire of censor boards.

In some ways, Gilda's struggle between immorality and morality reflected the battle many groups were waging against the industry. As *The New York Times'* Mordaunt Hall dryly put it: "She [Gilda] burns down a New Orleans hotel in the first five minutes trying to be a good girl."

Gilda's best efforts at staying decent lead her straight to the gallows. If a woman has to condemn herself to death to remain virtuous, what's the point? *Safe in Hell* fades out as Gilda ambles toward her fate—and a woman like her wouldn't reemerge from the shadows until Hollywood escaped its 1934 edict a good three decades later.

Nina Mae McKinney and Clarence Muse

One element of *Safe in Hell* most agreed upon by movie critics was Nina Mae McKinney's turn as Leonie. In his biography of his father, William Wellman Jr. argues it was the director's "lack of prejudice and desire to help the downtrodden" that allowed Leonie to speak without stereotypes; while that sounds a little arrogant, it has been reported that McKinney was conferred the power to alter her lines herself, an emboldening move probably granted due to her eminence at that time, as she was well-known as the first Black actress to star in a Hollywood musical, 1929's *Hallelujah*.

But the promising (for the 1930s) racial portrayals didn't stop there: The scene-stealing song Leonie croons, "When It's Sleepy Time Down South," was penned by Clarence Muse, who plays Newcastle. Like McKinney, Muse, a singer, composer, director, and law school graduate, sidestepped stereotypical language in this picture. While we tend to view this allowance as a rather radical move eight decades ago, it's ironic to note that McKinney's and Muse's characters are granted a degree of esteem that was even rare in the context of this picture. Without a doubt, they come across as two characters that viewers can most enjoy.

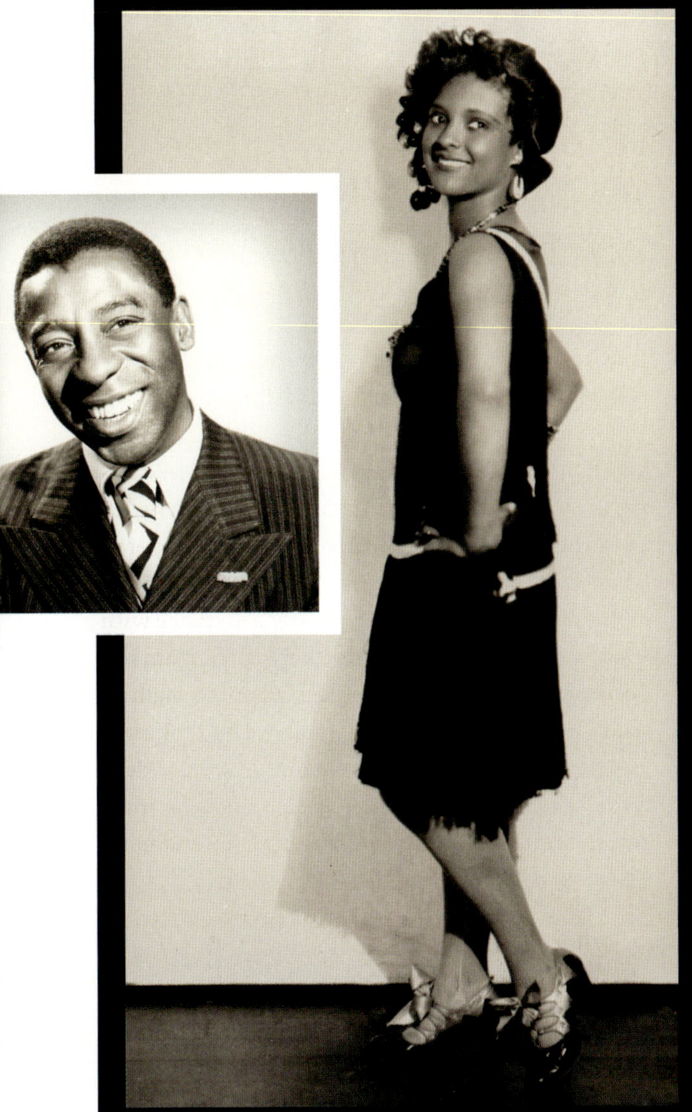

FROM LEFT: Clarence Muse in the 1930s. • Nina Mae McKinney in *Hallelujah* (1929).

FRANKENSTEIN

STARRING
Boris Karloff, Colin Clive, Mae Clarke, and Dwight Frye

DIRECTED BY
James Whale

RELEASED BY
Universal, November 1931

With the lightning-fast growth of technology in the postwar 1920s, there was a general sense that there was no end to what miracles science could deliver. Movies played upon this uneasy reality as horror films came into their own in the talkie era; when so much new technology seemed like magic, could humanity's ability to manipulate the boundary between life and death be that much further behind?

Frankenstein opens in a dreary graveyard on a godforsaken night. There, Dr. Henry Frankenstein (Colin Clive) and his companion, Fritz (Dwight Frye), await the dispersal of a cadre of mourners. You see, Henry has a compulsion, one that terrifies his fiancée, Elizabeth (Mae Clarke), and his stiff family: He has become obsessed with seeing beyond death. Nestled away in his gothic castle, Henry and Fritz assemble a creature, and one stormy night, their ambition is realized: They have brought the Monster (Boris Karloff) to life.

The thrill of the moment recedes when Henry learns that, due to Fritz's mistake, his creation has an "abnormal" brain of a criminal. Realizing his creation is imperfect, Henry abandons him, setting the confused and frightened Monster unwittingly down a path of death and destruction.

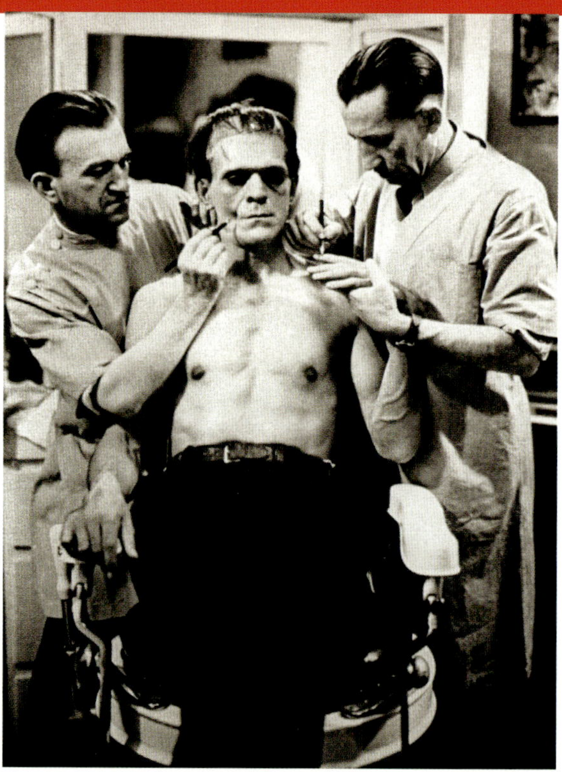

Boris Karloff surely enjoying hour after hour in the makeup chair.

This includes the tragic drowning of young Maria (Marilyn Harris), one of the few people not petrified of the creature but rather eager to befriend him. Horrified at the trail of devastation the Monster leaves, Henry joins a torch-wielding mob and finds himself facing off against his creation in a burning windmill.

When cash-strapped Universal Studios had a surprise hit with *Dracula* (1931), a cheaply produced screen adaptation helmed by Tod Browning and led

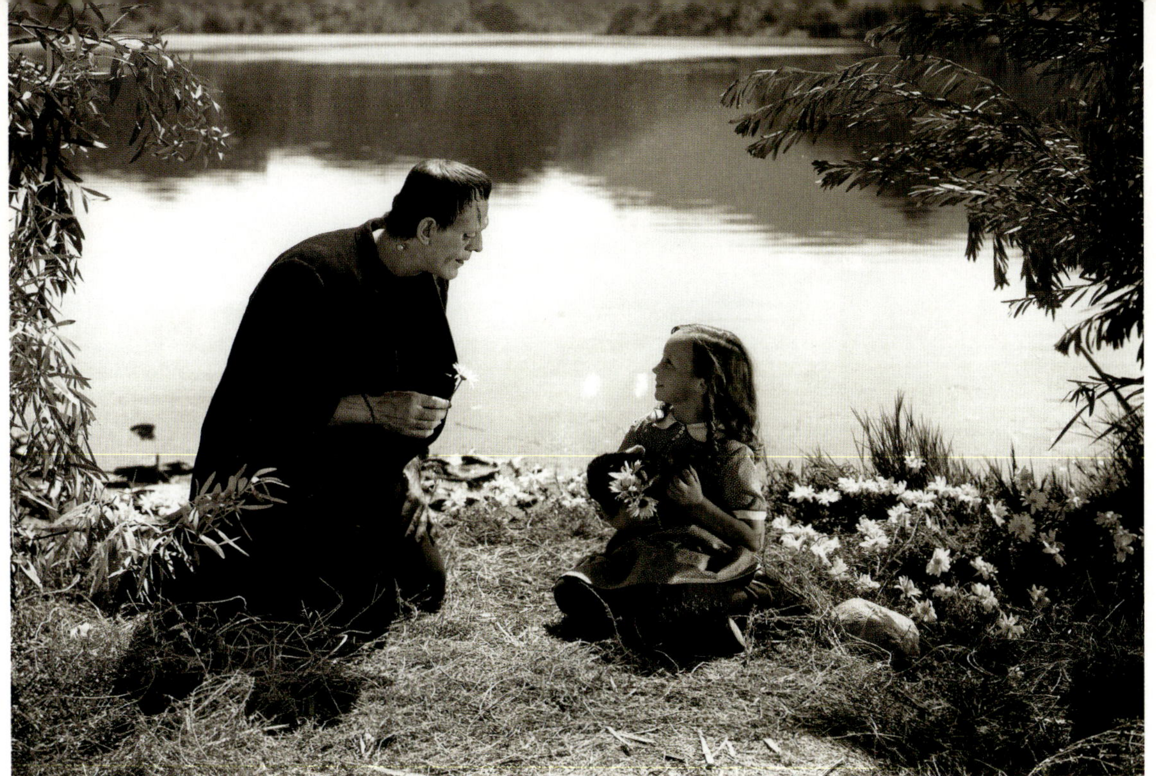

Such an idyllic scene between Boris Karloff and Marilyn Harris—that was censored by many states because of what happened next.

by a then-unknown Bela Lugosi, they sensed a fortune in the wings. It became the studio's top moneymaker for the year, and Carl Laemmle Jr. felt that "thrillers" like *Dracula* were the safest direction for the studio to take.

Director Robert Florey began to tackle the job of adapting Mary Shelley's 1818 novel, *Frankenstein; or, The Modern Prometheus*, a tome widely considered the first work of science fiction. There would be many differences between the novel and the film, such as discarding Shelley's monster's penchant for philosophizing; Florey kept the creature quiet, inserting silent movie pathos in its unseemly saga. Florey was eventually replaced by James Whale, coming off a pair of well-received dramatic features for the studio, *Journey's End* (1930) and the masterful *Waterloo Bridge* (1931).

Karloff would later mythologize about stepping into the role, saying that Whale had simply seen him in the studio lunchroom and found his features intriguing. Karloff's career before *Frankenstein* was a hodgepodge of character parts, and he spent decades supplementing his acting income by digging ditches and engaging in manual

"Have you never wanted to do anything that was dangerous? Where should we be if nobody tried to find out what lies beyond?"

—Dr. Henry Frankenstein, who is most certainly eager to dance with danger

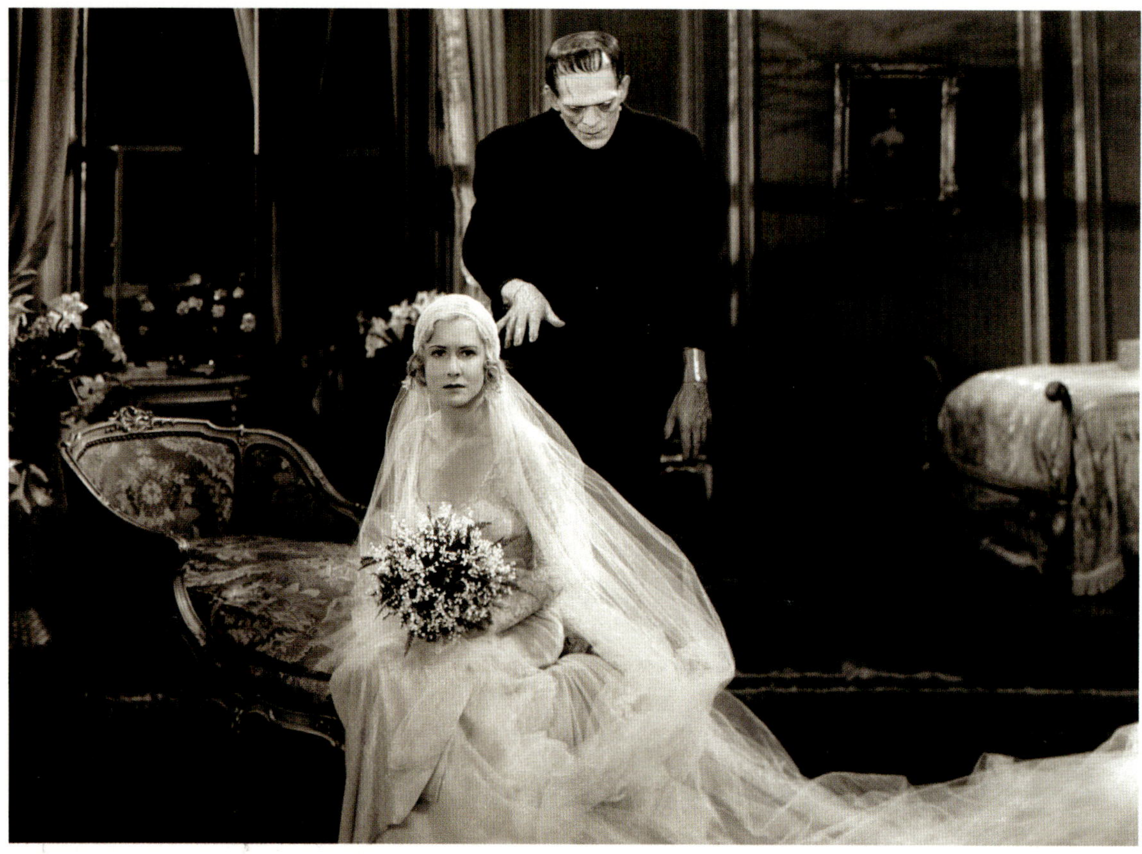

Don't look now, Mae Clarke . . .

labor. *Frankenstein* made the humble, shy, and reserved Karloff a star. He later acknowledged in an interview, "The Monster turned out to be the best friend I ever had."

That creature, made a haunting green color in posters and promotional material, was designed by Jack Pierce. The elaborate makeup, consisting of cotton, collodion, and gum, took Karloff four hours a day to put on. The results were iconic—and frightening. Karloff, who was trapped in clammy makeup for over fourteen hours a day, was banned from taking walks around the Universal lot after a secretary fainted at the sight of him. Guards were posted at the soundstage's doors, and Karloff was forced to take his lunch breaks in his dressing room. The small meals he ate eventually resulted in a weight loss of over twenty pounds.

The SRC had been caught with its pants down with *Dracula*, declaring the film satisfactory right before it was released to unsuspecting and, at times, hysterical audiences. Its massive success made them rethink their permissive stance. With *Frankenstein*'s implicit discussion of God and violating the sanctities of life, along with its general morbid atmosphere, local censors had no end of material to trim. Kansas was the most confrontational, at first banning the film entirely for its "cruelty" and how it "tends to debase morals." Even after negotiations with the SRC, Kansas threatened to cut out half of the movie, including basically all close-ups of the Monster, before Joseph Breen, in one of his earliest forays in working directly with censors, finally negotiated its release.

New York and Pennsylvania trimmed out Maria's drowning, showing only its aftermath, among other cuts. One must wonder what darkness could be conjured in the minds of the audience with this sequence missing. Several states and territories also removed Henry's direct invocation likening himself to God; while one would hope that these boards simply had a strong belief in subtlety, it's more likely that it was the blatant blasphemy that pushed them over the edge. (Meanwhile, Chicago, Ohio, and Virginia approved the film without eliminations!)

Of all the adaptations of Shelley's novel, Whale's perceptive interpretation indisputably stands as the most influential take on the material. (Not to mention, it helped expedite the Monster's permeation into pop culture, not only through countless references, reworkings, and parodies in film and television, but also music, comics, and even breakfast cereal.) While the movie differs considerably from Shelley's novel, it still contains many of the elements she originated and follows in her footsteps by exploring issues regarding the basic and tragic tenets of human curiosity. It's a movie about how people have an undeniable urge to explore and experiment, often without forethought or planning. Indeed, humanity's obsessive need to push the boundaries of what's possible has accelerated in the digital age, as social engineering and artificial intelligence are created at the behest of tech Svengalis who chase profits and ignore consequences, unleashing their horrors on an unsuspecting public.

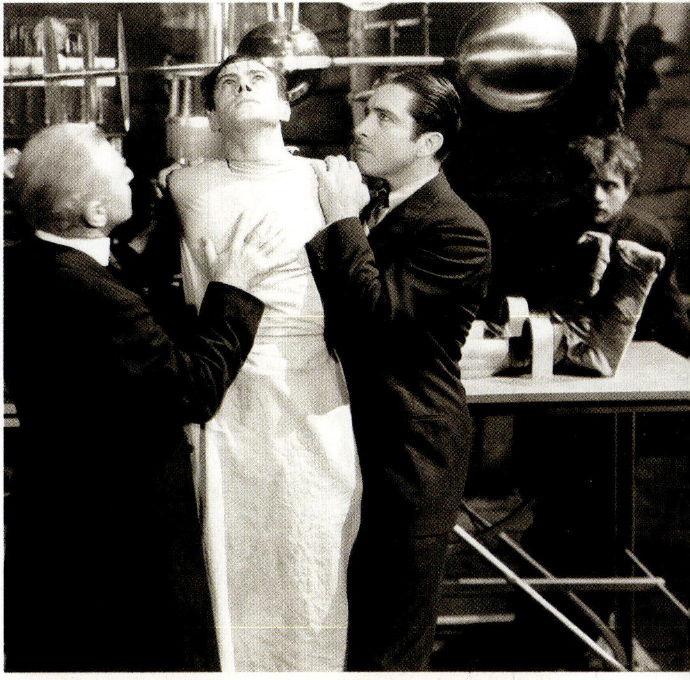

Several censor boards also did not appreciate Colin Clive's obvious god complex.

Frankenstein broke box office records, becoming one of the highest-grossing films of 1931 and keeping the fire lit for other chillers in the pipeline. Other studios, seeing dollar signs, would soon join in, testing the limits with vivisection, murder, and other psychological perils. But Whale's first entry into the horror genre still towers above its many imitators, seeking to find connection and communion with our own darker impulses lest we let them destroy us. *Frankenstein* begs for empathy in a world where only ambition rules.

DR. JEKYLL AND MR. HYDE

STARRING
Fredric March and Miriam Hopkins

DIRECTED BY
Rouben Mamoulian

RELEASED BY
Paramount, December 1931

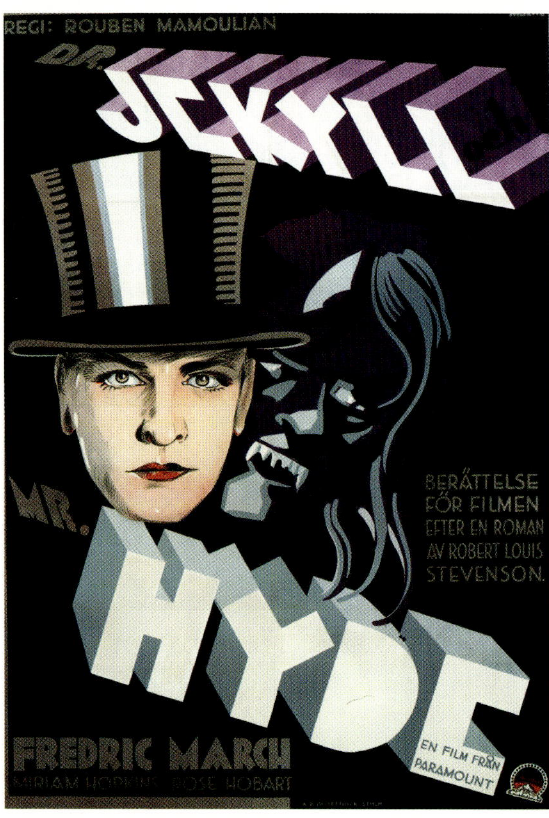

Swedish posters of the 1930s were so incredibly striking.

By the early 1930s, the works of Sigmund Freud had begun to twist their way into Hollywood. The belief that the mind is composed of forces outside of human control fascinated and repulsed filmmakers and, of course, led them toward taking old stories and ideas and making them more psychologically grounded—but also peppered with more sex. Paramount, known for its lavish and luscious star vehicles, was eager to hop on the horror bandwagon after *Dracula*'s success, and the pioneering work of Rouben Mamoulian, director of the innovative talkie *Applause* (1929), gave the studio the confidence to create something both terrifying and boundary-pushing for its time.

The film begins with upright Dr. Henry Jekyll (Fredric March) maintaining during a lecture that man, truly two beings, wages an eternal battle between one's good and bad self. Jekyll's righteous side tries to persuade the father (Halliwell Hobbes) of his fiancée, Muriel (Rose Hobart), to let them marry sooner to no avail—he's "got to have it" as one might say. Deprived, the resulting sexual repression roars to the surface with the appearance of Ivy (Miriam Hopkins), a singer and prostitute who Jekyll and colleague Dr. Lanyon (Holmes Herbert) rescue from a violent dispute. Ivy thanks Jekyll by seducing him, and he's all too happy to accept her show of appreciation.

To purify his mind and body, Jekyll intends to liberate his libidinous half with a tonic he's concocted. Upon testing it, he transforms into the animalistic Hyde and tracks down Ivy, forcing himself into her life and keeping her locked up for his depraved abuses. Seesawing between women

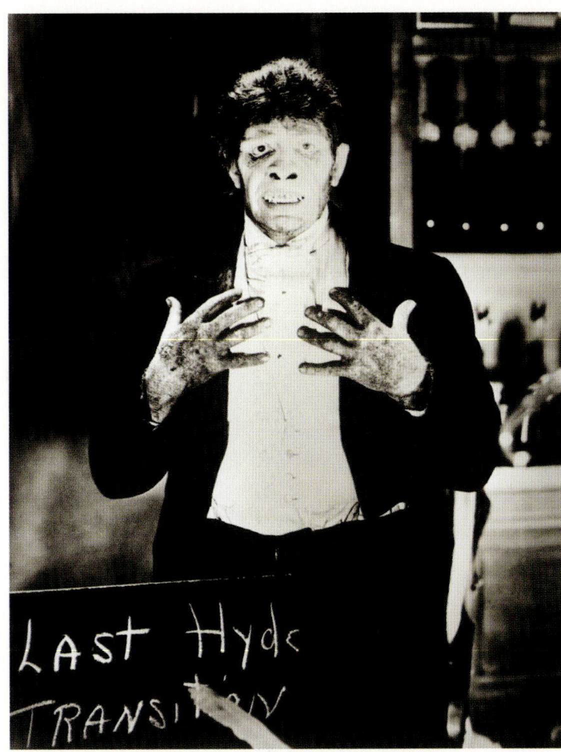

Fredric March showing off Wally Westmore's innovative makeup mid-transition.

"Perhaps you prefer a gentleman, eh? One of those fine-mannered, virtuous, and honorable gentlemen. One of those panting hypocrites who like your legs but talk about your garters."

—Mr. Hyde, displeased at being compared to his "better" half

and his two warring selves, Jekyll vows to conquer Hyde and no longer transform, but the experiment has gone beyond his control, and his attempts at repression only make things worse, resulting in Ivy's death and his own.

By 1931, Robert Louis Stevenson's 1886 novella *Strange Case of Dr Jekyll and Mr Hyde* was familiar to fans of the stage and screen, with the most recent film adaptation, starring the inimitable John Barrymore, appearing just over a decade earlier in 1920. Mamoulian kept several plot additions from prior versions, but he honed his focus on an exploration of the primitive versus spiritual. Hyde exists in all humans, Mamoulian declared, and ultimately, he's not a monster. While *Dr. Jekyll and Mr. Hyde* is closely associated with horror films, Mamoulian viewed the story as a "tragedy of man. Man with a capital M."

Upon review of the finished picture, the SRC's Jason Joy hoped for Paramount's sake that the "excellence of the production will offset any apprehension that the theme is too harrowing." Joy noted that horror films like *Frankenstein* were raking in "big money," but at the same time, he worried that "resentment [among the general public] is surely being built up. How could it be otherwise if children go to these pictures and have the jitters, followed by nightmares? I, for one, would hate to have my children see FRANKENSTEIN, JEKYLL, or the others . . ."

The "magnificently done" production, however, seemed to trump whatever apprehension existed, likely thanks to a public already familiar with the source material. Censor reception varied, though; the notoriously strict New York board approved the picture without eliminations, while elsewhere, close-ups of Ivy's violent strangulation sequence, her disrobing, her bare leg swinging from the bed, and her line "Come back soon" were frequent offenders. Abroad, Finland flat out rejected the film because it was "considered too terrifying."

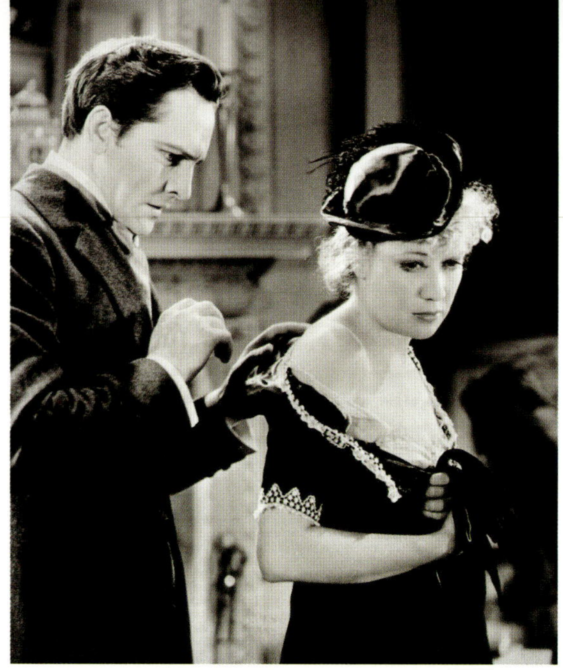

FROM TOP: Fredric March knows where this could lead. And Miriam Hopkins does, too. • Rouben Mamoulian's adaptation turned the sex and violence up a notch.

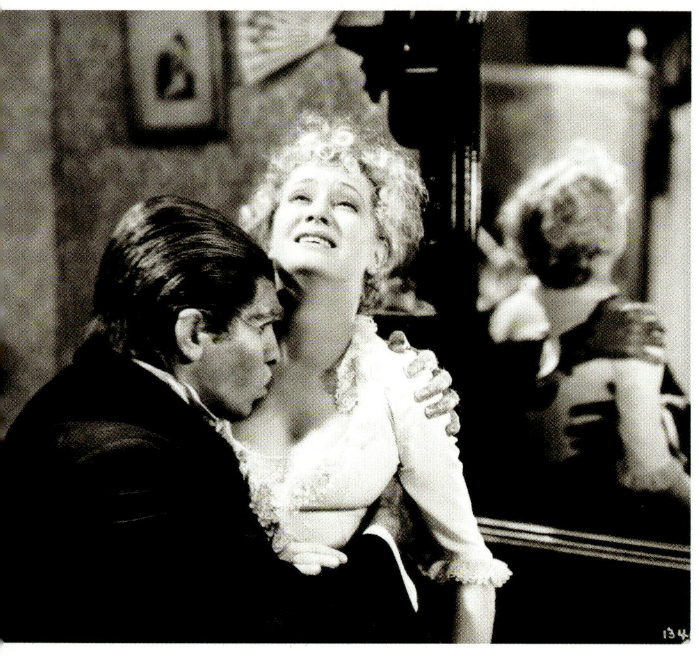

As a character, Hyde embodies an amalgamation of code violations, particularly regarding violence and sex, but the picture stands out from its contemporaries in other ways. For instance, in the film's celebrated first reel, the camera and the viewer proceed as Jekyll in the first person. This provides an unusual level of access and implication to the sadistic, hypersexualized acts later attributed to Hyde.

Then there is March's disquieting transition from Jekyll to Hyde, a finished sequence termed by *Variety* as "a triumph of realized nightmare." The one-take achievement was an innovative combination of Wally Westmore's revolutionary makeup and Oscar-winning cinematographer Karl Struss's use of colored lights and filters to expose and reveal the brute piece by piece. The evolution is agonizingly acted out by March, who rightfully earned his first Best Actor Oscar for his trouble. They would keep the secret of how this effect was achieved from the public for decades.

The themes in *Dr. Jekyll and Mr. Hyde* remain poignant nearly a century later as a window into how sexual frustration, righteousness, and societal pressures can lead to outbursts of violence. While Mamoulian's film asks us to sympathize and understand Jekyll's actions, it also knows that the blame for his decisions falls completely on his own shoulders. The movie may delight in showing off skin and sex, but it also knows that pushing too far beyond the confines of society can leave you rudderless, alone, and dangerous to all.

Paramount requested a reissue of *Dr. Jekyll and Mr. Hyde* in 1935, and the PCA mandated the removal of the scene in which Ivy undresses, but otherwise formally approved the movie. However, following MGM's purchase of the rights for their 1941 adaptation with Spencer Tracy, Ingrid

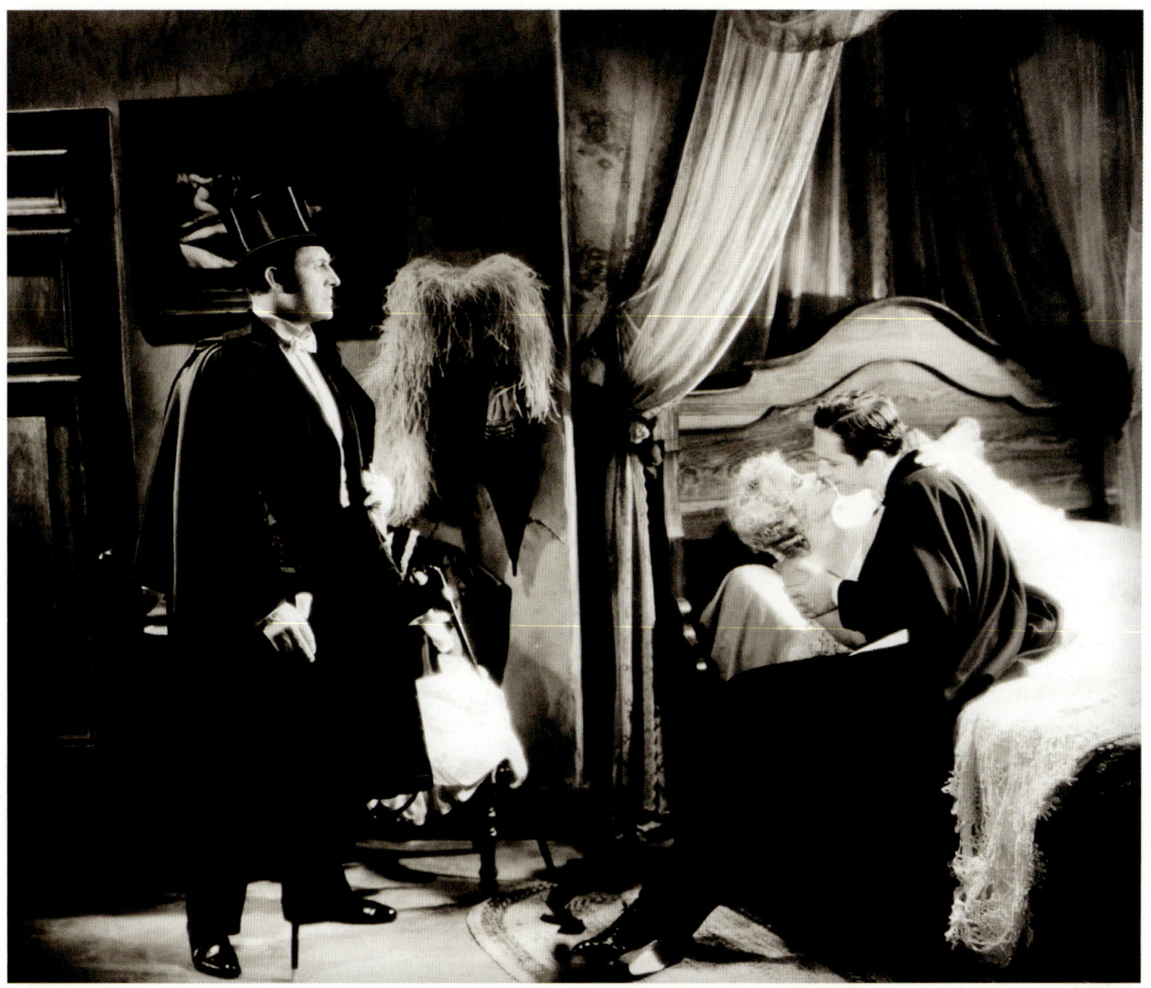

This is what happens when your future father-in-law makes you wait to get married—you land in the nearest prostitute's bed.

Bergman, and Lana Turner, the studio locked up all existing copies of Mamoulian's film, effectively suppressing the picture from public view until a print screened at a Mamoulian tribute at New York City's Museum of Modern Art in 1967.

Despite *Dr. Jekyll and Mr. Hyde*'s unfortunate lost time in vaults, the underlying story continued to inspire different takes on the tale over the years in a variety of formats and mediums. (For instance, along with fellow pre-Code essential *Frankenstein, Jekyll and Hyde* heavily influenced the creation of the classic Marvel character the Hulk.) Almost a century later, *Dr. Jekyll and Mr. Hyde* has not only had its missing scenes restored but found its place as one of the finest horror films ever made.

SHANGHAI EXPRESS

STARRING
Marlene Dietrich, Clive Brook, Anna May Wong, and Warner Oland

DIRECTED BY
Josef von Sternberg

RELEASED BY
Paramount, February 1932

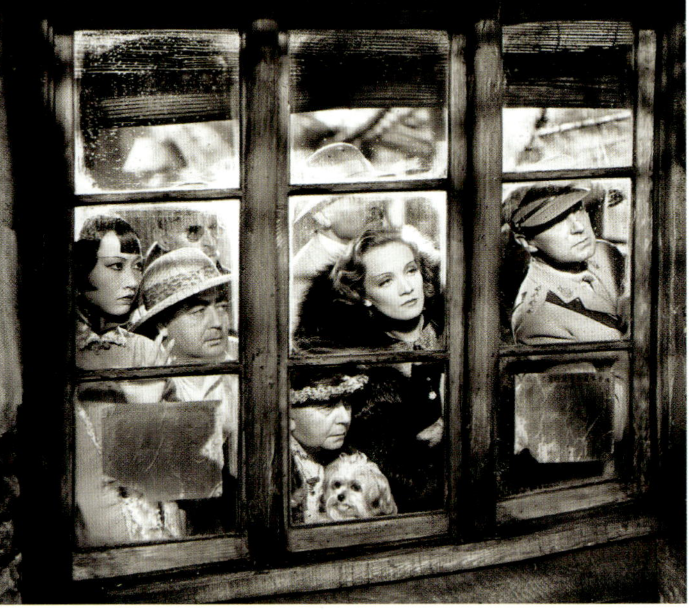

The *Shanghai Express* bunch.

Encased in shadows, pained love affairs, violence, and revenge, *Shanghai Express* is a dreamy voyage into the uglier side of humanity. Marlene Dietrich, at the height of her popularity and hypersexual allure, is cloaked in sumptuous Travis Banton-designed outfits as she fights for the man she loves against the backdrop of a perilous journey. Style and atmosphere permeate every scene in *Shanghai Express*, the pinnacle of Dietrich's inspired creative partnership with director Josef von Sternberg. Its moody, action-packed plot is lyrically presented in one striking, sophisticated picture.

Shanghai Express steams through a tumultuous China beset by bandits and civil war. The group of first-class passengers the tale follows is eclectic to say the least, all of them wary of one another's pasts and motivations. Cynical, unattached Brit Captain Donald "Doc" Harvey (Clive Brook) and Madeline (Dietrich), now known as Shanghai Lily, a German woman with a coquettish grin etched on her face and a flicker of mischief in her eyes, were once lovers, and their love story serves as the voyage's cornerstone. Besides a motley assortment of imperious Westerners, there's a mysterious Chinese woman named Hui Fei (Anna May Wong) and a half Chinese man named Henry Chang (Warner Oland), who isn't the ordinary fellow passenger he initially seems to be.

Trust issues formed the basis for Lily and Harvey's separation years ago, a point that rears its head again as Chang's rebel forces capture the train and hold Harvey hostage. Lily offers herself to Chang in a desperate bid to save Harvey, and eventually Hui Fei, raped by the power-hungry Chang, delivers the ultimate blow. Her act of revenge frees the voyagers, but the whole experience has resulted in a subtle shift in the way the passengers' greedy eyes see their adopted country of China.

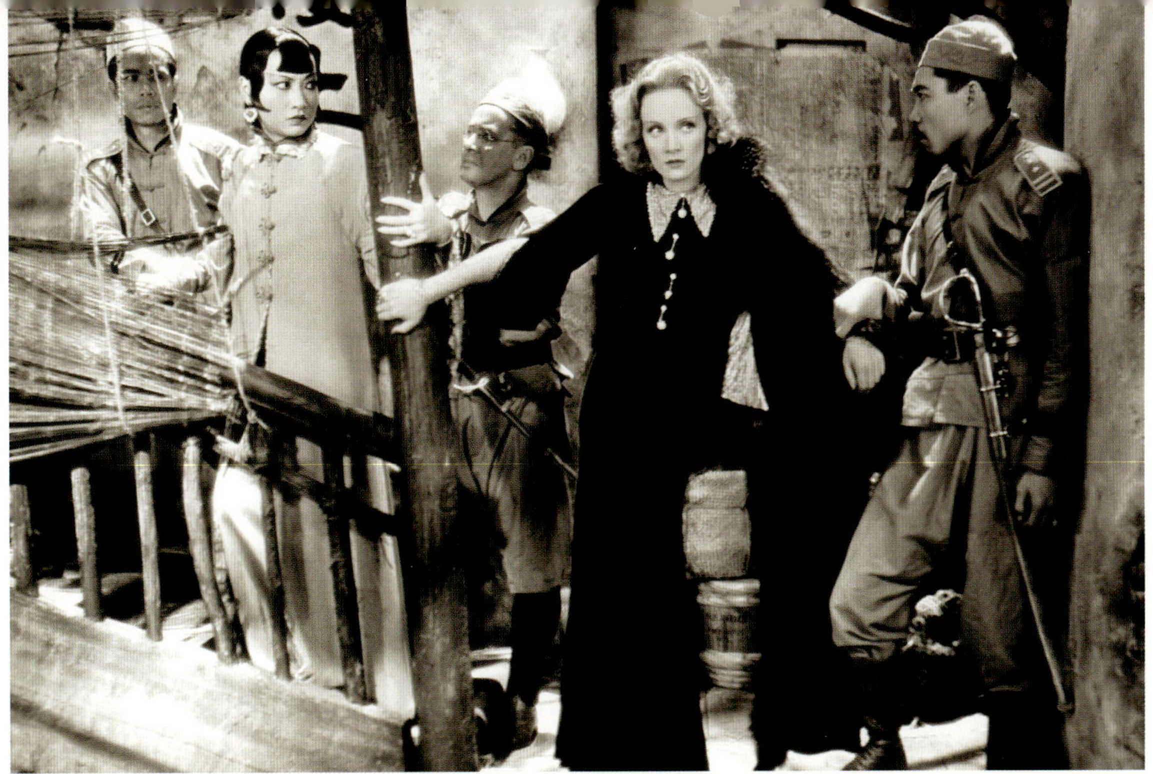

Marlene Dietrich and Anna May Wong take one (okay, many) for the team in this movie.

> "Everybody told me there wasn't the slightest danger. I made a point of asking."
>
> —the virtuous Mrs. Haggerty, upon learning that this train ride through war-torn China was indeed rife with danger

The collaborations between Dietrich and von Sternberg dominated the box office in the early 1930s after their first picture, *The Blue Angel* (1930), made Dietrich a star. Their other pre-Code partnerships, *Morocco* (1930), *Dishonored* (1931), and *Blonde Venus* (1932), are all equally lush and tantalizing. *Morocco* saw Dietrich don a top hat and tails to play a showgirl; she even kisses an unsuspecting female audience member squarely on the lips. Billed as an alternative and rival to MGM's Greta Garbo, Dietrich's Weimar-era sensuality and gender-bending was a sensation. Her presence was a perfect match for Sternberg's skill that relied on smoky frames and multiple planes of action. Both flourished under Paramount's loose structure that gave directors more leeway than other contemporary studios.

Shanghai Express encountered its fair share of hiccups as it made its way from page to screen. Two main issues plagued the film's censorship journey: the movie's portrayal of China and an initial plotline that saw the minister Mr. Carmichael (Lawrence Grant) as a petulant crook hiding behind a priest's collar. It turns out that the possibility of offending or misrepresenting not only a whole country but also a religion had the SRC on high alert. As a result, the Carmichael charade was

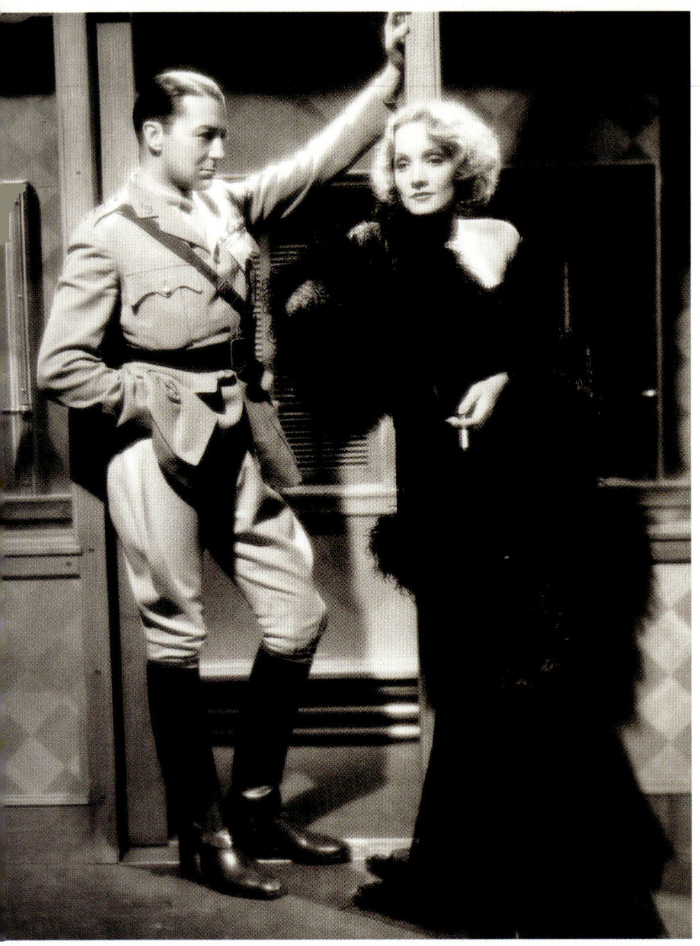

Sort of an inopportune time to rekindle a romance on a train hurtling through a revolution, Clive Brook and Marlene Dietrich.

dropped. But the SRC also voiced concerns about other elements, including a gag about a dog pooping, imagery of human heads on spikes, Chang's remark that he was not proud of his "white blood," and the film's most famous line, "It took more than one man to change my name to Shanghai Lily."

To add fuel to the fire, a Chinese publication accused Wong of disgracing her race with her role, prompting Paramount to beseech the SRC's assistance. "We have a pretty good contact with the Chinese Minister and will be glad to go to the bat with him after we have seen 'SHANGHAI EXPRESS,'" the SRC assured Paramount. In a 1937 letter, MPPDA foreign manager Frederick L. Herron recalled: "At that time they [Paramount] were told they would have to withdraw the picture from circulation throughout the world or else be barred from China." The situation proved so dire that the United States Embassy stepped in, and the ban was lifted—providing that Paramount put forth more positive portrayals of China going forward.

The movie retains a glowing appreciation from film scholars. Pauline Kael termed it a "glossy mixture of sex and intrigue." Mordaunt Hall's original review in *The New York Times* breathlessly called the picture "exciting" before proclaiming Dietrich's performance "impressive." The film won Lee Garmes an Oscar for his cinematography while also netting nominations for Best Director and Best Picture. *Shanghai Express*, for all its moodiness, was one of the highest grossing movies of 1932, an exotic diversion during the depths of the Depression that resonated for its icy-cool charms and sartorial beauty.

Shanghai Express certainly bears marks of its time, regrettably evident through numerous white actors donning yellowface and select derogatory dialogue, which still serve to capture how attitudes were and how they have evolved. At the same time, many of the film's elements proved influential and remain topical, from Garmes's commanding cinematography, particularly the chiaroscuro lighting that adds a proto-noir touch to the proceedings, to the way most of the characters assume dual identities as an act of survival. Furthermore, the trauma Hui Fei endures,

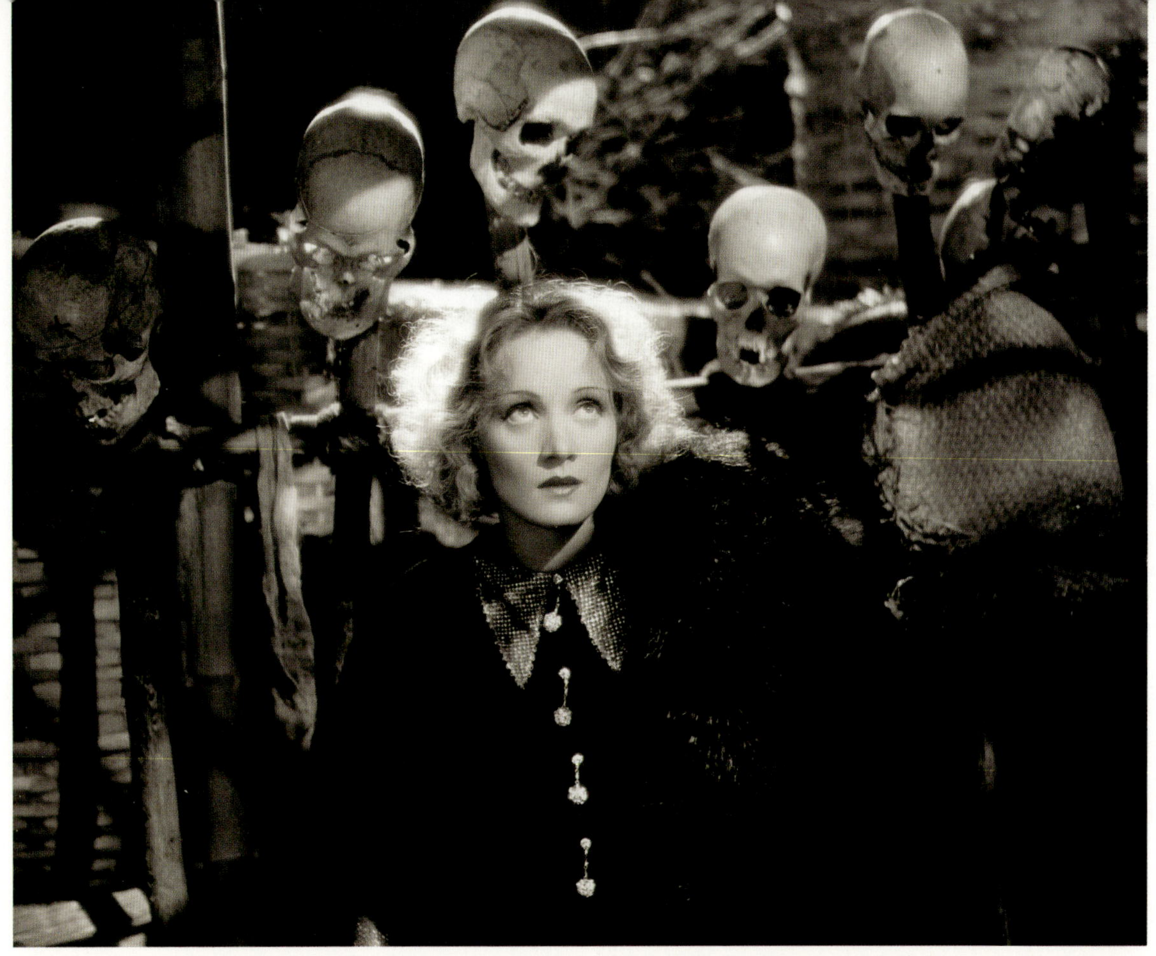

Fun fact: The SRC suggested deleting a scene featuring human heads on stakes in one of their early script reviews.

her refusal to be a victim, and the quiet wrath she employs taking Chang out cement her as a badass—and a very modern one, at that.

The illicit allure of *Shanghai Express* comes from its breathless style and enigmatic atmosphere. Like a lot of pre-Code films, it presents a woman whose reputation is seen as an obstacle and not a firm sentence. It further shows a woman's rage and ability to sacrifice, making a murderer a hero and redeeming a torrid past with the power of true love. The movie also does something rare for the period, coolly contrasting the colonialist views of the many passengers with jaundiced outcomes of their countries' policies. The worst among them pay for their arrogance, while the others bristle at the thought of any lessons learned.

Produced by one of the most glamorous and daring studios, starring the alluring Dietrich at the height of her popularity, and helmed by the innovative von Sternberg, it's no wonder *Shanghai Express* stands as a pristine picture. It both challenges and electrifies audiences while engulfing them in resplendent visual decadence.

FREAKS

STARRING
Harry Earles, Wallace Ford, Leila Hyams, and Olga Baclanova

DIRECTED BY
Tod Browning

RELEASED BY
MGM, February 1932

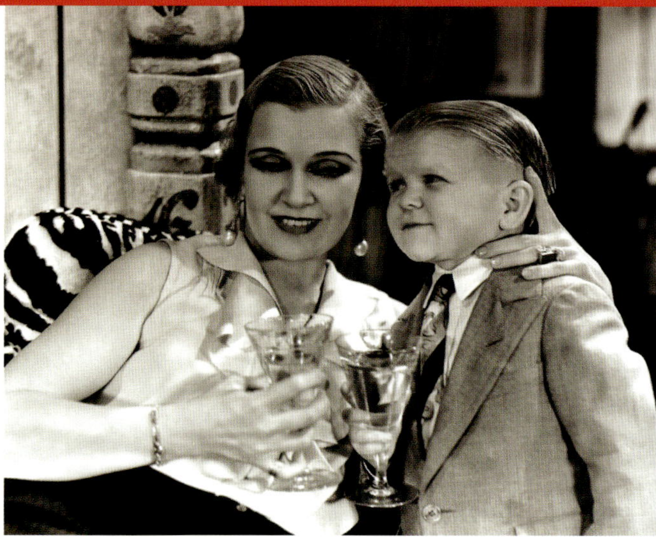

Shady Olga Baclanova likes money. And Harry Earles just came into some.

MGM was the only movie studio turning a profit in the early 1930s. With the Depression grinding away, every other company just dodged bankruptcy while the gloss of MGM and its finely tuned dramas kept audiences entranced. MGM also had a long history of working with both Lon Chaney and Tod Browning, two of the stalwarts of what were commonly called chillers, who collaborated together on *The Unholy Three* (1925), *The Unknown* (1927), and *West of Zanzibar* (1928). When Browning's *Dracula* saved Universal and set off a wave of imitations across Hollywood, MGM was no less immune to the prospect of further riches.

The result of that is *Freaks*, a film that was so outside the studio's glamorous ethos that it was virtually disowned. Ostensibly about circus performers and some extremely morbid revenge, the movie also serves as a humanizing portrayal of a group with disabilities who are so rarely represented on-screen with nuance or care. Even a century later with greater emphasis on inclusivity and diversity, there's nothing that has been or can be made again like *Freaks*.

"We didn't lie to you, folks. We told you we had living, breathing monstrosities."

—a carnival barker, promising something different for the audience

Told in flashback by a carnival barker, *Freaks* is the story of a love triangle in a traveling circus that ends horrifically—for the villains. Hans (Harry Earles), a man with dwarfism, has become enamored with the trapeze artist Cleopatra (Olga Baclanova). While Cleopatra carries on with the circus's strongman Hercules (Henry Victor), she learns that Hans has been willed a fortune. She decides to marry Hans, planning to murder him and take his money.

Hans is lovesick, which upsets Freida (Daisy Earles), another dwarf who has romantic feelings

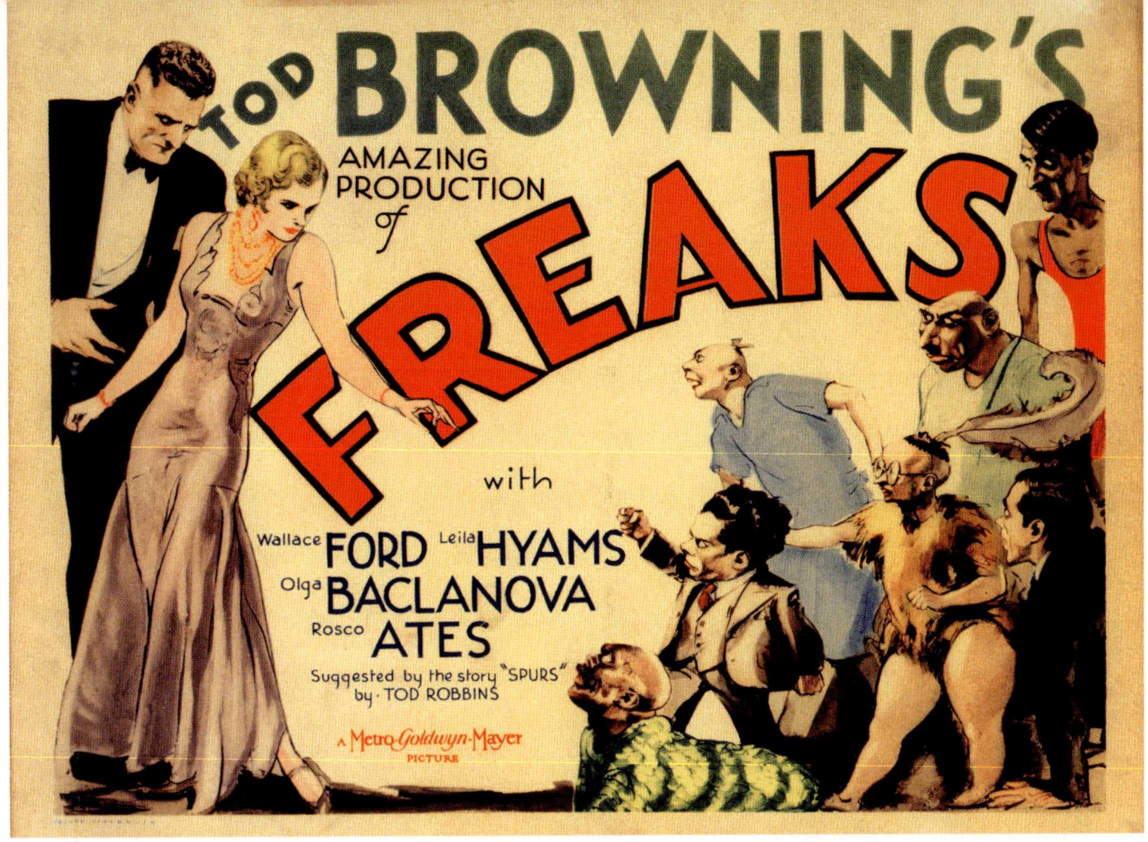

***Freaks* remains one of the only Hollywood features with a predominantly disabled cast.**

for him. While his fellow performers are open and accepting to Cleopatra, she angrily rages against the idea of being considered one of the "freaks." After they discover her attempted murder of Hans, the group gets their revenge on Cleopatra and Hercules one stormy evening, killing him and mutilating Cleopatra. Eventually, Freida and Hans reconnect and live happily ever after.

What this synopsis doesn't reveal is how much of *Freaks* is focused on the daily lives of its cadre of sideshow performers, many of them actual artists recruited by MGM. These included Johnny Eck (Half Boy), Olga Roderick (Bearded Lady), Prince Randian (the Living Torso), and Schlitzie, the most prominent of the featured "pinheads." Daisy and Violet Hilton (both credited as Siamese Twin), had been performing onstage since they were three and spent their life in virtual slavery to their manager; only a year earlier the duo sued to win their freedom and a share of their past earnings. Harry and Daisy Earles, who played lovers, were actually brother and sister, which accounts for some stiffness on her part. The two were part of "The Doll Family," four siblings with dwarfism who lived and toured in America after emigrating from Germany.

Browning himself quit high school to join a circus, working a variety of jobs under the big top for over a decade; his morbid fascinations during this period were confirmed by his new stage name—*Tod* is the German word for *death*. From there, he transitioned into slapstick comedy in 1909 and

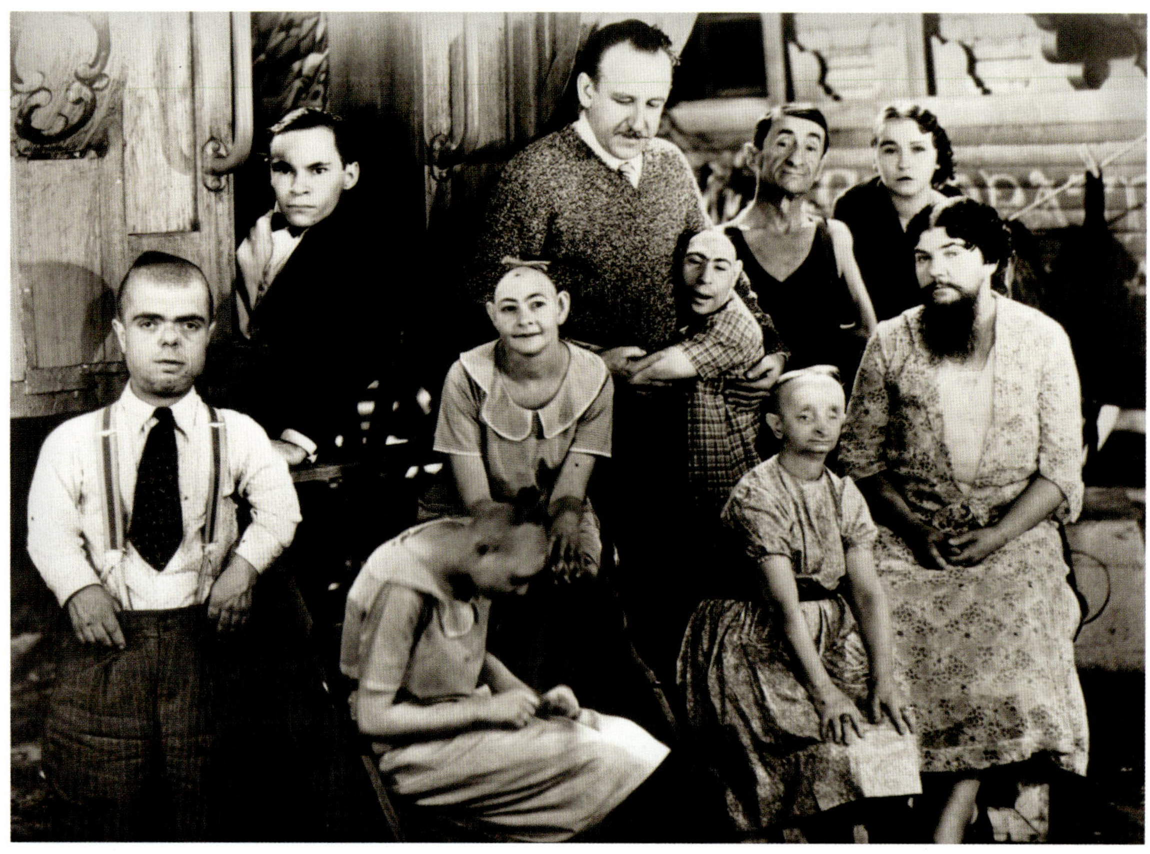

Director Tod Browning brought together an eclectic group of circus performers in *Freaks*.

shifted to movie directing in 1915. After the success of *Dracula*, MGM lured Browning back into their fold, acceding to his demand to film the short story "Spurs," which, along with Browning's own extensive circus experiences, formed the basis for *Freaks*. MGM originally planned on casting Jean Harlow, Victor McLaglen, and Myrna Loy before they began to worry about conflating their biggest stars with a production that reeked of exploitation.

Despite Browning's sympathies for the film's performers, few positives existed for them at MGM. The cast members were refused use of the MGM commissary as they reportedly disgusted the others there; F. Scott Fitzgerald, working as a screenwriter in 1931, apparently threw up after Daisy and Violet Hilton sat across from him and began to eat. Upon seeing the performers, studio head Louis B. Mayer went into a tizzy to try to shut down the film before MGM's production head Irving Thalberg stopped him.

Thalberg was notorious for how much he emphasized and relied on test screenings, reediting and restructuring films extensively based on audience responses. And the reaction to *Freaks* at a January 1932 preview was legendary. People fled the theater. One woman claimed that the picture caused her to have a miscarriage and threatened to sue the studio.

As a result, Thalberg took the film back and chopped nearly thirty minutes, completely reconfiguring the movie's structure. Cut footage altered the ending, which originally saw Phroso (Wallace Ford) and Venus (Leila Hyams) discovering the mutilated Cleopatra, while Hercules serenades her as a falsetto, implying that he'd been castrated. Other items Thalberg snipped included implications that Phroso was impotent and Venus was a nymphomaniac, as well as a scene of a love-stricken seal following the Seal Woman back to her wagon.

Freaks' legacy is as complicated as its tortured censorship history. Attempting to sell it as a purely exploitative horror film, MGM ran afoul of censor boards. The movie was even banned by the United Kingdom; it wouldn't be shown there until 1962. When Thalberg's gamble didn't pay off, MGM pulled the film from theaters. It was rereleased in 1933 without the MGM logo and later licensed to exploitation producers in 1948, who took it from town to town with sensationalized ad campaigns targeted to curious customers.

After the picture was shown at the 1962 Venice Film Festival, *Freaks* became a cult classic, often playing at midnight movie screenings and winning the acclaim of European film critics. The phrase "One of us, one of us!" chanted by the circus performers has entered common parlance, and references to the film pop up in television, comics, and music to this day.

However, the controversy around the picture has never died down. In 1971, Colonel Montague Addison, who had dwarfism, condemned *Freaks*, saying the movie "exploits and degrades us, in a manner that is hokey as well as offensive." Contemporary film writer Kristen Lopez demurred and explained that *Freaks* is appealing in seeing "how people with disabilities naturally adapt to their surroundings because they understand that the world is not built for them . . . There's an attempt to normalize in this movie that still feels very unique and revolutionary." Lopez added that "seeing a world where these characters work together, live together, and love together is very utopian for me."

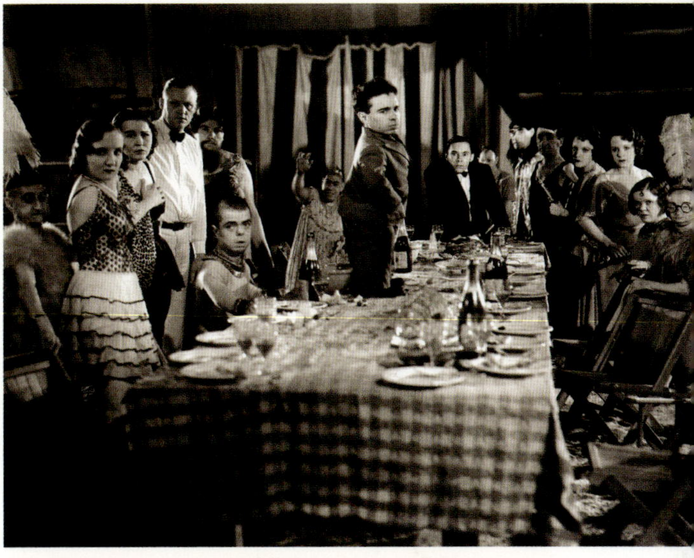

The wedding feast scene in *Freaks* and the "One of us!" chant has reached meme status.

Almost a century later, *Freaks* is still one of the few Hollywood-made films with a predominantly disabled cast. It remains a hotly debatable movie, one that has both seized and set off the popular imagination. Browning's attempt to not only bring a circus sideshow to life but also humanize its performers has and will continue to inspire filmmakers for decades to come.

MERRILY WE GO TO HELL

STARRING
Sylvia Sidney, Fredric March, Adrianne Allen, and Richard "Skeets" Gallagher

DIRECTED BY
Dorothy Arzner

RELEASED BY
Paramount, June 1932

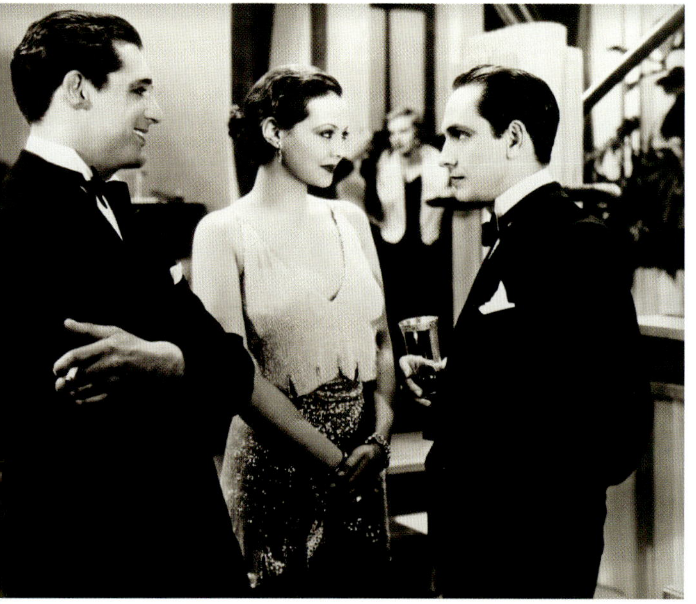

Sylvia Sidney gets back at Fredric March—with a smiling Cary Grant.

Merrily We Go to Hell boasts one thing no other entries in this book have: a woman director. This wouldn't have been surprising a decade before it was made or maybe about five or six decades after, but at the time, the studio system had methodically crowded women out of the filmmaking business. About half of all movies produced in the 1910s and 1920s were written by women, while hundreds more worked in creative roles at studios as script supervisors, editors, and directors.

The most prominent of these creatives in the early 1930s was Dorothy Arzner, whose ethos helped define Hollywood's sound era as well as serve as an inspiration for generations to come. While many films of the time focused on women and the level of freedom they should be allowed over their bodies, Arzner's work delineated the gender lines more sharply, with nuances that more concisely outlined systemic problems. In Arzner's worldview, men conspired with men for their own freedom and to escape judgment, while women were left to pick up the pieces.

Because of Arzner's influence, *Merrily We Go to Hell* is a fascinating look at the risks and dangers women must endure for love. Unlike hundreds of movies that would follow in the next few decades, the film showcases both the harms of alcoholism and the charms of the alcoholic. It is about the desperation to please someone you love while also admitting and accepting their weaknesses.

Merrily We Go to Hell kicks things off at a party, where Joan (Sylvia Sidney) meets Jerry (Fredric March). He's four sheets to the wind but a charismatic, handsome talker whom she connects with instantly. While she is a scion of the rich, he is a wannabe playwright, still smarting after the actress he loved, Claire (Adrianne Allen), left him.

Jerry and Joan marry—despite the fact that he arrives late and slips the top of a corkscrew on her finger—and she helps him sober up. For a brief time, they are happy, at least until his play is purchased and old flame Claire is cast as the lead, reawakening his miseries and their affair. Jerry now drinks out of guilt and shame, and the libations free him from worry, so much so that when Joan catches Claire and Jerry in the kitchen, he laughs it off and expects her to do so as well.

That she does, picking up male admirers along the way, but her attempts to connect with her husband or at least awaken some sense of jealousy fail. It's only when Jerry learns that Joan has given birth to his child that he snaps out of his cycle and rushes to the hospital to see her, if only she could ever forgive him.

The film's strongest feature is doe-eyed Sylvia Sidney. Born in the Bronx, Sidney got into stage acting supposedly as a way to fight shyness. She was spotted by a talent scout in 1926 and appeared in her first movie that year. She often played women who were put through the ringer in the likes of *An American Tragedy* (1931) and *Street Scene* (1931). Sidney would later famously claim that during this time she was being paid by the tear.

Based on Cleo Lucas's 1931 novel *I, Jerry, Take Thee, Joan*, the film's title was changed to the more evocative *Merrily We Go to Hell* for the screen. Speaking on it, Arzner slyly noted, "You'd have to know the times to know the title." Because of the contentious nature of the word *hell*, the *Los Angeles Times* refused to print the title in any advertisements for the picture, though the film's review in the paper escaped unscathed.

"Gentlemen, I give you the holy state of matrimony, modern style: single lives, twin beds, and triple bromides in the morning."

—Joan, just telling it like it is—at least in the world of this Dorothy Arzner film

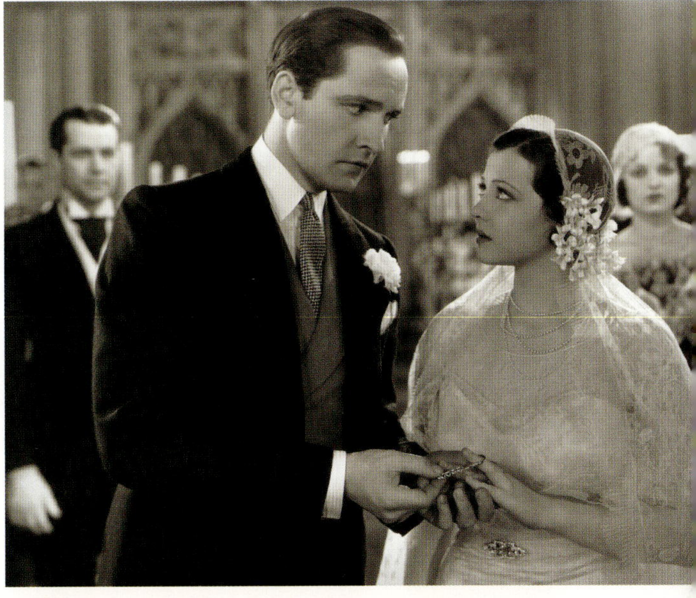

Fredric March gives Sylvia Sidney a corkscrew ring. Should she run now?

While the movie adaptation cleaned up the book's ending where Joan died and Jerry, in a drunken stupor, had forgotten about her death less than a year later, it is still hard to call the finale of *Merrily We Go to Hell* anything approaching optimistic. The movie's take on addiction is a harrowing one. Addicts can be charming and fun, but they are also deeply unreliable. Time and memories slip away from Jerry. It's usually said that one drowns their troubles in alcohol, but that is too passive for Jerry, whose precarious emotional state finds him helplessly stumbling about—through parties, through work, through

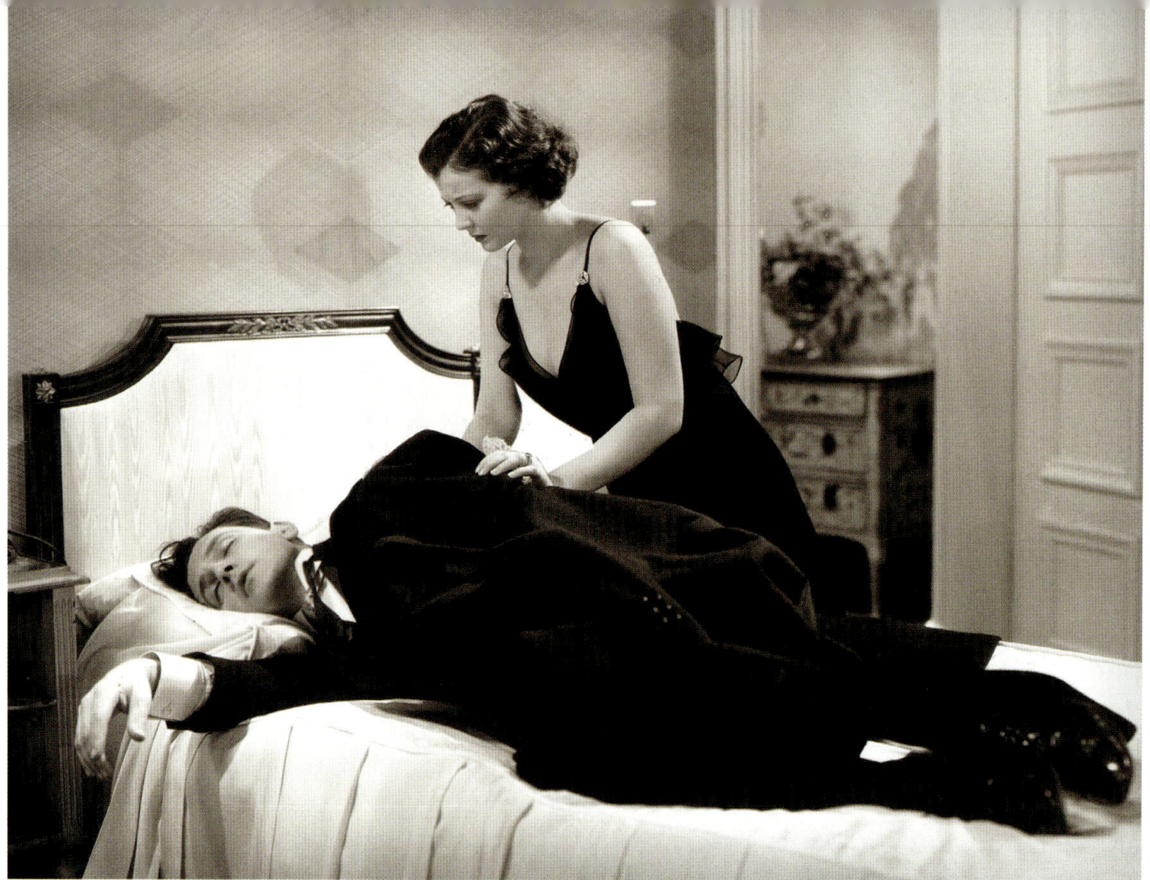

Turns out charming alcoholics don't make great husbands.

women—the entire film. Stories of addiction would be relegated to exploitation markets after 1934, and those would often focus on outrageous side effects or sexual deviance in order to draw in audiences. It wasn't until Billy Wilder's *The Lost Weekend* (1945) that this subject area returned to being fertile ground for filmmakers, and even then, Wilder could only get away with it because of his own directorial prestige.

Arzner also relied heavily upon an already-established trope of the pre-Code period: women leveling the playing field. They may be spurred on by men's certifiably horrible actions—as we've already seen in *The Divorcee* and *Madam Satan*—but the resilience and agency these ladies possess earn them praise and applause. (Yes, even if they bend to societal norms at the end.)

The movie doesn't pull any punches, outside the finale; Depression-era audiences probably could relate with such an uncompromising outlook, a frankness one can still spot in modern cinema, though it's generally relegated to the indie filmmaking world. *Merrily We Go to Hell* and much of Arzner's output may have been part of a dying gasp of women excelling behind the scenes in the 1930s, barely noticeable in the frontal facade of Hollywood proper, but the impact she left is still felt decades later, especially as women are finally starting to enter the directorial ranks in greater numbers again.

Dorothy Arzner

Dorothy Arzner was nothing if not unconventional. A lesbian who didn't hide her sexual orientation, Arzner took medical courses at the University of Southern California with the aim of becoming a doctor. But once she took a studio meeting with William C. de Mille and got to see his brother, Cecil, at work, she changed course. Arzner started working her way up the Hollywood ladder, starting as a secretary, then script supervisor, and finally film editor. Her uncredited directorial work on the Rudolph Valentino drama *Blood and Sand* (1922) won her prestige around the Paramount lot, though it wasn't until she threatened to move to Columbia that the studio relented to her demands and gave her the director's chair. She made her mark—and history—quickly, becoming the first woman to helm an all-sound feature, *The Wild Party* (1929).

Arzner's films, especially those she directed during the pre-Code era, foregrounded female struggles, from motherhood (1930's *Sarah and Son*) to class (1930's *Anybody's Woman*) to romantic trouble in the workplace (1931's *Honor Among Lovers* and *Working Girls*). Heck, she even helmed a movie about a female aviatrix, *Christopher Strong* (1933), that subverts convention in many ways.

Merrily We Go to Hell performed well at the box office, but it was to be Arzner's last picture at Paramount. As was happening across the industry, mandated pay cuts loomed as the Depression wore on, and Arzner left and became a freelancer. Arzner made a handful of films over the next decade and became the first female director to join the Directors Guild of America before retiring in 1943. She went on to teach film at UCLA in the 1960s, where she influenced many future directors, including Francis Ford Coppola.

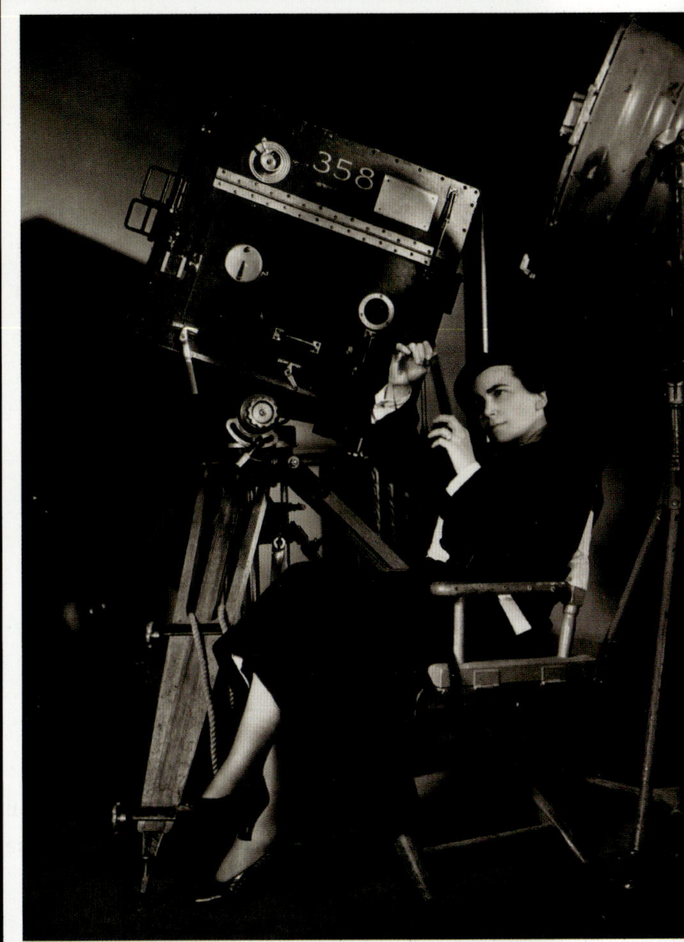

Director Dorothy Arzner on the *Merrily We Go to Hell* set.

RED-HEADED WOMAN

STARRING
Jean Harlow, Chester Morris, Leila Hyams, and Una Merkel

DIRECTED BY
Jack Conway

RELEASED BY
MGM, June 1932

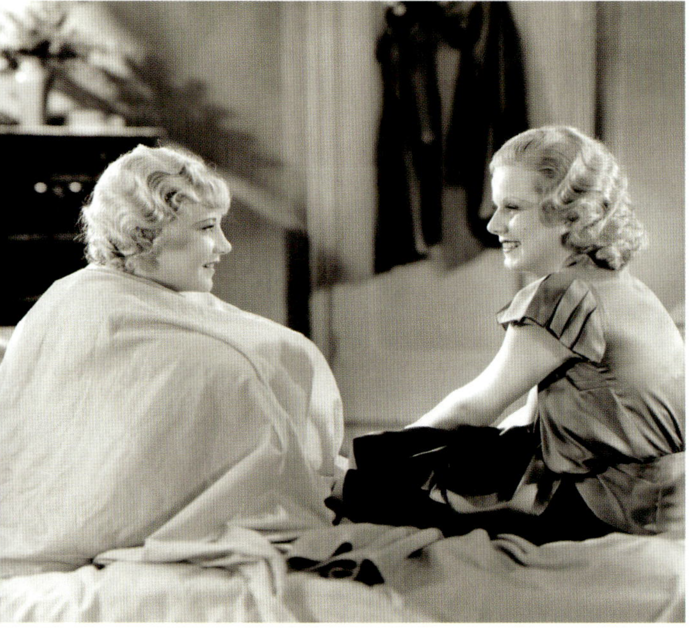

Una Merkel is covering up because she just gave her top to Jean Harlow. Girls will be girls!

"So gentlemen prefer blondes, do they?" Lil (Jean Harlow) cheekily questions as she pops up with her new fiery red mane at the beginning of *Red-Headed Woman*. Lil will see about that. This retort, penned by *Gentlemen Prefer Blondes* author Anita Loos, not only pokes fun at Harlow's blond bombshell image but also establishes the film's satirical tone right out of the gate.

While movies like *The Divorcee* couched their extramarital affairs in dramatics and questions of morality, there is scant little of that to be found in *Red-Headed Woman*, which works more as a burlesque of the notion of marriage than anything else. Lil is an opportunist, using her body and her ability to push the line to gleefully climb up the social ladder. She's also a monster egotist who would have killed in an era of social media and FOMO—and she didn't do too bad back in 1932, either.

Picking back up after Lil's ludicrously loud entrance, *Red-Headed Woman* follows the ferocious gold digger as she barges in uninvited to boss Bill Legendre Jr.'s (Chester Morris) home while his wife Irene (Leila Hyams) is away. But there's just one issue: Bill is *happily* married. The small detail doesn't deter Lil from seducing him full force with pity and sex till Bill eventually breaks down—just as Irene returns home early. Bill's attempts to reconcile are thwarted by Lil, who locks him in a room and drops the key down her blouse.

While Lil's endeavors to access high society don't pan out, her attempts at blackmailing Bill's influential older coworker work out well—until they don't, mostly when she gets sidetracked with his chauffeur. Scorned, Lil returns to Bill, just in time to shoot up his car as he drives off with Irene. But fear not, Lil lands on her feet: Two years later, she's spotted at a Paris racetrack, posing with a winning horse. She's obviously done all right for herself.

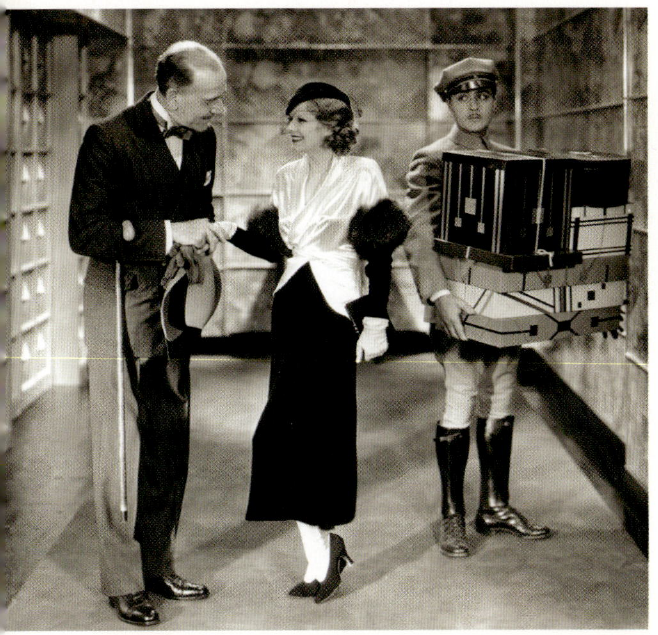

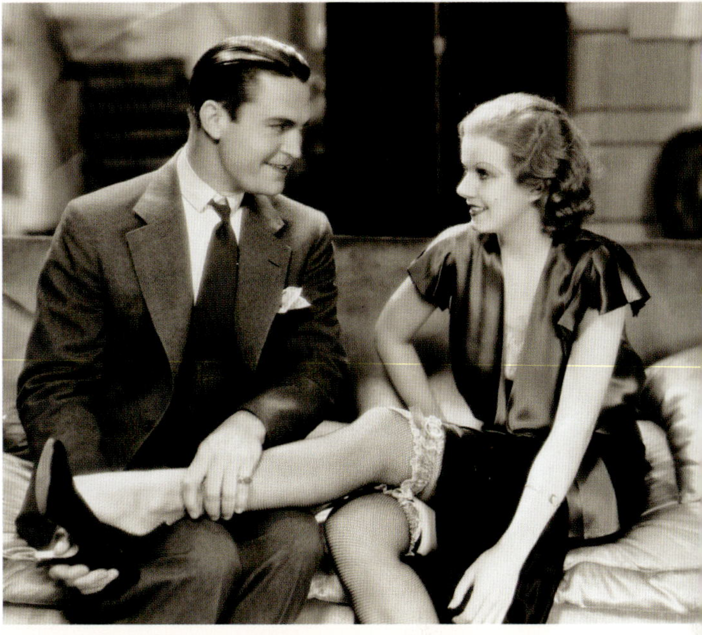

LEFT: Rich man Henry Stephenson, chauffeur Charles Boyer—they're all prospective lovers to Jean Harlow. **RIGHT:** Jean Harlow on the art of not being subtle, featuring Chester Morris.

Though *Red-Headed Woman* was a welcome change of pace for Harlow, the idea didn't overly excite her. That's largely because the sweet-natured star was about as far from Lil in real life as she could get, and the intricacies required to nail the role were intimidating. "The problem is to play her so that the audience likes her in spite of herself," Harlow commented to reporters. She proved she was in the right mindset when producer Irving Thalberg asked if Harlow thought she could make viewers laugh. "With me or at me?" she clarified. When Thalberg replied, "At you," Harlow countered: "Why not? People have been laughing at me all my life." She was good to go.

Not everyone was, though. *Red-Headed Woman* is "the worst script I have ever read," Jason Joy bemoaned to Will H. Hays when MGM sent the first screenplay to the SRC. They would be forced to do a complete rewrite. Joy suggested eliminating "the blatant sex quality" and injecting an air of satire, but he wasn't convinced even this could save the movie.

To stress the picture's lighthearted tone, Thalberg had Loos compose several additional outrageous bits to make it clear that Lil was a sardonic opportunist rather than a nymphomaniac, hopefully rendering her more palatable to audiences. Luckily, alterations in the new draft, which didn't

"A girl's a fool that doesn't get ahead. Say, it's just as easy to hook a rich man as it is to get hooked by a poor one."

—Lil, speaking the "truth" about the importance of marrying well

C O P Y

BOARD OF REVUES
406 City Hall
Atlanta, Georgia
June 22,1932

Dear Governor:

It is mighty hot to fuss and fume but here I am again with a complaint which is as high as heaven. I have just come in from previewing Jean Harlowe in THE RED HEADED WOMAN. I have the CODE before me and if I do not lose my job for letting this pass I certainly should and perhaps I will. I know nothing more provocative of putting the public strongly behind the Brookhart or any other censorship bill than this disgusting sex exploitation. I have read the code carefully and realize that this can get by and stay "within the law" tho #16 could be quoted if we came to the court. I wondered as the story progressed if there were no decent men in the world, if any one of them could ever withstand the appeal to the lowest nature.

Harlow's acting I suppose is superb. Not having known that type of woman, never having been thrown with women inherently rotten, as she must be, and whose behavior under such circumstances is therefore unknown to me, I suppose to those initiated her acting is superb.. Be it so, is it a good thing for young girls or young men to learn these tactics, is it even entertaining to the young mind to learn the mechanics of the profession Miss Harlowe so cleverly(?) portrays?

We have been working for years for clean decent pictures and here in 1932 we have THIS. I wonder if that resolution passed by the General Federation and which we have all worked for would ever have been passed had those women seen this picture along with a few others I could mention.

It is so disappointing, so disillusioning as to the real intent of the Industry that it almost makes us start a crusade for the Brookhart or any other censorship bill which would clean up such as this. I am so sorry I have to write this, but I would be untrue to all if I didn't. Can't we have decency? Look at this weeks Herald World see the percentages of the pictures which have made box office hits the country over, it is not this type of thing which has made the money and it seems that after all this is all that counts!

I am getting orders every day regarding things allowed. I have made excuses many and endless, but alibis are getting less potent every day. I do not know how I am to get by this time.

Sex! sex!sex! the picture just reeks with it till one is positively nauseated. Again Why?

Cordially,
(Signed)
Mrs. R.

LEFT: Mrs. R. (Mrs. Alonzo Richardson) did not have any kind words to say about the picture. **OPPOSITE:** The general comments here read: "I can't imagine a writer with a mind so low as to write a play of this kind, much less one who would produce it on the screen. It's disgusting. I think every American should be ashamed of the company that produced Red-Headed Woman."

arrive at the SRC until after filming commenced, made "all the difference in the world."

Even so, Joy prepared MGM for rough roads ahead on the censor front. Sure, the SRC found the finished product "replete with sexual inferences," but they believed the thematic implication—straight or farce—fell upon the viewer, including censors. In this vein, Joy advocated the moral watchdogs review *Red-Headed Woman* with an audience, as its "probable salvation" rests with them hearing spectators laugh at Harlow and sympathize with the wife. The MPPDA secretary agreed with Joy's strength-in-numbers idea, confirming that many moviegoers construed the picture as a "sex extravaganza rather than a sex problem."

The riotous treatment worked: *Red-Headed Woman* was a hit, and Harlow's first comedic-starring role transformed her career, all while dropping Hollywood's morality bar to a whole new low for the SRC to contend with. Despite the attempt to alleviate censorship trouble, Joy's fear of boards draining life from the picture or outright denying it proved true. Japan's rejection claimed Lil possessed "no sense of chastity at all and makes relations with all possible men to get herself on in the world or satisfy her desires" without any punishment. Pennsylvania's edits numbered three pages (including the removal of lines like "We're in each other's blood!"), while Maryland shortened scenes of Lil and Bill kissing. Dialogue such as, "If she wants to leave the barn door open, what's to keep a girl from goin' in," and insinuations like Lil dropping a key down her shirt were also frequent censor board targets. (Somehow, a fleeting view of

Reviewer's Report
The Atlanta Better Films Committee
on

Theatre Paramount Date June 24th 1932

Title Red Headed Woman

Stars Jean Harlow Chester Morris Company

~~Leila Hyams Una Merkel Lewis Stone May Robson~~

Gradings (Mark with Cross)
★—Exceptional
A—Very Interesting
B—Interesting
F—Fair
X —Not Recommended

Audience Suitability
M—Mature Audience Only
G—General Audience
HS—High School and Over
J—Juvenile (including all ages)

GRADING POINTS

	★	A	B	F	—
Entertainment Value					
Acting					
Plot					
Photography					
Educational Value					None
Moral Effect				Doubtful	

SUGGESTED FOR

Schools Junior Matinees

Names of Comedy or other Short Subjects:
1. News Reel Co. Paramount
2. Co.
3. Co.

General Comments: I can't imagine a writer with a mind so low as to write a play of this kind much less one who would produce it on the screen. Reviewed by Mrs Roy R. Smith

Use Other Side for Further Comments on Posters, Etc.

It is disgusting Mrs. Y. Clifton Perkins

I think every American should be ashamed of the Company that produced Red Headed Woman

Harlow's breast as she puts on a top Una Merkel's Sally just took off went undetected and remains in the picture today.)

After spending a few years in dramas and gangster movies, Harlow's brazen, uproarious turn finally proved that she was a star who could carry a picture and make audiences laugh, thanks to the addition of Loos's subtle, sophisticated innuendo. Critics praised Harlow's burgeoning comedic skills all the while highlighting just how incendiary *Red-Headed Woman* was. The *New York Herald Tribune* noted the Capitol Theater's "generously admiring audience" but questioned whether their amusement arose from Harlow's biting turn or rather "from the belief that she is the hottest number since Helen of Troy."

In toying with the boundaries of decency, *Red-Headed Woman* functioned as a tantalizing marker of the level of decadence Hollywood could reach. Make no mistake, other studios had their eye on what MGM got away with and plotted how they could up the ante. (See: Warner Bros.' 1933 film *Baby Face* later in this book.)

But voices of opposition tallied far and wide, representing an ever-growing apprehension with the moral state of Hollywood. For instance, Mrs. Alonzo Richardson from the City of Atlanta Board, who steamed, "Can't we have decency? . . . Sex! sex! sex! the picture just reeks with it till one is positively nauseated," later forewarned that "there is going to crystallize such a revulsion of feeling that the Industry is going to feel it in no uncertain way." She was right, but for now, the studios pressed forward pushing the bounds during some of the darkest days of the Depression.

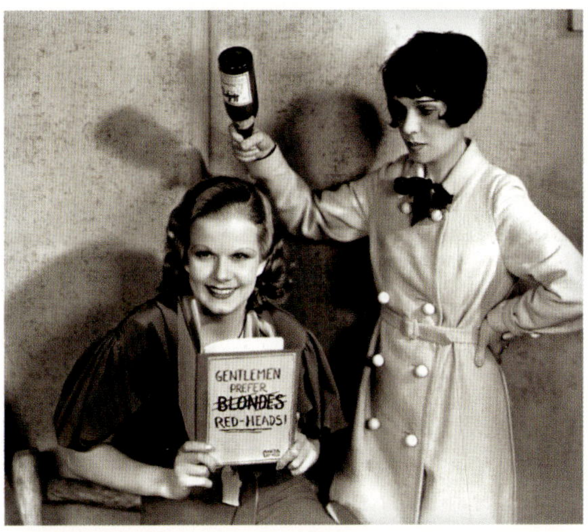

Writer Anita Loos goofing around with newly red-wigged Jean Harlow.

DOWNSTAIRS

STARRING
John Gilbert, Paul Lukas, and Virginia Bruce

DIRECTED BY
Monta Bell

RELEASED BY
MGM, August 1932

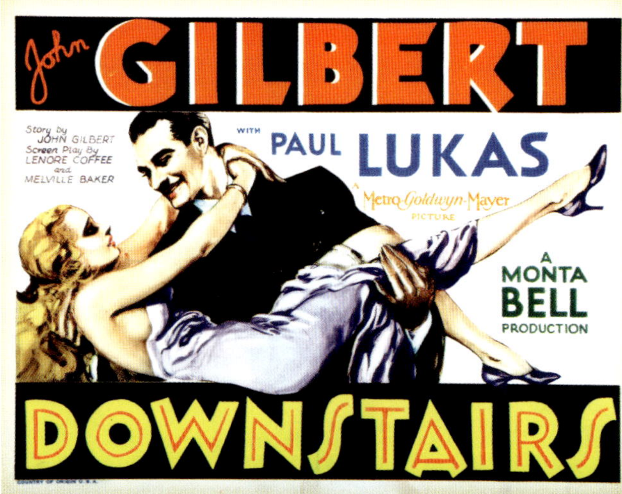

As the star and story originator, John Gilbert gets upstairs credit on this *Downstairs* lobby card.

"You think you can make love in the same frozen way you do everything else. And you think that's all I should ever have any wish for. Well, I tell you plain and straight right now—it's nothing of the kind."

—Anna, boldly declaring for herself that a good husband doesn't always mean a satisfied wife

The commonly accepted tale that talkies decimated and ended the careers of most silent screen actors remains largely overstated; while the careers of some silent icons did indeed wither, great stars like Greta Garbo, Norma Shearer, William Powell, and others saw their stock grow with the introduction of sound. However, the most visible victim of this transition was John Gilbert, at one time the screen's most sensuous silent lover. While his costarring roles with Garbo in pictures like *Flesh and the Devil* (1926) inflamed audiences of the silent era, his talkie debut, *His Glorious Night* (1929), left them laughing at the poor dialogue, clunky directing, and, worst of all, the sound of his voice. While it's a perfectly acceptable voice for a man, for the star of millions of women's fantasies, it was an unmitigated disaster.

Gilbert had been pitching *Downstairs* to MGM since 1927. With its euphemistic title, *Downstairs* is a film about power structures, violation, sex, romance, and the pain of lifelong subservience. It's extremely class conscious, while also offering a lens through which to view Gilbert's unwavering disgust with the studio system he served under and his unapologetic goodbye to his Hollywood silent screen heartthrob image.

Downstairs begins on the wedding day of Albert (Paul Lukas) and Anna (Virginia Bruce), the head butler and mistress's maid of a sprawling Austrian estate. The estate's head, Baron "Nicky" von Burgen (Reginald Owen) toasts the servants but, due to an inconvenience later in the evening, draws Albert back to wait on his own "upstairs" friends. This leaves Anna vulnerable to Karl (Gilbert), the new chauffeur, who had been spying on the couple's wedding night through the window.

Karl has a slick smile and a sociopath's disposition. Besides setting Anna in his sights, he quickly seduces "upstairs" and "downstairs" women, stealing from both, to lure Anna away from Albert. Anna is resistant at first, but during a cold night with Albert out of town, she succumbs. The next morning, Albert returns unexpectedly, and Anna's defense of her actions lay bare what Karl has that other men do not—a sexual fire that excites and dominates. The stewing Albert must now find a way to root Karl out of the household without Baron von Burgen knowing the truth or face remaining cuckolded the rest of his marriage.

Downstairs is an exceedingly nasty movie, a black comedy wherein the blackmailer brings both fiery life and destruction to a staid manor estate. Karl embodies romance and passion, a breakup of the complicit domesticity of the household inhabitants. He makes up stories and lies, and the movie lets the audience derive glee from the ways in which Karl manipulates each of his victims, searching for

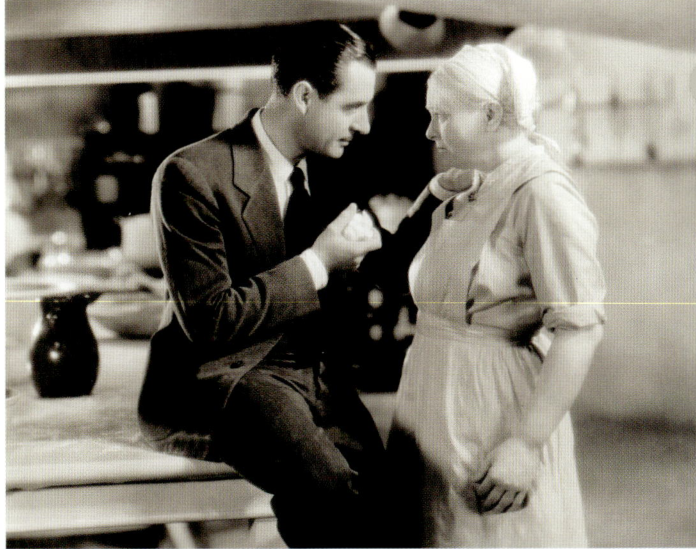

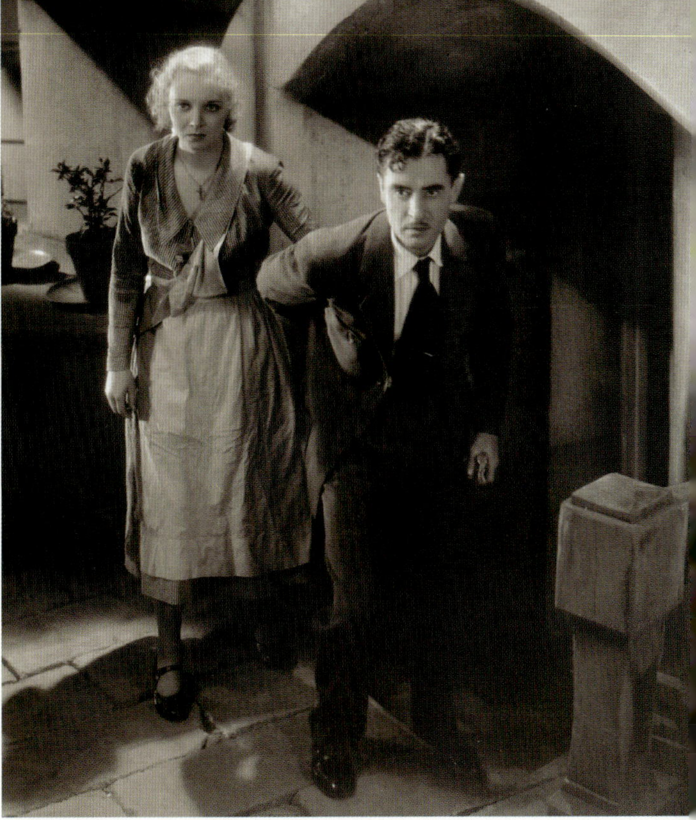

FROM TOP: Chauffeur John Gilbert can't keep his hands off the downstairs staff, including cook Bodil Rosing, who keeps money in her stockings. • Clearly something has happened between Virginia Bruce and John Gilbert, and no fair saying what.

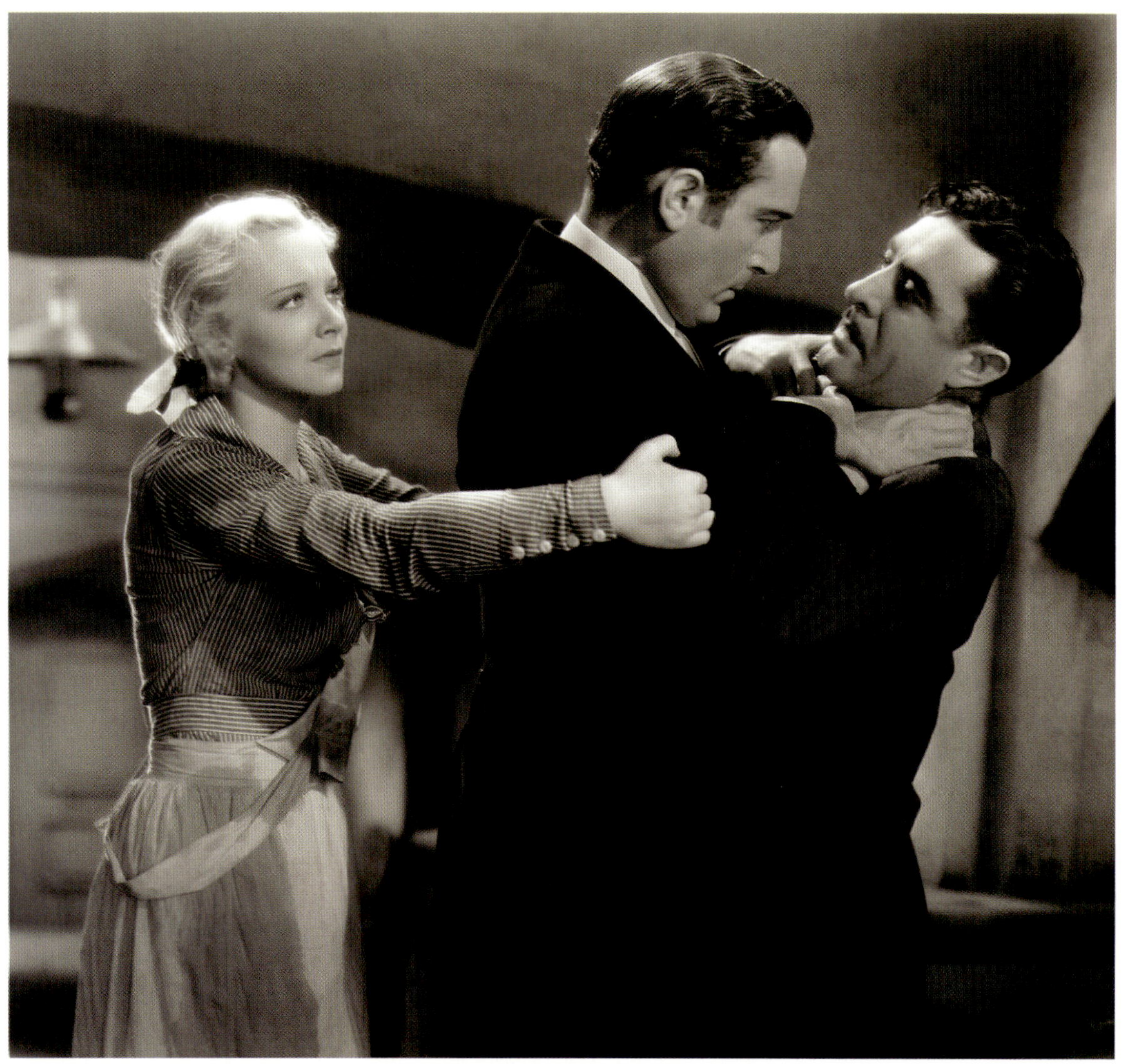

Jealous husband Paul Lukas can't keep *his* hands off John Gilbert after he learns that he slept with wife Virginia Bruce.

just the right place to find their weaknesses and exploit them.

Virginia Bruce was having a star-making year in 1932 between this film, *Winner Take All,* and *Kongo*, finally elevating her out of Goldwyn Girl chorus status. Her appearance in *Downstairs* set off a torrid romance and marriage with Gilbert (his last of four marriages). She left him in 1934 citing cruelty, and Gilbert died of heart disease only a year later in 1935.

Knowing that Gilbert came up with the story, it is difficult to watch *Downstairs* without drawing lessons and parallels from his rough time at MGM, particularly in terms of power and hierarchy. Look at Albert, the head butler: His life is one of prestige and authority but also unquestioning servitude. Baron von Burgen is a weak and silly man, unable to see the trouble in his house; the only time he becomes sexually excited is when he thinks about controlling the servants. This makes *Downstairs* as much an indictment of the underlings at MGM, including Irving Thalberg, who cocoon their leader into a fantasy world while fighting for the meager table scraps they're thrown.

Downstairs may present a more literal view of power and class structure through the upstairs and downstairs inhabitants of the baron's home, but the underlying struggles continue to be germane in modern life. From sexual harassment in the workplace to fighting imbalances of power to the disappearance of the middle class and beyond, society continues to grapple with the ripple effects of a changing world against a backdrop of rigid hierarchical systems.

On the censorship front, *Downstairs* faced an uphill battle. Questionable elements peppered the script, such as a few suggestive hand movements underneath clothing and the line, "The Countess said you gave her complete satisfaction." The SRC's Jason Joy remarked: "There is in this story a flavor of lecherousness on the part of Karl, and therefore careful treatment of the details is of the utmost importance." No kidding!

The SRC wasn't thrilled with the final product and its "vulgar tone," to say the least. In his review, James B. M. Fisher brusquely grumbled: "A stupid picture and one that is right on the line." Problematic material continued to emerge after filming, including Karl's line to Albert and Anna, "I don't have to wish you a good night," and "I could have had your wife any time I wanted." MGM presented multiple endings they were considering; the SRC preferred the eventual finale in which Karl gets beaten up and run out of the house—provided a scene showing him landing another job with another woman was deleted. (It wasn't.)

Aside from receiving a clean bill of health from the Kansas censor board—no eliminations—*Downstairs* fared rather poorly with local boards. Many aforementioned lines the SRC warned of were indeed excised. Other frequent offenders included the shot of Karl's coat thrown over Albert and Anna's wedding wreath in their bedroom and several lines from Anna's impassioned speech to Albert, such as, "There's a kind of way of making love that drives you mad and crazy, so that you don't know what you're doing. Are you going to throw me out in the street because I never knew this before?"

The way *Downstairs* toys with sexual and social dynamics, and the frankness with which it does it, is unlike anything American films would do for decades after 1934. The fact that the movie plays it off with the same knowing wink that audiences got from the far more playful *Red-Headed Woman* also speaks to how much more audacious Hollywood dared to be at this time.

All of Gilbert's machinations throughout *Downstairs* are fun to watch, with the movie functioning somewhere between a thumb to the nose and a poison pill to his career. Gilbert only starred in three more films after this, and his personal life spiraled. For fans of the silent era, Gilbert's star never diminished, and for fans of pre-Code Hollywood, his one-man rebellion against the system still amazes.

SCARFACE

STARRING
Paul Muni, Ann Dvorak, George Raft, Karen Morley, and Boris Karloff

DIRECTED BY
Howard Hawks

RELEASED BY
United Artists, August 1932

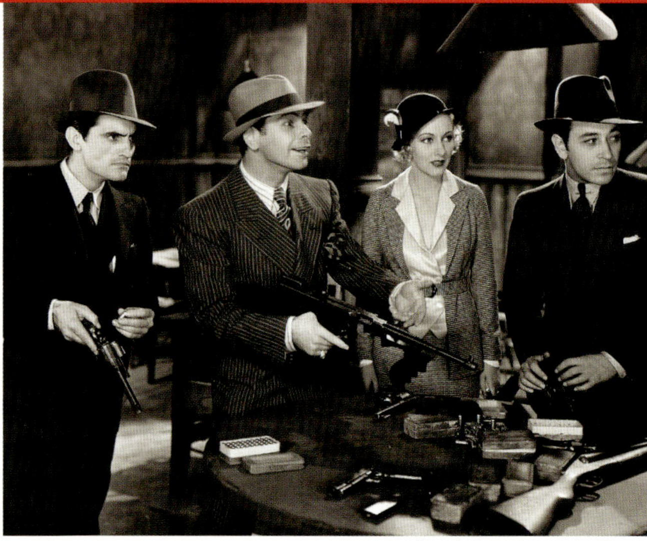

Paul Muni is a kid in a candy shop with his new deadly toys.

Gangster movies were on a moral time-out following the smash hits *Little Caesar* and *The Public Enemy*; two days after production commenced on *Scarface*, the New York Society for Suppression of Vice directed the New York censor board to ban all such films. But director Howard Hawks and writer Ben Hecht didn't intend to make *Scarface* a gangster movie. They fancied a reimagination of the Capone family through the lens of the incestuous Renaissance-era Borgia clan—relocated to Chicago.

Of course, a gangster picture that surpassed its predecessors in boldly violent sequences, objectionable characterizations, and the empathy it elicits for its lead is exactly what Hawks and company delivered. Given these unsavory elements, the SRC speculated on the dire consequences *Scarface*'s release would bring about for Hollywood. Indeed, the censorship battle waged between the SRC and headstrong producer Howard Hughes proved almost as damning and dynamic as the movie itself.

Cinematographer Lee Garmes's roving camera and gripping use of shadows sets a darkly prophetic tone in *Scarface*'s opening sequence, presenting the murder of gangster Big Louie Costillo (Henry J. Vejar) by his bodyguard Tony (Paul Muni). With Costillo out of the way, Tony teams up with Lovo (Osgood Perkins), but it's not long before the ambition, arrogance, and allure of power goes to his head.

Tony's relationships with women prove problematic, too, as he pursues Lovo's girl Poppy (Karen Morley) and exhibits inappropriately intense feelings for his sister, Cesca (Ann Dvorak), especially when she shows interest in Rinaldo (George Raft). Ensuing explosions of violence propel Tony to gangland supremacy, but his reign at the top is short-lived. As police close in on him and kill Cesca, Tony begins to crack, and he meets his end the same way so many of his victims did: in a barrage of bullets.

The two Howards made quite the team in 1932. Despite the fact that Hughes filed a lawsuit against the director in 1930, accusing Hawks's picture *Dawn Patrol* (1930) of plagiarizing *Hell's Angels* (1930), Hughes respected Hawks. Not to mention, he wanted in on those successful gangster pictures. Several writers had taken a stab at adapting Armitage Trail's novel of the same name, which bears little resemblance to the final picture, but their work failed to satisfy Hughes. Enter Ben Hecht, who crafted a detailed sixty-page treatment, and from there, Seton I. Miller and John Lee Mahin assembled a screenplay.

"We needed a fantastic *actor*, not just a personality," Hawks recalled of casting Muni. Hawks discovered him on the New York stage, and Muni's wife convinced him to test for the role. The director ran into George Raft at a prizefight, Ann Dvorak performed a dance similar to the one she seduces Raft with in the movie at a party at Hawks's home, and Boris Karloff just wanted to be involved.

Hawks's fusion of savagery and humor sets the picture apart from other pre-Code gangster entries. Gangsters "were just like kids," the director recalled, not the serious men often presented on-screen. This exultance is on full display when Tony discovers a rival gang's machine guns. To most, this type of euphoric demonstration wouldn't fit a hardened killer, but it did to Hawks—and it worked perfectly for the story.

As an independent producer, Hughes had a substantial amount of his money tied up in *Scarface* and fought tooth and nail to sensationalize the script. Warned at the start that the film's violence

"I don't know nothin'. I don't see nothin'. I don't hear nothin'. When I do, I don't tell the cops. You understand?"

—Tony, not sayin' nothin'

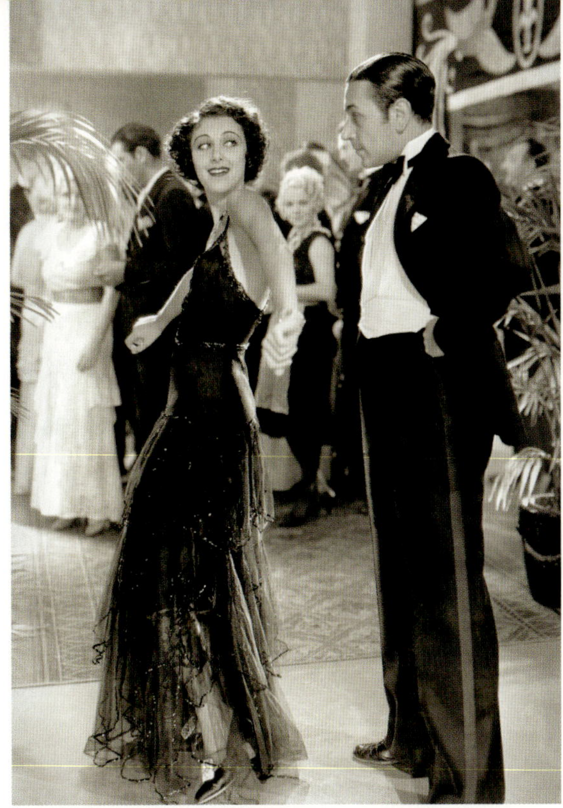

Ann Dvorak is very eager to seduce George Raft, and he is very willing to accept.

and sympathetic characterization of Tony would create severe impediments for distribution, the hardheaded producer clashed mightily with the SRC; in fact, *Scarface*'s PCA file exceeds 350 pages, likely the longest for any film made in the 1930s.

Suggested changes to minimize censorship challenges from the SRC included awkward insertions to emphasize law and order, the idea that Tony should be arrested at the end, and positioning the film as propaganda for gun control. Rounds of extensive revisions failed to appease the SRC, and a back-and-forth lasting months resulted in an MPPDA jury review of *Scarface*. All three jurors deemed the situation perilous.

At once anxious for the SRC to help "save it" from rejection by censor boards, Hughes also

.)CIATION OF MOTION PICTURE PROI ERS, INC.
5504 Hollywood Boulevard
Hollywood California
Gladstone 6111

October 3, 1932.

FEATURE	COMPANY	TERRITORY
"SCARFACE" ("The Shame of The Nation")	Caddo	PENNSYLVANIA 9-8-32

NOTE:- Underneath the Main Title: SCARFACE insert the words:- SHAME OF THE NATION. This also applies to all advertising used in connection with this picture.

Deletions:-

Reel 1- Eliminate scene of man in shadow holding gun, firing gun, wiping gun and throwing it to floor.
REDUCE to flash of three feet views of "Big Louie" dead on floor, as waiter discovers him.

Eliminate all views of gangsters in barber shop divesting themselves of guns and secreting them in laundry basket.

Reel 2- Eliminate dialogue as follows:-
Love:- "I see that Epstein got to you in time."
Tony:- "Yeah .... nice little fella. He give 'em a writ of hokus pocus."
Love:- "Sit down."
Tony:- "Thanks. He says, 'You stay here 'till the heat's off ...' he says.... Say ... that's purty hot!"

Eliminate underlined words:- "That's Poppy. Say, Poppy, meet Tony Camonte."

Eliminate all views of Poppy entering Love's bedroom, from bathroom, Poppy in negligee.

Eliminate underlined words in the following:-
Love:- "Here you are, Tony. It's a bonus."
Love:- "Now, listen, I'm going to cut you in on a percentage ... give you a raise ... doubles ... the south side is rolling jack .... all we gotta do is step in and take it."

Tony:- "Yeah ... and now he come to a dead stop ..."
Love:- "Listen, I'm gonna hold off that meeting with the boys a couple of days. After Big Louie's funeral is better, you know what I mean?"

Eliminate scene of Tony giving money to Guino Rinaldo in cab, and accompanying dialogue as follows:-
Tony:- "Here you are, li'l boy. Easy dough, eh? For just standing outside and listening to a gun go off?"

Guino Rinaldo:- "Cinch. When are we gonna get some more?"
Tony:- "We got plenty. This business just waiting for some guy to come and run it right. And I got ideas."

-continued-

LEFT: Some censor boards passed *Scarface* with no eliminations, some rejected it, and some butchered it, like Pennsylvania, submitting three pages of edits.

OPPOSITE FROM LEFT: Paul Muni is a tad too protective of sister Ann Dvorak—and grossly jealous of her suitors. • One way the SRC thought *Scarface* might pass local censor boards was by positioning the movie as anti-gun propaganda. Spoiler: That didn't work.

grew restless with the never-ending pile of issues, which eventually included a title change. Consequently, Hughes's publicity director came up with an idea: release the picture in areas without censor boards in hopes that positive public reaction would put pressure on the SRC to stand down on the mountain of difficulties they argued the picture still faced and give the film a pass. It worked—kind of. *Scarface* premiered in New Orleans on March 31, 1932, resulting in heaps of critical praise—and a thoroughly incensed SRC.

In a splendidly histrionic press release, Hughes determined "there will be no compromise with the censors." If only. While *Scarface* passed without edits in Virginia, Ohio, and Kansas, Pennsylvania censors decimated the film, and the Chicago and New York boards outright rejected it. (New York's ban was overturned with the addition of a moralizing foreword and a hanging for Tony.) Dialogue detailing the gangsters' barbaric acts proved the biggest issues; meanwhile, Tony and Cesca's uncomfortable relationship flew com-

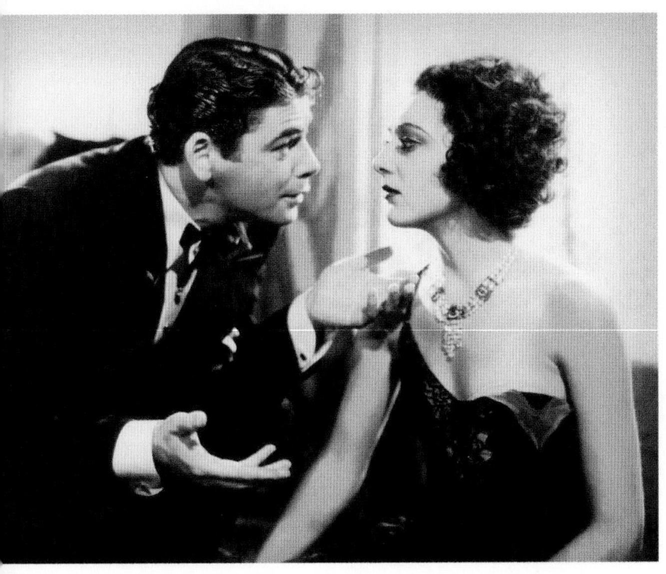

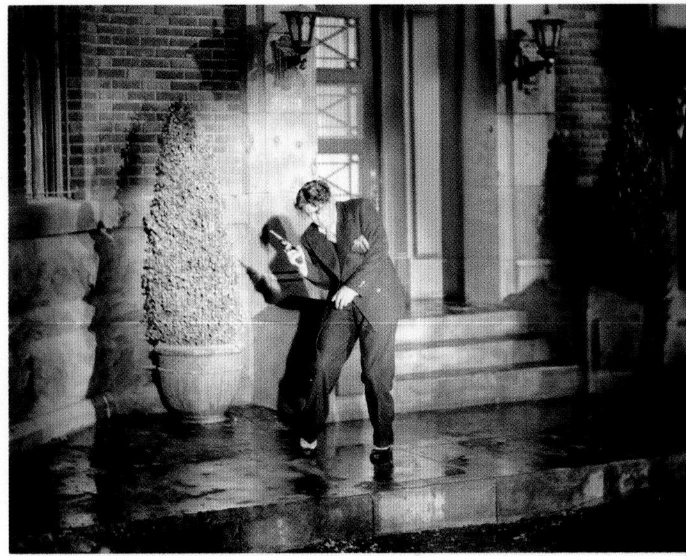

pletely over censor's heads. Ultimately, *Scarface* opened in most areas with fewer eliminations than the SRC originally feared, but the PCA denied the picture a seal of approval post-Code enforcement, and Hughes refused to chop the movie further for rerelease. Consequently, Hughes removed the film from circulation in 1947, and *Scarface* remained unavailable for public viewing until 1979, three years after his death.

"Regardless of the moral issues, *Scarface* is entertainment on an important scale," *Variety* exalted. The film's positive reception and stark violence, shrouded in an atmosphere at once darkly brutal but also highly stylized and amusing, raised the bar for gangster pictures and piqued other studios' interest in them at a time when the genre faced severe pushback from a number of censor boards and moral groups.

Like its lead character, the team behind *Scarface* played by their own rules and wrestled against authority. Hughes and Hawks boldly challenged the very machinery of the Production Code, while Hughes won supporters with an impassioned public tirade against censorship. "Hughes is the only Hollywood producer who has had the courage to come out and fight this censorship menace in the open," the *New York Herald Tribune* applauded. "We wish him a smashing success."

Despite Hughes burying *Scarface* for decades, the underlying story has grown incredibly influential. Brian De Palma's 1983 remake starring Al Pacino is a bona fide cult classic, inspiring everything from rappers to video games to impressionable young boys. Not to mention, the frightening rapture Tony displays for his "little friends" illuminates the persistent gun culture that still sparks heated debates in twenty-first-century America.

But the genesis for such a strong cultural resonance comes back to Hughes and Hawks. In creating a ferocious picture teeming with energy, style, and sympathy for the very last character censors wanted audiences to care about, they ensured the punch *Scarface* packs still shocks all these years later.

JEWEL ROBBERY

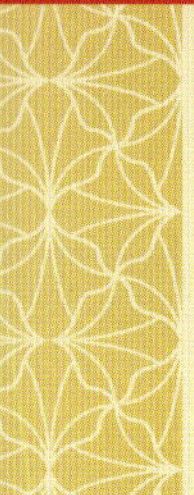

STARRING
William Powell, Kay Francis, and Helen Vinson

DIRECTED BY
William Dieterle

RELEASED BY
Warner Bros., August 1932

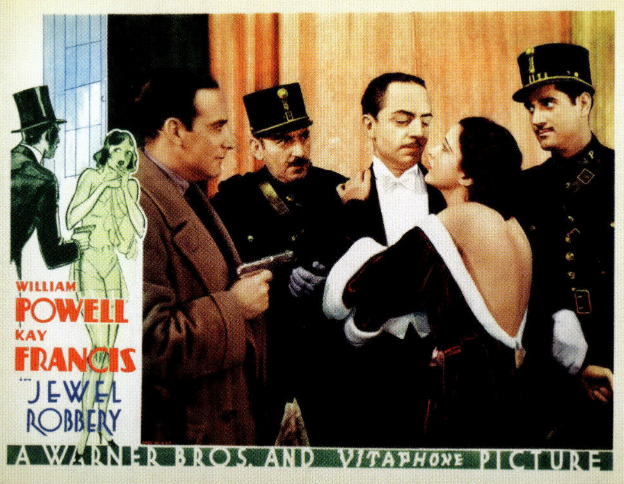

Robber William Powell is too tantalizing for bored, wealthy Kay Francis to give up. Cops be damned!

Taglines for *Jewel Robbery* proclaimed: "He stole her jewels—but that wasn't all!" It certainly was not, on-screen and off.

Jewel Robbery blithely flaunts several elements that violated the Production Code—sex, crime, and drugs—but it does so in such a buoyant way that the SRC fell prey to the grift. Like the smoke from the special cigarettes The Robber (William Powell) hands out like candy, the sly drug references in the picture floated right over the SRC's and most of the censors' heads.

In the movie, the Baroness Teri (Kay Francis) only wants one thing in life: a new diamond. Her lover has started to bore her and don't even start on her husband—it's all so rote. However, when the charming, dashing Robber holds up the jewelry store she's making a purchase in, she is intrigued and delighted. The Robber is efficient and erudite; before wrapping up, he mollifies his victims: Some he distracts with special cigarettes, some he ushers into safes, and Teri he just flirts with.

As the police investigate, The Robber woos Teri, first at her mansion under her husband's nose and then back in his resplendent apartment. He persuades her to take off to Nice with him before tying her up and leading the cops on a rooftop chase. Teri is rescued, but it's been such a stressful ordeal that she needs a vacation—and what better place than Nice?

Jewel Robbery debuted on the New York stage in January 1932, prompting the SRC to vet the story, registering worry from "the situation presented—a crook hero and a heroine who is evidently far from being a sober and virtuous wife." That type of warning failed to deter Warner Bros., as the studio secured the property and put it into production within two months. The studio cast the fan-favorite team of Powell and Francis as the leads, making this their fifth pairing.

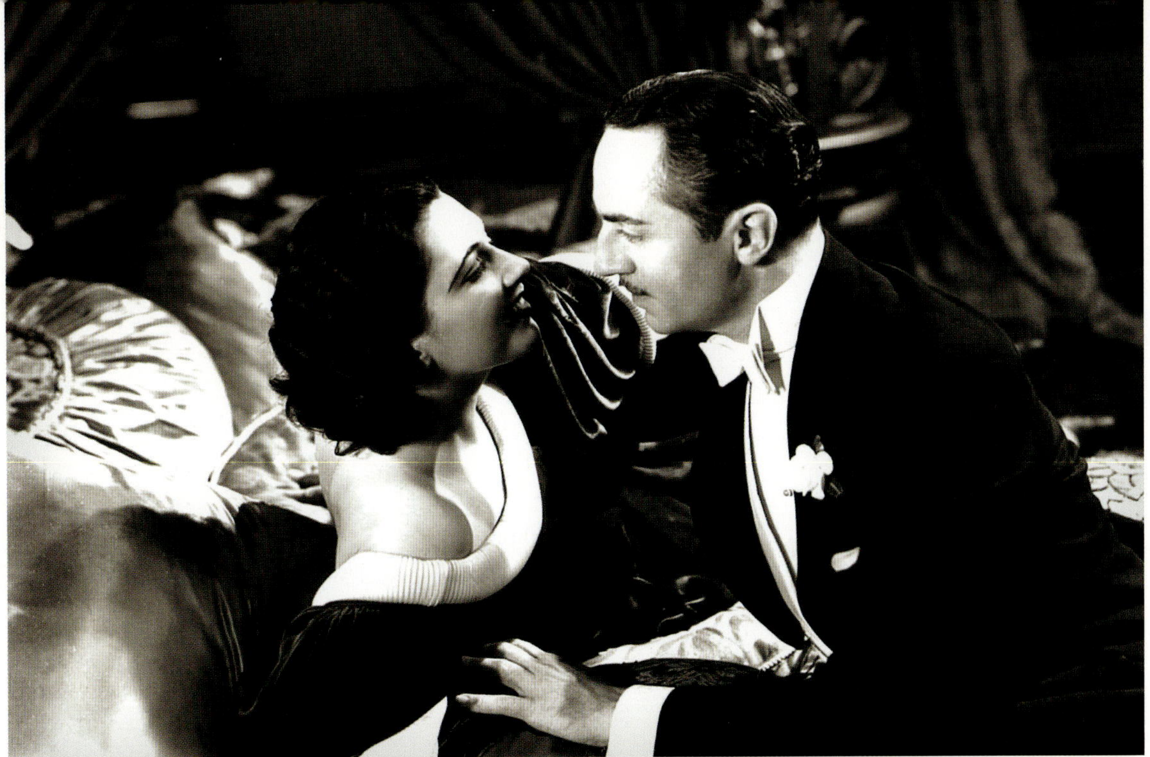

"Yes, we've been lovers in six pictures—but our romances never include the happy-ever-after sequence," Kay Francis told *Screenland* in 1934 of her partnership with William Powell.

While the cameras rolled, Jason Joy reminded Warner's production head Darryl F. Zanuck: "We know that you can and will make every effort to instill a quality of lightness . . . which will not allow it to drop below the borderline and become suggestive or vulgar." If you don't count The Robber's associates unveiling his bedroom five seconds after Teri gets there and about fifty other exchanges, then sure, Warner Bros. didn't make *Jewel Robbery* suggestive at all; Teri lusts over The Robber for only about 60 percent of the movie.

Once production was complete, the SRC reviewed *Jewel Robbery*—and indeed, they found it "very charming." While they affirmed that the picture didn't violate the Code, they pointed out questionable elements, though they didn't seem as adamant about some of the potential land mines as they did with dramas; "the lightness and gaiety with which they are used in this case seem to us to obviate any objection," the SRC noted. Apparently,

"As a matter of fact, I'm opposed to the American school of banditry. I studied in Paris. You have to work harder but you do acquire a certain finesse that is missing from the stick-'em-up and shoot-them-down school."

—The Robber, expressing his belief in the importance of style in your work

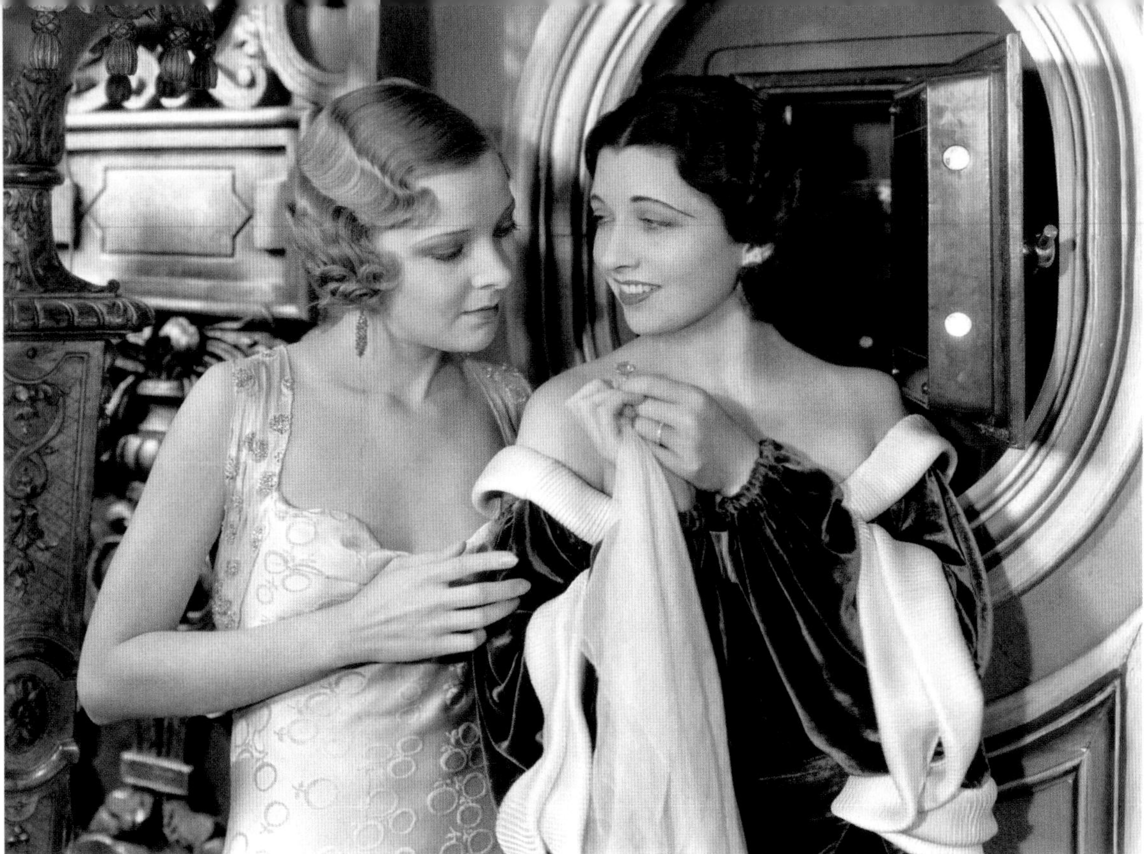

that affirmation also went for the witty Robber's "laugh-provoking" so-called cigarettes, which the SRC didn't think to question.

However, some censors took *Jewel Robbery* quite seriously. Local boards excised several lines from the picture, including, "Night is before us, and if you wish, by dawn we shall have a secret behind us." Visuals featuring guns also provoked ire from many censors; in fact, the New York board requested the deletion of basically every shot with a gun in the robbery sequence and went so far as to remove use of the words *robber* or *robbing*. (Never mind the fact that the main character is referred to simply as The Robber!)

Some audience members weren't as taken with the picture as the SRC was, either. One moviegoer felt compelled to complain to the MPPDA that the film "hasn't the slightest excuse for existence" as it rewards "dishonesty, disloyalty, and disobedience." He signed off, demanding, for dramatic effect: "HAVE SOMEONE DO SOMETHING ABOUT IT."

One blatant element that slipped by the SRC and most censor boards: the use of marijuana, which astonishes some modern viewers. While illegal substances had been dramatized since the silent days, many depictions either came ripe with caution (Lois Weber's 1916 feature *Hop, the Devil's Brew*, Mrs. Wallace Reid's 1923 production of *Human Wreckage*) or through exploitative means (1933's *Narcotic*, 1936's *Reefer Madness*). Several pre-Codes portrayed the devastating consequences of drugs, including *The Mad Genius* (1931), *Three on a Match* (1932), and *Heroes for Sale* (1933), but *Jewel Robbery* plays marijuana, effects and all, for straight-up comedy. This likely saved

OPPOSITE: Gal pals Helen Vinson and Kay Francis chat lovers and jewelry. **RIGHT:** William Powell makes this the politest *Jewel Robbery* possible for Kay Francis and company.

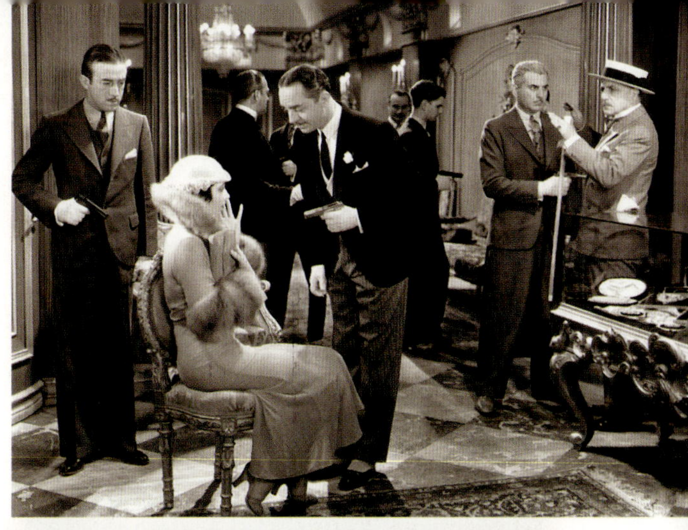

sequences where characters are under the influence from censure, though it begs the question: What did censors think caused those hijinks following puffs of The Robber's cigarettes? Marijuana wasn't a substance shown on-screen often in the early 1930s; while it can be assumed that some viewers had no idea what getting stoned meant, others surely recognized the reference.

Jewel Robbery may have snuck by the SRC in 1932, but the studio's 1937 rerelease attempt failed. The laundry list of violations included risqué dialogue, an insensitive view of marriage as an institution, the mocking of law enforcement, and the fact that The Robber faces no consequences for his various crimes. (Once again, no mention of drugs to be found!) Joseph Breen noted that the "light and airy fashion in which the crimes are committed serves to make the crime attractive"; ironically, that same blithe spirit was the reason the SRC initially passed *Jewel Robbery*. The Code remained basically the same in 1932 and 1937, but the interpretation—and enforcement—proved wildly divergent.

Jewel Robbery didn't pull off a large haul at the box office, but critics positively highlighted the picture's lavish plot and characters, Erwin S. Gelsey's buoyant dialogue, and Powell's urbane combo of menace and magnetism. The pervasive sense of mischief, and the perceived refinement that helped *Jewel Robbery* get away with it all—literally and figuratively—continues to make the film an engaging pre-Code entry.

William Powell and Kay Francis

Rarely will you find William Powell and Kay Francis on lists of Hollywood's most famous screen teams. And yet, they are one of the most beloved pre-Code pairs, appearing in six films from 1930–1932 (seven, if you count their brief roles in 1930's *Paramount on Parade*). Together, they possessed sophistication in spades—and credible sex appeal, to boot. The result was movie magic, whether the team played it light (1931's *Ladies Man*) or heavy (1930's *Street of Chance* and *For the Defense*).

The duo's most famous vehicle is the much-adored romance *One Way Passage* (1932), their final film, which finds Powell and Francis playing star-crossed lovers on a transatlantic ocean voyage, each holding a secret that will keep them from happiness. "Making a picture with Bill is always a grand adventure," Francis remarked in a 1934 *Screenland* interview. "He's generous to work with, has an unfailing sense of humor, is witty, has a fine code of honor, and is so essentially a gentleman under all conditions."

LOVE ME TONIGHT

STARRING
Maurice Chevalier, Jeanette MacDonald, Charlie Ruggles, and Myrna Loy

DIRECTED BY
Rouben Mamoulian

RELEASED BY
Paramount, August 1932

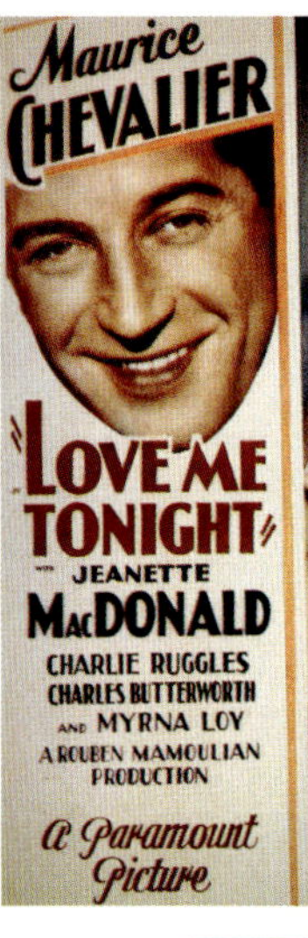

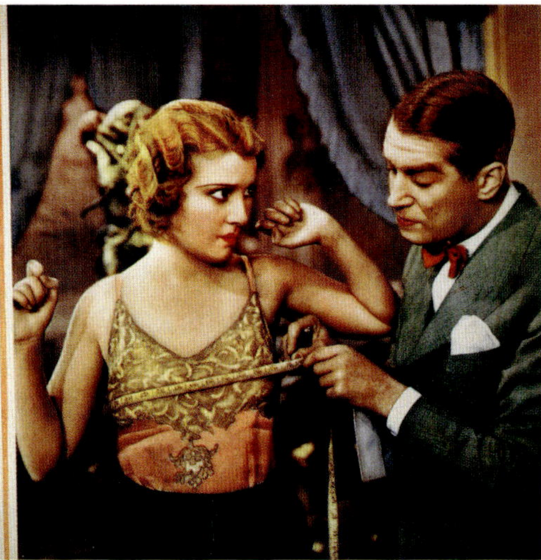

Maurice Chevalier is just looking at the tape measure. Promise.

The evolution of the movie musical in the early 1930s was a watershed time for the genre. After the disastrous musical craze of 1930, during which a rash of poorly produced melodious pictures resulted in burned-out audiences and further indebted studios, only the bravest (and freest) filmmakers dared to tread back into the territory. The improvement in sound technology by 1932 allowed for bigger, more open sets and more freedom in staging. Warner's *42nd Street* (1933) with Busby Berkeley's imaginative choreography beautifully demonstrates this, but just as influential was Rouben Mamoulian's charming fairy tale *Love Me Tonight*.

The film drifts to consciousness with a cacophony of natural sounds combined to make music, bringing the City of Light to life. Among the citizens is Maurice (Maurice Chevalier) with a song in his heart and a street of beautiful women to flirt with. Maurice's tailor shop is about to be saved by a large order from the Viscount Gilbert de Varèze (Charlie Ruggles). However, when Gilbert doesn't pay his bill, Maurice must trek to the estate of Duke d'Artelines (C. Aubrey Smith), Gilbert's uncle, to get his money.

Once arriving, Maurice is mistaken for a noble. Gilbert and his hot-under-the-collar cousin Countess Valentine (Myrna Loy) both rebel under d'Artelines but are at his mercy while he controls the purse strings. More laconic is Princess Jeanette (Jeanette MacDonald), who is distant and cold after her geriatric husband passed away, leaving her unable to comprehend the appeal of physical love. Maurice eventually wins her over through song, but when his true identity is finally revealed, Jeanette must decide if it is love or a noble bloodline that she really wants from a man.

The genesis of *Love Me Tonight* reaches back to 1929's *The Love Parade*. The film's leads, Chevalier and MacDonald, made a splendid pairing and were a hit at the box office. That movie proved a major turning point in sound production as well as the career of its stars and director, Ernst Lubitsch, who went on to make a series of light musical comedies that are still revered, including 1931's *The Smiling Lieutenant* and two other pairings of Chevalier and MacDonald, 1932's *One Hour with You* and 1934's *The Merry Widow*.

Lubitsch was conducting contract negotiations with Paramount at the time, so the studio opted to use Mamoulian. Having recently made the hit *Dr. Jekyll and Mr. Hyde*, Mamoulian was given a free hand in directing *Love Me Tonight* with few requirements other than featuring the two stars.

Mamoulian asked Broadway composers Richard Rodgers and Lorenz Hart to compose a score based on the concept of a "reverse Cinderella." The picture dips liberally into librettos, characters breaking into rhyming couplets and songs as the occasion demands. This makes the film what is widely considered to be the first integrated musical, where the music and lyrics directly reflect the action on-screen and advance the plot. Mamoulian used this in creative ways, such as with the elegant "Isn't It Romantic?" which begins on the lips of Maurice and then, through a series of strangers, arrives half a country away to the wistful Jeanette standing on a balcony.

Mamoulian also brought Myrna Loy on, borrowing her from MGM and changing her career trajectory overnight. Metro had pushed Loy in a variety of temptress or murderer roles, often putting her in yellowface for productions like 1932's *Thirteen Women* and *The Mask of Fu Manchu*. As the sexed-up Valentine, Loy broke out her comedic side, which allowed her to transition into classy roles, including her stint in the beloved *Thin Man* series (1934–1947). The studio originally demanded Mamoulian remove the character, but he instead prepared two versions

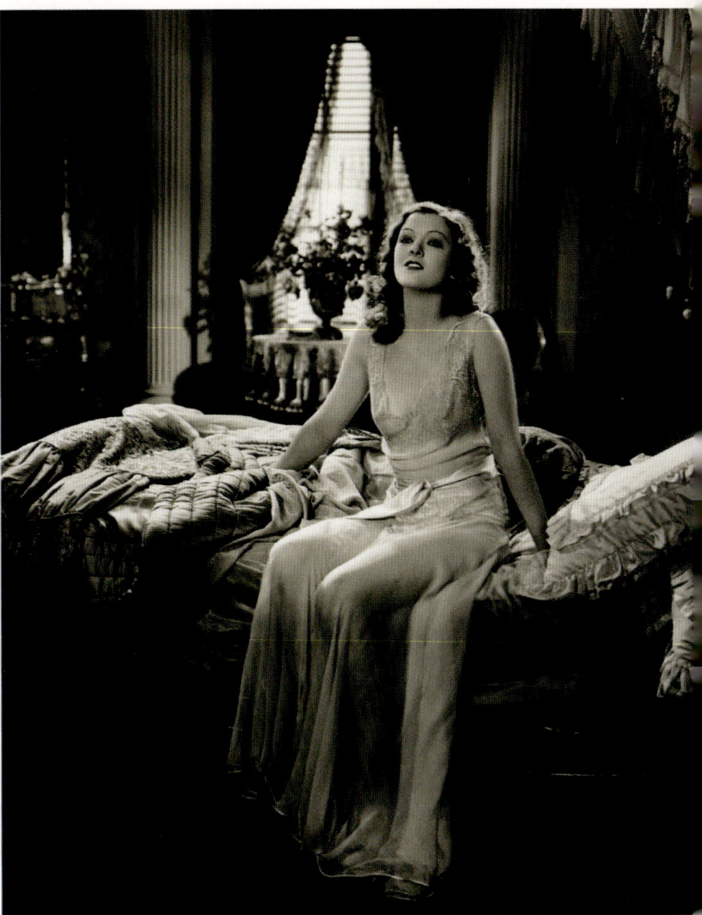

Censorship deprived the world of seeing Myrna Loy singing in this sheer negligee.

"A peach must be eaten, a drum must be beaten, and a woman needs something like that."

—Dr. Armand de Fontinac, reminding us we're reading a book about censorship in 1930s movies (and yes, this line was cut)

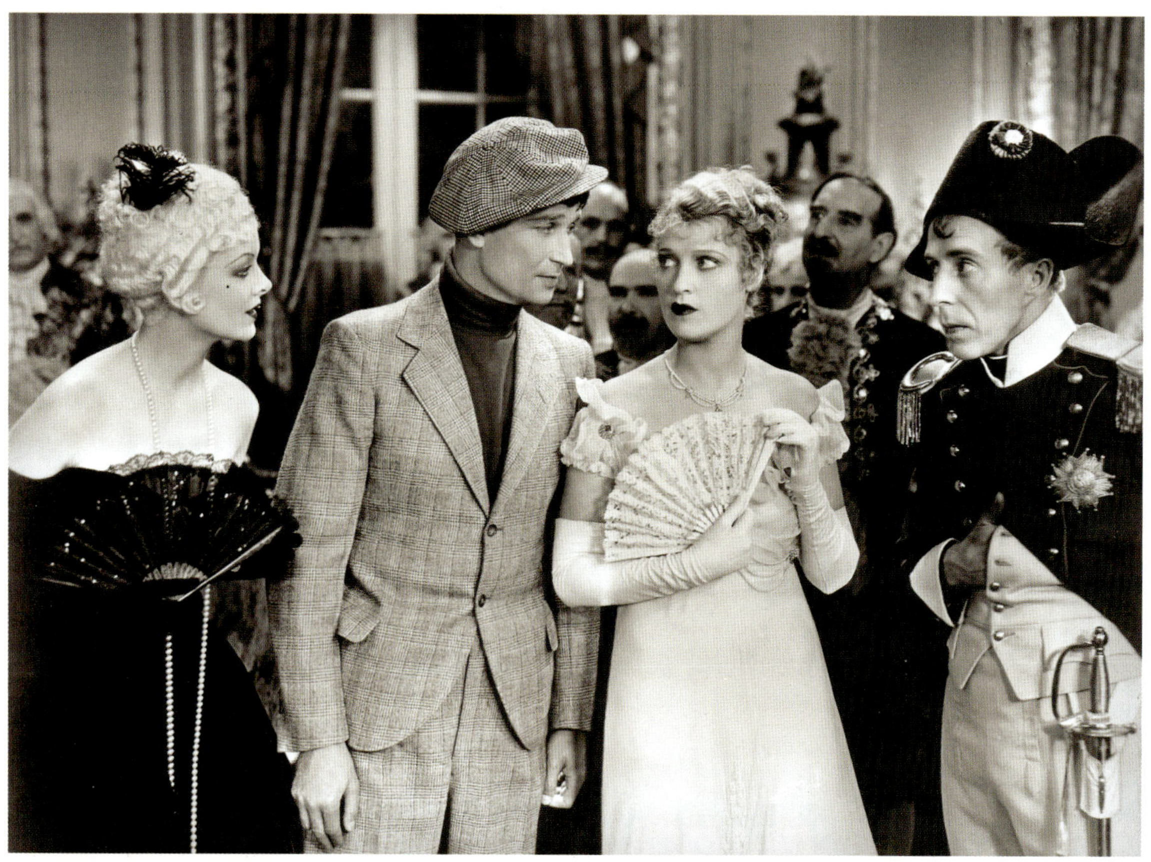

Everyone is sharing secrets, from Napoleon to Josephine.

of the script, with her part cut in the one that was handed to executives. The role stayed in once they saw how Loy dazzled in the dailies.

Mamoulian was a self-serious director working with a cast and crew used to collaborating with the more lighthearted Lubitsch. Upon MacDonald's suggestion, he eventually loosened up, but his endless script tinkering and other production turmoil resulted in the picture being delayed a number of times, ultimately costing nearly a million bucks in an era when most mid-range films totaled around $200,000.

Love Me Tonight was received rapturously, with Mordaunt Hall saying in *The New York Times*, "There are episodes in this production that merited applause and the only reason the audience failed to clap their hands was because they evidently thought they might miss a few words of dialogue or one of the melodious bits of music." The stars were notably less enthused, with Chevalier, embittered that he was not allowed any input during production, a dour presence on set. MacDonald left for Europe after the film's completion, saying that she would only do dramatic roles in the future and declaring, "I have gone far enough in lingerie."

Love Me Tonight enchanted the SRC and many censor boards, too. Most song lyrics submitted by Paramount were approved, though "A Woman Needs Something Like That" required vigilance. "There is such a real place in pictures for the delightful and clever Chevalier pictures that it is more than ever important not to jeopardize that field by going too far beyond the line between the risqué into the suggestive," the SRC cautioned.

At the end of the day, the SRC lauded Paramount: "If you should get into any difficulties with [local censors] on these counts—and this is one of the pictures which I am sure you won't want to see cut—you might have the censors look at [it] in the theatre with the audiences. I'm sure audiences are going to love it and will get no sense of suggestiveness out of the songs."

Indeed, *Love Me Tonight* was approved in its original form by New York, Quebec, and Kansas, but references to virgin springs and dialogue such as, "The old girl must have something" were frequently cut by boards in Ohio, Pennsylvania, and Australia.

After a 1936 note declared the picture suitable for rerelease with deletions, the PCA declined Paramount's request mere months later in early 1937, citing the film's suggestive dialogue as the culprit. "Some of the lyrics seem to be particularly offensive in this respect, and it would seem, from a cursory inspection, that any attempt to reedit it would ruin the picture," the PCA claimed.

Sadly, this film is one of the more egregious victims of the Production Code as it currently exists only in a trimmed version. When a condensed four-reel release was unsuccessfully floated in 1940 (Paramount was unable to sell a picture that short), a 1949 reissue for select art and specialty theaters still saw eight minutes of the film excised. Among the cut footage includes Loy's refrain in "Mimi" outfitted in a skimpy negligee, parts of the beginning and end of "A Woman Needs Something Like That," and more winking references to the virgin springs. This material is sadly still considered lost.

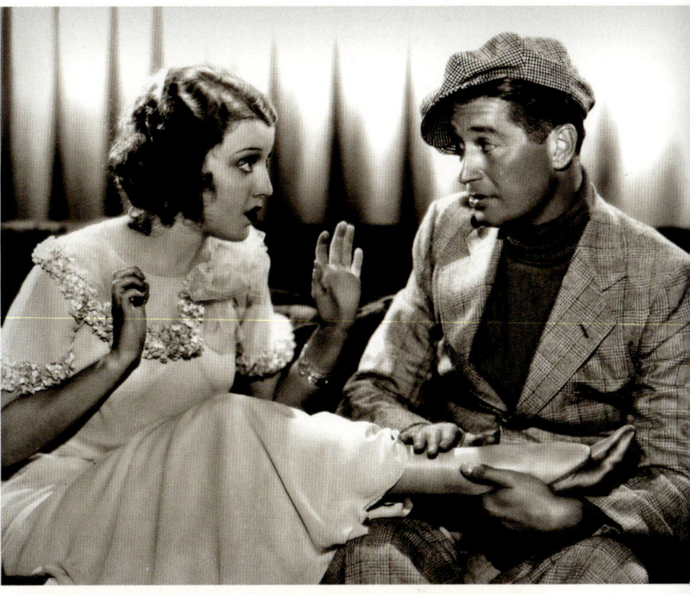

Jeanette MacDonald's ankles should be out of Maurice Chevalier's jurisdiction as a tailor. As a lover, well, that's another story.

Love Me Tonight is a rare film of wistful beauty, charm, and energy. Its innovations as a musical comedy are completely absorbed by modern musicals both onstage and off, from Rodgers and Hammerstein's smash hit *Oklahoma!* (1943) to modern classics like *The Book of Mormon* (2011); Vincente Minnelli even hailed it a perfect musical. The script's zippy freedom, the leads' amusing courtship, and Mamoulian's luminous touch continue to amuse and entice. Now isn't that romantic?

GRAND HOTEL

STARRING
Greta Garbo, John Barrymore, Joan Crawford, Wallace Beery, and Lionel Barrymore

DIRECTED BY
Edmund Goulding

RELEASED BY
MGM, September 1932

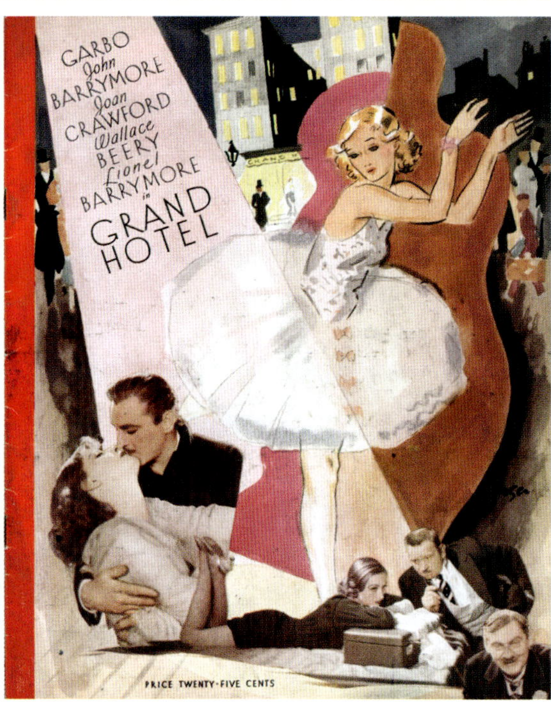

A star-studded spectacle calls for an astonishing souvenir program.

"Grand Hotel . . . always the same. People come, people go. Nothing ever happens."

—Dr. Otternschlag, with the biggest understatement of all time

Through its witty banter and plentiful dramatics, *Grand Hotel* explores a variety of issues, from the way money controls people's lives and how deceit taints human interactions, to the triumph of personal style over adversity. The result is one of the greatest Best Picture Oscar winners and a sober tale of both the immediacy and temporal nature of life.

Grand Hotel is the most expensive and trendy spot in the heart of Berlin. Inside, we follow five people as their lives intersect. The dying Otto Kringelein (Lionel Barrymore) is a poor accountant hoping to spend his last bit of cash at the lavish establishment. Flaemmchen (Joan Crawford) is a hardworking stenographer who wants to be an actress, but to make ends meet she cozies up to her clients. General Director Preysing (Wallace Beery) is a huffy industrialist who needs a merger to save his company but must resort to falsehoods to complete a business deal. The raffish Baron Felix von Geigern (John Barrymore) is a gentleman and a thief who works the hotel, often in that order. And then the ballerina Grusinskaya (Greta Garbo) is suffering from a crisis of popularity, putting her in a melancholy mood. Their stories unfold, leading the characters on different paths, some tragic and some hopeful.

Based on Vicki Baum's own experiences working at a pair of Berlin hotels, her 1929 book *Menschen im Hotel* was adapted for the Broadway stage in 1930. MGM had invested in the play and

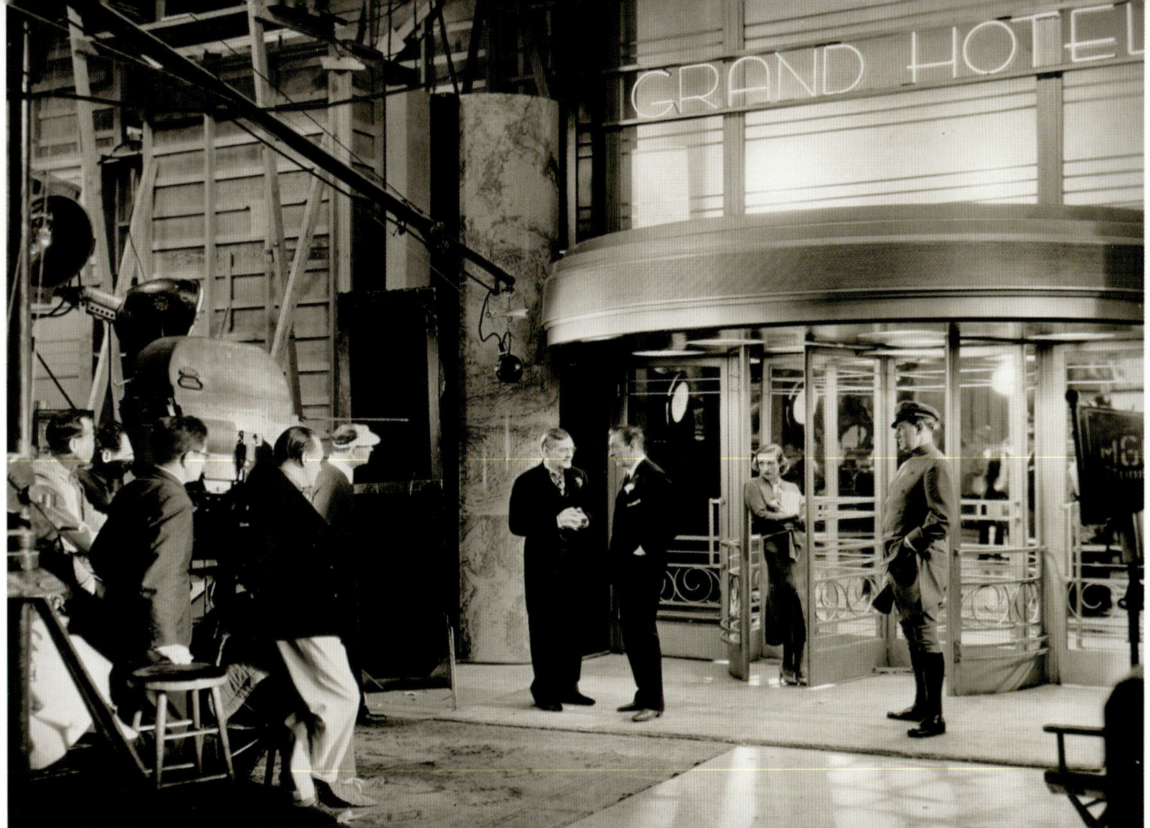

Things *certainly* happen in *Grand Hotel*!

acquired the screen rights to the novel. The story, which presented meaty scenes to each member of its lead ensemble, inspired Irving Thalberg to adapt it into an all-star motion picture.

The budget for these stars would be massive, as was the possibility of a massive clash of egos, but the payoff could be astronomical. For instance, Thalberg and others feared Garbo's famously reclusive nature would lead to conflict on set, but the shy Garbo instantly developed a rapport with John Barrymore. When Garbo became nervous filming their lovemaking scenes, Barrymore would whisper to her, "You are the most beautiful woman in the world." Their shared sequences genuinely reflected a respect and heartfelt love and, thereby, grounded the picture. Film critic Mick LaSalle noted, "[They are] a pair of exhausted, jaded adults who are rescued at their lowest moment, by love. If that's not the same as getting touched by God, it's a close second."

The only real conflict came from Beery, who was nominated for a Best Actor Oscar for 1930's *The Big House* and won the award for 1931's *The Champ*. He shot to stardom in the talkie era playing dim brutes with hearts of gold, and his casting confirmed his place in the studio's cache of top talent. To secure his participation in what is a villainous role, Beery was made one promise: He was the only actor in the film allowed to have a German accent. The placation still didn't totally calm him, as he stormed off the set at one point after accusing Crawford of being unable to act.

After previewing a rough cut of the movie, Thalberg was adamant that changes were needed in the romance scenes. Director Edmund Goulding, told by Thalberg to tone down some of the lengthier dialogue between the baron and Grusinskaya, crafted the line, "I want to be alone" and instructed Garbo to repeat it three times. It would become closely associated with the publicity-shy actress, earning all manner of parodies and tributes ever since.

When the SRC first reviewed *Grand Hotel*'s synopsis, they noted a scene in which Grusinskaya emerges from the bath and the baron spies her figure outlined in the shower curtain, deeming it "wholly unnecessary." (Another similar moment featuring "the figure of a nude woman," which was ultimately cut, came under fire by the SRC; "apparently the only excuse for the nakedness is the alleged box office pull," they charged.) Thalberg was also advised to handle the possibility that the baron spends the night with Grusinskaya delicately, as well as the scenes between Flaemmchen and Preysing in his hotel room. Those sequences, where Flaemmchen seems to be acquiescing to a sexual relationship with the industrialist for security, were the ones most commonly censored by local boards.

When MGM broached the subject of reissuing the film in 1936, the PCA came up with a host of demanded cuts, from references to Flaemmchen's figure, to Preysing snoring, to even removing the murder scene in the third act. MGM came to a "verbal understanding" with the PCA, resulting in the studio capitulating to about half of their demands—though the murder ultimately stayed in.

Grand Hotel was widely praised and beloved, raking in about $2.3 million the first year of its release against an exorbitant budget of $700,000. The film remains the only one to win Best Picture at the Academy Awards without any additional Oscar nominations. MGM revisited the story in

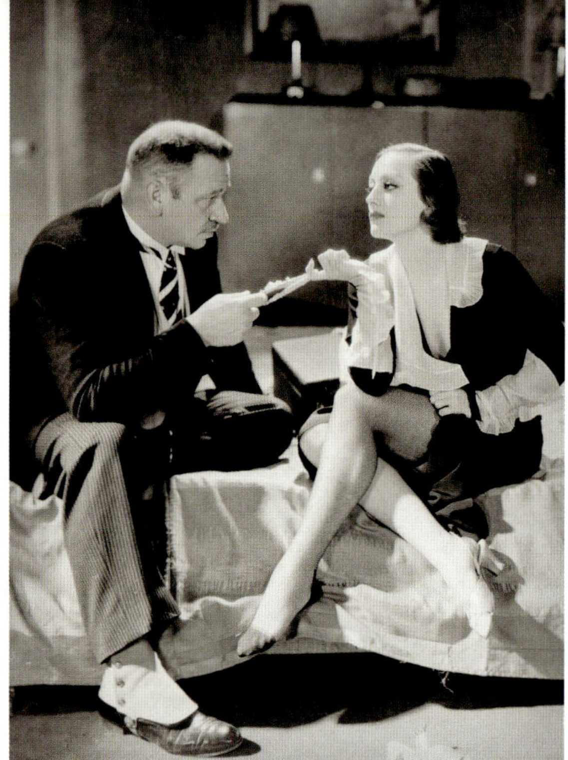

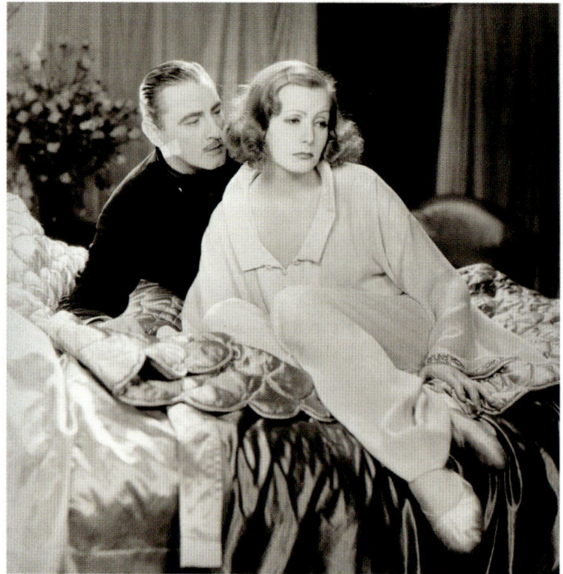

FROM TOP: Stenographer Joan Crawford and her legs set their sights on industrialist Wallace Beery. • Ballerina Greta Garbo broods in bed with part-time jewel thief John Barrymore.

Greta Garbo

Grand Hotel came at the peak of what was known as Garbo-mania. Born Greta Lovisa Gustafsson, the future star caught the attention of MGM chief Louis B. Mayer in her supporting performance in the Swedish film *The Saga of Gösta Berling* (1924). He brought her to Hollywood in 1925, and her beauty crossed with her withdrawn, melancholy attitude soon captured the imagination of moviegoers. *Flesh and the Devil,* her first film with frequent costar John Gilbert and only her third American movie, was a massive hit. By the time she appeared in *A Woman of Affairs* (1928), Garbo was MGM's top box office draw.

MGM was careful with Garbo's transition to talkies, coaching her thickly accented Swedish voice for over a year before she appeared in 1930's *Anna Christie*. Garbo soon commanded a great deal of power over her roles and could choose her directors, leading men, and writers. The high stature of her pre-Code dramas reflect this: She costarred with an up-and-coming Clark Gable in 1931's *Susan Lennox (Her Fall and Rise),* portrayed the infamous titular role in *Mata Hari* the same year, and took on the character of Sweden's own *Queen Christina*, hand-picking the out-of-favor Gilbert to play opposite her.

As European markets became less available to American films through the end of the 1930s, Garbo's popularity waned. Following an electric collaboration with Ernst Lubitsch for *Ninotchka* (1939), Garbo ended her movie career in the early 1940s, living in contented seclusion the rest of her life.

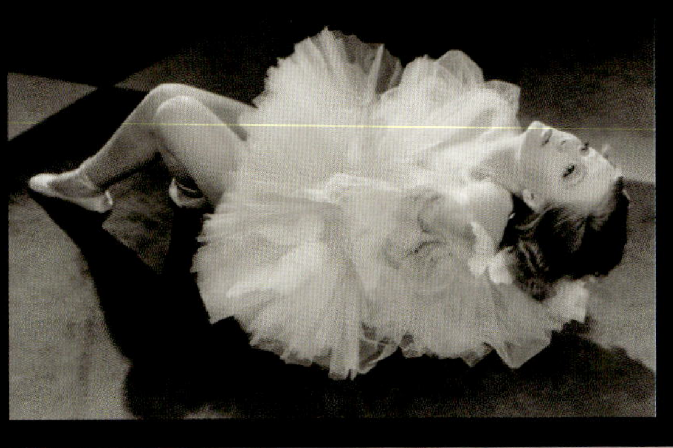

Greta Garbo is art.

1945 as *Week-End at the Waldorf*, and there was even another remake attempt in the 1970s with director Norman Jewison at the helm and none other than Dolly Parton in the Garbo role. The latter would have been set in MGM's Grand Hotel in Las Vegas, but sadly that version was never made. Can you even imagine?

Beyond the brand name, the legacy of *Grand Hotel* has had an acute effect on Hollywood over the decades, leading to a wide array of dramas with all-star casts, from the 1970s *Airport* series to heist films like the original *Ocean's 11* (1960) and its stylish 2001 remake. Trendsetting aside, *Grand Hotel* may be the peak of MGM's pre-Code output. It's a primary testament to the studio's versatility, showcasing beautiful sets, crisp sound and music, and immersive directing, delivering to audiences proof positive that the studio really did have more stars than there were in the heavens. *Grand Hotel* remains a crown jewel in MGM's legacy.

THE MOST DANGEROUS GAME

STARRING
Joel McCrea, Fay Wray, Robert Armstrong, and Leslie Banks

DIRECTED BY
Irving Pichel and Ernest B. Schoedsack

RELEASED BY
MGM, September 1932

"God made some men poets, some he made kings, some beggars. Me, he made a hunter. My hand was made for the trigger. . ."

—Zaroff, making one of those proclamations that helps you realize you're at the wrong dinner party

The pathology of a hunter may seem like an odd place for a modern parable, but Richard Connell's short story "The Most Dangerous Game" has long aroused the attention of readers and Hollywood for its potent themes and exciting thrills. The plot has been made, remade, and ripped off dozens of times. From episodes of the enduring TV hit *The Simpsons* to Katniss Everdeen drawing her bow in *The Hunger Games* (2012), stories of someone suddenly finding themselves as human prey have exhilarated audiences for over a century.

Even after the cultural fascination with big game hunting waned, *The Most Dangerous Game* remains powerfully rooted as a survival story, a testament to Americans' rugged individualism and eagerness to do good. The not-so-subtle messages about class warfare are made literal and imbue the dramatics with a charged sense of justice and "street smarts" triumphing over money and power.

In the film, great white hunter Bob Rainsford (Joel McCrea) survives a gruesome shipwreck and finds himself on a remote island being hosted by Zaroff (Leslie Banks), a Russian noble with an estate of Cossacks and servants who are stiff and aloof. Two other castaways, siblings Eve (Fay Wray) and Martin (Robert Armstrong), are also trapped on the island, and Eve has already sensed there is something unpleasant happening there. Zaroff is gleeful when he finds that Bob is another big game hunter like himself, but slowly it is revealed that the two have divergent standpoints on the matter: While Bob hunts for sport and thrill, he retains a philosophical distance. Zaroff has none, and he divulges that he yearns for the thrill of hunting the *truly* most dangerous game. No points now if you can guess what that is.

This movie, the first and most definitive filmed version of Connell's work, stays close to the original, with several changes that flesh out and deepen it, including the addition of Eve. In typical pre-Code fashion, the updates add a sexual dimension to the villain and his depravity, making it not just a psychological contest between two men but further redefining the stark difference in worldviews of people who see the human race as prey for their own machinations. This use of psychology to define and counter the villain and the hero had long-lasting impacts on how Amer-

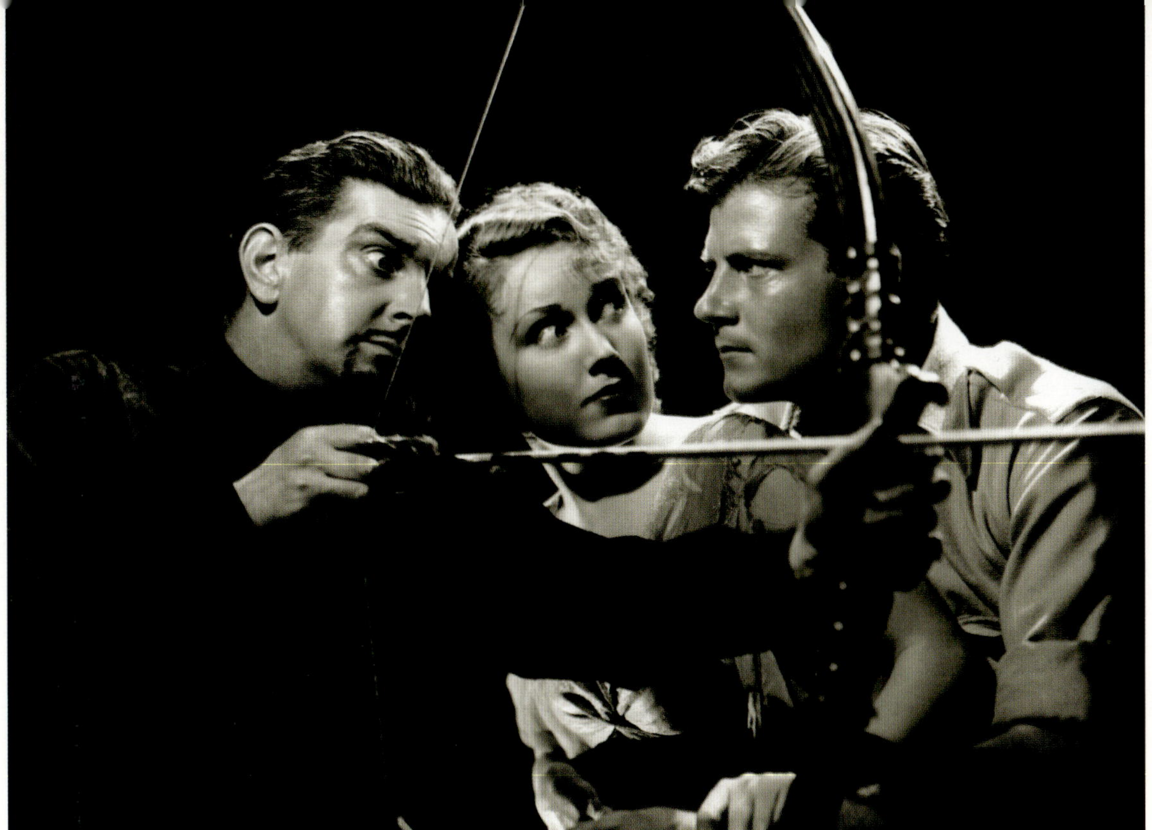

There's a lot to unpack in this photo with Leslie Banks, Fay Wray, and Joel McCrea.

ican movies would be told. (In fact, the plot and the film itself went so far as to stir the admiration and ghastly exploits of the real-life Zodiac Killer, as seen in David Fincher's 2007 *Zodiac*.)

Ernest B. Schoedsack codirected *The Most Dangerous Game* and *King Kong* (1933) simultaneously, leading to a number of interesting crossovers. Several actors, including Wray, Armstrong, and Noble Johnson, pulled double duty, with Bruce Cabot originally cast as Zaroff until Banks became available. Max Steiner scored both movies, sometimes even recycling musical themes. Several of the jungle sets were also reused; when Bob and Eve run across the log during their escape, you almost expect to see the sailors from the SS *Venture* running in from the other direction.

Some of this overlap could also be attributed to a sudden halving of the budget. This streamlining forced Schoedsack and codirector Irving Pichel to abandon whole scenes and characters, leading to an emphasis on action and suspense. Combined with the score, still a novelty at the time, the modern template for action pictures was born.

With a prominent scar and a goatee to visually tie him to Lucifer, Zaroff is the film's most interesting character, a noble who uses his immense wealth to hunt the unfortunate men he's lured there. One of cinema's first non-fantastical serial killers, he can be read as old-world aristocracy feasting upon the naivete of the young and less fortunate.

The addition of Eve allowed the filmmakers to explore some gnarly territory, as Zaroff clearly obsesses over the idea of sexual arousal being tied directly to the act of committing violence.

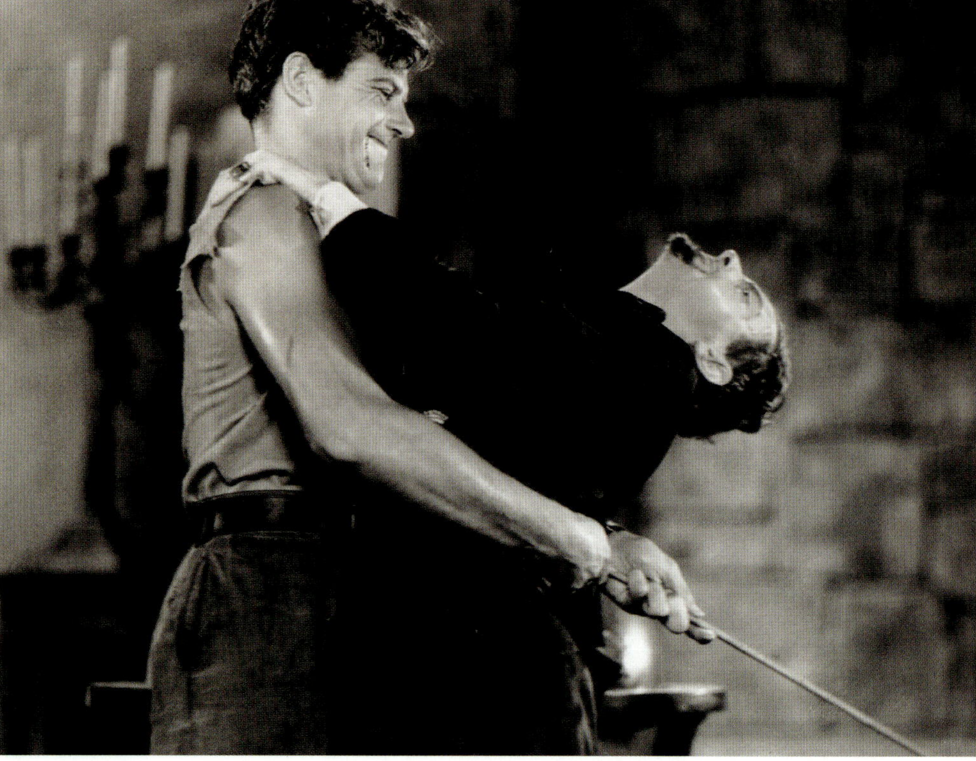

Hunter Joel McCrea did not take well to becoming the hunted by Leslie Banks.

"What is woman . . . until the blood is quickened by the kill?" he muses, his whole hunt of Bob hinging on the gratification he plans to get from Bob's murder and his planned rape of Eve. (Besides an orgiastic reaction after he thinks he's murdered Bob, Zaroff goes one step further by complacently lighting up a cigarette.) Zaroff, along with pulp icon Fu Manchu, would become a potent waypoint for every Bond villain and evil super genius on the screen for the next century, expressing disappointment that the hero refuses to see things their way before unleashing their sadism upon them with an elaborately rigged death trap.

Even with Zaroff's barely disguised kinks on display, *The Most Dangerous Game* proved surprisingly safe from censorship difficulty, with one exception. The SRC warned producer David O. Selznick to shoot the scene in the trophy room "in such a way as not to be gruesome."

This note hints at one of the more intriguing bits of missing cinema over the last century. It seems that trophy room sequence was filmed as scripted by RKO, but, between an early previewed version and the movie's wide release, over twelve minutes were cut from the film. In the version currently available, we see shrunken heads on the wall and another floating in formaldehyde, as well as skulls on the mantel and a skeleton in a human-size cage. The filmmakers deleted shots of an ebullient Zaroff showcasing fully realized taxidermy dioramas of his victims, including a man fighting off ravenous hunting dogs, and gleefully recounting details of their deaths at his hands. While the other scenes in the trophy room were ghastly, these addi-

Fay Wray

Though primarily remembered for her role in *King Kong*—later in life she'd tell reporters she'd say a prayer every time she visited the Empire State Building since she'd had a friend die up there—Fay Wray's Hollywood career was wild and messy and one of the best examples of the varied parts that women could be given in this period. Sometimes cast as a Latina, Wray may be best remembered for her scream, but she was able to bring charm and effortless sex appeal to her roles as well. Movies like *Ann Carver's Profession* (1933) gave her the opportunity to portray a powerful attorney while fare like *Viva Villa!* (1934) allowed her to really let loose as a sadistic mistress. *The Most Dangerous Game* would be the first of many horror films for her, including *Doctor X* (1932), *The Vampire Bat* (1933), *Mystery of the Wax Museum* (1933), and *Black Moon* (1934).

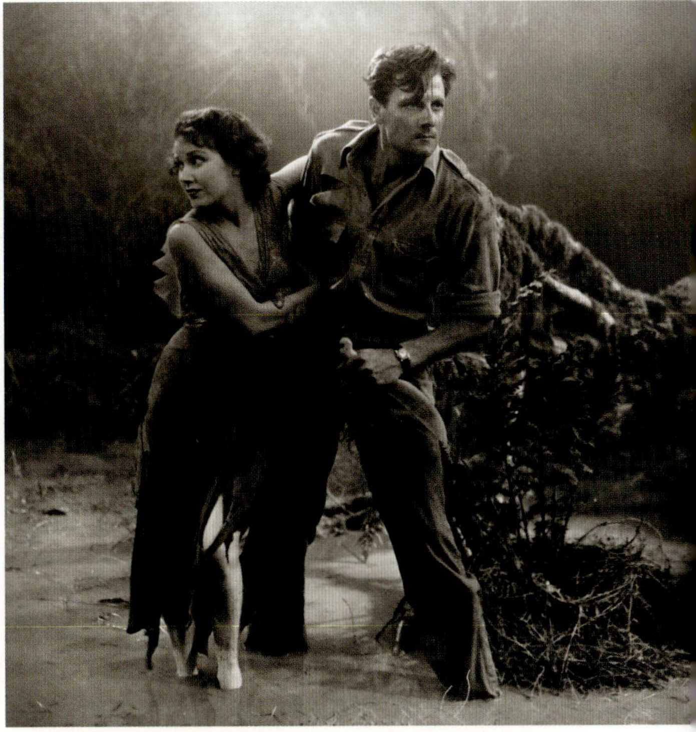

Fighting for your life against a maniac who's trying to *hunt* you in his own horror jungle is pretty exhausting.

tional demonstrations allegedly sent some audience members straight toward the exit.

With the most blatant sections removed, *The Most Dangerous Game* went broadly uncensored in the United States. Meanwhile, the response from most international boards was not as tepid. Ontario and Alberta struck down several sequences of men struggling and fighting, while Finland and Austria rejected the movie outright.

After the establishment of the PCA in 1934, the film was approved for reissue in 1935 uncut. However, a 1938 release made one change—underwater shots of sharks at the beginning, lifted from *Bird of Paradise* (1932), were printed as a negative image to lessen the horror as the predators consumed squealing sailors. This alteration wouldn't be undone for home viewers until the 1990s. (Interestingly, the lengthy trophy room excision and the shark edit are not noted in the film's PCA file. While a July 1933 piece in *Motion Picture Herald* references a seventy-eight-minute early audience test that resulted in a return to the editing room, the SRC raved about the film following the preview they attended around the same time.)

The Most Dangerous Game is a kinetic, exciting tale executed to perfection. One of the most stylistically complete and daring movies of the era, its influence will only continue to grow with time.

RED DUST

STARRING
Clark Gable, Jean Harlow, Gene Raymond, and Mary Astor

DIRECTED BY
Victor Fleming

RELEASED BY
MGM, October 1932

One of the most infamous films of the era, *Red Dust* centers on a love triangle between a married woman, a prostitute, and a conniving, sweaty plantation owner in 1930s French Indochina. The film is barely innuendo, featuring most of the leads undressing at one point or another, including a famous outdoor bath in a rain barrel that Jean Harlow herself would be parodying by the next year.

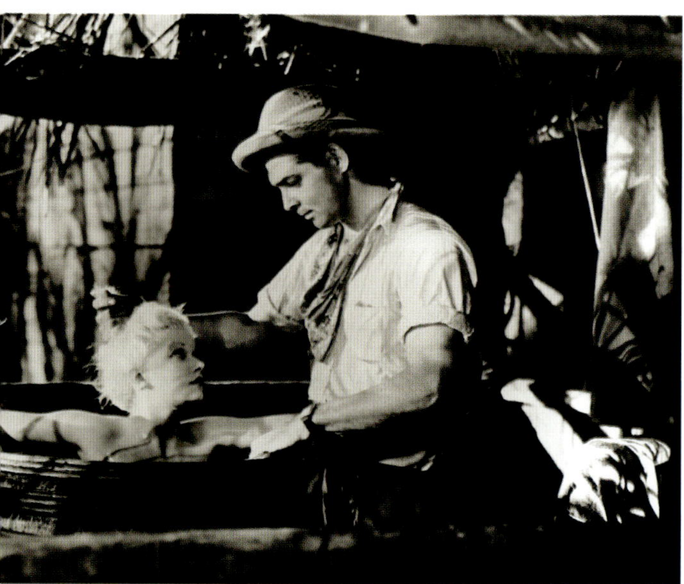

Red Dust opens on a flailing rubber plantation in Southeast Asia, where Dennis Carson (Clark Gable) rules as the often cruel, frustrated master. One evening, he finds that Vantine (Harlow), a prostitute on the run from the cops, has taken up residence in his home—and his bedroom. A pair of prim survey engineers, Gary (Gene Raymond) and Barbara (Mary Astor), arrive, and Dennis is immediately smitten with Barbara's manners and breeding. When Gary takes ill with fever and Barbara struggles to acclimate to the uncivility of jungle life, Dennis moves in while Vantine fumes. Dennis has to juggle his seduction of the classy Barbara (consummated, naturally, during a raging thunderstorm) and Vantine's jealousy. When Dennis is presented with the opportunity to murder Gary and make it look like an accident, he must decide what kind of man he really is.

Originally written as a vehicle for John Gilbert and Greta Garbo, *Red Dust* was filmed entirely on MGM soundstages. Its central building included overhead plumbing to provide rain and a working river, and moths were released before each take to add to the atmosphere. With the hot lights focused endlessly on the dirt and mud, the smell was supposedly nothing to write home about.

While neither Gable nor Harlow cared for the original script, the two became fast friends and their chemistry shone. It was during the filming of *Red Dust* that Harlow's personal life took a dark

Playful Jean Harlow does not amuse Clark Gable in the slightest.

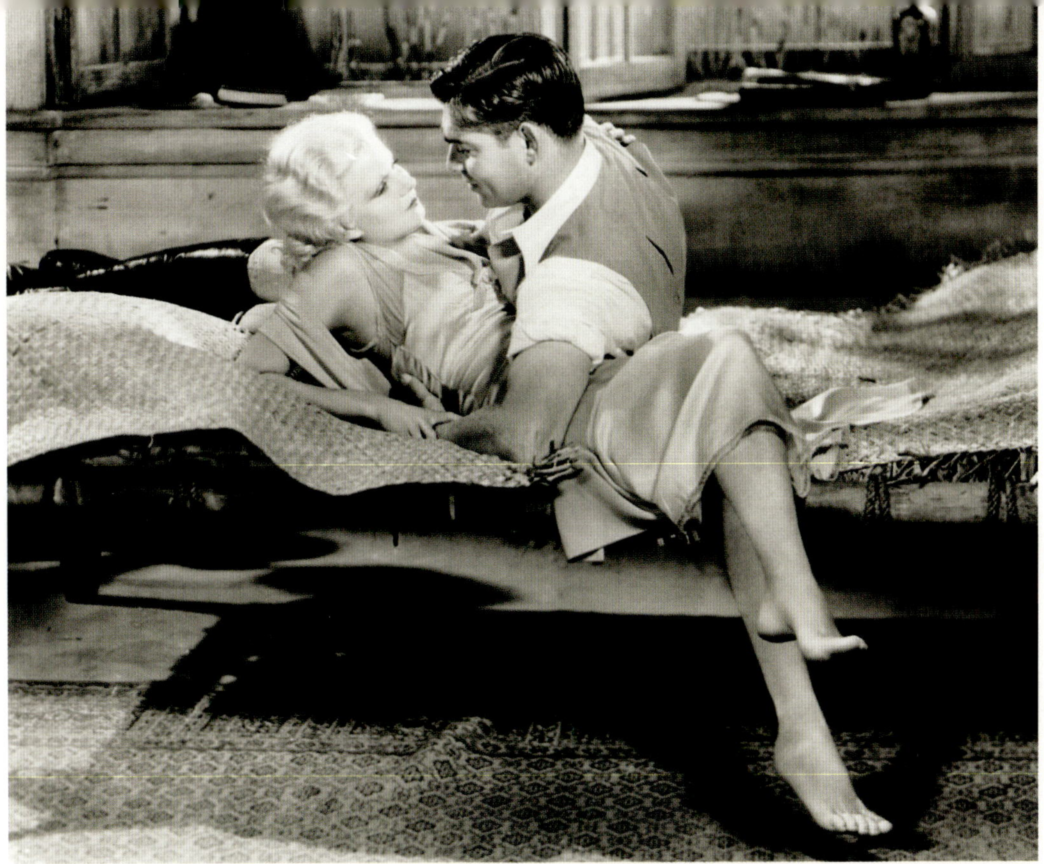

Prostitute Jean Harlow drops in on Clark Gable's plantation and finds her way just as quickly into his bed.

turn. Her husband of only two months, Paul Bern, was found dead in their home in September 1932. The aftermath was an example of the studio spin system at its most nefarious, with MGM executives and a studio photographer arriving on the scene before the police to search for clues (most likely tampering with evidence in the process), protecting Harlow—and MGM—from potential scandal. Bern's death was officially ruled a suicide by the coroner, with a note found at the scene implicating that he killed himself due to impotence. Unofficially, countless theories have been bandied about over the years, including one placing the blame on Bern's ex-common-law wife, but due to the studio's interference, the full truth of the situation will never be known for sure. To MGM's credit, their publicity machine engendered the nation's sympathy toward Harlow.

Harlow was shaken to her core, attempting to return to work a few days later only to collapse. Her first scenes back were those of her skinny-dipping in the rain barrel, and the time she spent with Gable joshing about helped her recover. Rumor

"What's the matter? Afraid I'll shock the duchess? Don't you suppose she's ever seen a French postcard?"

—Vantine, a woman of ill repute, who is more familiar with raunchy postcards than her romantic rivals

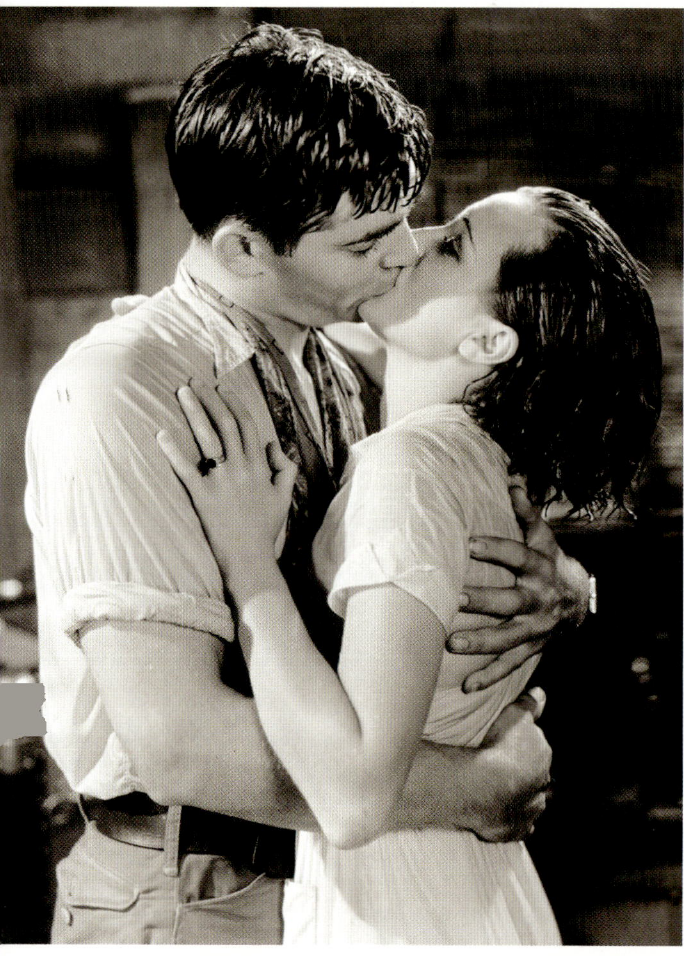

Mary Astor cheats on her sick husband with plantation manager Clark Gable in *Red Dust*.

has it that Harlow, topless, stood up in the barrel for one outtake shouting, "Here's one for the boys in the lab!" though it's never surfaced.

After censor backlash to *Red-Headed Woman* and Bern's suicide, Irving Thalberg worked to tone down *Red Dust*'s titillating sexual tension. Several early scenes in the movie were redone, including shots to give Harlow a more "decent" neckline and dubbing over a line that insulted the French.

In showcasing just how little backbone the SRC had to actually enforce the Code, MGM got away with submitting sections of the *Red Dust* script to the office as opposed to the whole thing—even as the film was in production. Early on, Vantine's character bore the brunt of concern. Despite MGM's assurance that she'd become a "finer character," worries persisted in terms of suggestive lines, revealing visuals (like her dress slipping up), and, of course, the rain barrel bath.

Luckily, the SRC's preview turned out better than they hoped, considering they never got a full handle on the script before production commenced. They lauded Thalberg for handling the sex situations with "finesse," noting that Harlow's honesty and humor hopefully will redeem "whatever danger may lurk in the portrayal of her profession." (The fact that the most passionate scenes occur between Dennis and Barbara alleviated much reference to prostitution.) Some in the SRC concluded that elements that might otherwise be objectionable "are done with such a light touch that the audience takes them as comedy rather than heavy sex."

Of course, not all censor boards agreed. While some went easy on the picture, like Kansas approving with no cuts, several others clocked multiple edits. Scenes of Dennis undressing and italicized parts of dialogue such as, "You ought to know *whether it's worthwhile or not*" faced excision in select areas. Meanwhile, *Red Dust* was rejected in Quebec (later overturned), British Malaya, and eventually Berlin the following year, because, per *Variety*, the picture was "deemed too hot for Nazified Germany."

The steaminess of *Red Dust*, peppered with wit and innuendo, sets it apart from many of its contemporaries. The movie plays on traditional

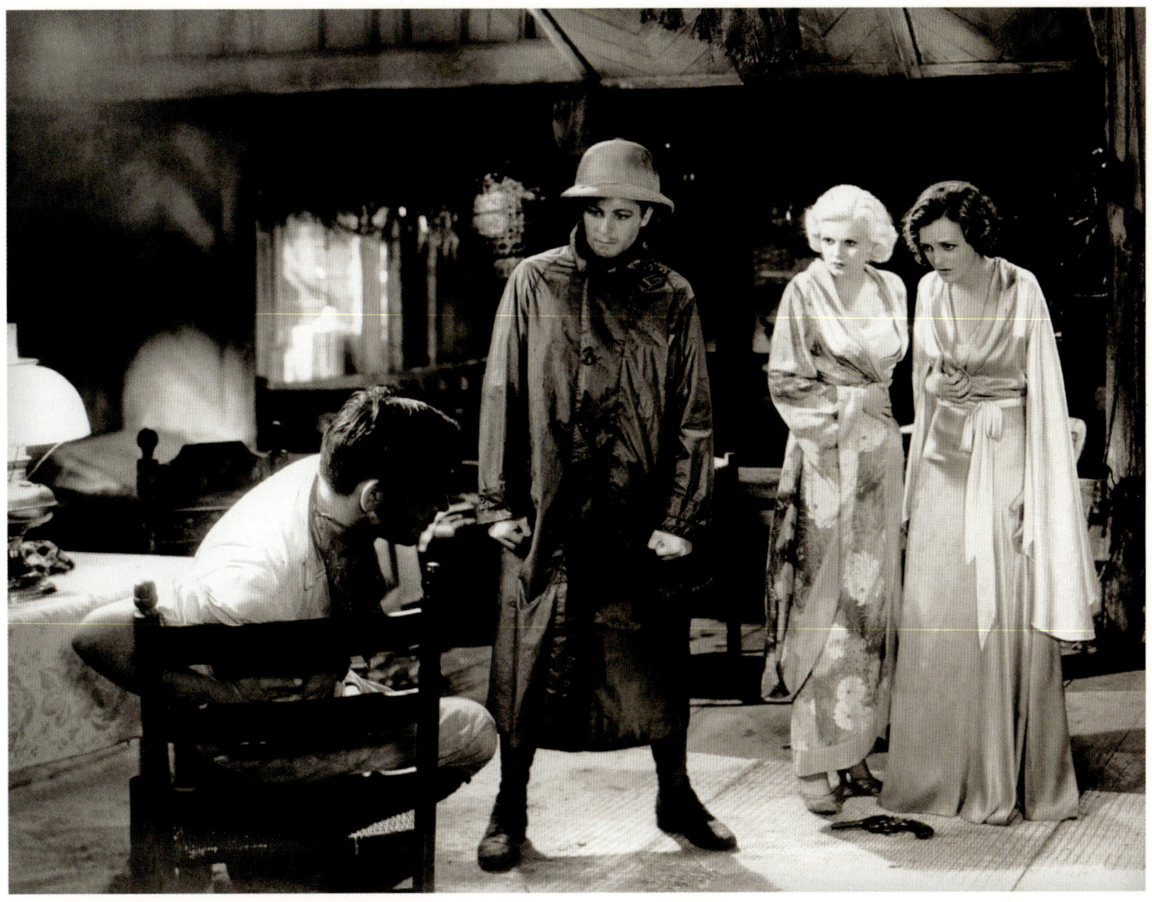

Honestly, Gene Raymond, Jean Harlow, and Mary Astor all had valid reasons for shooting Clark Gable.

thoughts on power structures, as Dennis rules his domain like a king, manipulating those around him to get what he wants. It's only through Vantine's heart of gold that he finally sees how thoroughly rotten both he and Barbara have behaved.

The film's views on colonialism in French Indochina, with regular disparaging remarks made about the native laborers and a truly unpleasant role for Willie Fung as a dim servant, reinforce how much cultural and racial perceptions have fortunately shifted. (John Ford's 1953 remake, *Mogambo*, also starring Gable, displays fewer overt racial stereotypes but still retains problematic elements.)

Red Dust's heated love triangle created a formative moment in both Gable's and Harlow's careers, turning them into two of the biggest sex symbols of the 1930s. The film was one of MGM's highest-grossing pictures of the year, bringing in a profit of about $400,000, and its sharp banter and titillating romance remain a touchpoint for the kind of lurid, moody dramas that would soon go out of fashion.

TROUBLE IN PARADISE

STARRING
Miriam Hopkins, Kay Francis, and Herbert Marshall

DIRECTED BY
Ernst Lubitsch

RELEASED BY
Paramount, October 1932

During the Great Depression, even the criminals were struggling. Ernst Lubitsch's *Trouble in Paradise*, which he later noted as the favorite of all his films, is a glimmering jewel in the crown of pre-Code cinema. While it wasn't wholly reviled by censors, it flew under the radar for the general public. Now it is firmly regarded as one of the first great romantic comedies of the talkie era and simply one of the most charming movies ever assembled.

The "Lubitsch touch," the sly sophistication the director playfully infused in his comedies, was firing on all cylinders in *Trouble in Paradise*. Lubitsch excelled at innuendo, and while post-Code films would be forced to rely on implication, Lubitsch utilized such sultry allusions in his pre-Code work to convey sex in the sexiest way possible—without showing a thing. The way Lubitsch's urbane sensibility tastefully turned subjects like romance, sex, class, and money into sparkling repartee served as a template for 1930s and 1940s screwball comedies and has remained an inspiration ever since. He was even able to make the fantastical affairs of upper-crust Europeans human and relevant with lines like, "Everything will be all right again. Prosperity is just around the corner," evoking hope then and now.

In *Trouble in Paradise*, Gaston Monescu (Herbert Marshall) invites the ravishing Lily Vautier (Miriam Hopkins) to his suite one moonlit night in Venice. Over the course of an intimate dinner, the two find that not only are neither of them the society snobs they pretend to be, but both are thieves. Now that Gaston and Lily have found each other, the world is their oyster, and they spend the next year committing robberies around Europe. After lifting an egregiously priced handbag from Mariette Colet (Kay Francis) in Paris, however, they find that the hefty reward for the handbag is too good to resist. Gaston returns it, only to find that the sultry Mariette keeps a loose grip on her money. He signs on to be her secretary at once, planning a fleecing that should put him and Lily back on easy street. Ah, but if it weren't for the way Mariette's eyes sparkle . . .

"Darling, remember, you are Gaston Monescu. You are a crook. I want you as a crook. I love you as a crook. I worship you as a crook. Steal, swindle, rob. Oh, but don't become one of those useless, good-for-nothing gigolos!"

—Lily, warning her crooked lover away from the easy path in life

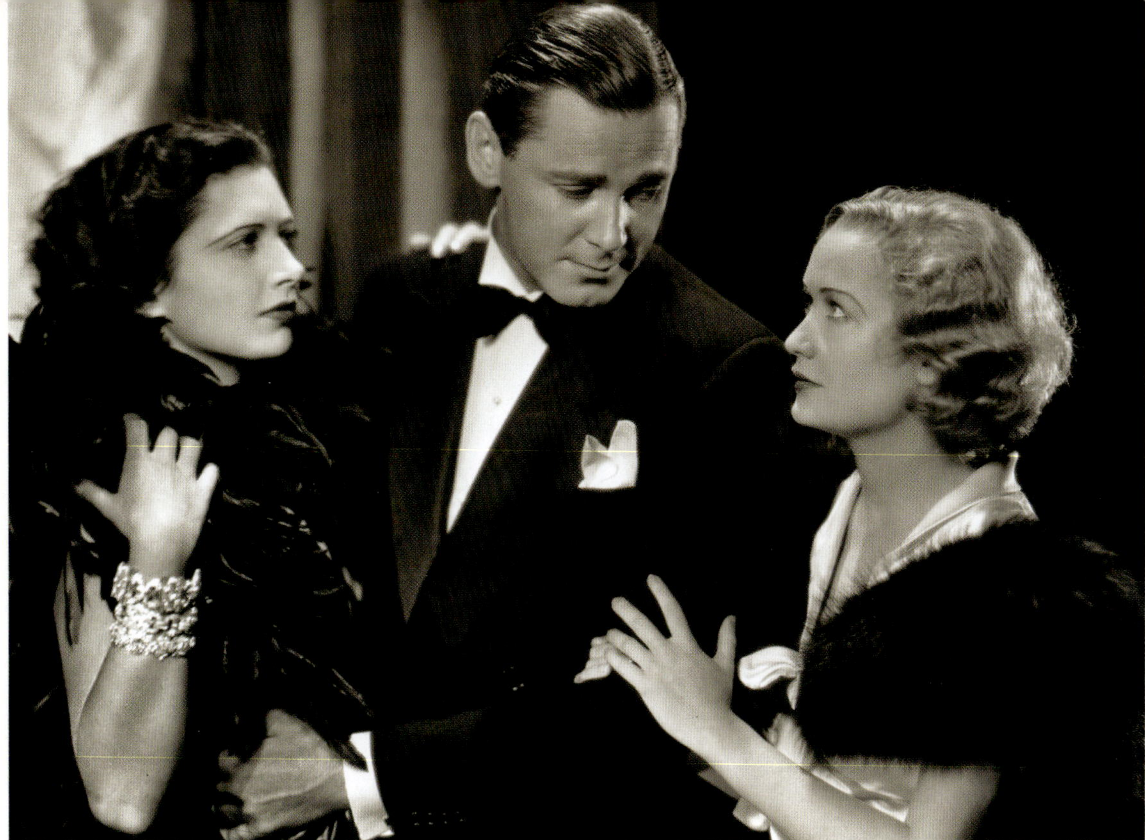

Herbert Marshall faces the ultimate predicament in *Trouble in Paradise:* Choose perfume executive Kay Francis or fellow thief Miriam Hopkins.

Paramount's movies of the early 1930s were meticulously crafted, often elaborate affairs that cost the studio more money than it had. Due to its partnerships with German filmmakers, the studio became a storied home of expatriates, with some commenting that the Paramount ideal of Europe often triumphed over the real thing in the imagination of its audiences.

Though reportedly based on the 1931 Hungarian stage play *The Honest Finder*, the only element kept was the basic premise. The film's cowriter with Lubitsch, Samson Raphaelson, supposedly never even read it. (The movie originally retained the play's title, but even that was jettisoned, with *Trouble in Paradise* only emerging a few weeks before release.) Together, Raphaelson and Lubitsch designed the picture as a satire of whodunnits, riffing on the gentleman-thief genre that was popular at the time. The script was written over the course of four months at Lubitsch's Santa Monica beach house, with Lubitsch pushing for "how do we say it different *and good*."

This approach created many moments of cinematic poetry, from the film's opening shot of Venice revealed by way of a garbage collector to a full minute where the camera stays on a beautiful deco clock as we listen to dialogue unspool. Along with Travis Banton's shimmering gowns and Hans Drier's elegant sets, Lubitsch's deft crafting gives the picture a dreamy, magical atmosphere; as Peter Bogdanovich expertly noted, "It's a film about

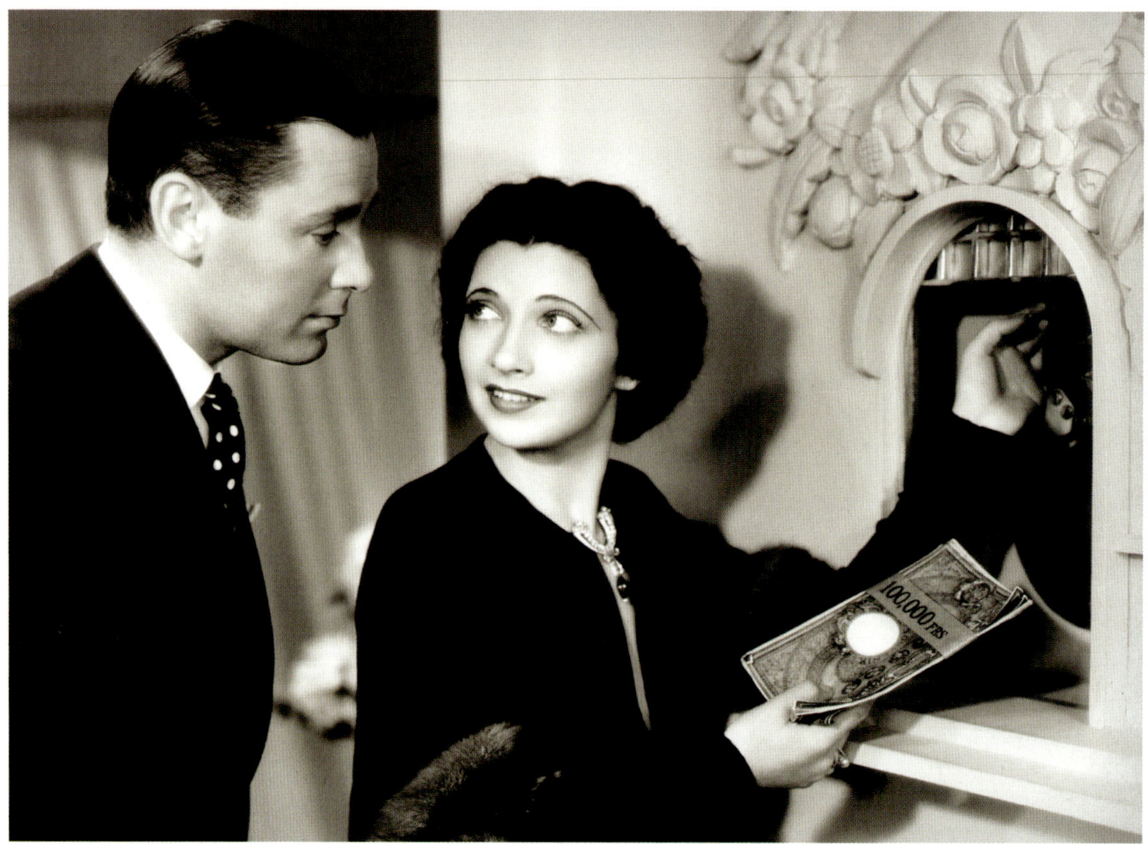

ABOVE: Never show a man your safe within the first 24 hours, Kay Francis. **OPPOSITE:** So much conveyed just through shadows.

thieves but you never see anyone steal anything." On top of that, the cast's chemistry was so immaculate that there were even rumors that Marshall was carrying on simultaneous affairs with Francis and Hopkins, though that seems unlikely.

As was generally the case with comedies, the SRC was mostly smitten by *Trouble in Paradise*. The main objections raised didn't come from glorifying the thieves or the rather explicit partner swapping, but instead from the film's early scenes set in Venice, spotlighting the garbage collector and excitable hotel staff, and the potentially offensive portrayal of police in a "so-called musical comedy manner." The office suggested painting Venice in a more colorful, romantic light, expressing a worry that Italians may not take the gentle ribbing of Venice well, especially after Paramount had gotten into trouble with its earlier release *This Is the Night* (1932).

Lubitsch's style certainly worked in his favor when it came to the topic of censorship. Early on, the SRC pointed out, "Of course we realize the light Lubitsch touch is rather the all-governing factor insofar as domestic censorship is concerned." Complaints lodged from local censor boards were minor, with lines like, "But I don't want to be a lady,"

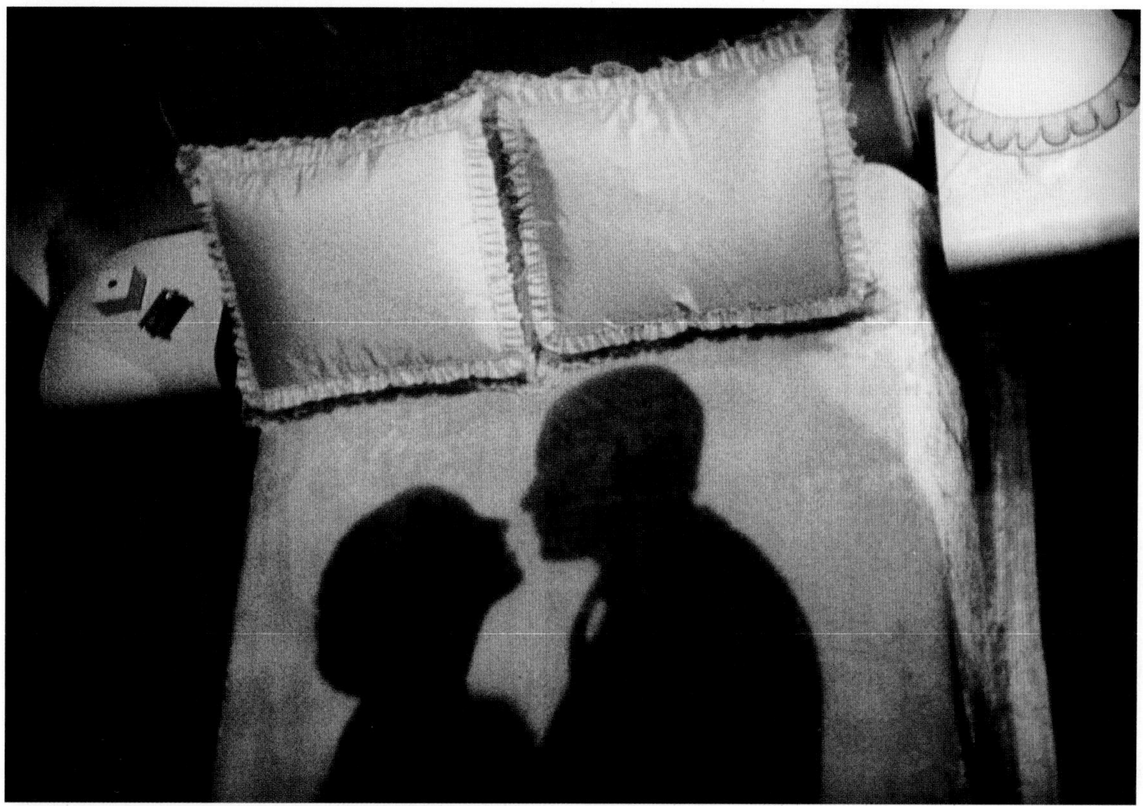

"I like to take my fun and leave it," and "We'll celebrate the second anniversary of the day *we didn't get married*" facing the chopping block in several states.

Despite initially breezing by most censor boards, *Trouble in Paradise* faced hurdles when Paramount attempted to reissue the movie in 1935. The PCA didn't even suggest any edits; they simply blocked the film for rerelease on the basis that it was not acceptable under the current application of the Code. They would even deny Paramount the option to remake the picture as a musical in 1943, explaining: "It contains definite indications of illicit sex relationships without sufficient compensating moral values whatever . . . Your two sympathetic leads are thieves whose crimes are made to seem acceptable, and go unpunished at the end." The film did not return to theaters again until 1968. Furthermore, it was never released on VHS, leaving only sporadic theatrical revivals and a 2003 DVD release to finally reaffirm its place in cinema history.

Lubitsch's pull with Paramount at the time amounted to total control. He was his own producer and wrote his own scripts; in fact, the first draft of *Trouble in Paradise* was the only one. Though Lubitsch lost the studio nearly $800,000 on all of his 1932 productions alone, including the Best Picture Oscar nominee *One Hour with You,* Paramount and Hollywood treasured him. *Trouble in Paradise*, with its understated social and sexual politics and incredible charm, is one of the most stylistically brilliant pictures Hollywood ever produced.

THREE ON A MATCH

STARRING
Joan Blondell, Ann Dvorak, Bette Davis, Warren William, and Lyle Talbot

DIRECTED BY
Mervyn LeRoy

RELEASED BY
Warner Bros., October 1932

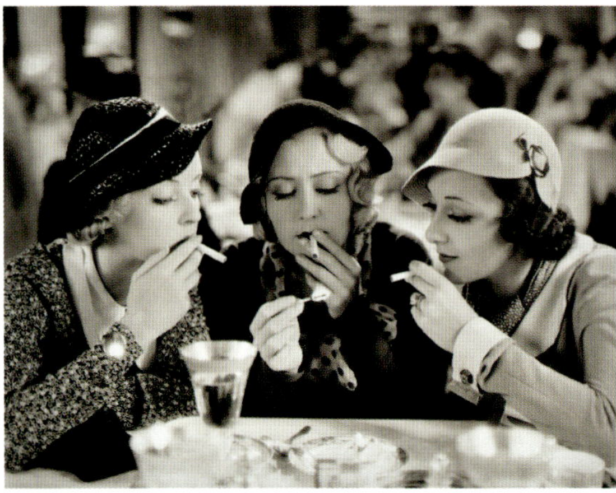

School chums Bette Davis, Joan Blondell, and Ann Dvorak ignore the three-on-a-match superstition . . . which proves true.

An illicit relationship, drinking, drugs, gangsters, blackmail, kidnapping, a murder plot against a child, and a suicide. Sounds exhausting, doesn't it? Even for a typical Warner Bros. pre-Code entry, *Three on a Match* jam-packs these salacious topics in a tightly wound picture that dashes through two decades worth of history in sixty-three minutes, ably aided by a stable of Warner stars.

Though the aforementioned list reads like a roll call of Production Code violations, one element in particular, the kidnapping, presented the greatest trepidation prior to release. The reason: *Three on a Match*'s debut closely followed the Lindbergh baby kidnapping, a tragedy that was a monthslong media circus nicknamed the "crime of the century." Timing was certainly not on Warner's side, but the attention paid the subject helped facilitate the picture's surprisingly painless censor reception.

The stage is set in *Three on a Match* when former school chums Vivian (Ann Dvorak), Ruth (Bette Davis), and Mary (Joan Blondell) reconnect and find their paths have taken some turns. Class valedictorian Ruth works as a stenographer, bad girl Mary straightened out into a chorus girl, and Miss Popular Vivian has it all—including successful husband Robert (Warren William) and son Robert Jr. (Buster Phelps)—or so it seems.

Bored with her comfortable life, Vivian takes off with Mary's pal Mike (Lyle Talbot) with Robert Jr. in tow. The hedonistic lure leads her right down the rabbit hole: She drinks too much, discovers drugs, antagonizes the wrong gangsters, and neglects her son, not necessarily in that order. Though Robert Jr. is extracted from the situation, he's soon kidnapped by Mike, who hopes the ransom will cover his gang debts. As the police close in and the gang gets antsy, Mike is ordered to kill the child—unless his mother can step up to save him.

On May 12, 1932, the body of twenty-month-old Charles Lindbergh Jr. was discovered in New Jersey.

"Will you stop remindin' me of Heaven when I'm so close to the other place?"

—Mary, trapped in a girl's reformatory school before her life begins to turn itself around

Three days prior, the SRC reviewed part of the *Three on a Match* script, clocking usual issues such as drunkenness and suggestive dialogue. But when the SRC watched the finished film in August 1932, they were astonished at two elements: a kidnapping and a plot against a child's life. Sensitive subjects combined with inopportune timing led the SRC to warn the studio about following such a tragedy with a similar subject: "With the present fear on the part of parents . . . public resentment is apt to be strongly against such a picture."

Following a reedit in September and subsequent approval from the SRC, Darryl F. Zanuck entreated Jason Joy to "put in a plug for 'THREE ON A MATCH'" with the New York censor board, as he believed the film had box office potential and a moral to boot: It presented kidnapping as an "unhealthy occupation" from which nothing good could come. Joy agreed, sending his colleague Vincent Hart to the board with a plea for special consideration. Sure enough, *Three on a Match* passed New York—without a single cut. Delighted, Warner Bros. dispatched Hart to Pennsylvania, Maryland, and Ohio at their expense, where he advocated for the film's ethics and Warner's prudent handling of the subject.

Seemingly, the censor tour worked; *Three on a Match* passed in the states visited with very few or no edits. That said, the picture fared surprisingly well in general with most domestic boards, with references to drugs and shots of Vivian's

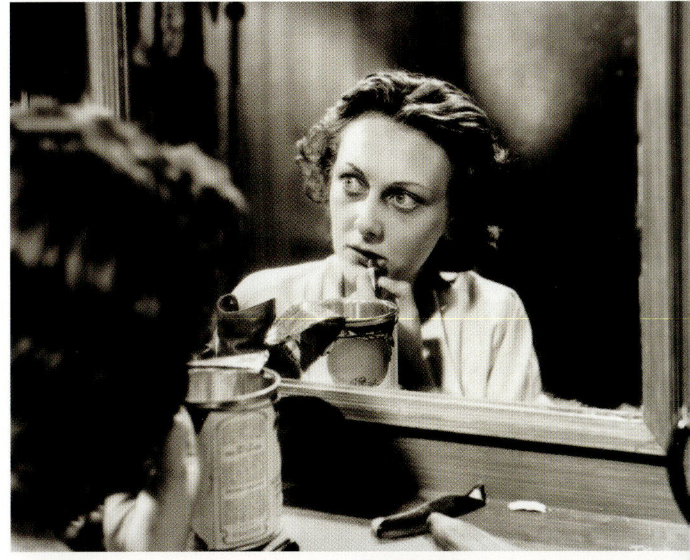

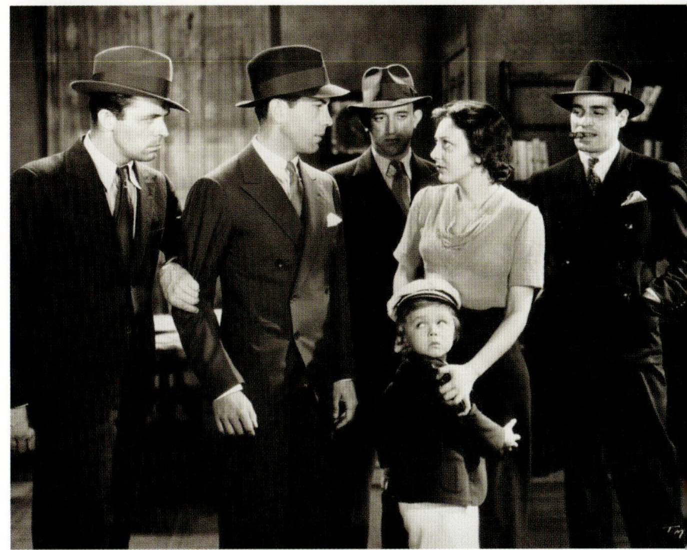

FROM TOP: The struggle is real. Being a rich wife and mother is boring compared to the world of booze and drugs. • Drugged-out mother Ann Dvorak is no match for gangsters (including a young Humphrey Bogart) who plan to kidnap her son, Buster Phelps.

Warner Bros. Pictures, Inc.
WEST COAST STUDIOS
BURBANK, CALIF.

OFFICE OF ASSOCIATE EXECUTIVE

Sept. 21, 1932.

Colonel Jason S. Joy
Ass'n Motion Picture Producers, Inc.
5504 Hollywood Blvd.
Hollywood, California

Dear Colonel:

I wish you could get in touch with whoever the New York Censor is now and, in a roundabout way, put in a plug for "THREE ON A MATCH" and, as a matter of fact, do this in other spots wherever you can as I am personally of the feeling that this picture is going to be a box-office knockout and if we get by without much censorable grief from it, I am certain it will not do any damage at all. After all, it certainly proves that kidnapping is a very unhealthy occupation from which nothing comes but misery, grief and no reward whatsoever.

Best regards,

Sincerely,

Darryl Zanuck

CLASS OF SERVICE DESIRED	
DOMESTIC	CABLE
TELEGRAM	FULL RATE
DAY LETTER	DEFERRED
NIGHT MESSAGE	NIGHT LETTER
NIGHT LETTER	WEEK END LETTER

Patrons should check class of service desired; otherwise message will be transmitted as a full-rate communication.

WESTERN UNION

NEWCOMB CARLTON, PRESIDENT J. C. WILLEVER, FIRST VICE-PRESIDENT

CHECK

ACCT'G INFMN.

TIME FILED

Send the following message, subject to the terms on back hereof, which are hereby agreed to

Mr. Vincent Hart,
28 West 44th St.,
New York City.

THE STUDIO VERY GRATEFUL TO YOU FOR WORK YOU HAVE DONE ON THREE ON A MATCH STOP THEY REQUEST YOU AT THEIR EXPENSE TO DO THE SAME THING WITH THE BOARDS IN PENNSYLVANIA MARYLAND AND OHIO STOP PLEASE DISCUSS WITH MAURICE AND WIRE ME CONFIRMATION ALSO DATES REGARDS

JASON

FROM TOP: Oftentimes, the studios ignored the SRC's suggestions—until they needed their help getting their picture past local censor boards. • The SRC was happy to have the MPPDA do the studios' bidding—in this case a mini censor board tour to promote *Three on a Match*—for a price.

final scene raising the most concerns aside from the few kidnapping-related notes. Chicago proved the outlier; the film was rejected there.

To think that a picture packing this much degeneracy got off scot-free in most places or with a slap on the wrist is quite astounding when comparing it to films released a mere two years later. Perhaps the SRC's persistence on the kidnapping front led to state boards focusing most of their attention there while other potential issues slid by? Regardless, Zanuck's request and Hart's promotion proved the lengths the SRC went to help studios, even if in hindsight it seems that they, or rather the PCA, were waging a moral war against the industry.

Three on a Match stands out as an atypical entry on most of the leads' résumés. Fast-talking Blondell lands right side up as a concerned, kind stepmother. Pre-Code stalwart William also appears against type as a decent, loving husband. As for Davis, she's given so little to do that you can hardly discern the fire that catapulted her to stardom later in the decade.

Then there's Dvorak, who walks away with the picture while shouldering the brunt of the immorality as she listlessly stumbles into the abyss. Pre-Codes are known in part for their candor, but a displeased woman afforded every comfort who caves to her baser instincts and blows it all for illicit sex, depraved thrills, and yes, blow—that's a rarity. While Helen Twelvetrees (1931's *Millie*) and Clara Bow (1932's *Call Her Savage*) experienced similar pre-Code plunges, theirs were at least initiated by issues with men, marital woes, and/or personal tragedies; in this case, Dvorak's ugly, no-holds-barred pragmatism only underlines Vivian's strictly subjective, hollow discontent and devastating desperation.

During its initial release, *Three on a Match* received mixed reviews for what *Film Weekly* called its "pointless and unpleasant" story. The generally chipper Mae Tinee of the (then) *Chicago Daily Tribune* graded the picture a "moderately interesting and very well acted melodrama," but critiques rarely rated above that level. Remarkably, child actor Buster Phelps received more standout notices than any of the other players in the majority of 1932 reviews.

With half of the main cast fondly remembered for their pre-Code work and future film icons as well (including Humphrey Bogart, playing one of the gangsters), it nonetheless took decades for *Three on a Match* to find its home among the cream of the crop. A century later, it takes its rightful place beside the most lurid, seedy, and dynamic of the period, just as engaging and shocking as ever.

Ann Dvorak

Ann Dvorak's star shone brightly—and briefly—during the pre-Code period. After appearing in a few films as a child actress, Dvorak made her way back into show biz as a chorus girl in the late 1920s, appearing in the background of dozens of pictures. She became fast friends with actress Karen Morley, who landed a role in *Scarface* and made it her mission to orchestrate a way for her talented pal to meet director Howard Hawks. Dvorak certainly made an impression on him: During a party at Hawks's home, she asked actor George Raft to dance. He initially said no—and she proceeded to slink about him seductively, just as she does in the movie. That caught Hawks's eye and would make her a star.

After her success in *Scarface*, Dvorak's contract was sold for a record sum to Warner Bros., who put her to work in moody dramas, notably *Three on a Match* and *The Strange Love of Molly Louvain* (1932). But the studio wasn't pleased that she broke her contract for a yearlong honeymoon with Leslie Fenton in 1932—and that was the beginning of the end for her at the studio. Litigation eventually ensued over her contract, and while she still played some plum parts, including Myra in 1934's *Heat Lightning*, she quickly found herself relegated to subpar roles, languishing mostly in B pictures from the mid-1930s through her retirement in the early 1950s.

I AM A FUGITIVE FROM A CHAIN GANG

STARRING
Paul Muni, Glenda Farrell, Helen Vinson, Noel Francis, and Edward Ellis

DIRECTED BY
Mervyn LeRoy

RELEASED BY
Warner Bros., November 1932

"Well, there's just two ways to get out of here. Work out, and die out."

—inmate Bomber Wells, on the prospective futures for all men assigned to the chain gang

It seems hard to believe, but people used to be afraid of the sheer concentrated power of film. The medium held such a distinct and unchallenged grip on society that everyone saw both its danger and potential. One of the most potent examples of cinema's ability to not just change the world but inflame it was *I Am a Fugitive from a Chain Gang*, which exploded across the country, demonstrating to the nation—and especially anxious politicians and censors—just what a well-crafted and ambitious motion picture had the power to do.

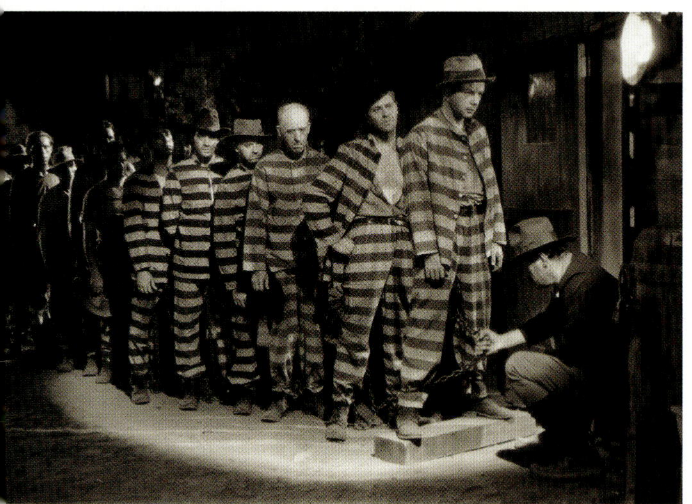

The film follows the story of Jim Allen (Paul Muni), a penniless and jobless veteran of the Great War. While hitchhiking through Georgia, Jim gets caught up in an armed robbery and mistaken for the thief, resulting in a sentence of ten years of hard labor. Realizing he can't survive the brutality of the chain gang, Jim is encouraged by his friend Bomber Wells (Edward Ellis) to escape.

After an elaborate breakout, Jim begins a new life under an assumed name. He finally realizes his dreams of being an engineer, but he's betrayed by an opportunistic woman, Marie (Glenda Farrell), who exposes the truth about his past and lands him in the state's worst labor camp. Rather than succumb to the system, Jim and Bomber escape yet again, though Bomber is fatally wounded in the pursuit.

The story picks up a year later, with Jim hiding in the shadows, bidding his ex-fiancée, Helen (Helen Vinson), a final goodbye. On the run again, he is a desperate, broken man. When Helen asks a fleeing Jim how he survives, he looks back, a ghost in the darkness, snarling: "I steal!"

The degrading wait for an ankle bracelet check takes its toll on the chain gang.

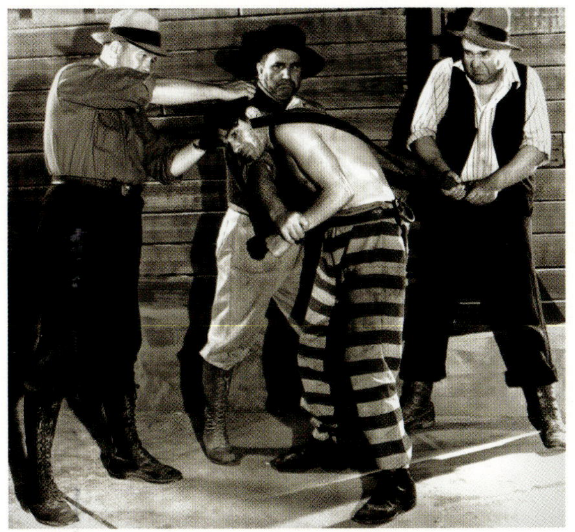

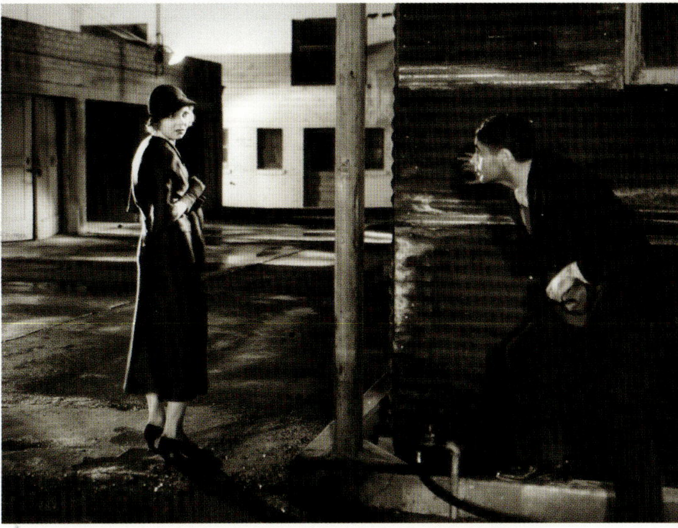

FROM LEFT: ***I Am a Fugitive from a Chain Gang*** **clearly displayed how brutal chain gangs are. • Paul Muni ultimately lives a life lurking in the shadows.**

The movie was adapted from the book *I Am a Fugitive from a Georgia Chain Gang!* by Robert Elliott Burns, based upon his real-life experiences. A World War I vet, Burns became a drifter after suffering a case of shell shock. He helped hold up a grocery store in Atlanta that netted the participants a total of $5.81; for this, he was sentenced to six to ten years of hard labor. Much as in the movie, Burns escaped and found work in Chicago, before he was caught and returned to Georgia, where he launched a second, dramatic getaway. After that, he moved to New Jersey and took up odd jobs as he wrote his book.

The decision to make *Fugitive* into a film was fraught with controversy. The SRC was quick to warn studios against purchasing it, with Jason Joy emphasizing that the conditions of the prison camp and the escapes could not be shown in any great detail or risk the wrath of Southern states who "can stand any criticism as long as it isn't directed at themselves." Joy, who condemned chain gangs, knew the film would create an uproar. "While it may be true that the systems are wrong, I very much doubt if it is our business as an entertainment force to clear it up," he lamented.

Warner's own story department voted against making the movie under the Code, concluding that "all the strong and vivid points in the story are certain to be eliminated by the present censorship board." Director Roy Del Ruth, the highest paid director at the studio at the time, also passed on the project. However, Jack Warner, who admitted that the film "will make us some enemies," concurred with Darryl F. Zanuck that the project was too important to ignore.

Zanuck assigned up-and-coming director Mervyn LeRoy to the film, removing him from preproduction on *42nd Street*. Paul Muni, fresh off his magnetic performance in *Scarface*, was skeptical, unsure of how seriously to take the young

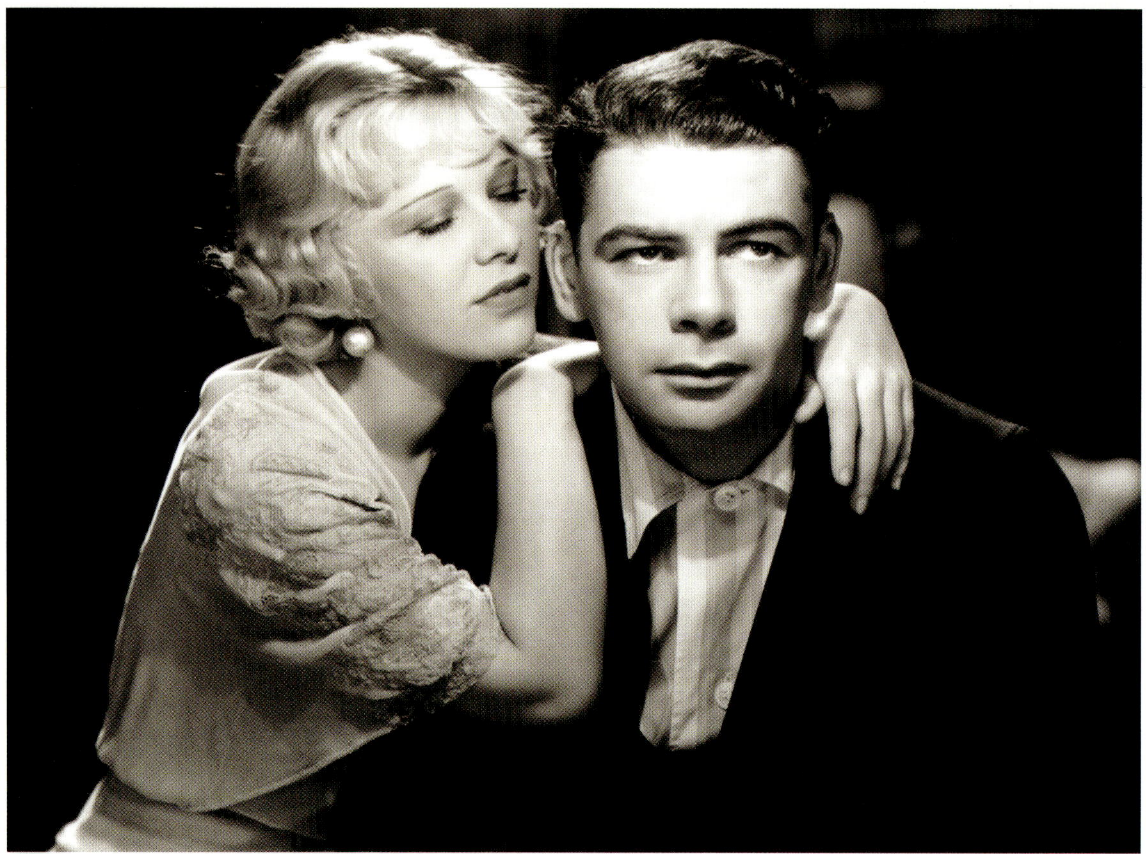

Glenda Farrell is up to no good; even Paul Muni can sense it!

director. However, Muni threw himself into the role, consulting with prison guards, including those who'd overseen chain gangs, and insisted on performing all the film's hard labor himself.

Author Burns helped craft the treatment, served as a consultant on the movie, and worked with Muni to find authenticity in his character. He visited the set under the pseudonym Mr. Crane, though he was terrified of being found out by the authorities. The picture's success turned Burns into a public figurehead for reforming the chain gang system, leading to his third arrest in December 1932 in New Jersey. The governor refused to extradite him, and eventually, Burns had his sentence commuted with time served in 1945.

Joy continued to try to defuse the time bomb of a film, desperate to avoid any direct conflict with Georgia by insisting that the movie remain as geographically neutral as possible. To do this, he suggested minimizing the number of Black prisoners shown in hopes of obscuring its location. Despite his admonishments being ignored, Joy gave the completed picture a favorable review and felt that the film's social value and adherence to truth would help deflate many local censorship concerns.

The movie was a blockbuster for the studio. It won Best Film of the Year from the National Board of Review (who also called it "one of the best films ever made in this country") and netted Academy Award nominations for Best Picture and Best Actor. At the same time, the state of Georgia was thrown into uproar. Newspapers ran headlines declaring the movie "Yankee lies!" while other social forces crafted petitions to abolish the chain gang system. Georgia politicians tried to ban the film and even sued Warner Bros. to prevent its release. Two prison guards also launched million-dollar libel suits against the studio, though none of these attempts to suppress the movie were successful.

Jack Warner would later call the picture "the first sermon I had ever put on film." Some critics praised the movie enthusiastically and hailed it as a tool for great social change, while others expressed their disappointment. For instance, pioneering documentary filmmaker Pare Lorentz wrote in *Vanity Fair* that the film never examines why society allows institutions like the chain gang to function and thrive but instead simply illustrates their wrongness.

Decades later, *I Am a Fugitive from a Chain Gang* retains its impact, with critic David Thomson declaring the movie "is still a slap in the face." Through tyranny and cruelty, the system created the criminal it claimed to pity all along. The prison system remains hotly contested, whether politically or socially, with pictures like *Brute Force* (1947), *Cool Hand Luke* (1967), and *Escape from Alcatraz* (1979) intent on portraying the oftentimes inhumane environment inmates must endure.

Through Burns's crusade, chain gangs were abolished from the South by the mid-1950s, an impressive feat that the film spearheaded, while in Hollywood studios became more sensitive toward pictures that advocated direct action. That said, chain gangs have resurfaced in the last few decades in select states that paint themselves as hard on crime, and some prisoners are still forced to work under dangerous conditions with little public scrutiny.

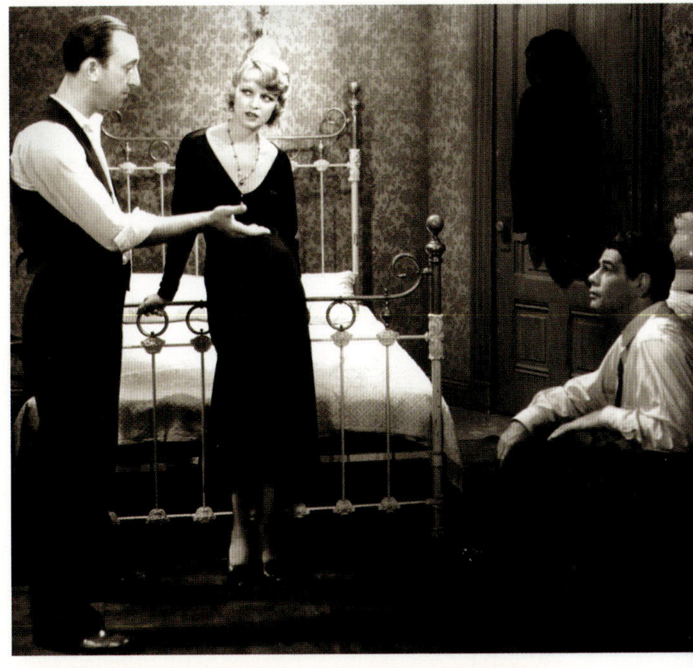

Allen Jenkins helps recently escaped Paul Muni out with accommodations, which comes with Noel Francis, who provides compassion and something else, too.

I Am a Fugitive from a Chain Gang is Warner's best and most successful polemic, a gritty and unapologetic tale that stays close to the facts and the emotional weight of living in Depression-era America. It's an unblinking look at how government systems can dehumanize their constituents and the ways in which compliant people allow it.

CALL HER SAVAGE

STARRING
Clara Bow, Gilbert Roland, Thelma Todd, and Monroe Owsley

DIRECTED BY
John Francis Dillon

RELEASED BY
Fox, November 1932

"Why were you whipping him?"

"I was practicing in case I ever get married."

—Pete to his daughter, Nasa, on seeing her beating the ever-loving tar out of Moonglow

By the early 1930s, Clara Bow had withered into a mere symbol of roaring twenties' overindulgence. At the beginning of the decade, she'd endured mentally and physically ravaging breakdowns, sinking confidence, scandals, and lurid tabloid reports that tossed about lascivious accusations of drug abuse, incest, exhibitionism, threesomes, bestiality, and then some. The allegations read more salacious than Bow's bawdiest pre-Code films and tossed the superstar's reputation into a tailspin.

Upon release from her Paramount contract in 1931, Bow sought escape from her woes on a remote ranch. But Hollywood beckoned her back, with independent producer Sam Rork landing her a two-picture deal at Fox guaranteeing Bow $75,000 per film and approval of script, cast, and director. The first property she picked: *Call Her Savage,* a tale ripe with drama. Jason Joy wrote of Bow: "I am confident her re-appearance will be a revelation to the country." Indeed, the world waited with bated breath for Bow's return to the screen after a whole year and a half absence.

"The sins of the father shall be visited upon the children, even up to the third and the fourth generation," *Call Her Savage* warns. Lo and behold, Ruth (Estelle Taylor), the daughter of devious Silas (Fred Kohler), is left under the watchful eye of Ronasa (Weldon Heyburn) while husband Pete (Willard Robertson) is away. Rest assured, Ronasa takes very good care of Ruth.

Years later, Ruth and Pete's hot-tempered daughter, Nasa (Bow), nicknamed Dynamite by schoolmates, defies Pete and weds wicked Larry (Monroe Owsley), who only married her to get back at his girl, Sunny (Thelma Todd). Nasa enjoys free rein of Larry's bank accounts until he falls deathly ill. Not long after, Nasa becomes a mother, but tragically her child dies in a fire while Nasa works the streets to make ends meet.

Childhood pal Moonglow (Gilbert Roland), dubbed a "half-breed," informs a devastated Nasa that she's just inherited her late grandfather's fortune. The highs she experiences turn into lows, and eventually Nasa buckles under the demon of drink, but she rallies to her mother's deathbed only to discover a bombshell: Her birth father was Ronasa. Like Moonglow, Nasa's considered a "half-breed"; they were meant to be together all along.

For her leading man, Clara Bow selected Gilbert Roland. Audiences of the day would have overlooked

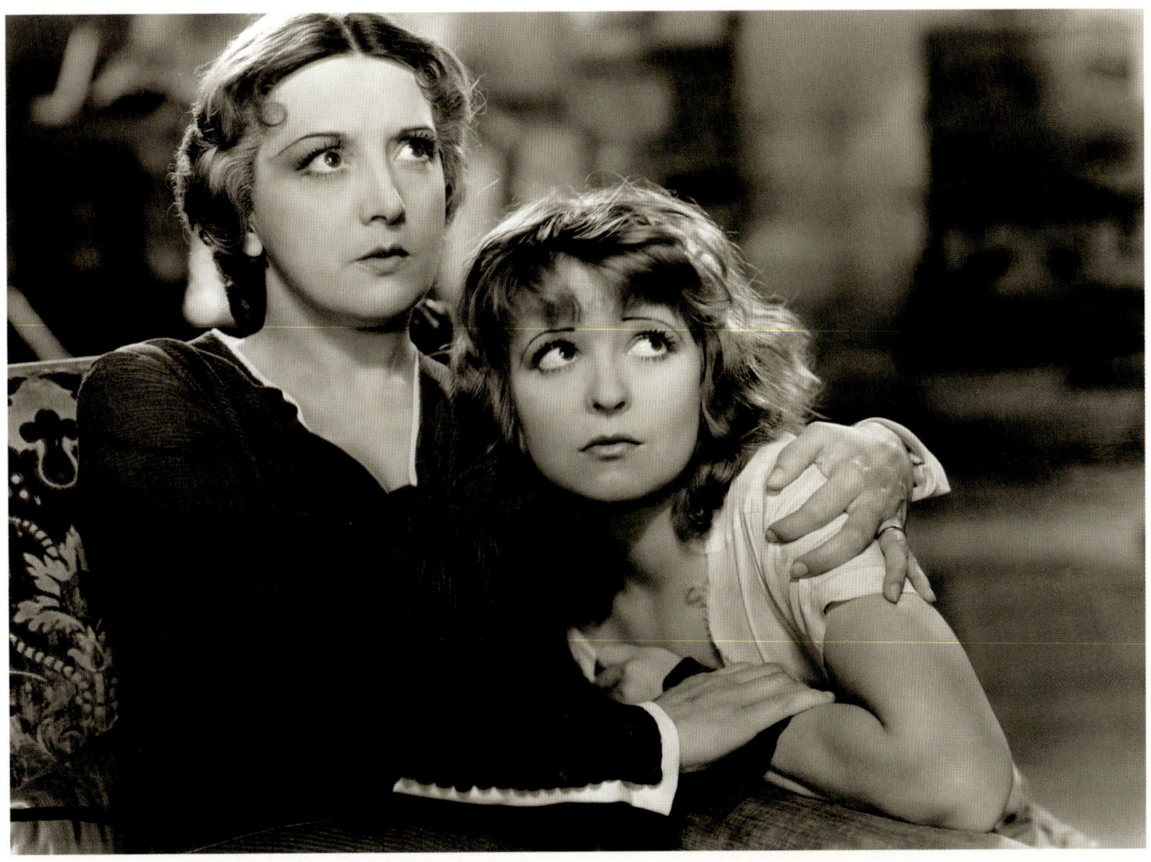

One of the only protective forces in Clara Bow's life, mother Estelle Taylor—who also kept a big secret from her.

the fact that an American woman and a Mexican man were playing Native Americans, as Hollywood frequently whitewashed minority roles. In fact, some fans must have been ecstatic with the casting, as Bow and Roland enjoyed a much-publicized love affair and engagement in the 1920s. Due to her father's interference and Bow's own dalliances, they split but remained friends for life. (By 1931, Bow had settled down with Rex Bell, who was on set and hobnobbed with Roland the first day.)

The stakes were high for Bow, and with the added pressure her return elicited, she found Nasa emotionally demanding. On top of that, the microphone anxiety that plagued her early talkies persisted, so much so that she demanded a closed set in her contract. But she was up to the task, and when the cameras rolled, there was no trace of her apprehension. Bow's star still shone bright.

Tiffany Thayer's novel *Call Her Savage* contained a "great deal of unsuitable picture material," according to the SRC, but Fox nevertheless wanted it for its title recognition and choice story elements. (One unsavory feature modern audiences recognize right off the bat is the film's disparaging

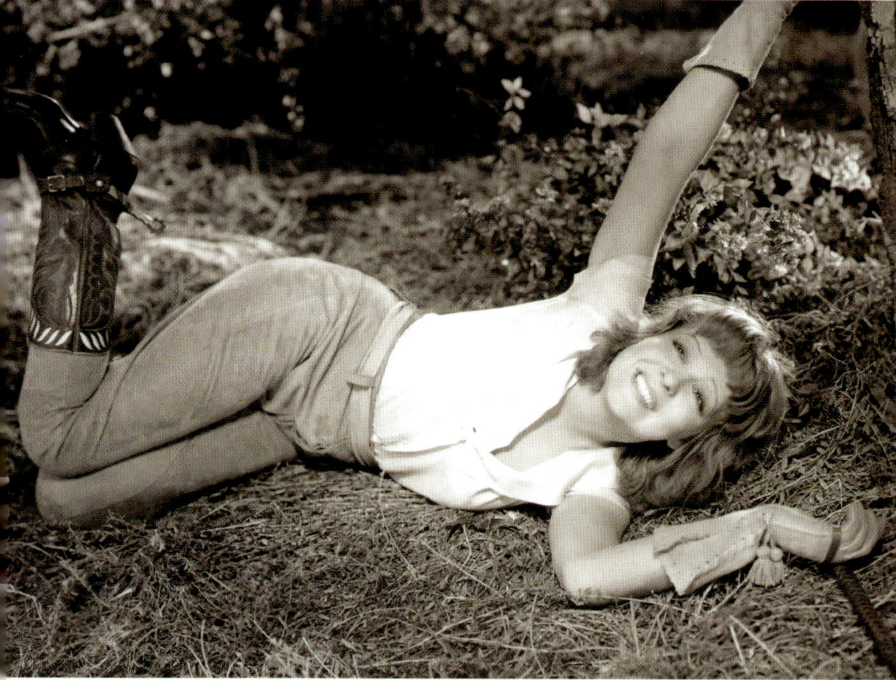

Nerves? What nerves? Clara Bow's anxiety for her Hollywood comeback in *Call Her Savage* did not appear on-screen.

view of Native Americans, starting with the "savage" stereotype asserted in its title and throughout.) Despite Joy reporting that the source material "is about as far wrong as it is possible to be," they conceded the treatment could be admissible with minor edits. Scenes of Bow bathing and beating horses, as well as insinuations of prostitution and venereal disease, raised red flags, prompting the office to stress caution and suggest cuts.

Ironically, *Call Her Savage* soon found a champion in Joy—yes, the same man who labeled the picture "as far wrong as it is possible to be." In the fall of 1932, when *Call Her Savage* was undergoing review at the SRC, Joy jumped ship for an executive position at Fox, with James Wingate taking his place. Joy informed several censor boards of his upcoming move while slyly lobbying for his new employer. He singled out *Call Her Savage* in particular, expressing hope "that the picture will be judged as a whole for the character study that it is, all parts of which inter-link importantly." The Montreal censors were on board, replying, "after what you say, I think that you have reason to hope it [*Call Her Savage*] will be seen in the light that you expect." Once planted on Fox soil, Joy shared his insider knowledge with the studio in hopes they "will be successful in getting the censors to see it our way."

Except that didn't turn out to be the case. Several boards cut references to prostitution and a vicious sexual attack, while British Columbia rejected the film, citing infidelity, brutality, "adultery by the mother with an Indian. A lot of nudity scenes, story of a kept woman, and the heroine winds up as a street-walker. A sordid picture dressed up in tinsel." In April 1937, Joseph Breen denied Fox the ability to reissue *Call Her Savage* due to the "sordid story dealing with illegitimacy, attempted rape, prostitution."

Critics alternately praised and trashed the story, but the majority trained their focus on the star. As the *New York Herald Tribune* remarked, Bow is "such a vivid and arresting screen personage, who plays with so much amiable vitality that she remains an invariably interesting performer to watch." Even though many reviewers found her

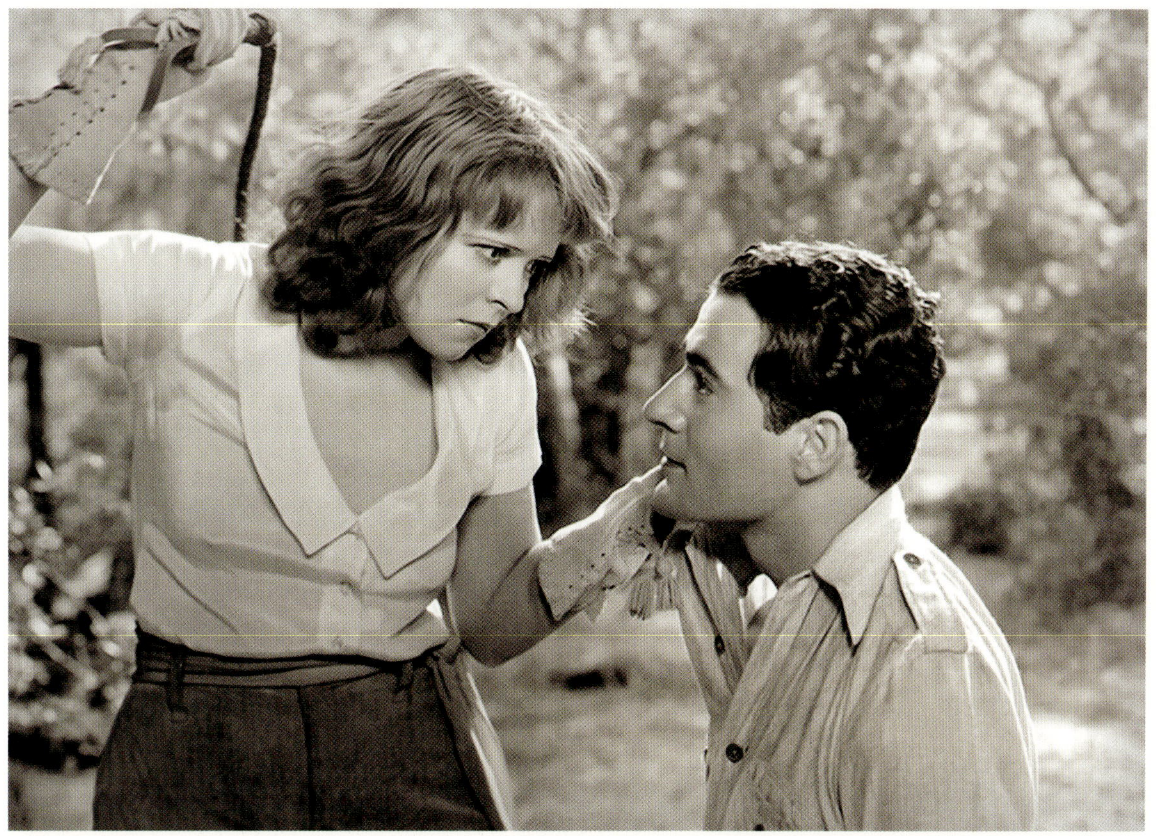

The indomitable Clara Bow attempts to tame Gilbert Roland in *Call Her Savage*.

stimulating performance a revelation, it didn't seem the critical reception would matter much, as fans came out in droves for their long-awaited glimpse of the star back on the silver screen. Fox boasted of box office records and holdovers in many cities, while *The Film Daily* reported that *Call Her Savage* set a one-day attendance record at New York's Roxy Theatre with a crowd of 18,171 on opening day—which just so happened to be Thanksgiving.

Despite the hype and marketing, *Call Her Savage* wasn't a financial mega hit for Fox. Nonetheless, packed theaters made it clear that the "It Girl" still had "it" and could attract an audience. Consequently, Fox exercised Bow's option for a second picture, *Hoopla* (1933), which performed well at the box office.

What most fans couldn't predict was that it would be Bow's swan song. Following the fulfillment of her two-picture deal, she finally made good on a prior pledge: She retired and vanished from Hollywood forever. But with her comeback in 1932, the world was at her doorstep, and *Call Her Savage* served up controversial Bow as boisterous, bawdy, and melodramatic as fans could have hoped.

THE SIGN OF THE CROSS

STARRING
Fredric March, Elissa Landi, Claudette Colbert, and Charles Laughton

DIRECTED BY
Cecil B. DeMille

RELEASED BY
Paramount, November 1932

> "My head is splitting . . . the wine last night, the music . . . the delicious debauchery!"
>
> **—Emperor Nero, clearly living his best life**

Cecil B. DeMille's expertise was in taking biblical subjects and imbuing them with vice and grandeur. Sure, his films may be filled with nudity, sex, and violence, but they were telling important stories about the Bible; there's a sort of genius hucksterism underwritten by the audacity of DeMille's pictures. His big-budget extravaganzas remain among the most treasured and imitated of the great Hollywood religious epics, both because of the artistry and the careful commercial calculations.

Adapted from an 1895 stage play, *The Sign of the Cross* is set during the reign of Nero (Charles Laughton). Seeking to stamp out the nascent Christian religion that threatens his dominion over the Roman people, he orders anyone identifying as Christian to be hunted down and killed. One such Christian is Mercia (Elissa Landi), who tries to interject when one of her friends is captured. The hedonistic Marcus (Fredric March), Nero's right-hand man, sees this and intervenes on her behalf, falling irreparably in love with her.

Marcus and Mercia's courtship is strangled by their differing perspectives, with Marcus doing everything he can to seduce Mercia to his way of life, even enjoining Ancaria (Joyzelle Joyner) to

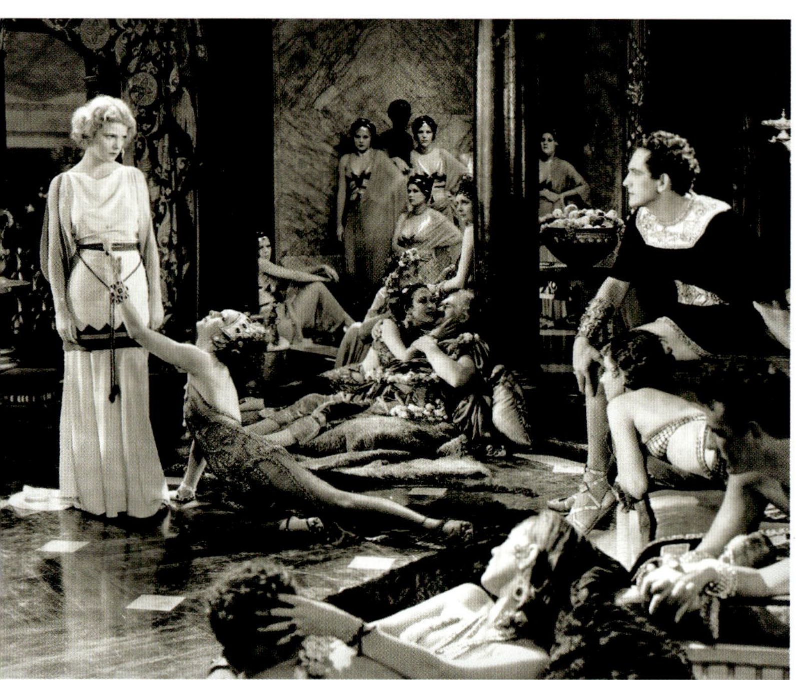

Joyzelle Joyner giving it her all to lure Elissa Landi to the land of sin, as Fredric March eagerly hopes for. Alas, purity prevails.

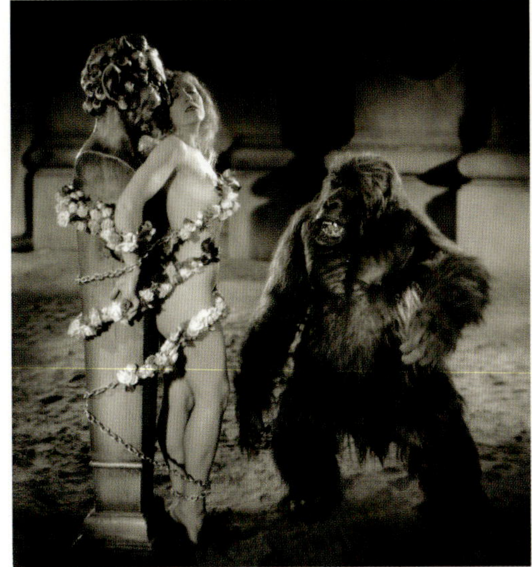

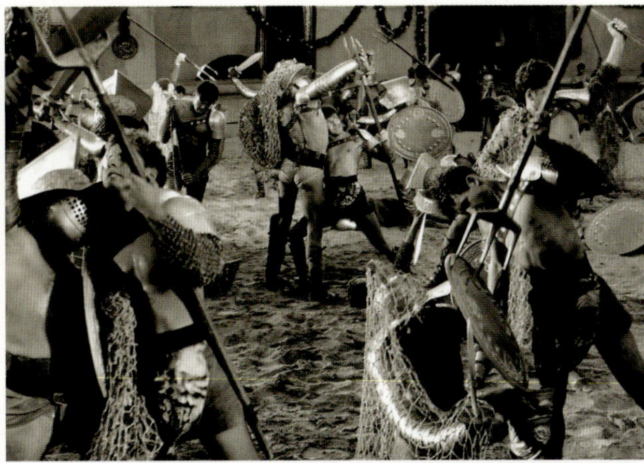

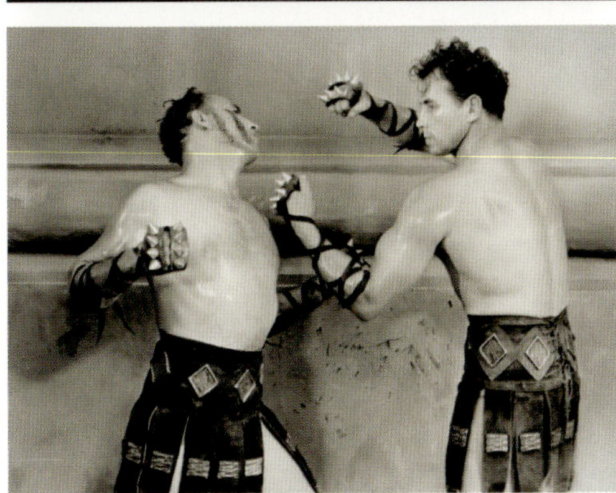

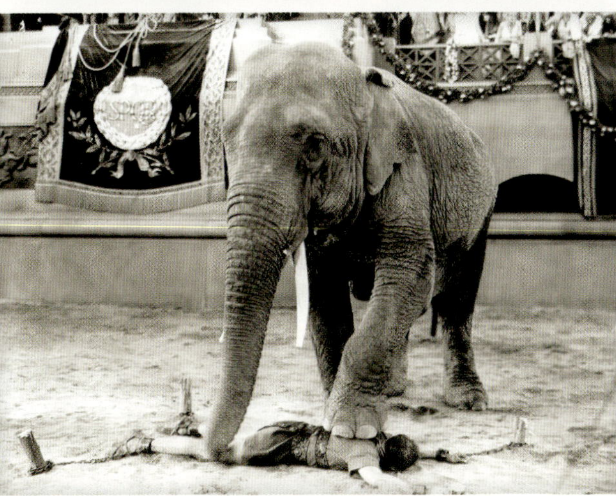

How many ways can one portray the violence and eroticism of ancient Rome? Plenty, especially if the director is Cecil B. DeMille.

entice her with her famous "Dance of the Naked Moon." This fails, as Mercia remains virtuous. At the urging of Empress Poppaea (Claudette Colbert), Nero's wife and would-be lover of Marcus, Mercia is sent to the Colosseum with her Christian compatriots to be killed. Marcus eventually decides to put his faith in her and their love, sacrificing his life along with Mercia's.

DeMille, who had helped cofound Paramount, returned to his former roost in a state of disgrace. His pictures at MGM, including *Madam Satan*, had flopped, and he'd found himself severely restricted in their producer-first system. Returning to Paramount, he was given a short leash but was determined to redeem himself. Having seen *The Sign of the Cross* on the stage, DeMille envisioned it as a continuation of his silent epics *The Ten Commandments* (1923) and *The King of Kings* (1927), saying, "*The Ten Commandments* is the giving of the law. *The King of Kings* was

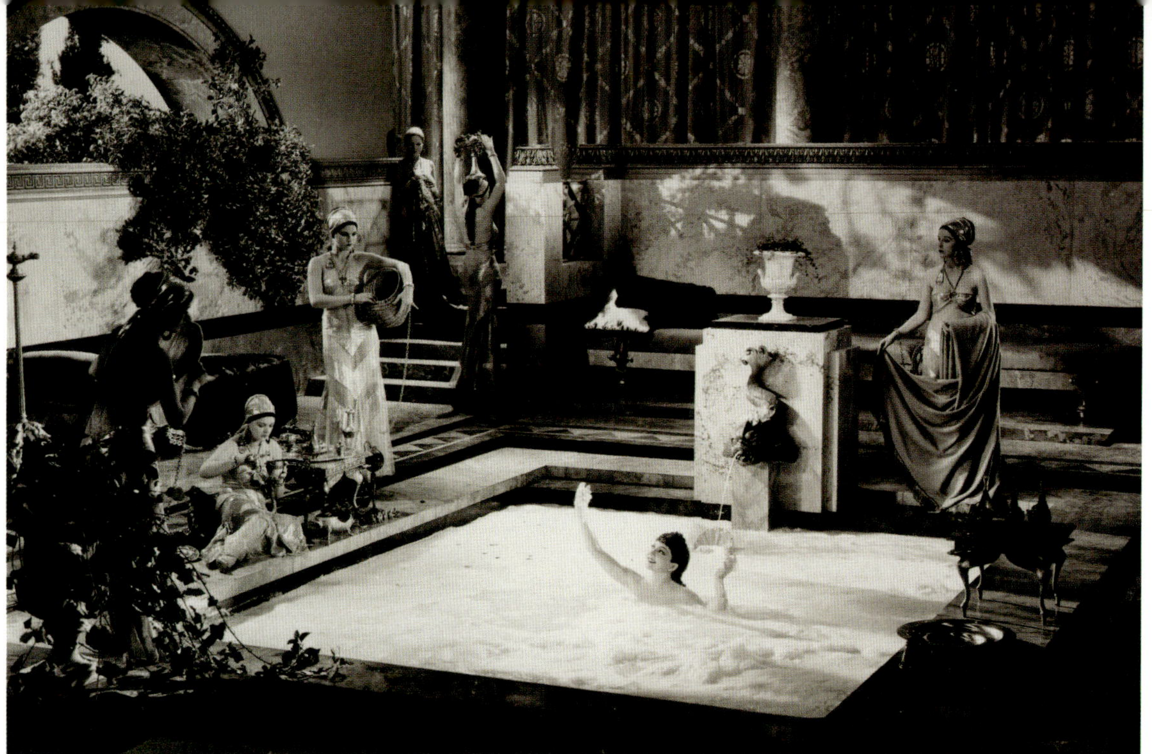

Being naked in a milk bath is one way to get a censor's attention, Claudette Colbert.

the interpretation of the law, the fulfillment of its promise. *The Sign of the Cross* will be the preservation of the law, the struggle of humanity to live up to it."

The Sign of the Cross is one of the most spectacular pictures of the early 1930s, all despite a surprisingly limited budget. Paramount was going through receivership at the time and only offered DeMille $650,000 to work with—with DeMille himself expected to pay for half that amount with personal loans and guarantees. One famous legend is that DeMille had assistant director Roy Burns keep track of the money as it was being spent, and when he was told the money ran out, he yelled "Cut!" and that was a wrap.

Every cent is on the screen, with DeMille, art director Mitchell Leisen, and cinematographer Karl Struss studying German techniques of forced perspective to make their small sets seem enormous. DeMille was careful, however, in paying handsomely for an A-list cast, including Fredric March, fresh off his Academy Award–winning performance in *Dr. Jekyll and Mr. Hyde*.

Viewed in modern times, *The Sign of the Cross* still has the power to shock with its unfiltered depiction of ancient Rome. The film's grim portrayal of ethnic cleansing would mirror world events from the Holocaust to the present day. Furthermore, the movie's sexuality, extravagance, and violence revel in a level of decadence less common in the pre-Code period but much more familiar in the twenty-first century. The gruesome Colosseum sequences, which stretch about ten minutes, include scenes of Amazons beheading pygmies and nude women being left vulnerable to crocodiles and curious gorillas.

Besides what's already been mentioned, the film is infamous for how it introduces Poppaea—nude in a bathtub of ass's milk, coyly toying with showing her breasts full-on. (There's also the hint that she's showing off her body for her female handmaidens.) When a friend, Dacia (Vivian Tobin), arrives, she orders her to strip down and join her in the bath. And of course, Ancaria's lesbian-tinged "Dance of the Naked Moon," along with Nero's overly attentive, nearly nude servants, reminds us that queer undertones are nothing new to cinema—or civilization.

Despite a bevy of potential censorship land mines, DeMille's prestige and his relationship with Jason Joy helped the movie sail through the SRC with few notes. However, religious groups were less eager to let the movie pass without a mention. Methodists, Protestants, and Catholics took their turns reprimanding *The Sign of the Cross* for its lewdness. Jesuit priest Daniel A. Lord called the film "intolerable," while Catholic layman Martin Quigley, editor of the *Motion Picture Herald*, felt that the film would encourage evil in its audience. (Coincidentally, Lord and Quigley coauthored the Production Code.) An attempt by the Paramount advertising department to send the script to a reverend in hopes that he'd promote the picture in his sermon backfired horrifically when he lambasted, "It is a cheap and disgusting attempt to present lewd performances under a sacred name and shielded by an ignorant notion of religion." For maximum effectiveness, he signed off: "Yours in disgust."

From the general public, reactions to the picture were sharp, but mixed. *Variety* declared the movie "censor-bait," but that didn't exactly turn out to be the case. While the SRC flagged select lines, a shot of a naked girl from behind, and parts of Ancaria's dance as potentially dangerous before filming, they weren't overly concerned with DeMille behind the camera. Ultimately, *The Sign of the Cross* wowed the SRC, with James Wingate reporting that DeMille "has refrained to very good advantage, from running wild with Roman orgies and the other high-jinx which might have been expected in this type of subject."

Most censor boards agreed; Kansas, Pennsylvania, Quebec, and New York approved the picture without edits. Ohio originally did the same—and then they came back with cuts to Ancaria's dance and a close-up of Dacia's legs as she enters the bath. Massachusetts cut many frames of bare abdomens, several murder scenes, and the shot of a lion mangling a man. As Massachusetts usually requested, these cuts only applied to Sunday screenings.

When the studio attempted to reissue *The Sign of the Cross* in 1935, Ancaria's entire dance was eliminated, and in 1944, Dacia's robe falling came out, too. Curiously, the studio decided to add an eleven-minute prologue at a cost of $125,000 to the 1944 rerelease, showing American soldiers leaving to bomb Rome, linking the past with the present in an attempt to display how early Christians sacrificed their lives just like American soldiers for the "sake of tolerance and freedom."

The Sign of the Cross was a lightning rod of controversy upon its release, particularly for pious viewers, both as an ode to the philosophy of Christianity and as a sex-and-violence-filled extravaganza. While DeMille certainly won this battle, reestablishing himself as one of the industry's top directors, the fact that he took his material to the home turf of so many of Hollywood's religious opponents gave them more fuel in their fight that would eventually lead to the full enforcement of the Production Code in 1934.

THE BITTER TEA OF GENERAL YEN

STARRING
Barbara Stanwyck, Nils Asther, Toshia Mori, and Walter Connolly

DIRECTED BY
Frank Capra

RELEASED BY
Columbia, January 1933

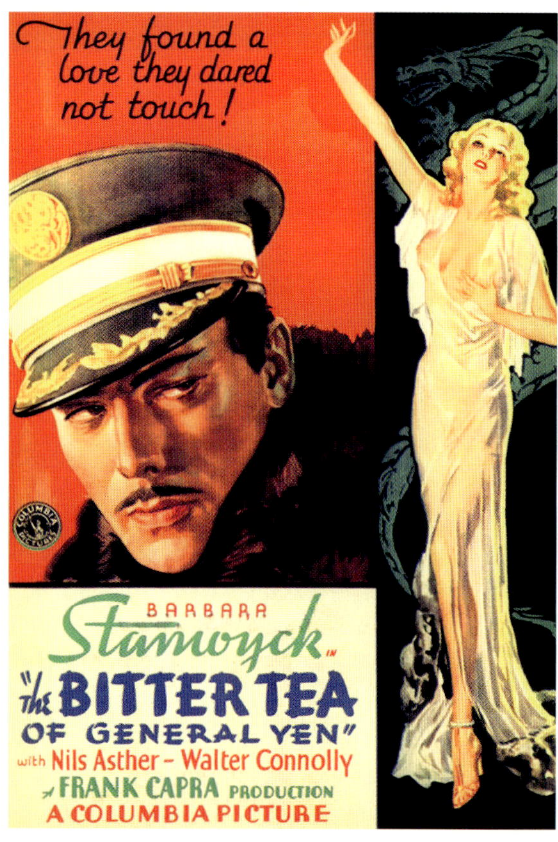

Oh, they touched that love.

"Conquest of a province, or the conquest of a woman . . . What's the difference?"

—General Yen, extolling on the philosophy of his desires

Probably the most politically incorrect entry in this book, *The Bitter Tea of General Yen* is a fascinating document, a treatise on racism so thoroughly enmeshed in its own era that its own hypocrisies only add to the many dimensions of interracial lust and the American superiority complex that the film eagerly exploits.

Besides being a moody and lush piece of art, *The Bitter Tea of General Yen* demands a confrontation with audiences' own beliefs and prejudices. Made at a time when the United States didn't accept Chinese migrants but eagerly sent out missionaries, it's an essential piece of interwar reckoning with America's place in the world.

The Bitter Tea of General Yen opens with Megan Davis (Barbara Stanwyck) arriving in China to marry her long-distance sweetheart Dr. Robert Strike (Gavin Gordon). However, she finds herself lost in the nation's civil war and kidnapped by the dashing General Yen (Nils Asther). Yen is in the middle of a battle for his province, propped up by the frank American wheeler-and-dealer Jones (Walter Connolly) and circumvented by his concubine Mah-Li (Toshia Mori). As Yen attempts to seduce Megan and overcome her revulsion, she advocates to him ideas about faith and kindness—ideas that may well get him killed.

FROM TOP: One probably shouldn't ask how Barbara Stanwyck and Nils Asther met. • Nils Asther and Walter Connolly plot their next big caper with Toshia Mori listening in—but Asther can't decide if it's better to focus on conquering the province or conquering a woman.

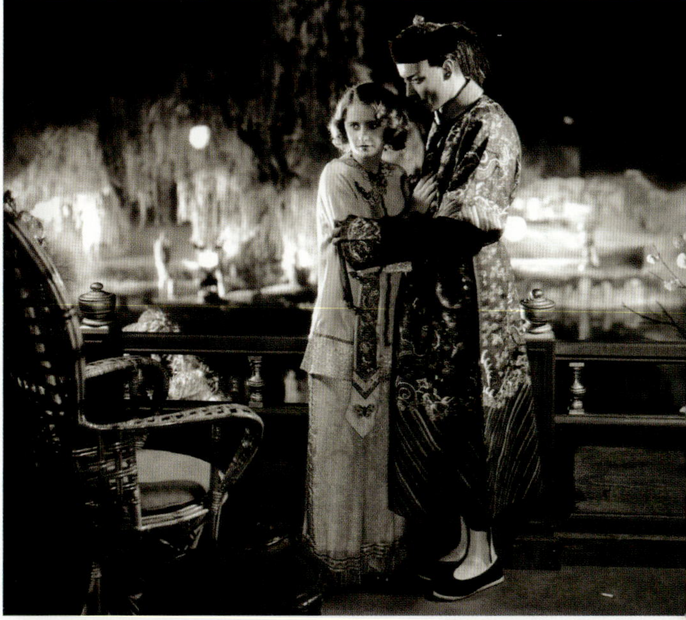

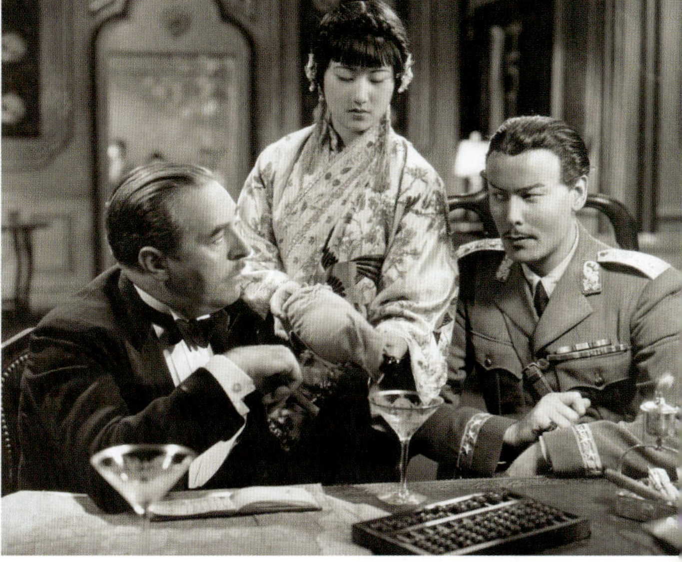

The central philosophical arguments between General Yen and Megan cross many rivers, from romance to respect and how those feelings are earned or given. At first, both have a deep disassociation with one another—he viewing her as a conquest, she viewing him as a stereotypical barbarian. Over the course of the film, their willingness to discuss and help each other ends in a romantic tragedy, but one that shows how far both have influenced each other. Yen doesn't win Megan over with revolutionary swagger but rather his faith in actions over words. He intentionally allows for his own defeat as a lesson of understanding to prove to her the error of her notions.

Directed by Frank Capra, *The Bitter Tea of General Yen* is one of the most honest movies of the time in tackling American hypocrisy at home and abroad. Capra is one of the best remembered filmmakers of the Golden Age; *It Happened One Night* (1934), *Mr. Smith Goes to Washington* (1939), and *It's a Wonderful Life* (1946) are his most famous chronicles of Americana. But layered in all of Capra's films is a deep cynicism about the country. America isn't great for the sake of greatness—it's great in the ways it can allow people to overcome greed, cruelty, and indifference through the power of the individual.

Capra, who immigrated from Italy when he was five and served in World War I, had a college degree in engineering and used a ruse to slip his way into the film industry in the mid-1920s. He viewed his story as going from rags to riches and often felt a tension between the sophistication of his fame and the poverty he was raised in.

By the early 1930s, Capra's films were the most expensive and luscious that Columbia Pictures

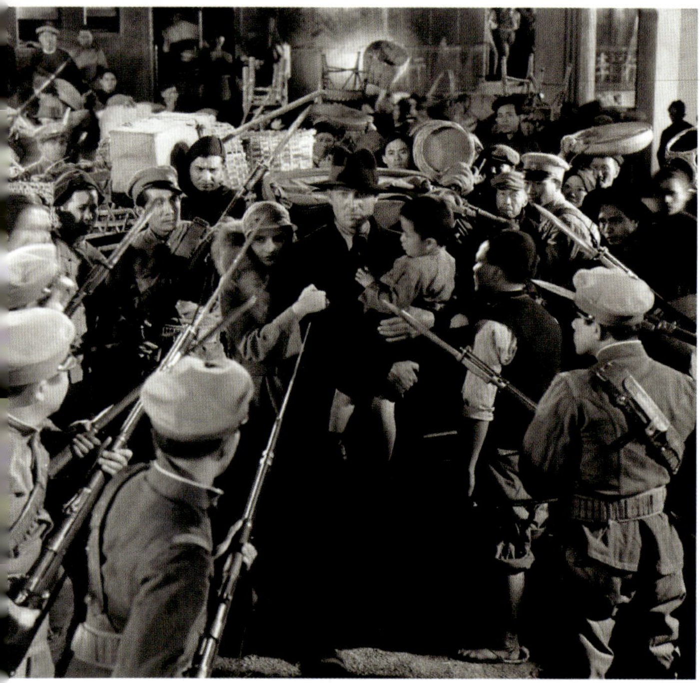

A warm welcome for the missionaries.

produced, mainly as a play for Capra and studio head Harry Cohn to earn respect from Hollywood and the public. In that way, Capra chose this project in hopes it would net him an Oscar.

Instead, the reception was disastrous. Despite being the first film presented at Radio City Music Hall, its engagement was shortened, with the venue taking a $20,000 loss on the booking. While Capra hoped the romantic story would titillate, it seems to have simply gone too far for the time.

Nils Asther, a Swedish actor, plays General Yen in yellowface, his severe makeup easy to contrast with the dozens of Chinese and Asian American extras who fill the crowded screen behind him. The decision to cast a Swede as a Chinese man was a practical solution that many in Hollywood had to bend to in the early- to mid-twentieth century: To stave off audiences' offense at an interracial romance, having two white actors in those roles could create a rhetorical distance and help escape criticism. It's a bizarre approach that made sense to Hollywood for decades, but one that is plainly offensive to modern audiences.

The film's romanticized view of miscegenation—made in a time when interracial marriage was not only illegal but also brought a host of social repercussions—was surely a big gamble and a major factor in the movie's disappointing box office. Oddly, though, it didn't play a big role in the film's reception by local censor boards.

The SRC deemed the script satisfactory, suggesting a few changes, and delivered high praise on the finished product. That said, the groups portrayed in the film were a little more particular: Protests were clocked regarding the characterization of missionaries, and the Chinese Legation in Washington requested some deletions, including scenes of shooting prisoners of war, the line "human life is the cheapest thing in China," dialogue calling the Chinese treacherous and immoral, and reference to "yellow swine." It's somewhat perplexing that the SRC didn't flag these elements as potentially problematic, given how overly conscious they were when it came to the "foreign angle."

An execution scene with shots of men falling to the ground, Stanwyck in lingerie, and the aforementioned treacherous and immoral sentiment frequently came under fire when the picture went to local boards, but that was nothing compared to the denunciation Joseph Breen had for the movie in 1950. At a time when many pre-Codes had already been approved (with edits or not) or rejected for reissue, Breen charged *The*

Barbara Stanwyck

It's hard to argue that Barbara Stanwyck's pre-Code output isn't among the starkest and most exciting of the early 1930s; she appears in no less than five entries in this book, for starters. Frank Capra auditioned the Brooklyn-born starlet who had been orphaned at a young age at the start of the talkie revolution—and was unimpressed. When Stanwyck's husband, Frank Fay, persuaded Capra to watch one of her other screen tests, he realized that he'd found a star and cast her in *Ladies of Leisure.* She ended up appearing in five of his films, four of which were pre-Codes, including the scandalous *The Miracle Woman* (1931). Whether playing a working woman (1931's *Ten Cents a Dance* or *Night Nurse*), a persevering single mother (1932's *Forbidden* or *So Big!*), a mail-order bride (1932's *The Purchase Price*), or a criminal (1933's *Ladies They Talk About* or 1934's *Gambling Lady*), Stanwyck imbued her characters with a sense of fierce strength and independence. And we obviously can't forget to call out 1933's bed-hopping *Baby Face*, one of the most notorious pre-Codes.

Stanwyck's ability to switch from dramatic to comedic served her well, and her career reached its peak in the 1940s with films like *The Lady Eve* (1941) and *Double Indemnity* (1944). She won an Emmy in the 1960s for *The Barbara Stanwyck Show* and continued to push boundaries in movies and TV until her passing in 1990.

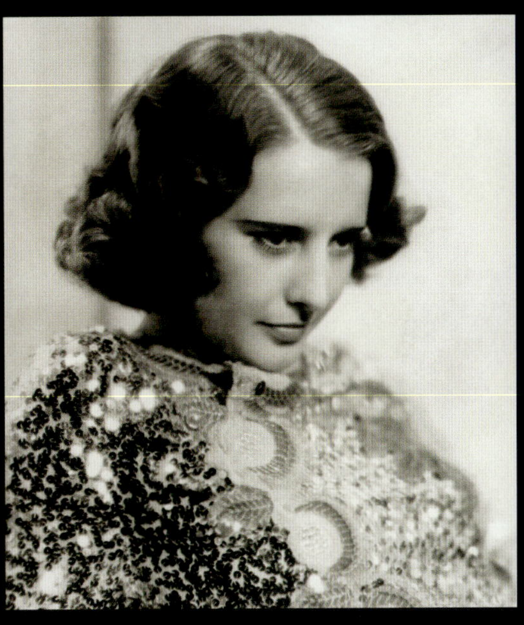

Barbara Stanwyck is the second most represented actor in this book—and for good reason. (Number one is Joan Blondell, who appears in six films out of the fifty highlighted.)

Bitter Tea of General Yen with depicting countless contentious elements, which led him to suggest the studio halt their rerelease plan. Marks against the film included Connolly's "unscrupulous character," the negative portrayal of Americans in China, the unflattering characterization of missionaries, a scene involving a truckload of prostitutes hauled in for soldiers, a suggestive sequence of Stanwyck in a bath, and the "whole unhappy period" of the Chinese Civil War. (That's basically the entire film.)

Despite the picture's cool reception, few movies capture the mystery of a hazy summer night and a pointed discussion like *The Bitter Tea of General Yen*. Capra's forward-looking film challenges its audience to consider their own worldview and where, ultimately, they will all end up.

LADIES THEY TALK ABOUT

STARRING
Barbara Stanwyck, Preston Foster, Dorothy Burgess, and Lillian Roth

DIRECTED BY
Howard Bretherton and William Keighley

RELEASED BY
Warner Bros., February 1933

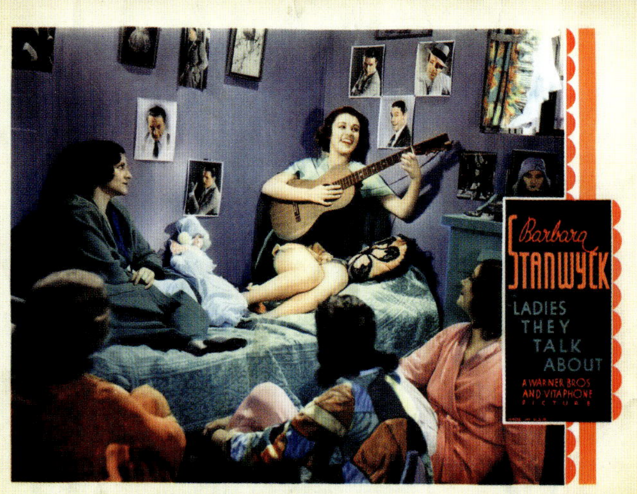

Is this a women's prison or a summer camp? This lobby card with Lillian Roth crooning to a photo of Joe E. Brown makes it seem like the latter.

The women-in-prison picture has a long, inglorious history, from Academy Award–nominated fare like *Caged* (1950) to the exploitation-heavy films produced in the 1970s to the popular 2010s show *Orange Is the New Black*. The genre is full of clichés, presenting the hard-bitten lifer to the sadistic matron and everything in between. With these pictures allowing filmmakers to comment on class consciousness, hot-topic political issues, and open explorations of women's sexual yearnings, it's little surprise that the genre took off for the first time in the pre-Code era. Throughout the early 1930s, women in varying degrees of "trouble" often languished momentarily in prisons, reformatories, or homes for unwed mothers, so it was only a matter of time before Hollywood filmed it.

Nan Taylor (Barbara Stanwyck) has problems in *Ladies They Talk About*. The daughter of a preacher, Nan was nabbed as the figurehead of a gang of bank robbers. After confessing to evangelist David Slade (Preston Foster), who's smitten with her, she's shipped off to San Quentin, vowing vengeance on David for sealing her fate. The new fish in lockup, Nan is shown the ropes by Linda (Lillian Roth) and adjusts to her new surroundings quickly; her natural hard exterior comes in handy for dealing with Susie (Dorothy Burgess), whose fixation on David and his weekly radio sermons puts her at loggerheads with a vengeful Nan.

Also giving the prison some color is former brothel owner Aunt Maggie (Maude Eburne) and Prisoner Mustard (Madame Sul-Te-Wan), a lifer who has few cares left to give. They're managed by prison matron Noonan (Ruth Donnelly) and, incredulously, her fearsome parrot that she keeps on her shoulder to shriek at misbehaving inmates. When a prison break gone wrong leaves two of Nan's former crew dead, she places the blame on

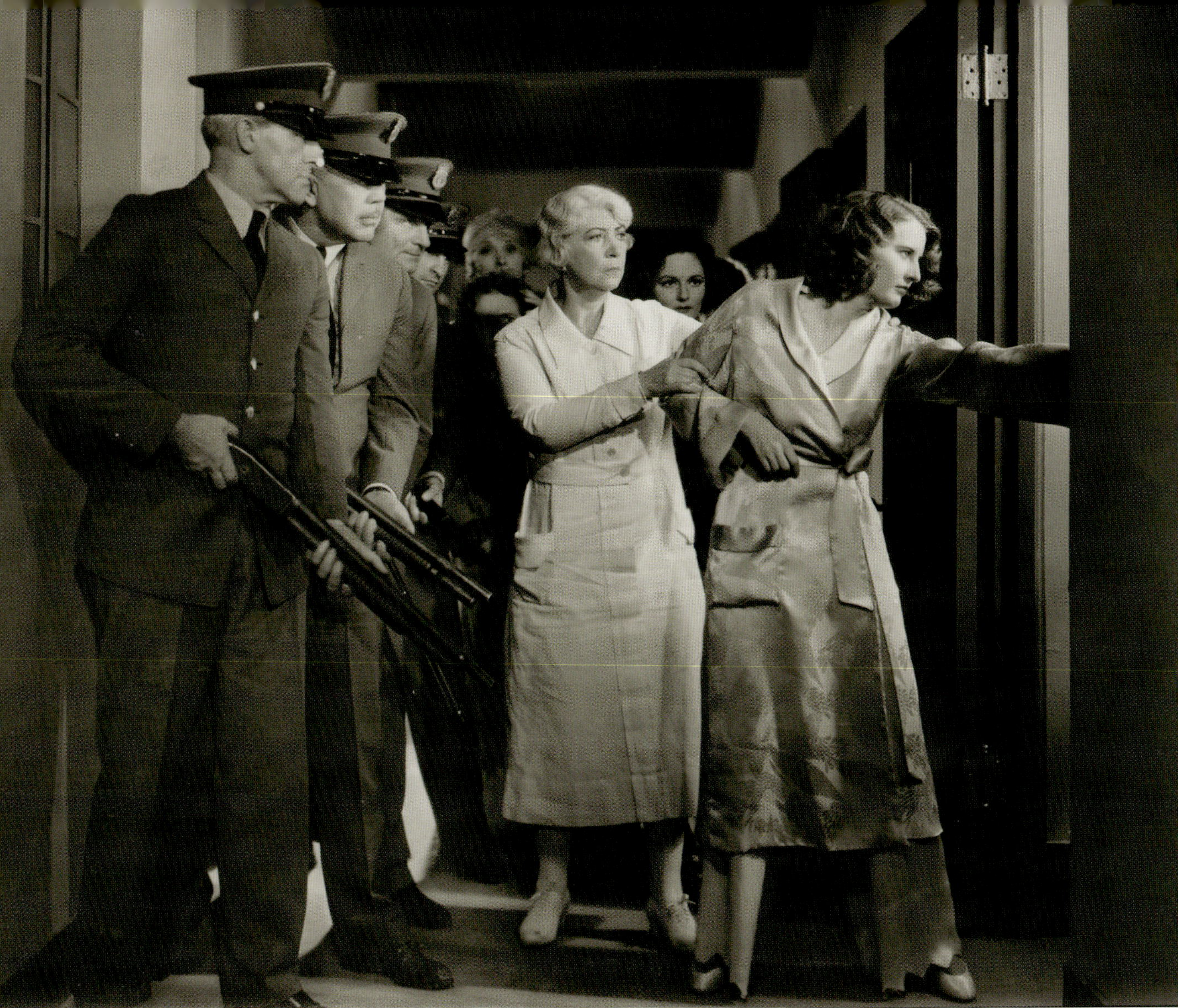

Understandably, Barbara Stanwyck is not too keen to start her prison term.

David, thinking he uncovered their plot. Upon her release, she confronts David, he confesses his love, and she shoots him—and instead of turning her over to the authorities this time, he announces they'll be married. Romantic, isn't it?

The original play for *Ladies They Talk About* comes from actress Dorothy Mackaye's personal experience serving ten months in San Quentin. She'd been put away for the conspiracy to cover up the part her lover, actor Paul Kelly, played in beating her husband, Ray Raymond, to death in 1927. Mackaye performed the lead role herself in a Los Angeles production, which led to Warner Bros. buying the rights.

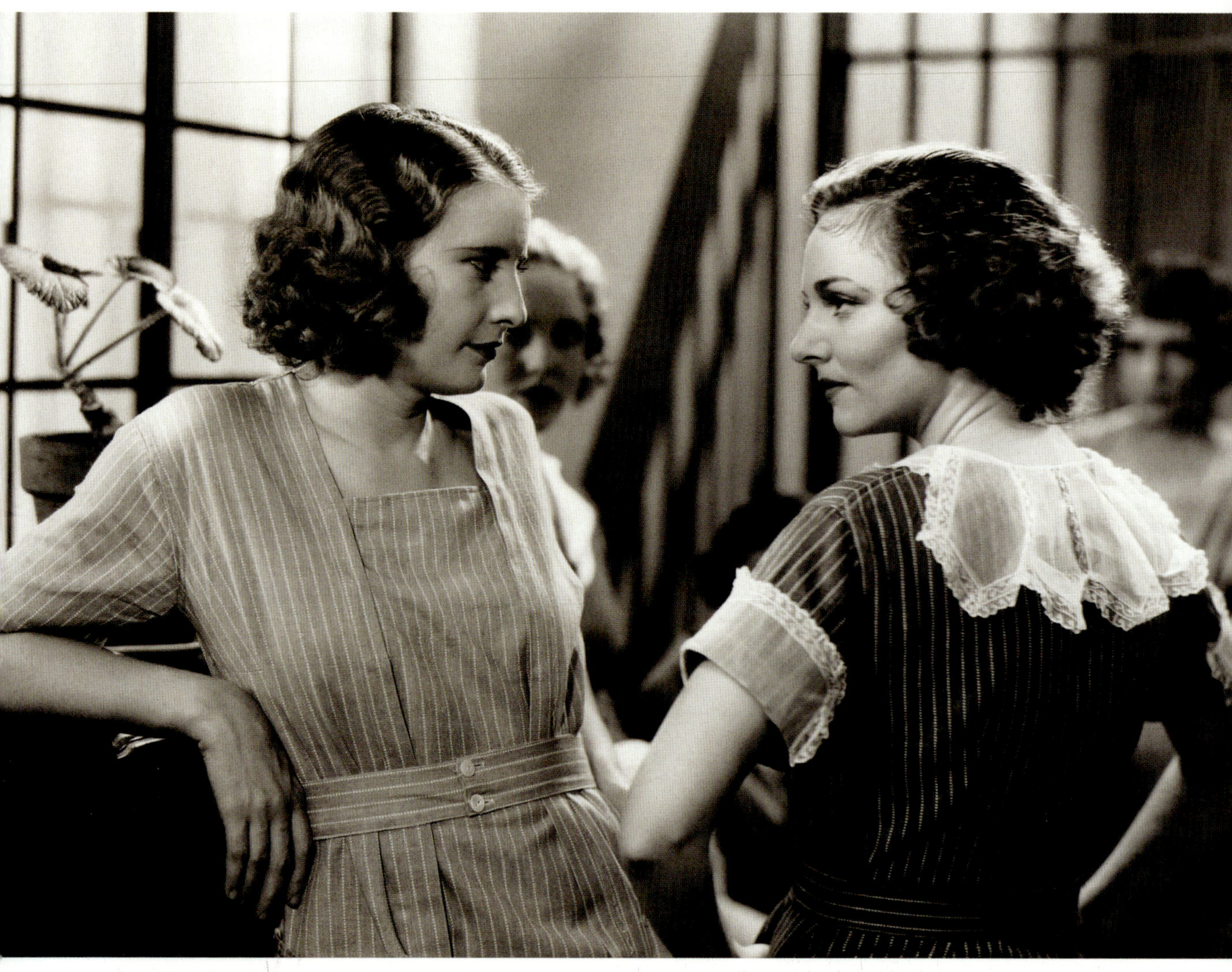

It's unwise to cross Barbara Stanwyck; this is a lesson Dorothy Burgess must learn.

Barbara Stanwyck welcomed the change of pace *Ladies They Talk About* offered after "dowdy" roles in *So Big!* and *The Purchase Price*, and the tale's sassy sophistication suited her well. "I never was the type to make men think," Stanwyck said of the role, "but perhaps I can make them react . . . I'm a product of crowded places and jammed-up emotions where right and wrong weren't always clearly defined and life wasn't always sweet, but it was life." That certainly describes the paradise version of prison that Nan and company occupy, in which a former society lady is allowed to keep

"Listen. Don't think you can walk in here and take over this joint. There's a lot of big sharks in here that just live on fresh fish like you."

"Yeah, when they add you up, what do you spell?"

—Susie and Nan, sizing each other up in the clink

a dog *and* a servant in stir. What a walk in the park compared to the likes of *The Big House* (1930) or *20,000 Years in Sing Sing* (1932)—save for a burly, cigar-chomping prisoner Nan is warned about ("Watch out for her. She likes to wrestle.") and volatile Susie.

The studio's request to film in the real San Quentin was turned down by the state prison board; the picture was instead shot at the studio in Burbank. Early in the movie, Roth gets a song, "If I Could Be with You (One Hour Tonight)" (yes, this women-in-prison flick comes with a tune!). Warner Bros. was well-known at the time for reusing its songs across its motion picture catalog to save money, and the scene also has Roth crooning to headshots of other Warner stars, in particular Joe E. Brown. It's a blatant advertisement for the studio's own output, though the spotlight on the bigmouthed comedian, usually noted more for his juvenile fare than his sex appeal, makes the number that much more bizarre.

While *Ladies They Talk About* is fairly chaste compared to other entries in this book, it still set off some alarms at the SRC. The film's opening, in which Nan calls in a false police report to distract the cops and ensure the coast is clear for their robbery, was notably controversial. Parts of the Production Code were written to specifically highlight the dangers in showing how criminals committed crimes in fear that'd spark imitators, and as expected, state and local boards mangled this sequence. In fact, Ohio cut the scene completely, opening the film in the bank. During the robbery itself, phrases like "Stick 'em up" and "I'll blow your insides all over the wall" were eliminated in many states.

Other problematic material also came from the jailbreak, though objections weren't as fierce since the getaway was ultimately unsuccessful. New York still eliminated scenes about the map Nan makes of the women's side of the prison, scenes showing women digging for their escape, and Nan getting a copy of the key from the matron—so practically the entire sequence, rendering it almost incomprehensible.

Almost every board had its pet quibbles, except Kansas, which passed the film without deletions. Chicago removed a shot of brass knuckles, Quebec and Ohio excised the wrestling line, and Pennsylvania deleted all references to a "beauty parlor," which was code for a brothel. Quebec also took out all scenes of Nan talking about murdering David, probably making the ending even more surprising. But perhaps the most humorous censorial decision came from Australia, which had Roth's musical ode to Joe E. Brown removed completely.

For as ridiculous as *Ladies They Talk About* is at many turns—we can't end this entry without mentioning the matron's parrot once again—it was yet another example of Warner Bros. exploiting a genre to the hilt. Hints of lesbianism, crimes galore, and shooting your future husband were all par for the course, and maybe you and the gal pals could get a couple of laughs in along the way.

EMPLOYEES' ENTRANCE

STARRING
Warren William, Loretta Young, Wallace Ford, and Alice White

DIRECTED BY
Roy Del Ruth

RELEASED BY
Warner Bros., February 1933

One of the most audaciously cold films ever made, *Employees' Entrance* is a singular paean to the cruel and calculated businessman. While it is arguably a black comedy, its protagonist is a brutal man whose business sense saves thousands of jobs despite the sexual and moral depravity he not only employs but elevates at every turn.

In the movie, Kurt Anderson (Warren William) rules a large department store with an iron fist. Anderson's employment maxims, which include the belief that useless employees should kill themselves lest they become a burden, drive the store's fortunes to dizzying heights. Anderson finds unemployed Madeline (Loretta Young), alone and in desperate need, and offers her a trade of sex for a job. Madeline grows to like the job but detests Anderson and his overt, unsympathetic methods. When she weds Anderson's gullible protégé, Martin (Wallace Ford), they keep the marriage secret. One evening at a party, the couple has a spat, and Anderson moves in on Madeline. When Martin finds out what Anderson has done, the man's future—and the store's—hang in the balance.

For as callous as Anderson is, this is when the film's actual villains appear: a cabal of bankers eager to cut the store's expenditures to line their own pockets. Anderson has to pull together his resources as Madeline takes poison to subsume the guilt of what's happened, and Martin realizes what a monster he's idolized. Miraculously, Anderson keeps his job and the store afloat, kicking Martin and Madeline out the door to their own somewhat happy ending.

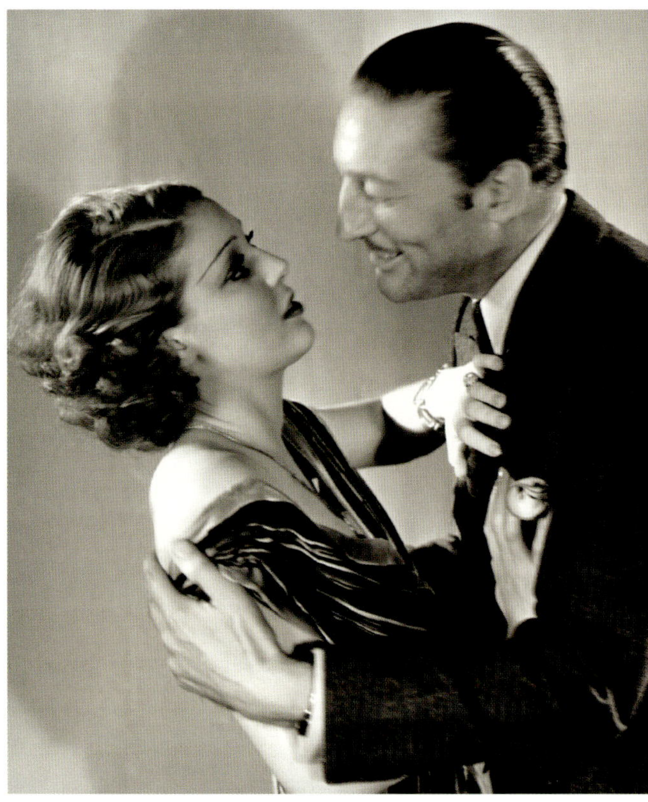

The businessman preys on his employee as Warren William looms over Loretta Young.

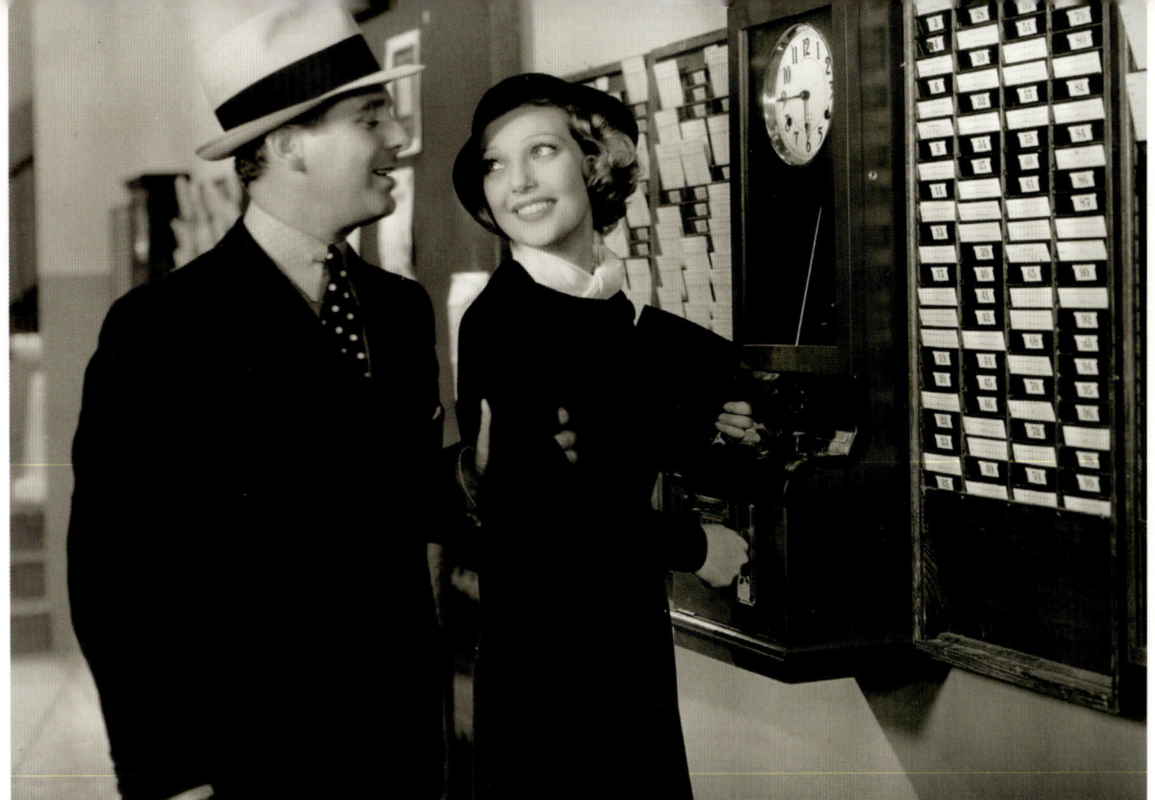

Working with your spouse is great! Unless you have to hide your relationship, like Wallace Ford and Loretta Young must do.

"You bankers make me sick. You don't know how to run your own business, and you want to tell everyone else how to run theirs."

—Kurt Anderson, putting Depression-era thoughts into bitter words

Anderson's repertoire, which includes using sexual harassment, date rape, and a cold disregard for life to blackmail and undermine his rivals, would appear galling for a villain in practically any picture, let alone in *Employees' Entrance*, where he becomes one of the most intriguing antiheroes of the time. Though Anderson is ruthless, he does have a specific code of honor, one where he keeps his employees on payroll so long as they are good employees. By the film's end, he even allows Martin to save face by letting the man shoot him, with Anderson growling, "You can't even shoot straight, can you?!"

Much of the sympathy for Anderson comes from a trend in early 1930s films that fawned toward authoritarians. Documentaries like *Mussolini Speaks* (1933) gave audiences a taste of how leaders and their veritable iron fists could solve problems, while movies like *Gabriel Over the White House* linked decisive, undemocratic leadership with stability, safety, and prosperity. *Employees' Entrance* would be one of the last films in this brief cycle, with Franklin D. Roosevelt's swearing in to the presidency in March 1933 reviving the national faith in democratic institutions

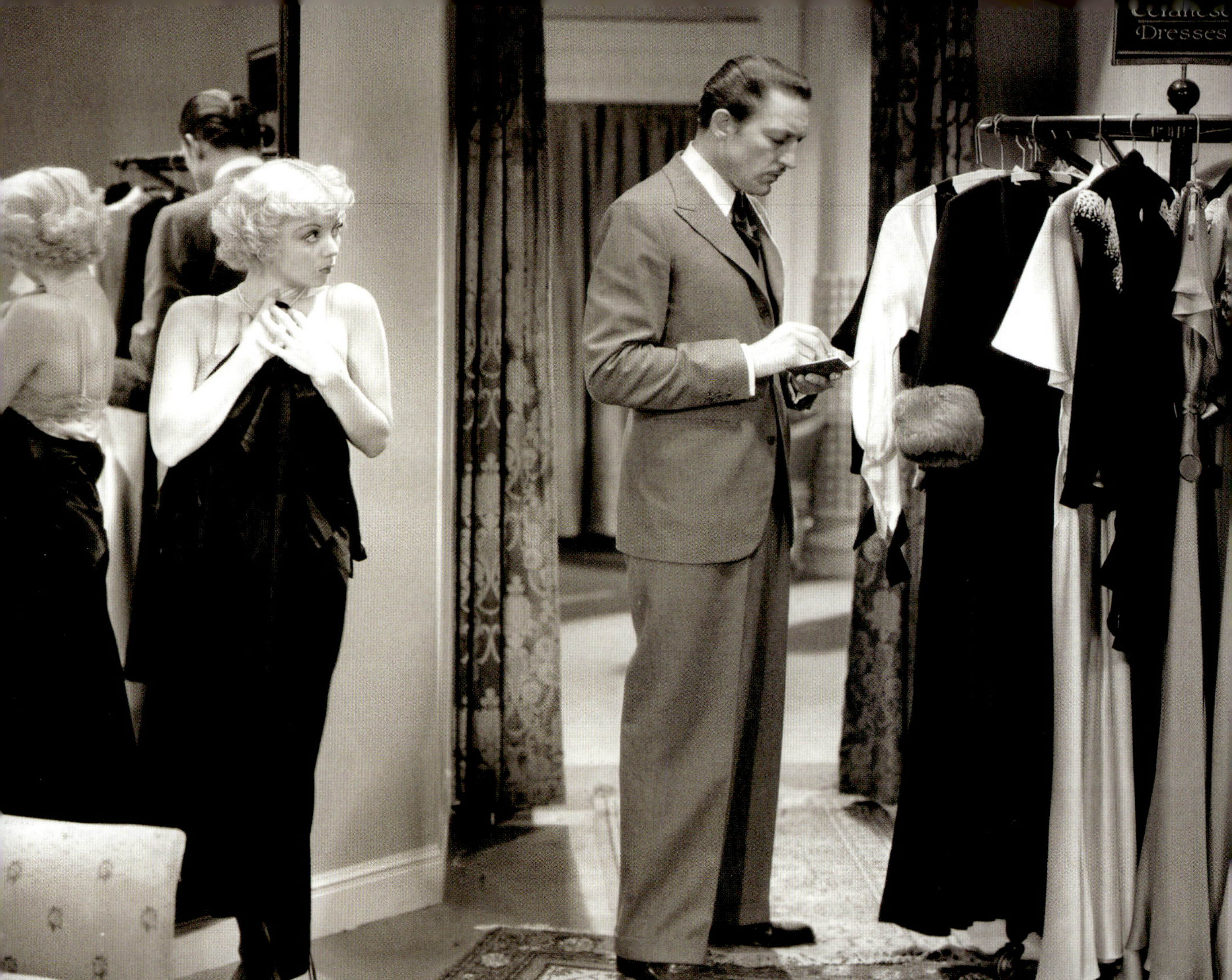

Being the boss back in the day may have meant you could march into the changing room; here, Alice White looks on unamused as Warren William checks the stock.

that Herbert Hoover's ineffectual response to the Depression hadn't.

The most telling feature of the movie, and one that sets it apart from several similar Warren William vehicles of the time, is that Anderson is still alive and in charge at the film's end. Even with a gunshot wound, he is no less fazed or thwarted in his rampage of casual and calculated cruelty. Rather than the typical comeuppance, he is merely nicked and free to resume his cold ways. That's a pre-Code ending if we've ever seen one.

Based on a play by Dave Boehm and shot over twenty-three days, *Employees' Entrance* interestingly mirrors a number of Jack Warner's own onerous business practices, including coercion, blackmail, and exploiting the desperate. The drastic pay cuts mentioned in the movie would be mimicked by the studio itself around the time of

Warren William

Edward G. Robinson was originally set to star in *Employees' Entrance*, but it's impossible to imagine him in a role that so perfectly encapsulates the oeuvre of the nominal king of pre-Code, Warren William. Often playing a brazen seducer or a villain—but always the protagonist—William was nearly forty years old when his immoral roles at Warner Bros. made him a star. His parts, often unscrupulous moguls, lawyers, or employers who seduced and destroyed their underlings, are some of the most reliable of the era, including *Beauty and the Boss* (1932), *Skyscraper Souls* (1932), and *The Match King* (1932). William's wolfish demeanor gave him latitude that few other actors possessed and a self-confidence that erased any doubts. For these incredulously callous roles, no one could present the wit, heart, and smarm like William.

William's stardom diminished quickly after the Code became enforced. He would appear in dull programmers like *Arsène Lupin Returns* (1938) or outright tragedies like *Satan Met a Lady* (1936) to round out his Warner Bros. contract before taking on the role of the debonair Lone Wolf for a series of nine films, the best being the first one, *The Lone Wolf Meets a Lady* (1940).

the film's release, leading to consternation and the ousting of production head Darryl F. Zanuck. How much of the picture was coincidentally autobiographical of the Warner Bros. troubles is strictly up for interpretation, but the parallels are intriguing.

Employees' Entrance set off a few alarms at the SRC in its script phase. Jason Joy disapproved of the movie's profanity, including uses of "floozy" and the phrase "Oh my Lord." Dialogue about mounting a campaign against birth control didn't make the cut, and a comedy scene about a young boy going to the bathroom apparently met the same fate.

State and local censors were unified in their attempts to make the sequence of Anderson raping the unconscious Ruth less suggestive, frequently removing all scenes of the two making their way to a hotel room. A lot of the film's more provocative dialogue got chopped in various localities, with the line "When I get tired I'll pay you off" (suggesting that Anderson would keep Alice White's Polly as a long-term escort) a popular offender in Chicago, British Columbia, and for Sunday audiences in Massachusetts.

Contemporary viewers remain stunned by the movie's content, with film historian John McElwee musing, "You need watch few movies or television today to recognize production codes still in place . . . It's one-of-a-kind disavowal of chalk-lines we walk that gives *Employees' Entrance* ongoing power to shock." Indeed, Anderson is basically a walking HR violation. It's hard not to contemplate his uncouth escapades through the lens of a post-#MeToo world, but in reality, men like him—and their sexist actions—were tolerated and accepted by many in the 1930s.

Employees' Entrance grows richer with age. A revelatory document of a number of virulent strains of misogyny and power all told unapologetically, the movie continues to deliver a jolt to audiences, rewriting expectations and transgressing the typical Hollywood ending in a way that could only happen in the pre-Code era.

GABRIEL OVER THE WHITE HOUSE

STARRING
Walter Huston, Karen Morley, and Franchot Tone

DIRECTED BY
Gregory La Cava

RELEASED BY
MGM, March 1933

"He's doing the things you wanted. And if he's mad, it's a divine madness. Look at the chaos and catastrophe the sane men of this world have brought about."

—Pendola Molloy, basically arguing that the ends justify the means, even if the man who touts those means is unhinged

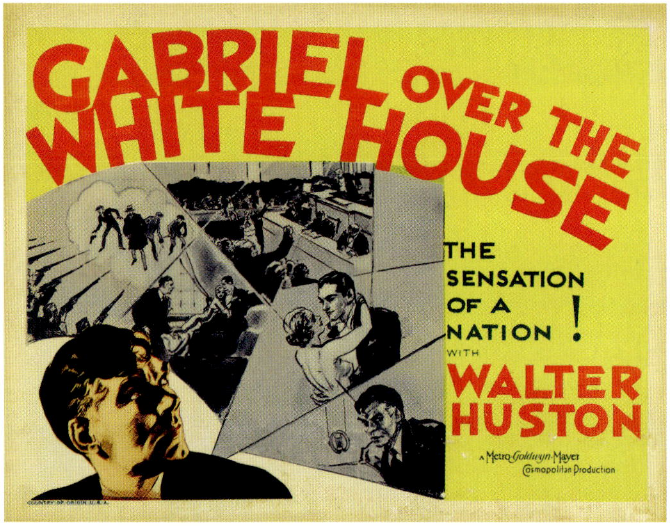

Walter Huston certainly has a lot to reflect on from his wild presidency.

One of the most prescient American films ever made, *Gabriel Over the White House* captures what would soon be known as "the American century" in a way few other movies could by tapping into the anxious desperation of a country at a crossroads during the Depression. From a drive-by shooting at the White House to the president's destruction of his own warships to threaten the world into disarmament, the film holds nothing back.

A bonkers political roller coaster with the faintest of religious undertones, *Gabriel Over the White House* finds Judson Hammond (Walter Huston) inaugurated as the president of the United States. Surrounded by his eager secretary, Hartley Beekman (Franchot Tone), and his mistress, Pendola Molloy (Karen Morley), he's ready to start the job—which means buddying up to his cabinet and tossing out all those campaign promises.

Immediately, it's obvious that Hammond's not fit for office in a country that desperately needs a visionary leader. But that all changes after the commander in chief crashes his car while recklessly speeding. Doctors think there's no hope, but he wakes—the result of divine intervention, we are led to believe—prepared to take action.

But the way Hammond wields his power, even if it's for good, raises eyebrows. He fires those who disagree with him, dissolves Congress, and declares martial law. Hammond leverages his authority, cutting through red tape to get things done, which includes executing gangsters and threatening countries that haven't paid their war debts. As Hammond finally gets foreign delegates to sign a debt-and-disarmament deal, he suffers a heart attack. He briefly wakes as his former self, signaling that the spirit of Gabriel has left him, and dies thereafter.

Unlike the bureaucratic drip of real-world politics, *Gabriel Over the White House* was an exceptionally speedy endeavor. Thomas W. Tweed's originally anonymous novel of the same name hit American shores at the start of 1933. In painting a desolate future of mass unemployment and skyrocketing crime, Tweed, a former aide to British Prime Minister David Lloyd George, latched onto a prophecy many Americans feared in the early 1930s: that the encumbrance of the Great Depression would destroy democracy.

Wanting to make a bang with his first film for MGM, producer Walter Wanger requested the book rights within days of arriving on the lot. Sensing just how timely the story was, Wanger transported Tweed's futuristic 1980s plot to the modern day and instructed writer Carey Wilson to play up the realistic parallels. Cameras rolled within one month's time. After a tight ten days of shooting and a total of $180,000 spent, production wrapped on February 26. On March 31, *Gabriel Over the White House* hit US screens, less than three months after MGM bought the property.

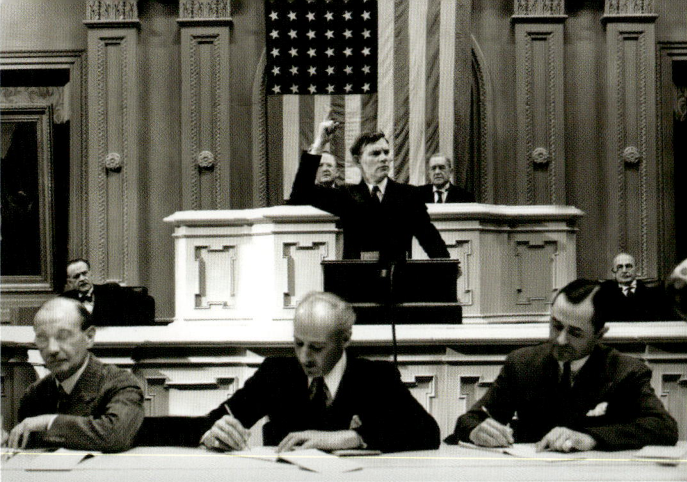

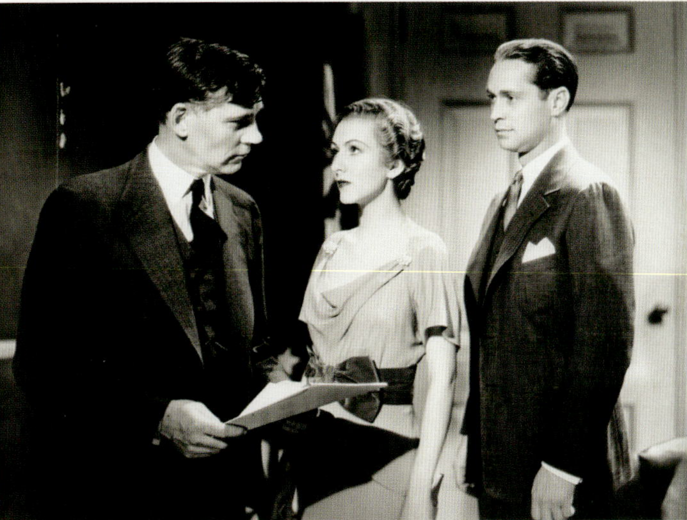

FROM TOP: A president dissolves Congress and makes his own rules to save the world as Walter Huston takes America into his iron hold. • Sure, he's the president, but can't he have a sidepiece, too? Karen Morley plays the boss's mistress until he decides to get to work; then she falls for Huston's secretary, Franchot Tone.

Financial support came courtesy of William Randolph Hearst, whose production company Cosmopolitan Pictures made its home on the MGM lot. Hearst and Wanger both expressed interest in the property and teamed up on "one of several cinematic inauguration gifts" Hearst would bestow upon Franklin D. Roosevelt. Hearst's money and general endorsement also came in the form of copious script notes and promotion across his publications.

The president-elect also contributed advice and input—just as he was about to start his term

[1933]

Gabriel Over the White House

EXCERPT FROM MR. HAYS MEMORANDUM OF MARCH 7th ON
GABRIEL OVER THE WHITE HOUSE

I- Essential that the picture be changed in the early footage to indicate that there is some intelligence and wisdom and high purpose rather than to avoid even the promises, let alone execution, of proper duty.

(a) The card game in the first Cabinet meeting.

(b) The President's own attitude.

(c) The President's utter disregard for present conditions.

The picture ought to be changed to the extent of causing the audience to believe that there is at least a small amount of sense of duty in a man that could be elected president today of this Republic.

II- The unemployment problem: "There can be some modification of the way this is handled. You don't have to say 'rotten government' and several instances of dialogue can be changed and other modifications. The majority opinion in the country, supported by all the papers, except two circuits, thought the necessity was such it was necessary to show some force during the occurrence of the recent Bonus Army."

III The debts: We run the risk of the President's belief that we are shaping public opinion contrary to what he may have to do. It will of course offend the nations involved and that offense might result in their restrictions on the distribution of our pictures.

Reiterating the problem:

1. The picture should be so modified as to give, in its early footage, an impression of proper respectability and righteousness in the present government which has to lead us out of the emergency.

2. That such changes be developed as will offer the solutions in the way that
   A- Are correct;
   B- Do not offend the majority opinion in the country;
   C- Do not offend those responsible for the solutions or make it harder for them to do that which they have to do and in which they have to be supported by the people or there will not be any tomorrow.

The SRC frequently gave studios feedback on scripts, which the studio could incorporate or, more likely, completely ignore.

on March 4, no less. Roosevelt's participation at such a busy time mirrors the momentum he soon applied to the implementation of the New Deal.

Journalist Jeff Greenfield remarked in a 2018 conversation at the University of California, Santa Barbara that *Gabriel Over the White House* was really the "only officially pro-fascist movie Hollywood made." With a script that boldly commented on contemporary social problems—unemployment, bootleggers, apprehension of another global war—and attempted to answer them in such an authoritarian manner, censorship concerns were inevitable. James Wingate confessed that the SRC couldn't "deny the screen the right to portray a dramatic solution of present-day economic problems," but the office forewarned of danger in tackling such timely, divisive subjects, such as the jobless uprising. "God knows there are enough people who are afraid of something of that sort without stirring it up on the screen," a member of the New York censor board confided to Will H. Hays.

Corruption was another sticking point, especially exposing deceitful elected officials. After viewing the film, Hays worried that audiences might construe it as an indictment of a weak government and its employees, firmly suggesting MGM "indicate that there is some intelligence and some wisdom and some high purpose rather than to avoid even the promises, let alone execution, of proper duty."

The SRC also noted potential difficulty with the way the picture painted international relations. In particular, a scene in which a bothersome political colleague is palmed off to England as an ambassador raised flags. "We have a hell of a nerve to put anything like this in one of our pictures, and at the same time beg these different Embassies and Legations of ours to help us out . . ."

Colonel Frederick L. Herron, who headed the foreign office of the MPPDA, bristled.

Wanger and Hearst were well aware of the controversial subject matter, especially as they supported Roosevelt, whereas MGM's Louis B. Mayer backed Hoover. At a preview, Mayer was reportedly so upset at the way the film took a swipe at Hoover's presidency that he apparently ordered MGM executive Eddie Mannix to "put that picture in its can, take it back to the studio, and lock it up!"

With such vehement opposition from Mayer, Wanger reluctantly softened political episodes. Hearst wasn't fully satisfied, either, accusing Mayer of diminishing the potency of a big speech "because you have been afraid to say the things which I wrote and which I say daily in my newspapers and which you commend me for saying, but still do not sufficiently approve to put in your film." The changes proved helpful, though, as the picture made it through most state censor boards relatively unscathed.

A prophetic film such as this warranted a range of critiques, but most proved positive. "If Mr. Roosevelt ever folds up or runs out of ideas—there seems no likelihood of it—I'm all for drafting Mr. Walter Huston as President Extraordinary [*sic*] and giving him free hand to do just what he does in this picture," the *Chicago Daily Tribune*'s Mae Tinee extolled. After living three full years of the Great Depression with little hope in sight, *Gabriel Over the White House* must have felt incredibly enticing in 1933, showcasing the desire for a strong leader who wielded power unilaterally. By the time the film finally hit theaters, Americans had already cast their votes for change. That said, the involvement of both Hearst and, to a lesser extent, Roosevelt, in the creation of a film that so overtly embraced elements of fascism and socialism indicates just how dire the situation had gotten—and how open some Americans were to a leader like Hammond.

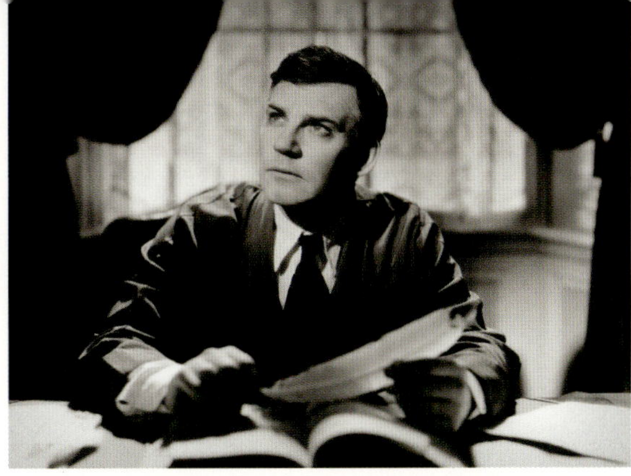

Heavenly intervention fixes American politics as Walter Huston is influenced by the angel Gabriel (it seems).

Modern audiences may extract some lessons from the movie too. Wingate remarked that the film's commentary on timely subjects "may lead to the radicals and the communists, and others who believe in governmental changes by other than constitutional methods, doing the same thing, thus helping to lessen the confidence of the peons in their form of government." As America continues to grow more polarized, modern parallels to the film can feel unnerving, with those operating at the fringes on both ends of the political spectrum having voiced support for ideas similar to those expressed in the movie.

By the time *Gabriel Over the White House* premiered, the American public had amassed three years' worth of grievances during an era when countless lives and livelihoods were squandered or destroyed. The film captures that despondency and hunger for action in an incredibly dynamic, albeit alarming and fantastical, way. Power didn't necessarily corrupt in this movie, but it's a reminder of just how much it can in the wrong hands—and that's a message that still resounds incredibly loudly.

KING KONG

STARRING
Fay Wray, Robert Armstrong, and Bruce Cabot

DIRECTED BY
Merian C. Cooper and Ernest B. Schoedsack

RELEASED BY
RKO, April 1933

"Some big, hardboiled egg gets a look at a pretty face and bang—he cracks up and goes sappy!"

—Carl Denham complaining about Jack Driscoll's attitude toward Ann Darrow, though it could certainly speak to another character's looming feelings as well

Fay Wray and Bruce Cabot look less than thrilled to be tangled up in some monkey business.

Like its titular character, *King Kong* remains an imposing American giant. A splashy spectacle of a film, it was one of the first talkies to unite sound design, state-of-the-art special effects, and fast-paced filmmaking to deliver an unmitigated thrill ride. An extremely expensive gamble for the floundering RKO Pictures, it paid off and remains one of the greatest action-adventure movies ever made.

While it's easy to trace the many trends *King Kong* started in terms of blockbusters and special effects-heavy productions, the social cues that underline the picture remain timeless. It is a film of desperation and exploitation, where a starving actress and a lonely monster find their fates intertwined.

King Kong follows filmmaker Carl Denham (Robert Armstrong) as he sets out for a mysterious island along with his crew and actress Ann Darrow (Fay Wray), whom he finds stealing an apple off an applecart. Upon arrival, the movie crew blunders into a native ritual surrounding a creature named Kong. Members of the tribe kidnap Ann, and she is snatched up by the massive gorilla and taken deep into the forest. Kong, alone with Ann, is enchanted by this foreign creature. Led by Jack Driscoll (Bruce Cabot), the crew overcomes various fantastical creatures to rescue her and subdue Kong. A triumphant Denham plots his next outrageous project—turning the greatest wonder the world has ever seen into a star attraction on Broadway—but that backfires enormously when Kong escapes and takes Ann with him for a trip up the Empire State Building.

Coming from an era where adventurous filmmakers traversed the world to bring new and exciting pictures back to stunned audiences, the Carl Denham character was a figure cut from real life, most clearly from *King Kong*'s coproducer/codirector Merian C. Cooper, a former fighter pilot, documentary filmmaker, and adventurer. Taking a cue from the popular exploitation movie *Ingagi* (1930), a fake documentary that supposedly showed a woman being forced to mate with a gorilla, Cooper decided that he also wanted his picture to feature a "love story" that would titillate the audience.

While Fay Wray was one of Hollywood's most prolific actresses at the time, there's little doubt as to what film she's best remembered for. Cinema's original "scream queen," Wray earned a reputation as the damsel in distress in many a thriller, which sometimes belittled her talent. Wray experiences quite the emotional journey in *King Kong*, swaying from desperation to hope to terror to relief and then some. Kong may overshadow the proceedings, but her range—and that scream—still impress.

They actually did make a Broadway show based on this movie, so this is somehow very self-referential.

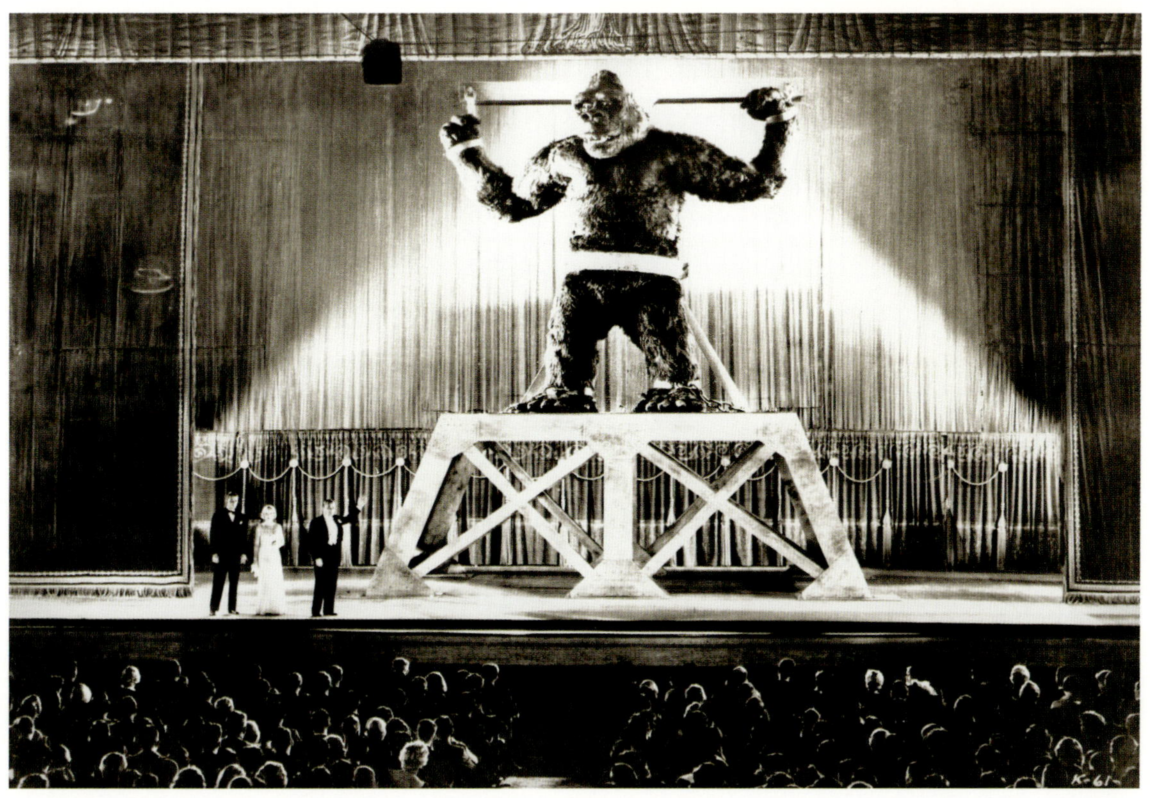

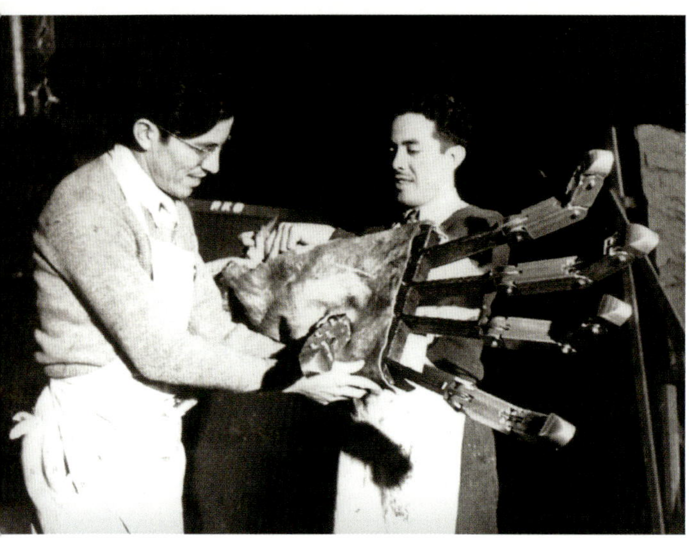

Gotta hand it to them with this one! That's special effects technicians—and brothers—Victor and Marcel Delgado working on Kong's articulated armature.

Kong and his prehistoric cohorts came to life through an unprecedented combination of stop motion, matte paintings, rear projection, and miniatures. The creature was designed by Willis O'Brien, who spent his early years as a ranch hand and guide to paleontologists in Oregon. Cooper commissioned pulp writer Edgar Wallace to pen the script, but Wallace died after the first draft was turned in. Several other RKO writers cycled through, with the film's final polish coming from Ruth Rose, codirector Ernest Schoedsack's wife and a novice screenwriter who helped tighten the story's pace. Besides creating the opening scene between Ann and Denham, she further cemented how the characters mirrored the real world, tying Denham to Cooper, Driscoll to Schoedsack, and adding details of her own life to Ann.

The meticulous Cooper focused on the effects sequences while Schoedsack directed the live-action components. Cooper's and Schoedsack's enthusiasm for the production was evident on set; they even acted out the battle between Kong and the Tyrannosaurus rex to be used as reference. Their most surprising part in the picture, however, is the cameo roles they play as the two pilots who finally manage to fell Kong in New York.

King Kong went hundreds of thousands of dollars over budget, which led to Cooper paying Max Steiner out of pocket to create the film's score. Steiner ignored Cooper's suggestion to reuse old music and composed a symphonic score from scratch, one of the first ones crafted for a sound picture.

When *King Kong* opened, it brought in $100,000 its first week, the biggest opening for any film up to that point. It eventually pulled in around $5 million, making it a certified blockbuster. Decades later, critic Roger Ebert would add the movie to his roster of Great Films, noting that *King Kong* "pointed the way toward the current era of special effects, science fiction, cataclysmic destruction, and nonstop shocks." The movie further proved its cultural relevance when it was added to the National Film Registry in 1991.

When RKO inquired about rereleasing the film in 1938, the PCA demanded cuts. They removed a number of brutal scenes, including shots of a woman Kong drops in New York and imagery of natives getting crushed on the island. The moment where Kong undresses Ann and sniffs her clothing was also excised. A 1942 reissue went one step further by darkening certain scenes to make the explicit violence more difficult to discern. These shots were restored in the late 1960s.

One scene that hasn't been restored, and most likely never will be, is the infamous "spider

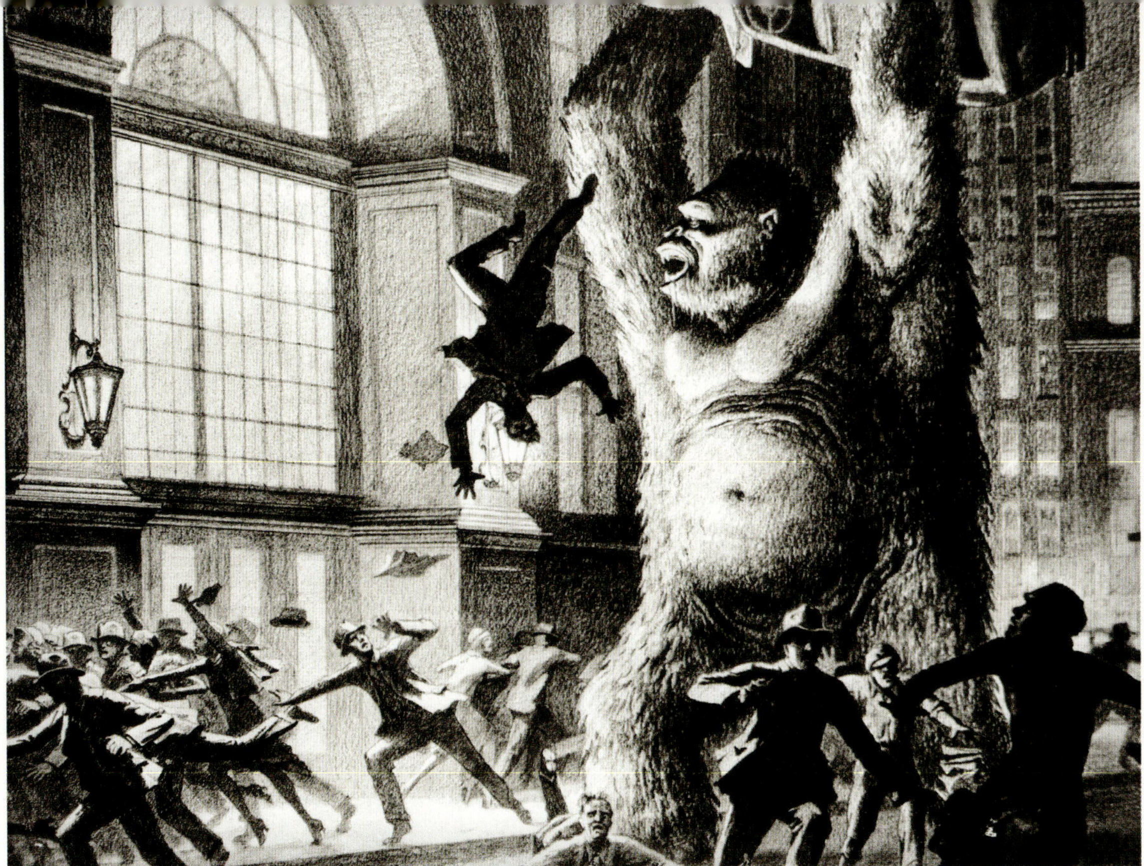

Concept art for the film illustrates how much Kong would grow in future drafts.

pit" sequence, which was believed to have taken place after Kong shook several sailors off a log, sending them plummeting into a pit where they were consumed by a variety of repulsive creatures. The scene is generally thought to have been cut prerelease to help with the film's pacing, but some viewers in the early 1930s swore they saw it in theaters. Whatever the true story is, no stills or footage of this sequence have ever been found.

King Kong would be followed by a minor sequel, *Son of Kong* (1933), and has been remade countless times, either in the Hollywood blockbuster mold where he leaped between the World Trade Center towers or farmed out to Japanese kaiju filmmakers who pitted him against Godzilla or a Mechani-Kong. The giant ape has made appearances on Broadway and even starred in an animated musical for children with Dudley Moore as the voice of Carl Denham—though that one had a decidedly happier ending than its pre-Code cousin. Kong movies continue to be produced, whether they are pastiches or special effects extravaganzas, period pieces or throwbacks. King Kong may be the liveliest nonagenarian still in the game.

Out of all the pre-Code era films, none have enjoyed quite the legacy or caught the cultural imagination with such an unremitting tenacity as *King Kong*. Besides its ability to wow, *King Kong* has served as a model for hundreds of action-packed blockbusters and tales of antiheroes since. And amazingly, for a film that has been remade and revisited so much, it hasn't been topped yet.

THE STORY OF TEMPLE DRAKE

STARRING
Miriam Hopkins, William Gargan, Jack La Rue, and Florence Eldridge

DIRECTED BY
Stephen Roberts

RELEASED BY
Paramount, May 1933

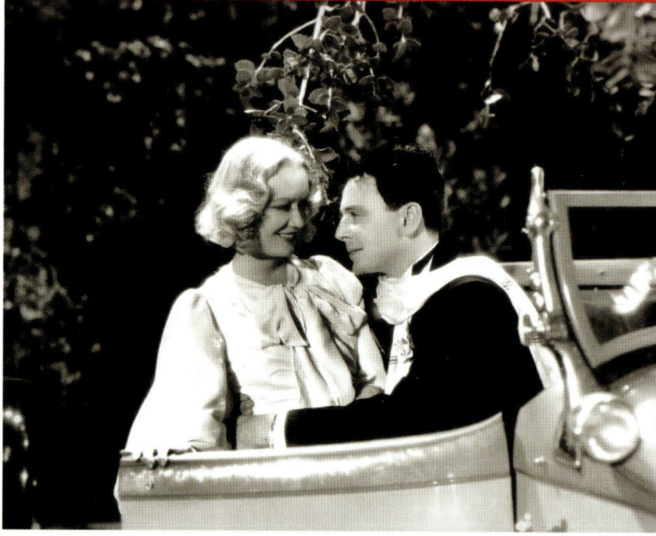

Miriam Hopkins leaves beaus wanting in *The Story of Temple Drake*. This one, William Collier Jr., ends up getting drunk and changing the course of her life.

The Story of Temple Drake is one of the darkest, moodiest, and most controversial movies of the early 1930s. That's compounded by the fact that it spent decades locked in vaults, unavailable for rerelease and then only in murky copies with pops and hisses. One of the most pivotal films in the history of American cinema, *The Story of Temple Drake* is a quiet, intense picture about a woman's honor in the New South and her unconventional redemption that still shocks.

In *The Story of Temple Drake*, Judge Drake (Guy Standing) enjoys a reputation of honesty; his granddaughter has a reputation of a different kind. We meet Temple Drake (Miriam Hopkins) flirting with a beau, adoring that fleeting feeling of leaving a man craving her in every way. Her wild, impetuous streak leads to her repeatedly turning local lawyer Stephen Benbow's (William Gargan) proposals down.

One reckless night, Temple gets into a car crash with a drunken beau that sends her into a different world. A menacing figure, Trigger (Jack La Rue), rescues them—or so they think. Trigger and Tommy (James Eagles) lead them to a dilapidated mansion full of bootleggers; the only woman in the house, Ruby (Florence Eldridge), spits venom at the privileged Temple but has Tommy keep watch over her. Temple is finally hidden in the corncrib to sleep without constant male visitors, but Trigger finds her in the morning, shoots Tommy, and rapes her.

The traumatic event leaves Temple inverted and morose. Trigger puts her up as his prisoner in a boardinghouse, until Stephen tracks him down for Tommy's murder. Temple convinces Stephen that she's there voluntarily to save his life, but after he leaves, she kills Trigger and makes her way back home. There, Stephen pleads with Temple to come clean as a witness to clear the wrong man for Tommy's murder, but the guilt on her conscience is almost too much to bear.

Hopkins's divine talents carry *The Story of Temple Drake*. There's no grand speech that explains her motivations, her thoughts, or feelings. Much of the film, Hopkins leaves her face as a passive mask, dropping emotions the moment she's unobserved by another character. We remain on the outside of her just as much as those in the movie do, turning her into a cipher whose internal desires are driven more by the diffusion of camera light and the melodramatic cinematography.

While many gangsters of the era were dangerous and sexy, Trigger is a straight-up monster—arrogant, cruel, and way too happy to live up to his nickname. (George Raft turned down the role due to its unpleasant subject matter.) But his intimidating exterior belies how pathetically needy he is. Trigger thinks he can threaten the world and get what he wants, only to learn how delicate his control really is. He even appears slightly meek after raping Temple, offering her coffee, repelled by his own natural sympathy and her reaction to what happened.

Paramount assembled a capable team for the picture, including Oscar-winning cinematographer Karl Struss, who had filmed *Sunrise: A Song of Two Humans* (1927) and *Dr. Jekyll and Mr. Hyde* (1931). Struss, who believed in using in-frame objects to separate the characters, gives the film a stylistic connection to *Jekyll and Hyde*, though in *Temple Drake* it lived through the prism of an old dark house rather than a supernatural emergence of the id. Both pictures feature frustrated protagonists pounding at the walls of conservative sexual and gender roles, as well as concentrated cinematography that traps the audience. In the case of *Temple Drake*, the extreme close-ups of Hopkins's and La Rue's faces in the boardinghouse—while

"It's like there were two me's. One of 'em says: Yes. Yes. Quick. Don't let me get away."

"And the other?"

"I won't tell you. But what it wants or does or what'll happen to it, I don't know myself! All I know is I hate it!"

—Temple Drake and Stephen Benbow, discussing the delights whose name you dare not speak

she pleads to be let out and he manipulates her to stay, Stockholm syndrome style—place us in the middle of their unnerving duel.

The Story of Temple Drake was based on William Faulkner's salacious 1931 novel *Sanctuary*, which was still so controversial that the title is omitted from the film's opening credits. That Paramount was in desperate enough straits to adapt this work into a movie in 1933 speaks both to the precipice of their financial situation as well as how willing they were to gamble on such risqué material. The SRC's Lamar Trotti called it "utterly unthinkable as a motion picture," with Will H. Hays agreeing, testifying: "We must not allow the production of a picture that will offend every right-thinking person who sees it." Hays, not consulted by Paramount as they readied a script, tried to block the film from getting made, to no avail; at the very least, Hays pleaded that the strictest supervision must be taken with the movie.

The SRC thoroughly emphasized the dangers involved with attempting such a story while pushing for changes. The original title, *The Shame of*

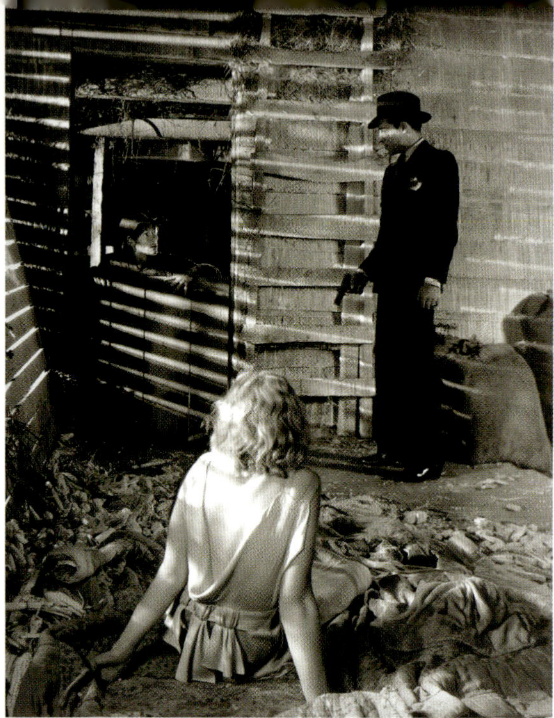

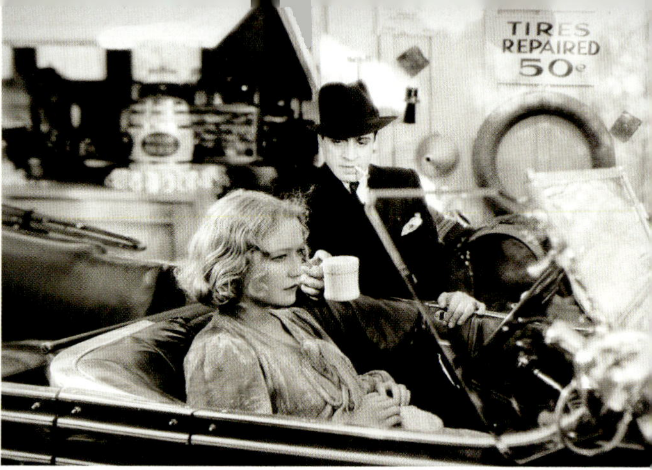

FROM LEFT: Jack La Rue terrorizes Miriam Hopkins in a scene whose adaptation could only allude to the horrors described in William Faulkner's novel. • *The Story of Temple Drake* presents Miriam Hopkins's suffering in the aftermath of her rape so brutally that Jack La Rue's Trigger momentarily feels the need to be nice to her.

Temple Drake, was considered too scandalous; the novel's brothel is sold as a boardinghouse; and the infamous rape is heavily implied with corncobs scattered about, a clear allusion to how an impotent Trigger uses them in the book. Paramount and the SRC bandied back and forth countless times, the SRC suggesting edits that the studio either ignored or the SRC felt didn't go far enough. For instance, one ending the studio put forth found Temple engaged in welfare work in China. That ticked the moral values box—as long as it was clear the law was satisfied in regards to Trigger's death. (As if what Temple endured wasn't enough.) In the end, SRC officials were split as to whether the film technically abided by the Code, eventually declaring no. "It is a sordid, base and thoroughly unpleasant picture that will add nothing to the advancement of the screen," Joseph Breen charged.

Per usual, Paramount applied for a license to exhibit the film in New York, and then something unusual occurred: They withdrew the application to make further modifications. Prior to that withdrawal, the New York censors noted several questionable situations, admitting they felt it "would need to have a pretty thorough renovation before being presented for licensing." After yet another review of the picture, the SRC issued suggestions based on urgency; essential deletions centered on the rape and boardinghouse scenes. Select changes were agreed upon, and the final version was approved by the New York board.

Of course, that's not the end of the story. Local censor boards ranged in their reactions from a few cuts (Virginia) to three pages' worth (Pennsylvania) to outright rejection (India, Holland, Latvia). Main points of contention were—you guessed it—the rape and boardinghouse sequences. Ohio censors even grumbled, "Sex pictures are now on a plateau and when are they going to start declining?" Well, that started around May 1934, when the Catholic Legion of Decency listed sixty-three pictures banned for members; *The Story of Temple Drake* was among them.

Viewers did not respond positively to the film's repellant subject matter, either. Critics were either baffled by the elliptical nature of the filmmaking or simply revolted by the sum of its parts. With the official enforcement of the Production Code in the summer of 1934, *Temple Drake* was listed as one of the biggest offenders, a film not to be reissued even with cuts. While this saved the picture from being mangled, it also kept it out of the public eye for decades. In 2011, the Museum of Modern Art restored *Temple Drake*, but even then, the film wasn't available on home media until 2019. This left Hopkins's brilliant turn forgotten by the earliest generations of film scholars.

Temple Drake didn't just push the envelope when it came to what was shown on-screen; the film is also groundbreaking in depicting a rape victim who voices as much—her line "he attacked me" was deleted in Alberta—and ultimately is not ashamed of what befell her. It's a modern sensibility, as the #MeToo movement has shown—and it's a rarity for the period, as well. While rape was subtly hinted at in some pre-Codes, the implication was never this blatant, the violation rarely verbally addressed, audiences seldom saw the immediate emotional impact on the woman, and, certainly, no one ever articulated how proud they were that the victim came forward (to save an innocent man's life, in this instance). Seeing such an honest portrayal in a 1930s film, in which a woman grapples with coming clean because she knows the effect it will have on her reputation and family, is profound and powerful. It may be just a movie, but the strength Temple displays, in a time when rape was routinely swept under the rug, remains incredibly impactful.

For all its unassuming quiet, *The Story of Temple Drake* would be pointed to, along with *Convention City*, as one of the key films that led to the end of the pre-Code era. In addition to its censorship issues, the movie clocked several complaints from the public. P. S. Harrison, publisher of the influential trade journal *Harrison's Reports*, wrote an open letter to Paramount after they acquired the title, bluntly stating: "If you allow the making of this book into a picture, I believe you will do the greatest harm to the motion picture industry that has ever been done in its entire history." Paramount's willingness to tackle such unsavory material, treat it with nuance and respect, and blast it out for public consumption was the loudest warning yet that studios would continue to test the limits. Censors and reformers across the country had a new flashpoint.

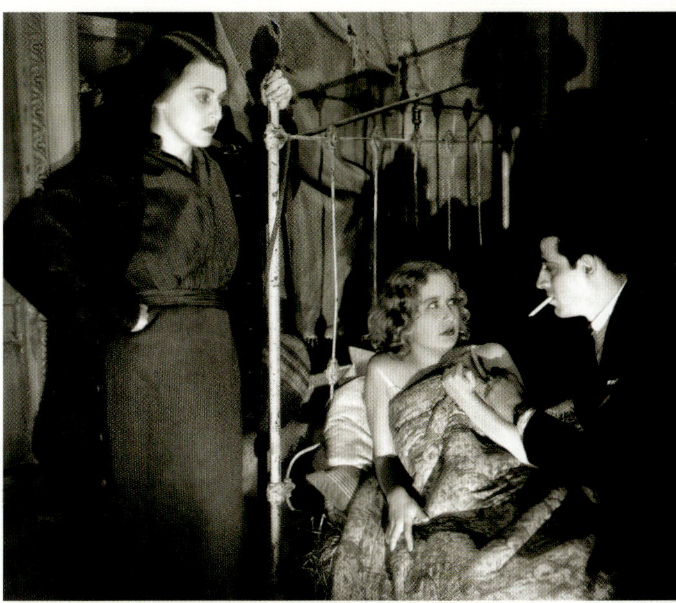

Trapped without her fancy manners and accoutrements, Miriam Hopkins gets folded into the sleezy Southern underworld while Florence Eldridge looks on.

SO THIS IS AFRICA

STARRING
Robert Woolsey, Bert Wheeler, Raquel Torres, and Esther Muir

DIRECTED BY
Edward F. Cline

RELEASED BY
Columbia, April 1933

Bert Wheeler and Robert Woolsey were one of the most popular comedy teams of the early 1930s. Though mostly forgotten a century later—their output could be *wildly* inconsistent, to say the least—the comics helped keep RKO solvent during its early years with Wheeler playing the effeminate dope of the duo and Woolsey the braggart hiding behind a pair of oversize horn-rimmed glasses.

After negotiations between the team and RKO stalled over pay, the actors hopped to Columbia Pictures to make one movie, which proved to be one of their most profitable and undoubtedly scandalous films. Even the SRC was caught off guard at just how vehemently the movie was received. State censor boards, most notably New York, declared the film nigh unsalvageable. Because of the controversy, *So This Is Africa* was hacked from its original run time of ninety minutes to a little over sixty, with cuts swooping in right before punch lines and entire subplots tidied up to near extinction. *So This*

If you're thinking this is monkey business, no, that's the Marx Brothers movie that came out two years before.

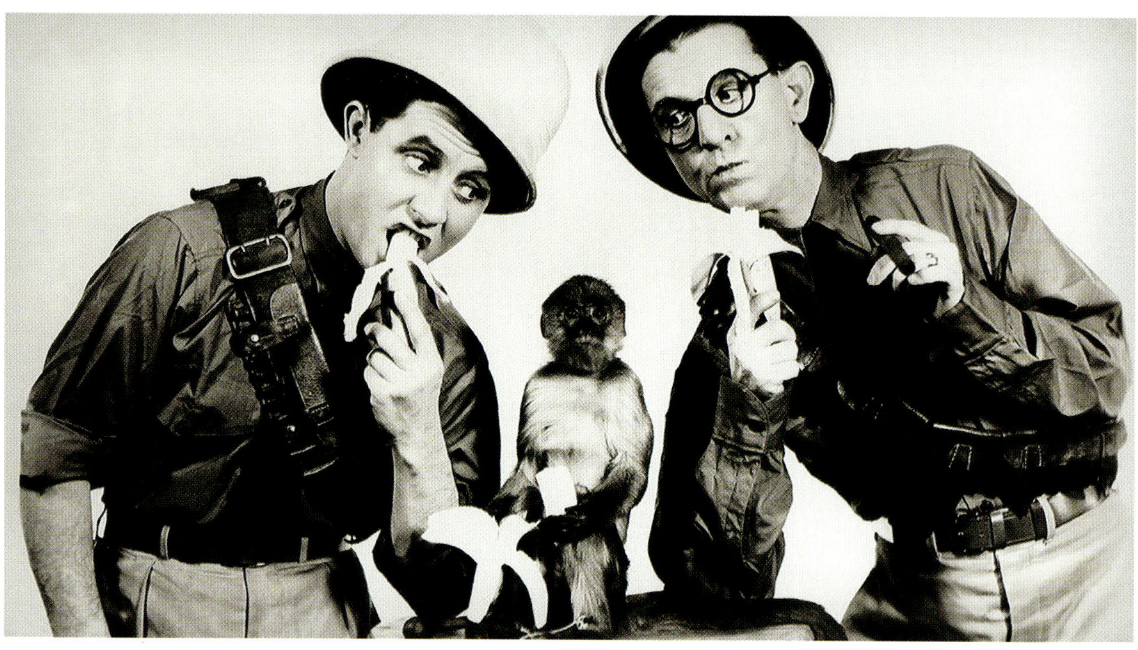

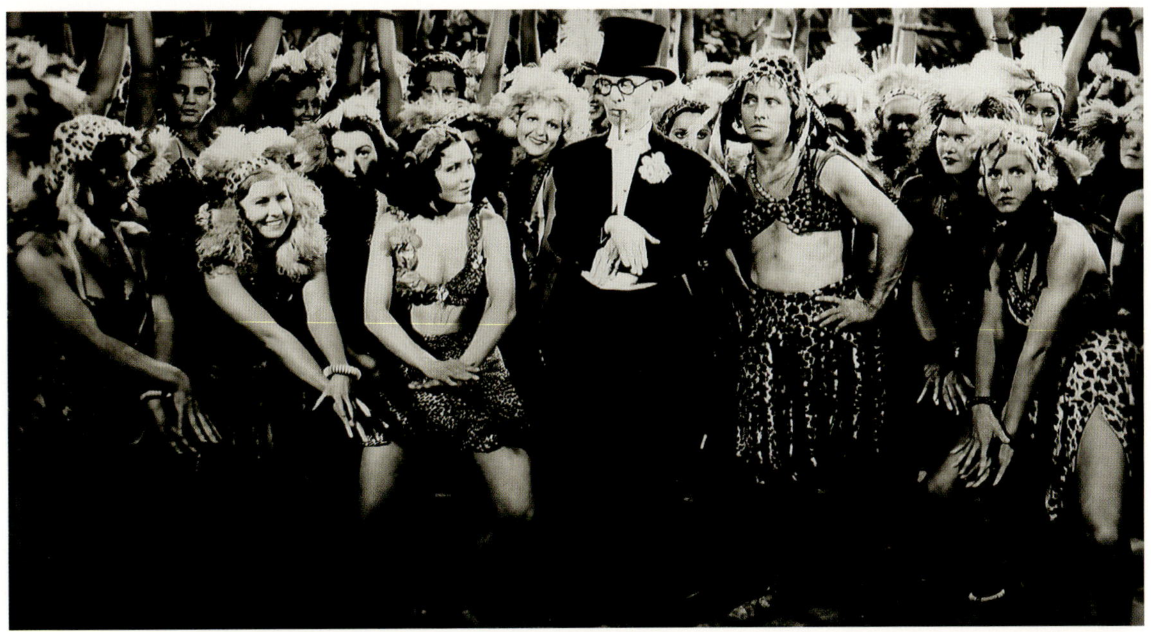

Wheeler and Woolsey meet "the natives."

Is Africa is a testament to how far the loosey-goosey 1930s films could go with blue jokes and just how they could be punished—and rewarded—for satisfying an audience's dirtier impulses.

How is the movie itself? Well, almost the entire first third consists of the duo, Alexander (Woolsey) and Wilbur (Wheeler), looking for a horse to murder so they can feed a group of lions they care for in their New York apartment. (Really.) The men are then met by famed African explorer Mrs. Johnson-Martini (Esther Muir), who has been hired to make a nature documentary but is deathly afraid of animals. Naturally, they all head to Africa to fake their film in an authentic setting.

The second half of *So This Is Africa* is a wild, breathless pastiche of the many inane jungle pictures that flooded cinema in the early 1930s. Wilbur has a run-in with vine-swinger Tarzana (Raquel Torres) who forces him into his tree house for overnight mischief; her gorilla companion, Josephine, instantly takes a liking to Alexander. The men are then captured by a tribe of (all-white) female Amazons who plan on "loving" them to death once the sun sets. To escape their gruesome fate, Wilbur disguises himself as an Amazon and is forced by the tribe to marry Alexander. From here,

"You girls are all alike, that's all you think of. Kissing, hugging, hugging, kissing. It's stuff like this that gives the jungle a bad name!"

—Alexander, confronting the romantically inclined Mrs. Johnson-Martini; for shame!

it looks like things are headed toward an inescapable conclusion that will finally make good on all the duo's homoerotic undertones.

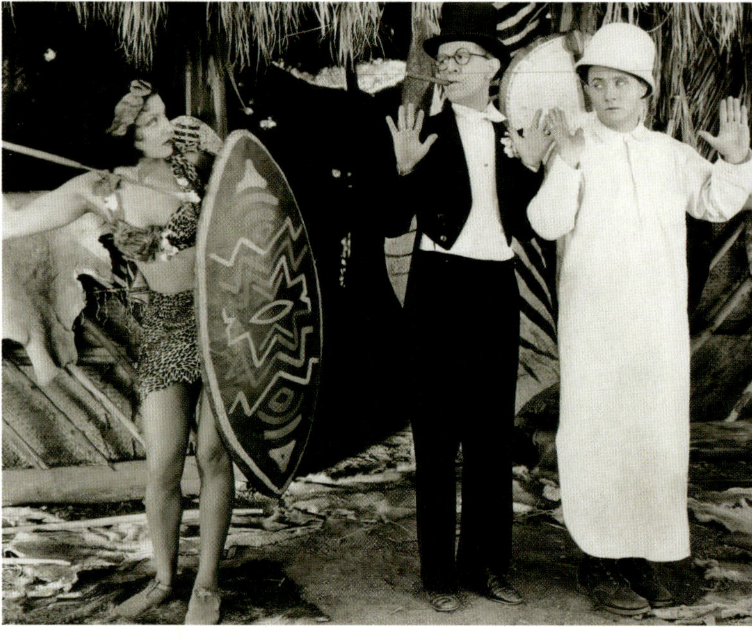

Raquel Torres takes control of a less-than-prepared Wheeler and Woolsey.

So This Is Africa came at a peak during what was known as Hollywood's "pansy craze." While the Production Code specifically forbade portrayals of "sex perversion," effeminate (and implicitly homosexual) men were staples in pre-Code films such as *Call Her Savage* (1932), *Our Betters* (1933), and *International House* (1933). Fox was the most transgressive, even having two men agree, as a way to suspend their romantic rivalry, to "Let's be gay!" in *My Weakness* (1933). The end of *So This Is Africa* reveals just how far gender fluidity played out in Wheeler and Woolsey's pictures, where a person's sex was mostly an act, and a pretty silly one at that.

Because of the cuts inflicted upon it, much of *So This Is Africa* comes with the feeling of delirium. With nearly thirty minutes deleted from the picture, dozens of beats and moments were lost. Since Wheeler and Woolsey were no longer under contract to Columbia, there was no possibility of reshoots; any and all the extant material that could get past the censors made it into the movie.

The SRC reviewed the script, originally titled *Bottoms Up*, cautioning against several jokes but most adamant about one that could be regarded as derogatory toward Italians. They also asked that sequences of the dancing native girls be filmed in distant long shots, and that one scene that involved a theater burning down be handled delicately lest the audience think the theater they were in was likewise on fire. (Noticeably, there are no scenes set in a theater in the print that survives.) James Wingate approved the finished picture and told Harry Cohn that *So This Is Africa* appeared free from censorable elements. He would nearly lose his job in the ensuing debacle.

The fireworks began when the National Board of Review completely disparaged the movie, which "outrages every common standard of decency" and "has absolutely nothing to recommend it." The New York censors were just as blunt, citing obscenity and immorality as the reasons it was initially rejected. Columbia worked closely with the board to get the picture passed but were rebuffed at every turn, with the censor board admitting that they didn't believe the film could be saved, as it was "filled with licentious and lascivious scenes, dances and escapades accompanied with lewd and indecent dialogue." (It eventually passed.) The Pennsylvania censors recorded eight pages of edits—for comparison, most boards deleted less than one page worth of content during this period—and Kansas, the board that most frequently approved movies with no cuts, found two pages' worth of issues.

Harrison's Reports, a trade journal, posted a notice in early March 1933, asking "WHAT ARE YOU GOING TO DO WITH 'SO THIS IS AFRICA'!?" while offering tips to exhibitors in their efforts *not* to show the picture. They summed up their feelings about the movie in the opening: "'So This Is Africa!' is so vulgar, so coarse, so low, that ninety-five per cent of those of you who have your theatre in a small town will not be able to show it. If you should show it, I am sure that it would take months and months before you could offset the ill feeling that will be created among the people of your community. They will class you as coarse and vulgar, as a being without any finer feelings, without any civic pride, without any moral responsibility. They will, in fact, think you a moral leper."

Cohn and Columbia panicked, slashing the film down as best they could. The results are noticeable; for instance, at one point, a plague of locusts swarms around Mrs. Johnson-Martini, Alexander, and Wilbur, and after they pass, both men are nude, the area below their waists obstructed by a now-shaved dog. "Where's Mrs. Martini? Where's Mrs. Martini?!" cries Alexander. The movie cuts here, but the original script revealed her behind a tree, similarly disrobed. Alexander then waggles his eyebrows and smiles, "Mrs. Martini sure knows her locusts."

Apparently, Alexander's contact with Josephine the gorilla also went much further in the original film, as select state censors eliminated scenes of an embrace, Alexander pleading, "Not tonight, Josephine . . . I'm not going upstairs," and Alexander grumbling, "Africa's killing me, boy. It's killing me. I can't stand it," after emerging from behind a tree with her.

The public, catching wind of the scandal, turned the film into a blockbuster. Mordaunt Hall noted in *The New York Times* that "the two comedians will not fail to stir up merriment," while *Variety*, which reviewed both versions—the uncensored prerelease picture and the shortened movie released in 1933—turned its back on the truncated print, calling it ragged and endless. Exhibitors who had been warned to avoid being labeled "moral lepers" leaped at the chance to exploit the picture. One RKO theater in St. Paul even acquired five monkeys from the local zoo and placed them in a cage in their lobby. "Wheeler and Woolsey in 'So This Is Africa' are more fun than a cage full of monkeys!" the sign declared. Bless the poor usher who had to tidy up after that. Another exhibitor in Louisiana showed the movie, even after rumors that an exhibitor in Mississippi had been arrested for screening it, and reported, "I've never heard such roars of laughter."

The full, complete cut of *So This Is Africa* has never been found, and we are stuck with what is left: a bizarre, indecipherable comedy. Even then, the film set a new standard in blue, ribald humor, a dangerous lightning rod for moral crusaders that wouldn't be topped for at least a few more months.

GOLD DIGGERS OF 1933

STARRING
Warren William, Joan Blondell, Aline MacMahon, Ruby Keeler, Dick Powell, Ginger Rogers, and Guy Kibbee

DIRECTED BY
Mervyn LeRoy (Busby Berkeley, musical numbers)

RELEASED BY
Warner Bros., May 1933

The musical, as a genre, was dead by 1931. The entrance of sound in 1927 with *The Jazz Singer* had given viewers a thirst for song-and-dance numbers, and the response was a glut. Costly new equipment coupled with the studios' quickly declining fortunes as the Depression took hold meant that their glitzy, prohibitively expensive musical productions began to crash and burn with regularity.

It wasn't until Warner Bros. decided to actively revive the genre in 1933 with a big, splashy gamble called *42nd Street* that the musical truly tapped into its potential. Utilizing the kaleidoscopic vistas of choreographer Busby Berkeley and the tropes of the backstage musical, the players of the Warner stable crafted an enjoyable concoction.

Put into production before *42nd Street* wrapped, *Gold Diggers of 1933* amplifies that movie's gonzo choreography while adding a layer of social commentary that fit snuggly with Warner's house

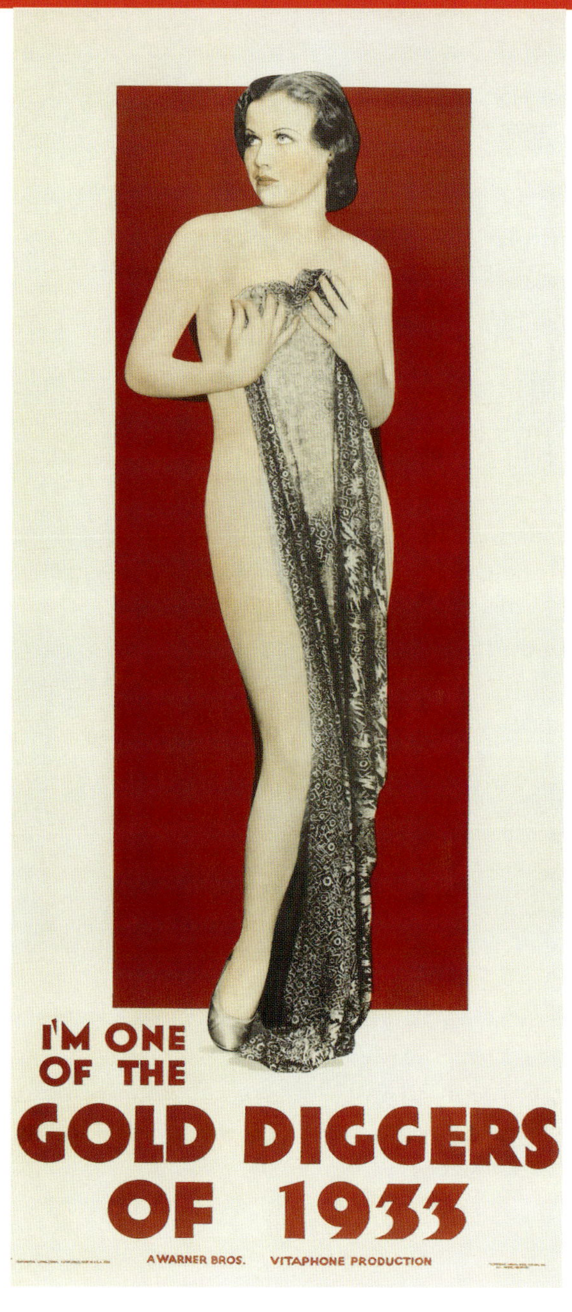

Talk about attention-grabbing!

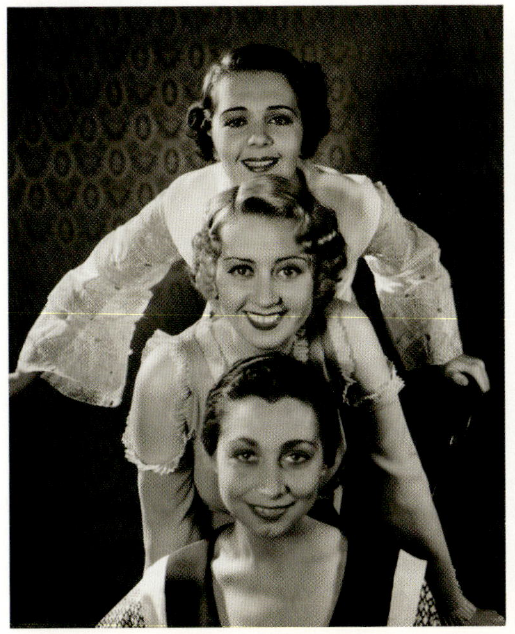

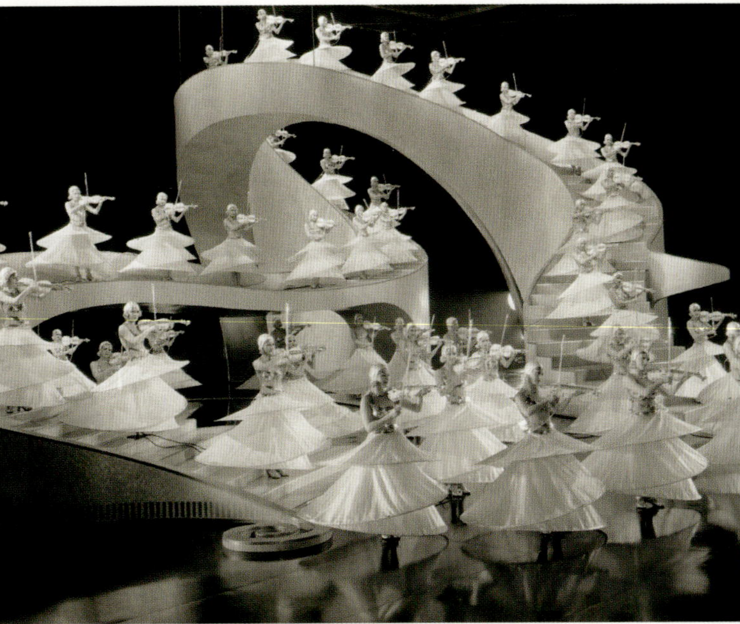

FROM LEFT: Ruby Keeler, Joan Blondell, and Aline MacMahon prepare to laugh and get rich by any means necessary. • "Shadow Waltz" is an instance of the film flittering between elegant, thoughtful, and lowbrow.

style. The result is a film uniquely a combination of glamorous musical, delightful farce, and pleading, yearning wail for the dispossessed in the world. It was so insane it just had to work.

The plot of *Gold Diggers* is a nice mix of glib and stark, a tiptoe between the excess of wealth and the sudden stark realities of the Depression. It opens with a nice twist of irony—the forever remembered "We're in the Money" number kicks things off, only to see the stage be raided by the sheriff's department. The production, it seems, hadn't been paying its bills.

From there we follow four chorus girls, Carol (Joan Blondell), Polly (Ruby Keeler), Trixie (Aline MacMahon), and Fay (Ginger Rogers), who go from stealing milk off the neighbor's porch to in the money overnight thanks to a Broadway smash. But the secret to the play's success is that the songwriter, Brad (Dick Powell), is actually a scion of a wealthy Boston family, and soon his elder brother, J. Lawrence Bradford (Warren William), and family friend Fanuel (Guy Kibbee) are hounding him to withdraw from the play and break up with Polly, who he's fallen for. An identity mix-up leads to Carol taking Bradford for a ride as the gold diggers teach the upper crust a thing or two, and everyone ends up married or on their way to the altar by the closing number.

"The Depression, dearie."

—Fay, summing up everyone's problem with everything

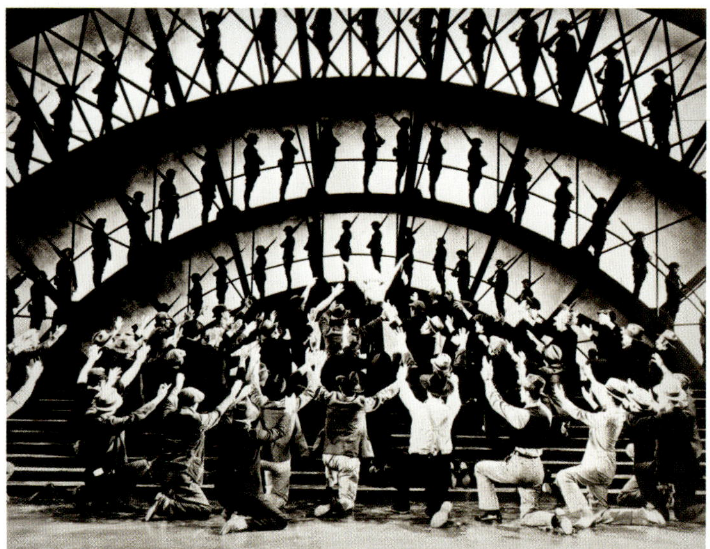

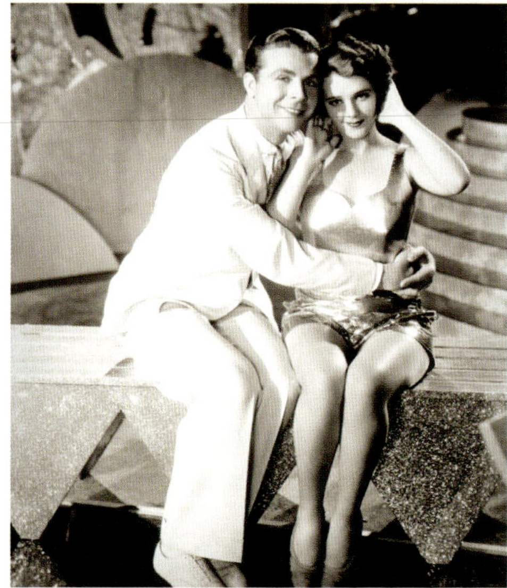

FROM LEFT: Joan Blondell and a massive chorus finish the film with a paean to the Forgotten Man. • Before revealing a sexy new use for the can opener in "Pettin' in the Park," Dick Powell and Ruby Keeler relax.

The cast is a who's who of pre-Code Warner Bros., with Powell and Keeler playing the straight lead couple backed by MacMahon as a chiseler supreme and Blondell as a good girl who doesn't mind teaching a few judgmental people a lesson (or wearing some stunning lingerie). These two ladies match and defeat William and Kibbee as two stuffed shirts. The dialogue is wry and snappy, and by the end of the film, the derisive "your kind" switches from the gold diggers to the rich snobs.

But that description only tells half the story, as it's interspersed with a number of show-stopping Busby Berkeley sequences. "Pettin' in the Park" is a naughty interlude that involves roller skates, nude silhouettes, and tin can brassieres—a peak pre-Code display. The "Shadow Waltz" number veers in the opposite direction—regal and lyrical, it showcases neon-lit violins sweeping in darkness to a dreamy tune. The opening "We're in the Money" is a fever dream of monetary excess with women draped in coins and dollar bill signs. And the film's final number, "Remember My Forgotten Man," is a sobering reminder of the stark realities of 1933.

With a forty-five-day shooting schedule under two directors, Mervyn LeRoy for the comedy and Berkeley for the musical numbers, and a budget of $433,000, the movie earned over $2 million, further cementing the rebirth of musicals in their new-and-improved form. Berkeley, who cameos near the end of the film, was finally given the freedom to create some of his most fabulous tapestries. He fanatically strove to achieve what was in his mind's eye, at one point drilling through the soundstage roof to get the full shot he desired.

The film's musical numbers were shuffled several times, with the script originally ending with a reprise of "We're in the Money." It was production head Darryl F. Zanuck who, after seeing the dramatic effect, moved "Remember My Forgotten Man" to the end and altered the message of the movie. It was no longer a comedy set during the Depression, but a movie about it. The film's final number circles it back to the beginning, a recognition that, while *Gold Diggers* makes us laugh, there is pain beneath it all. It's a movie that knows its audience; its last moments are an olive branch, a rousing cry for help and a nod of understanding.

Riding high on the day's attitudes, *Gold Diggers* lampoons wealth with smiles (on bodies not wearing much else), which censor boards probably did not appreciate. Its marketing often capitalized on this with a massive advertising campaign, which included a beauty contest that took eighteen of the background "gold diggers" and had them compete on the national stage for a movie contract. The film's posters and standees equally fixated on advertising the female body, including a countdown set on top of the silhouette sequence from the "Pettin' in the Park" number.

Gold Diggers was one of the first films made with footage specifically aimed at different territories to help it avoid censorship issues. As we've seen, individual boards cut pictures at their will, costing studios a pretty penny. The SRC was ideally helping to forestall that, and they did to an extent by warning studios what boards were apt to cut, but some studios didn't take their advice, and films were still chopped per local censors' whims. Catering their prints more specifically to guidance on what particular boards regularly removed gave Warner Bros. a little more leeway in tailoring their releases, bearing the brunt of cost up front rather than at the end. (For instance, the Kansas board frequently cut excessive drinking.) Even so, the entire "Pettin' in the Park" number was deleted from the film's 1937 rerelease under the PCA's discretion. Playful sexual banter, nude silhouettes galore, and cheeky tin costumes the men endeavor to break open—it was all a tad too overt for the PCA's liking.

But perhaps the most politically audacious part of the film comes during "Remember My Forgotten Man." The spectacle, with a mournful Blondell backed by a beautifully baritone Etta Moten, crafts a melancholy look at the rise and fall of the American soldier. Inspired by the then-recent Bonus Army march that saw Hoover's government sending in troops to drive out camps of homeless veterans, the number is compact and executed with the usual Berkeley gee-whiz musical touch. As one set of soldiers marches gallantly along a treadmill toward battle, another set marches back home, broken and battered. Berkeley, a veteran of the Great War and a former drill instructor, cast more than 150 extras and created an expressionistic masterpiece. Through stirring visuals and lyrics, "Remember My Forgotten Man" comes closer to capturing the essence of the Depression than any bleak statistic ever could. The song's solemn plea for dignity hit home with audiences who felt its message in their bones—and its impact continues to touch modern viewers who relate to the song's criminalization of the homeless and general air of malaise following disastrous global events.

Warner Bros. took a gamble in mixing harsh reality with glitzy escapism, and it pays off big in *Gold Diggers of 1933*. The movie spawned several post-Code enforcement sequels, including an outing to Paris, that tone down the glamour, commentary, and charm, all too neutered by the Code. This leaves the 1933 entry as an exemplar of its time, an essential piece of cinema—fun, zippy, sobering, and thoughtful. It must be seen to be believed.

HEROES FOR SALE

STARRING
Richard Barthelmess, Loretta Young, Aline MacMahon, and Robert Barrat

DIRECTED BY
William A. Wellman

RELEASED BY
Warner Bros., June 1933

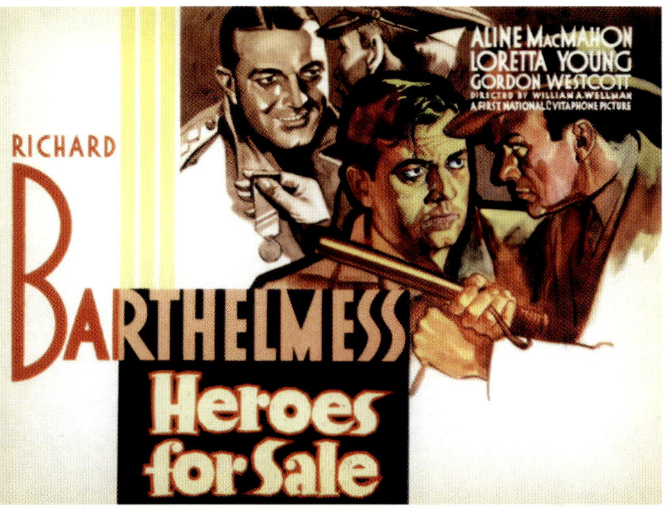

From war hero to forgotten, troubled veteran: That's a descent many men knew all too well.

A film that deftly encompasses the ominous pessimism that defined the era, *Heroes for Sale* touches on subjects ranging from labor unrest to veteran homelessness to drug addiction to communism and handles them with an admirably cold candor. Running barely more than an hour, the movie is one of the most arresting and immediate documents of the Depression.

In *Heroes for Sale*, Great War veteran Tom Holmes (Richard Barthelmess) suffers from a lingering injury that leads to a harrowing morphine addiction. After undergoing treatment, he begins life anew in Chicago. There, he finds cheap lodging run by the charitable Mary Dennis (Aline MacMahon) and becomes smitten with another boarder, laundress Ruth (Loretta Young). There's also a combative communist named Max (Robert Barrat) who hangs around, tinkering with inventions and threatening to overthrow the government as soon as he has time.

Tom lands a job working with Ruth at the laundry, they eventually marry, and he finds himself climbing up the ladder to the executive ranks. When it looks like one of Max's inventions can revolutionize the laundry business, Tom negotiates a deal to use the machines in the factory—as long as no workers are fired. That holds until a penny-pinching corporation swoops in and dismisses the staff, leading to a riot that ends in Tom's arrest for incitement and Ruth's death.

Tom goes to jail for five years, while Mary cares for his young son. Max's invention makes both men rich, but Tom wants none of it, giving the money to Mary to open a soup kitchen. Upon his release, Tom is identified as a possible communist and left wandering the country, passing signs telling jobless men to move on. Nevertheless, the indomitable Tom refuses to give up, citing Roosevelt's inaugural address, asserting that no matter how many hits you take, you can't let it defeat you.

"What do you think of all this? The country can't go on this way. It's the end of America."

"No. It may be the end of us, but it's not the end of America. In a few years, it'll go on bigger and stronger than ever."

—Roger Winston and Tom Holmes, under a bridge, in the rain, expressing a shred of optimism in a dangerous and difficult time

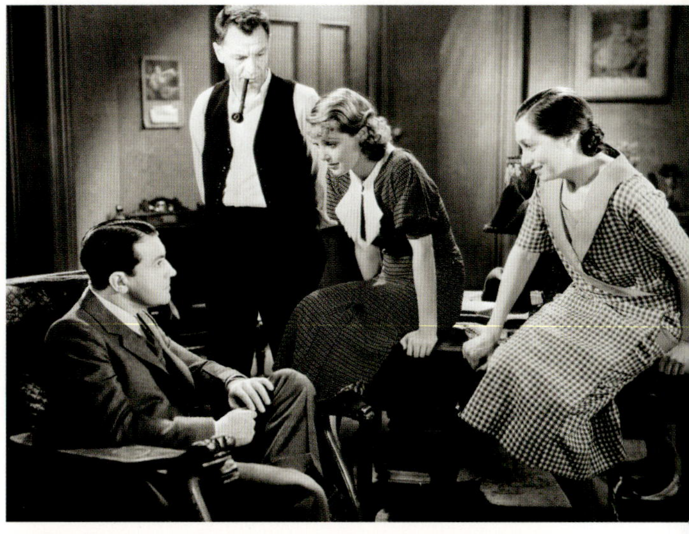

Richard Barthelmess gets glowing attention from Loretta Young and Aline MacMahon.

Confronting a litany of problems that America faced in 1933, *Heroes for Sale* reads less like a cohesive motion picture than a list of symptoms tied to a fatal disease. Described as "journalistic" cinema, the movie rarely builds, but rather jumps from controversy to controversy at a breathless pace.

Warner's cheap and quick style beget tight, compact films, often focusing on presold concepts (*gangsters! crime! lavish musicals!*) that could generate traction at the box office. *Heroes for Sale* is the perfect specimen of this early-1930s style, where plots are cobbled together and invested with an abundance of creative energy for short, staccato bursts of real life, retold with an unwavering and unchecked reverence.

Just as Depression-era audiences could identify with many of the elements and frustrations in *Heroes for Sale*, so can those viewing in the twenty-first century; many of the issues covered in the film regularly remain front-page news, from the tragic rise of drug addiction to antidemocratic takes on government to the skyrocketing fear that machines, via artificial intelligence, will supplant humans in the workplace. When the leader of an angry mob shrieks, "The machines did it! The machines ruined us!" that same agitation and terror manifests mightily a century later. Not to mention, the general mood of discontent that permeates *Heroes for Sale*—the characters facing incredible hardship following a devastating World War and Depression—are emblematic of the fear, confusion, and lack of confidence so many assert in the early-twenty-first century in a world turned upside down by a global recession and pandemic.

The concept, suggested by Warner's production head, Darryl F. Zanuck, originally stretched the story from World War I to the march of the Bonus Army in July 1932. Over forty thousand people participated in the march, almost half of them WWI vets in need, gathering in Washington, DC, to protest unpaid wages from Congress. Herbert Hoover instead ordered the army to clear the protesters out. While the Bonus Army sequences were jettisoned to better align the movie with the

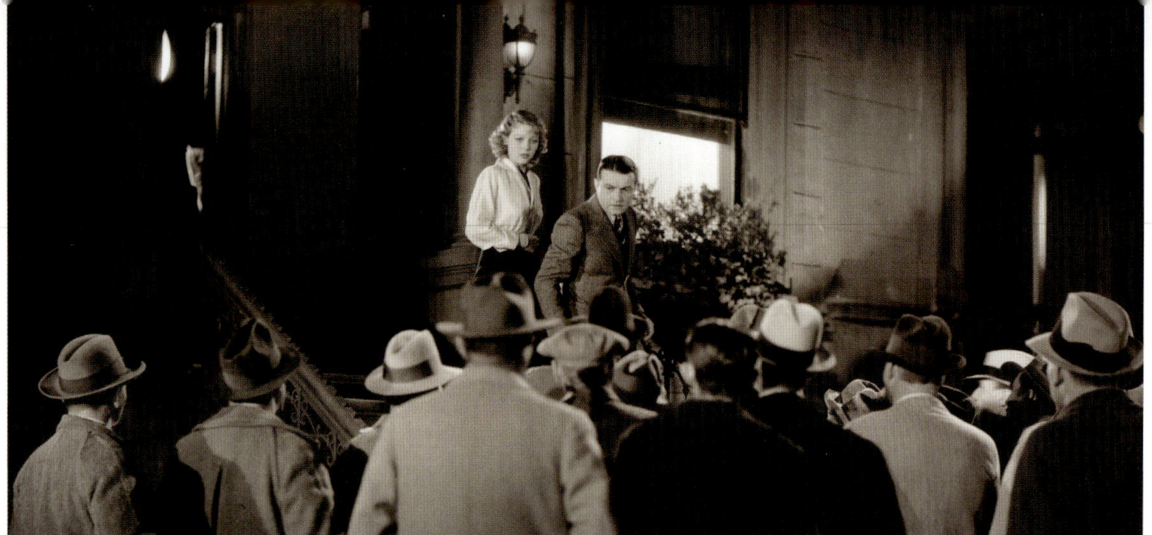

Richard Barthelmess confronts the crowd of discontented workers he both created and whom will soon destroy his life.

incoming Roosevelt administration, the influence remains. (Speaking of alignment, Zanuck had director William A. Wellman shoot an alternate finale where Tom reads Roosevelt's full inaugural address from a discarded newspaper.)

Originally titled *The Forgotten Man* and then *Breadline, Heroes for Sale* began filming the day after a federally mandated bank holiday shuttered many of the nation's banks in March 1933 to help stave off further runs and closures. The movie was shot in twenty-three days, and the resulting film is riveting, an undigested and raw revue of fifteen years of American exceptionalism.

Everything in *Heroes for Sale* is set against Tom. The army, which leaves you for dead. The government, which beats you senseless and runs you out of town. The people, who turn against you and let you rot. While there are a lot of shocking moments, the film's emphatic depiction of morphine addiction remains most harrowing. Tom's struggles with drugs are shown vividly—it's "like a million ants eating me alive," he cries—and felt keenly.

While it's not hard to read the movie as a document of a society in which all good has fled, *Heroes for Sale* also makes many cogent points about how money corrupts the best of intentions. Tom is a hero because he rejects money that he finds unseemly, while Max is a buffoon for taking it. One of the better-remembered exchanges from the film is when Tom, in prison, glares at Max, who is dressed to the nines for a visit. "You used to hate the capitalists," he says with a nod. Max puffs up and replies, "Naturally. That was before I had money."

From the script phase, *Heroes for Sale* set off alarms at the SRC. One scene in particular, where Tom visits a drug dealer, had to be altered. Further suggested changes relayed to Zanuck included eliminating shots of hypodermic needles, excising views of a man drawing a nude woman, and replacing all references to communists and capitalists with "radicals" and "employers." Besides avoiding showing a needle, none of these other suggestions were heeded.

After viewing the film, the SRC was complimentary but concerned about another element: the way the police were portrayed. They suggested Zanuck trim the scenes where police are shown as "overly officious and unfair in carrying out their duties." Throughout the picture, the cops are the brutal enforcers of state and corporate violence, and sequences of this would be eliminated in New York.

For the most part, *Heroes for Sale* fared quite well with local censor boards. The picture was approved in several areas with zero cuts, while select pieces of dialogue such as, "When you get to be my age, you'll have a bomb in every pocket!" and reference to war heroism as "a couple of medals and a lousy ribbon" were popular deletions in Pennsylvania and Ontario. Quebec's board was one of the most brutal, removing mentions of morphine, communism, and the entire riot. In spite of these difficulties, the film was granted reissue in 1936 by Joseph Breen—no cuts needed.

Heroes for Sale would be Zanuck's last film as the supervisor at Warner Bros. Having built the studio style and ethos since the 1920s, his conflicts with Jack Warner and their decisions on implementing employee pay cuts reminded him just how precarious his own position was.

As a picture that fully wears its insecurities on its sleeve, *Heroes for Sale* may be one of the purest of Warner products from the era, relentlessly grappling with hard-hitting, downbeat issues, even if the movie dares to end on an optimistic note.

Richard Barthelmess

Richard Barthelmess always looks like he's ready to take a punch, and he found no better vehicle for his quiet, intense charm than *Heroes for Sale*. A longtime screen veteran by 1933, Barthelmess had been one of D. W. Griffith's favorite actors, appearing in silent epics such as *Broken Blossoms* (1919) and *Way Down East* (1920). Barthelmess's prestige gave him more command over his Warner Bros. projects than many of his costars, and the material he selected was always more controversial and smarter than the average studio output at the time. This included movies like *The Last Flight* (1931), where he played a broken World War I aviator aimlessly drinking through Europe, and *Massacre* (1934), where he portrayed a Native American fighting against government corruption.

Barthelmess's career as a leading man dissipated as Paul Muni's star ascended and the studio stopped making the kind of movies that Barthelmess excelled in; he flexed his talent best playing characters who were slowly wound up to the point of explosion, often in fury at unjust decisions or cruel personages. Luckily, he invested wisely and retired in 1942, making one of his last appearances as the old pro flyer in Howard Hawks's *Only Angels Have Wings* (1939).

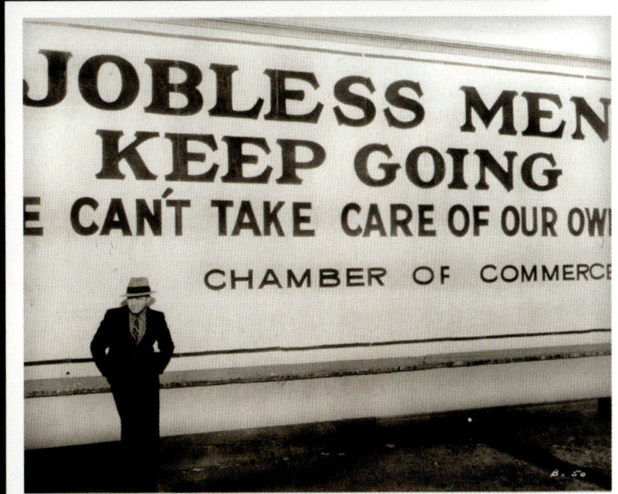

Richard Barthelmess poses in front of a prop sign—but one not uncommon to see around the country.

BABY FACE

STARRING
Barbara Stanwyck, George Brent, Theresa Harris, and Donald Cook

DIRECTED BY
Alfred E. Green

RELEASED BY
Warner Bros., July 1933

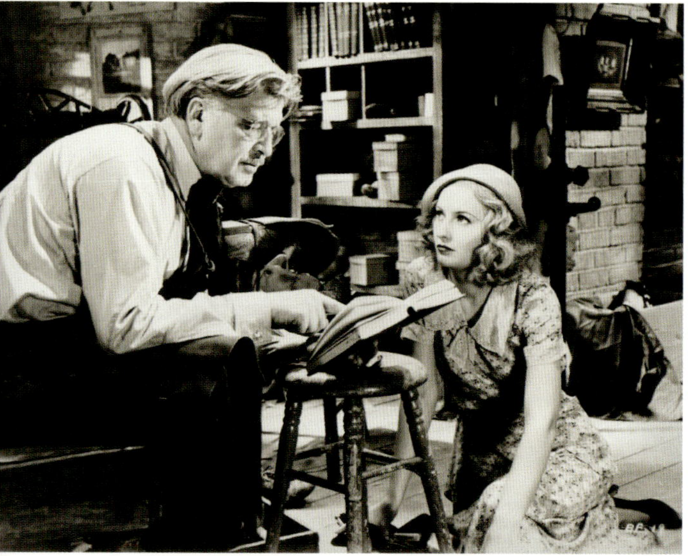

Barbara Stanwyck learns that a little knowledge is a dangerous thing in *Baby Face*.

Boasting a plot revolving around a woman who uses her body and her wiles to climb the corporate ladder, *Baby Face* ranks among the most scandalous of the pre-Code period—and indeed, it still shocks in the twenty-first century. But that's topped by a fact even more fascinating, especially for pre-Code fans: Two versions of *Baby Face* survive today, the film released in 1933 and available for decades thereafter, and an uncensored prerelease version uncovered at the Library of Congress in 2004.

A mere five minutes separates the two versions. Doesn't sound like much, right? It may not, but the ensuing censorship struggles and alterations made for release offer a peek into the inner workings of the pre-Code era. So, in this chapter we're going to shake things up and examine the main modifications between the two surviving versions of *Baby Face*. Think of it as a pre-Code history lesson come to life, an opportunity to survey the footage deemed inappropriate and what made the cut, which you can evaluate visually, too, as both versions are available on DVD. Do the changes really make that much of a difference? Let's see just how immoral things get.

In *Baby Face*, Lily (Barbara Stanwyck) toils away in a dirty speakeasy owned by her father, Nick (Robert Barrat), who pimps her out to customers. Following his death, a kindly cobbler, Cragg (Alphonse Ethier) encourages Lily to get the hell out of Dodge and to leverage her sexuality to get what she wants. Read: wealth and luxury.

With her Black companion Chico (Theresa Harris) in tow, the duo head to the big city, where Lily begins her ascent up the societal ranks by sleeping with everyone and anyone who will help her quest. But she also finds herself in a bit of a scandal prompted by the murder-suicide of a bank's vice president and president, both of whom she played.

We always think that Nat Pendleton looks like a centaur with this staging. And we don't think that's totally on us.

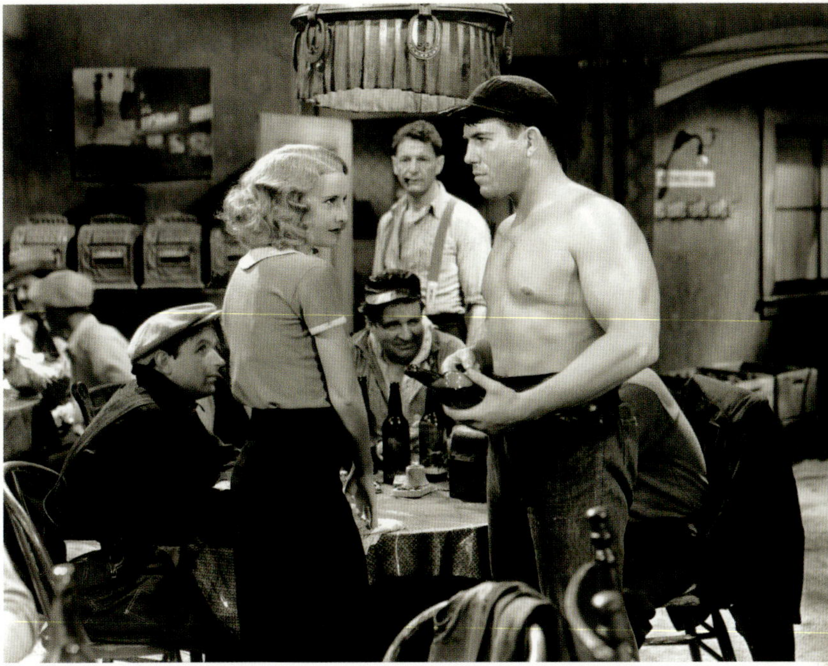

Lily assumes the bank will throw money at her so she won't publicly share the lurid story, but the organization's new president, Trenholm (George Brent), doesn't fall for her innocent victim act. Instead, he transfers her to their Paris office where she can earn an honest living, but there's just one complication: They fall for each other. When Trenholm is indicted for his board's theft of bank assets and pleads with Lily to give up her wealth to save him, she hesitates—will love win out?

Baby Face set out to push the envelope. In one outline, screenwriters Gene Markey and Kathryn Scola noted that the director should "go as far . . . as the censors will allow," and in her story notes, Stanwyck personally proposed that Lily's father force her to sleep with his patrons, among other suggestions that raised red flags. Consequently, the SRC advised Darryl F. Zanuck to limit the sex element and emphasize that Lily's success will not bring her happiness.

Apparently, Warner Bros. failed on that front, because the film was submitted to the New York censor board and rejected on the grounds that it was "'IMMORAL' & 'WILL TEND TO CORRUPT MORALS.'" The SRC advised the studio not to resubmit until changes were made; one particularly glaring issue was that neither Lily's man-eating methods nor her lavish profiteering are ever condemned.

When it came to alterations, initially the SRC trained their focus on Cragg and his influence upon Lily. They suggested Warner Bros. insert a scene where Cragg visits Lily in wealth in New York, telling her, "I know you wouldn't do anything wrong. You're too good a girl . . . Some other girls, with all

"Yeah, I'm a tramp, and who's to blame? My father. A swell start you gave me. Ever since I was fourteen, what's it been? Nothing but men! Dirty rotten men! And you're lower than any of them. I'll hate you as long as I live!"

—Lily, commenting on her father's parenting with a hint of grievance

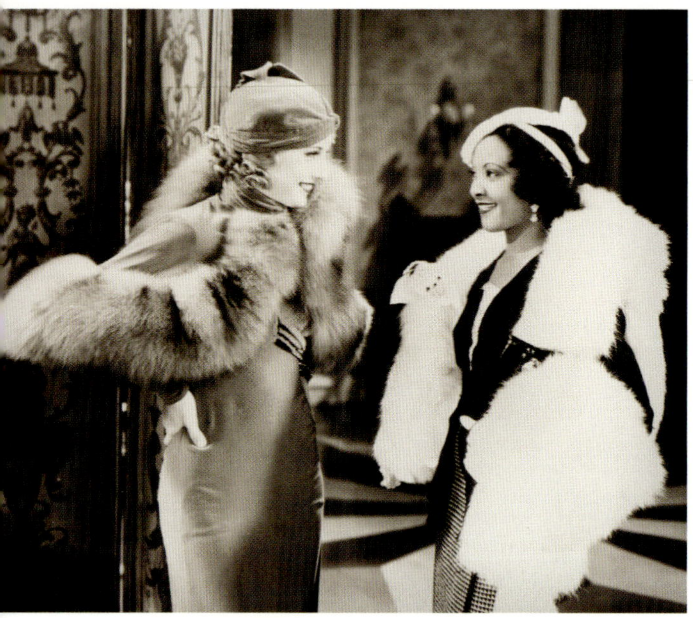

Barbara Stanwyck started from the bottom and now she's here—and of course she's bringing Theresa Harris with her. (Though, because it was the 1930s, Harris played her maid, one who also donned furs on her day off.)

this success and glamour, might lose their heads and do things they'd be sorry for later. But not my Lilly [*sic*]." The SRC also penned a letter from Trenholm to the bank board at the end, detailing how Cragg took him and Lily in and they are getting to the "business of raising good babies." Perhaps this went a bit too far for the studio; they heeded neither suggestion, but others they did take.

Three sequences underwent drastic modification in order for *Baby Face* to pass state censor boards. The first concerned Cragg's speech utilizing Nietzsche to counsel Lily to exploit herself, pointing the film's moral compass just past wicked early on. Cragg's tough-love advice could sound paternal, but it's still pretty damning; sure, he doesn't sell Lily's body like her father, but he encourages her to do the same—this time for herself. Accordingly, the SRC asked Warner Bros. to insert dialogue to turn Cragg's guidance into a stern moral warning, penned by none other than the crusading Joseph Breen. While many lines and shots remain the same in both cuts, the new dialogue brazenly injects a virtuous tone.

The scene directly following, in which Lily and Chico hop a train to New York, also faced the chopping block. In the prerelease print, a brakeman threatens to kick the duo off, but Lily instantly commences her seduction; the emphasis on her beckoning glances, the brakeman's gloves dropping to the floor, and Chico's knowing smirk encourage the audience to fill in the tantalizing blanks. In the theatrical release, this conquest completely vanishes.

The final major amendment involved the ending. The scripted finale found Trenholm dead and Lily free to enjoy her wealth, but that simply would not fly. The version that first went before the cameras takes place in an ambulance, where Lily's world no longer revolves around money. The theatrical cut, though, brought things full circle: After the ambulance, the bank's board of directors meets and reports that Lily and Trenholm are broke and "working out their happiness together" as the scene cuts to a long shot of a steel town. Lily may be back where she started, but she's there as an honest, upright citizen—and married, to boot.

Though *Baby Face* was technically admissible under the Code, Breen warned the studio that the movie's theme still "suggests the kind, or type, of picture which ought not to be encouraged." To Warner's relief, after several months and countless edits, *Baby Face* was formally approved by New York censors. The film still came under fire, with

CHANGES IN DIALOGUE AND CUTS ON "BABY FACE"

OLD DIALOGUE AND SCENES — REEL ONE	ELIMINATIONS
How's things, baby? Let's me and you take a little walk over by the quarry, huh?	Let's me and you take a little walk over by the quarry, huh?
It's by Neitzche. The greatest philosopher of all time.	It's by Neitzche. etc. Entirely out.
Yeh. Well, I never did get much good out of books.	Entirely out.
Pan Shot of Lilly - starting with her feet and ending on her face.	Substituted closeup of Lilly's face
Politician whispers to Lilly's father and gives him money.	Cut just as politician leans toward father. No money changes hands.
Yeh, you're exclusive. You are. The sweetheart of the night shift. Come on. You're wasting my time. Everybody knows about you.	Eliminated the words"night shift" by cutting to father waiting outside
Politician follows Lilly into kitchen and puts arms around her. She hits him with a beer bottle.	Entirely out.
REEL TWO	
Yeah? I'm a tramp. And who's to blame? My father. A swell start you gave me. Eversince I was fourteen, what's it been? Nothing but men, dirty, rotten men. And you're lower than any of them. I'll hate you as long as I live.	Eliminate "ever since I was fourteen"
More chance than men. A woman, young beautiful, like you, can get anything she wants in the world. Because you have power over men. But you must use men, not let them use you. You must be a master, not a slave. Look. Here. Nietzsche says: "All life no matter how we idealize it is nothing more nor less than exploitation." That's what I'm telling you. Exploit yourself. Go to some big city where you will find opportunities. Use men! Be strong! Defiant! Use men to get the things you want --	Substituted More chance than men. A woman, beautiful like you, can get anything she wants in the world. But there is the right and wrong way -- remember the price of the wrong way is too great. Go to some big city where you will find opportunities. Don't let people mislead you, you must be a master -- not a slave. Keep clean, be strong, defiant, and you will be a success -------

A side-by-side comparison of some of the cuts made to the unreleased version of *Baby Face* to finally pass the New York censor board.

the Ohio, Virginia, and British Columbia boards barring the movie and the Catholic Legion of Decency placing the film on its banned list in 1934.

From script to release, the censorship battle over *Baby Face* demonstrates how the tides were turning. The studios, perhaps more than ever, were willing to push their luck with racy films during some of the Depression's darkest days, but censor boards and religious groups were pushing back. Even the seemingly miniscule thematic adjustments the studio made in *Baby Face* exhibit how the industry was dealing with the strain, doing the bare minimum to get films past important boards so they didn't lose money in key areas, like New York.

Baby Face received mixed reviews, with most critiques spotlighting how shocking the picture was. *Liberty Magazine* enthusiastically declared: "Three cheers for Sin! If you don't think it pays, get a load of Barbara Stanwyck as she sins her way to the top floor of Manhattan's swellest bank." Others echoed what the censors dreaded, that the movie's immorality would inspire imitators, as Mae Tinee reported in the *Chicago Daily Tribune*: "Barbara Stanwyck handles her role of perpetual prostitute in a manner so astute and workmanlike as to make the picture a positive menace to silly or unreasoning young girls . . . If, after all these years, producers are to make pictures like 'Baby Face' because pictures like 'Baby Face' are what the public demands, then I throw up my hands. [Now I suppose you'll all go and take a look at the film and thus encourage the industry to turn out some more like it]."

Though the censored cut of *Baby Face* attempts to inject a level of morality into the proceedings, it doesn't stand a chance against Lily's brazen methods; an upstanding ending can't erase seventy minutes of unscrupulous actions, especially ones that result in luxury. In retaining its sin and sizzle despite mandated cuts, *Baby Face* narrowly won this battle, but the industry would ultimately lose the war in just a year's time.

THE EMPEROR JONES

STARRING
Paul Robeson, Dudley Digges, and Fredi Washington

DIRECTED BY
Dudley Murphy and William C. de Mille

RELEASED BY
United Artists, September 1933

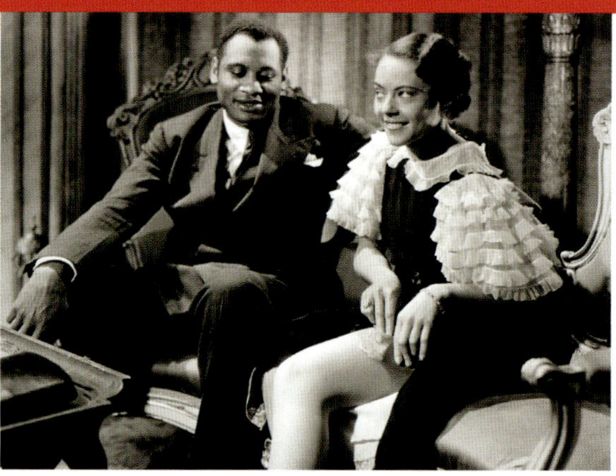

Paul Robeson takes a peek at Fredi Washington's makeup.

Discussions of race and racism in the pre-Code period invariably must note the lack of films headed by non-white actors and actresses. While comics performing or appearing briefly in blackface was prevalent at this time—Eddie Cantor and Al Jolson would make careers out of these portrayals—Hollywood had a more difficult time crafting works for Black audiences. Part of this was simple profit-driven capitalism: Positive portrayals of Black characters imperiled box office returns in Southern states, whose theater chains clamped down on any probing of racial relations. While some movies, like *Safe in Hell* or *Baby Face*, pushed boundaries by including Black characters as friends of the leads, they rarely had agency or their own agenda. This had to change.

Black audiences in all parts of the country were still segregated from their white peers. Similarly, Hollywood left the production of movies for Black viewers to a cadre of independent filmmakers who dealt with smaller budgets and less corporate oversight. While a number of pre-Code films would clumsily attempt commentaries on race relations, most were made to play strictly to a white audience and their rampant biases.

"Talk polite, white man. Talk polite. Do you hear me? I'm boss here now."

—Jones, in a rare 1930s racial role reversal with Smithers

The Emperor Jones is an intriguing exception, a movie boasting a commanding Black lead based on a hit Broadway show—directed by two white men. Produced independently in New York, the picture was shot in ten days and showcased one of the first leading roles for a Black actor in a widely distributed American movie. Much like the play, though, the film was extremely controversial.

In *The Emperor Jones*, Brutus Jones (Paul Robeson) is a self-absorbed Black man on the cusp of "making good" and escaping his small-town life in Georgia. Though he promises to be true to his wife, the lure and excitement of Jazz Age Harlem overcomes his minimal resistance, and he makes moves on Undine (Fredi Washington), the girlfriend of his best pal Jeff (Frank H. Wilson).

Jeff learns of Jones's fling, they fight, and Jones kills Jeff in self-defense. Jones is sentenced to hard labor, and after being ordered to beat a helpless prisoner, he kills his guard and escapes on a steamer, jumping ship at an obscure, former colonial island to avoid arrest.

Once there, Jones takes up with a white trader named Smithers (Dudley Digges) whose stock in trade is exploiting the island's backward government. Sensing an opportunity, Jones leverages his wits and the native population's archaic fears to declare himself emperor. His multiyear reign is filled with violence and cruelty, eventually prompting a revolution. As Jones flees through the jungle, he battles visions of his past sins, slowly losing his mind along the way.

Eugene O'Neill found his first major success when *The Emperor Jones* opened on Broadway in 1920. The story was inspired by two Haitian figures, Henri Christophe and Jean Vilbrun Guillaume Sam. The former was born into slavery and became King Henry of Haiti in 1811, dying by suicide with a silver bullet in 1820. The latter, who served as Haiti's president for four months in 1915, ordered the execution of 167 political prisoners, a move that led to his death by Haitian rebels.

Charles S. Gilpin portrayed the lead onstage to great acclaim, but he and O'Neill battled over the play's language. O'Neill's work was generously peppered with the use of a derogatory term that Gilpin altered to "negro" in his performances. Their falling-out led to the title role being recast in 1925 with football star and singer Paul Robeson in the lead and the slurs intact.

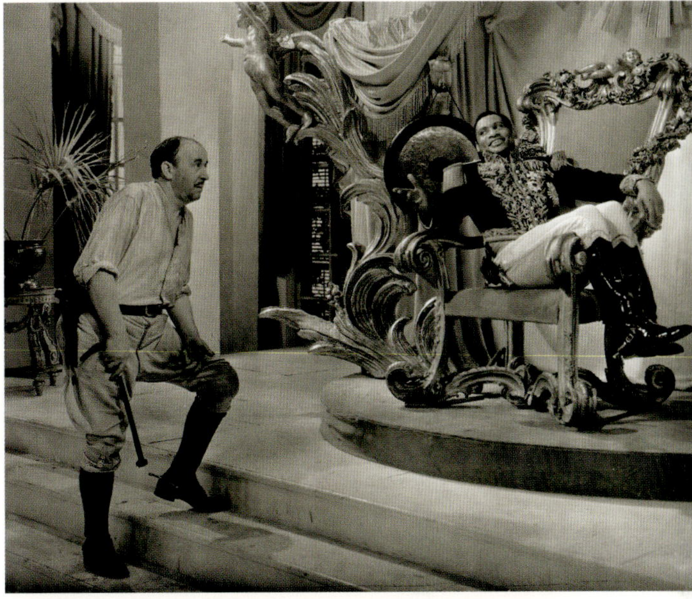

Dudley Digges makes his best appeal to Paul Robeson.

Director Dudley Murphy, known for his stylish, avant-garde independent films, pursued O'Neill for nearly a decade to adapt *The Emperor Jones*. Displeased with his limited experience in Hollywood, Murphy perceived himself as an outsider, which drew him to the story. He also helmed two shorts highlighting Black musicians, 1929's *Black and Tan* and *St. Louis Blues*. As other white artists did, Murphy's films "often conflated Blacks with performance and spectacle," Murphy's biographer Susan Delson wrote. He "seized upon a highly stylized view of Black culture" in his movies, as opposed to an aim of uplifting the Black community. With this, Murphy's own biases reinforced stereotypes of Black stories as exotic, relegating them to the "other."

O'Neill agreed to let Murphy adapt the play, as long as Robeson remained the lead and the actor's name appeared above the credits. Though

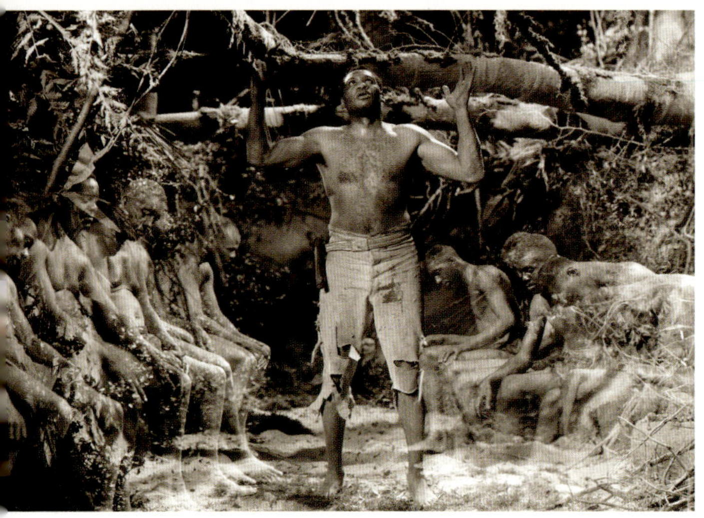

Paul Robeson slowly loses his mind in the film's haunting finale.

production was initially planned for Haiti, the location ultimately moved to New York, partly because Robeson had it forbidden in his contract for filming to take place below the Mason-Dixon line. Shooting in New York also allowed Murphy to exploit the thriving entertainment scene of Harlem; real Cotton Club dancers appear during the cabaret sequence, as well as a very young Harold Nicholas of the Nicholas Brothers fame.

Jones's egotism, from his predilection for mirrors to his disdain for his fellow Black people, makes him ripe for a downfall. The character was written as a self-reflexive interrogation of white capitalism. As Jones attempts to climb the ladder of success, armed only with his wits and fortune, he finds his way blocked by the narrow role society lets him and men of his race hold.

Unsurprisingly, for as controversial as *The Emperor Jones* had been onstage, contention surrounded the film version—in more ways than one. While the picture's PCA file is curiously free from SRC suggestions, save for commentary on whether uses of the words *Lord* and *God* were objectionable, it's been reported that the SRC indeed made many recommendations, the most startling having to do with Fredi Washington. A light-skinned Black actress, Washington was subjected to reshooting her scenes in blackface, as the SRC apparently was worried that ignorant audiences would view scenes between her and Robeson as miscegenation.

The film's most crucial sequence, and the only one where Jones acts outside of his own self-interests, comes when he kills the chain gang guard by bludgeoning him with a shovel. Censors removed the moment of impact from the picture, leaving an awkward cut to cover that precise instant before Jones flees.

The movie's finale was edited as well. In the original play and as initially filmed, one hallucination that Jones suffers was a visage of him on a slave ship being sold at auction. This imagery, which would better link up to his monologue on the history of the slave trade and its power over his existence, was excised for being too vivid.

One scene that remained despite protests from the SRC was when Smithers is commanded to light a cigarette for the emperor; the moment of racial role reversal caused anxiety, but the filmmakers felt it was important to demonstrate Jones's power. (Massachusetts excised this scene—in Sunday prints only, as was the norm for this state.)

It's possible that these initial changes relieved most of the movie's censorable elements—or perhaps state censors chose not to give this film as much thought—as local boards deleted very little from the picture. "Dancers wriggling and contorting their bodies" and money exchanges ("Here's forty dollars and goodbye") proved among the

Paul Robeson captures Jones's petulant behavior, hidden behind his fancy airs.

most popular targets when *The Emperor Jones* was sent to censor boards for review.

But the most controversial aspect of *The Emperor Jones* remained its language; this is one element that divided Black audiences' response to the film. While the picture was simply passed over by white theater owners in Southern states, United Artists removed each and every use of the N-word, as originally written for the play, for Black theaters. Despite a smaller release, *The Emperor Jones* performed well in select markets, including New York, though overall, it wasn't the overwhelming triumph the filmmakers hoped for.

Like the play, the adaptation proved divisive—and it does to this day. Many praised Robeson's performance and the opportunity for a Black man to play a lead role, while others decried the racist tropes the story reinforced (and several, still, agreed on both points). In 1936, the Universal Negro Improvement Association condemned the movie as "an international conspiracy to disparage and crush the aspirations of Negroes toward higher culture and civilization and to impress upon them their inferiority."

Despite its contentious elements, *The Emperor Jones* stands as a unique, remarkable, albeit controversial, achievement to this day. The picture is at once a dissection of capitalism, colonialism, and the limited opportunities granted to Black people, while also the product of the views of its white filmmakers and writers. Though *The Emperor Jones* would be the last widely distributed American film featuring a Black leading man for nearly two decades, it remains a fascinating relic still worthy of modern examination.

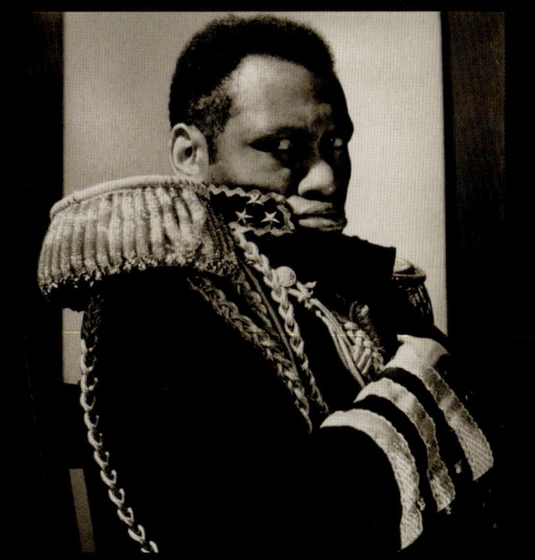

Paul Robeson

Paul Robeson, whose father escaped slavery, was born in 1898. He was a tireless worker, earning valedictorian honors in high school and at Rutgers University. He played football, joined the debate team, and sang to earn money. Robeson eventually graduated from Columbia Law School but found racism in the legal field too oppressive. He instead went into acting, landing a lead part in Eugene O'Neill's 1924 miscegenation drama *All God's Chillun Got Wings*. The controversy around that play delayed its premiere, giving Robeson time to star in the revived *The Emperor Jones*, for which he received rave reviews. In 1925, he made his film debut in Oscar Micheaux's silent drama *Body and Soul*. As the decade rolled on, Robeson would make iconic appearances on the London stage in *Show Boat* (1928) and *Othello* (1930). By the early 1930s, he was one of the most popular and respected Black artists the country had ever produced.

ANN VICKERS

STARRING
Irene Dunne, Walter Huston, Bruce Cabot, and Edna May Oliver

DIRECTED BY
John Cromwell

RELEASED BY
RKO, September 1933

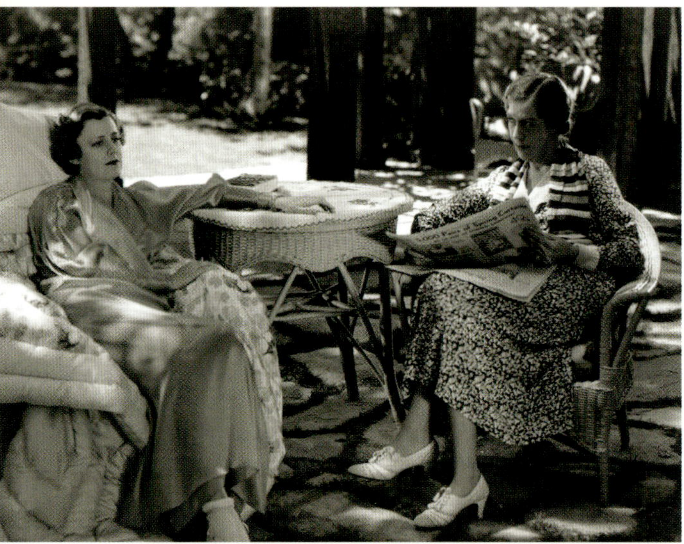

Edna May Oliver provides respite to Irene Dunne in the aftermath of her abortion.

"Problems continue to present themselves with amazing frequency," the SRC reported when the script for *Ann Vickers* landed on their desks. While the SRC heard cries from a growing number of groups bent on a moral makeover of the movies, Hollywood did its best to ignore the noise and resumed churning out the sex and sin with alarming frequency. But recent pictures that pushed the boundaries, such as *Baby Face* and *The Story of Temple Drake*—both of which the SRC were juggling around the same time as *Ann Vickers*—were starting to catch up with the studios.

Within the first ten minutes of *Ann Vickers*, the title's namesake (Irene Dunne) receives a marriage proposal from Captain Lafayette Resnick (Bruce Cabot). She's just started her career, so Ann turns him down. But soon she's pregnant with his child, and though he's got one foot out the door, he dutifully extends the marriage offer again. Ann rejects that one, too, and her confidant, Malvina (Edna May Oliver), whisks Ann away to Havana to get an abortion.

Ann soon secures a job as a sociologist in a prison, but her attempts to mitigate the harsh environment with humane methods get her fired. Ann's fortunes turn when her book exposing penal brutality earns her an honorary doctorate and a prison reform position. However, it's not long before she falls in love with married Judge Bernard "Barney" Dolphin (Walter Huston), who is under investigation for accepting stock tips. Their secret relationship results in a baby boy. Barney soon gets sent to prison, and because she stands by him, Ann is forced to resign from her job, resorting to writing with the hope that she and Barney will eventually be reunited and become a family.

Ann Vickers packs a hell of a lot of drama into seventy-six minutes. After reading an early script, the SRC's Joseph Breen termed Ann's trajectory "progressive prostitution" and decried

"But I found a new, modern virtue to name my daughter. Pride. The pride of life. Pride of love. Pride of work. Pride of being a woman. Those will be her virtues. Pride Vickers. She's become so real. If only she hadn't . . . died. Oh, Malvina. I wish I had her. I wish I had her."

—Ann Vickers, grappling with a host of emotions after terminating her pregnancy

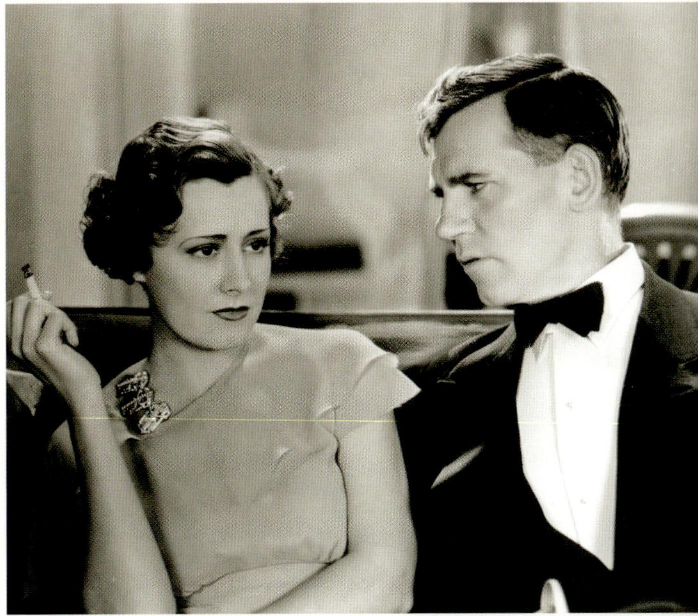

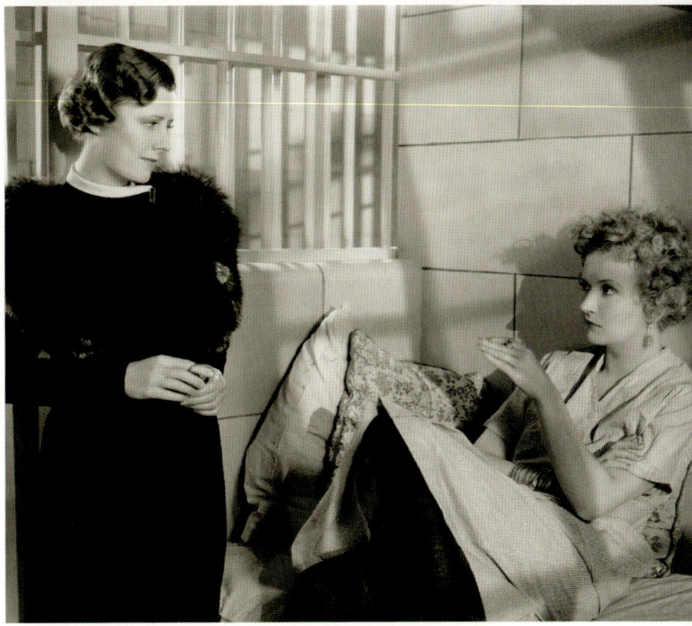

FROM TOP: Irene Dunne finally finds happiness with the judge, Walter Huston . . . who happens to be married and headed to trial himself. • Irene Dunne vows to help a female inmate get off the "snow," and we wonder how many viewers thought that was winter-related.

RKO's attempt to drum up sympathy for the character. In terms of sympathy, Breen was not wrong. In fact, both Ann and Barney, despite their missteps, are presented as well-intentioned, *good* people. Of course, the irony here is that their respective jobs find them imposing upstanding morals upon the public, while controversial personal choices deemed ethically improper destroy their private lives.

Ann Vickers quickly turned out to be one of the SRC's largest headaches. Breen provided incredibly harsh feedback, presaging the iron fist he would rule with as head of the PCA the next summer: "Not in years have I read anything quite so vulgarily [*sic*] offensive. The whole thing is so definitely out of line that I respectfully suggest that you lose no time in letting the R.K.O. people know that this script simply *will not do* and must be radically changed if its production is to be carried through. I see great trouble, both for the industry and the company, if this script, based upon a current best seller *which is known to be vile and offensive,* is not checked at once."

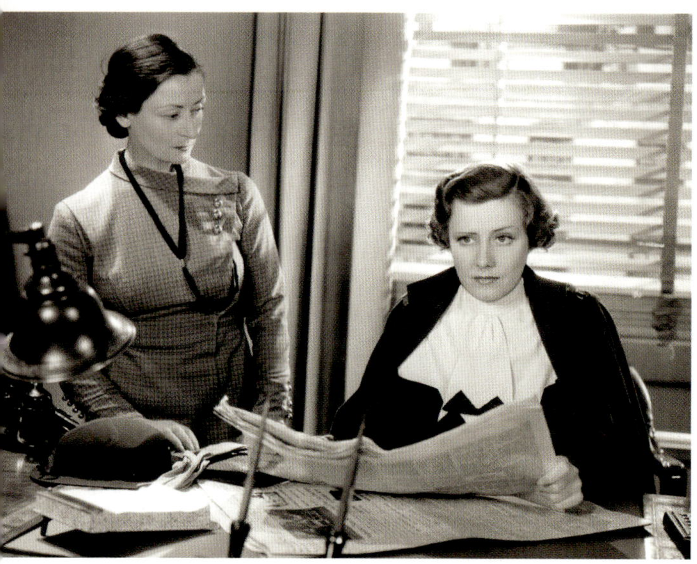

Social worker turned prison reformer Irene Dunne will get the job done come hell or high water.

RKO proved hard to budge, stating they'd "rather not make the picture" than stray from the Sinclair Lewis source novel. The SRC held fast, too, though. James Wingate asserted that Ann required "an honest statement of remorse for having broken the laws of God and man in this respect," as they used adultery "as a justifiable means out of an impasse."

Though they put up a good fight, in the end RKO capitulated on several points, and the SRC eventually deemed *Ann Vickers* satisfactory under the Code. However, in both 1935 and 1937, Breen suggested RKO withdraw their rerelease requests. His justification mirrored the exact same issue the SRC tried to mitigate in 1933, that the movie excuses adultery with no compensating moral values. Ann's professional defeat wouldn't suffice under Breen's reign.

Censorship battles aside, *Ann Vickers* proves an interesting study in the characterization of Ann herself. In rather standard pre-Code female fashion, the film's lead is feisty and determined. At the same time, she's genuinely career-oriented and earns her way to the top through dedication, passion, and hard work. An accomplished, opinionated, independent career woman? No wonder so many try to knock her down! Ann's stature and attempts to change the status quo come off as threatening, especially in her male-dominated profession.

Dunne's mindful performance and some truly stirring monologues from Jane Murfin's script give the role a solid bump and an incredibly modern sensibility. Nowhere is this more evident than in Ann's rousing first-act speech in the aftermath of her abortion. Though her heartbreaking address reveals how strongly she wanted to keep her daughter, Ann truly stands for that which she so strongly advocates. Ann forgoing marriage for her career, her call to put motherhood aside (for now), and the agency she exhibits making the painful decision to terminate her pregnancy are rare episodes, even for a pre-Code. So are the complex mix of emotions she displays in the aftermath, so resilient while at the same time absolutely shattered. The subject of abortion, never spoken by name and only a brief episode in the picture, rarely received this type of nuanced, poignant portrayal that paints it as the difficult event it is for most women. A century later, this scene retains the power to garner sympathy from women who continue to struggle with these choices amid renewed debate over allowing a choice at all.

As wholly progressive a woman as Ann is for most the picture, the film's final moments have her fortitude unfortunately undermined by

To: Dr. Wingate
From: Mr. Breen.

I read last night the "estimating script" of the R.K.O. Production, ANN VICKERS.

In my considered judgment, this script is definitely in violation of both the letter and the spirit of our Production Code for the following reasons:

1. The action by which it is definitely suggested that the leading character not only co-habits with two men, to whom she is not married, and has a child by each of them, but maintains this illicit relations with one of the characters, who is married, while she, herself, is the wife of another man, seems to me to fit in well with Mr. Hays' characterization of the plot of another picture recently produced - "progressive prostitution". All this in my judgment is definitely in violation of that portion of our Code which prohibits themes "tending to destroy the sanctity of marriage" which, the preamble to the Code suggests, "is the very foundation of society."

2. The patent attempt to build up sympathy for this leading character. This sympathetic build up is likewise a definite violation of our Code inasmuch as its purpose and intent is to soften and mitigate the grossness of her crime. The Code says somewhere that the sympathy of the audience should not be thrown on the side of evil.

3. The excessive brutality suggested in the several prison scenes is not only a Code violation but, likewise, highly censorable.

The entire script is filled with innumerable suggestions that are definitely in violation of the spirit of the Code - if not of its actual letter - and much of both action and dialogue is highly censorable. Not in years have I read anything quite so vulgarily offensive. The whole thing is so definitely out of line that I respectfully suggest that you lose no time in letting the R.K.O. people know that this script simply will not do and must be radically changed if its production is to be carried through. I see great trouble, both for the industry and the company, if this script, based upon a current best seller which is known to be vile and offensive, is not checked at once.

May 5, 1933.

Future PCA head Joseph Breen did not think highly of *Ann Vickers*.

the abrupt recognition that Barney and their son saved her from her "prison of ambition." It's a cringeworthy pivot for sure, originating with Lewis's novel, but one that aligns with the SRC's view of keeping Ann broken and relegating her to a mother role compliant with 1930s gender norms. However, the audience can find hope in the fact that Ann continues to work in her field and support her family and presumably will continue to advocate for those in need.

It's important to note that by 1933, some viewers were also voicing their exasperation with perceived cinematic depravity, *Ann Vickers* included. The author of *The Billboard* article "Shoddy!" watched *Ann Vickers* with an exhibitor friend who negatively reported: "I may be old-fashioned, but I not only wouldn't run it, I would advise every exhibitor in America to cancel it. It just isn't the thing to put into a theater—picture or otherwise."

Not all distributors felt that way, and *Ann Vickers* enticed enough movie fans to pull in a profit of about $65,000. Such a small number also demonstrates that sensationalism was no longer enough to ensure big box office returns. Just as Ann and Barney pay a price for behavior deemed unseemly by the moral guardians of the film, Hollywood was losing ground in a growing battle with righteous moralists rallying for censorship.

I'M NO ANGEL

STARRING
Mae West, Cary Grant, Edward Arnold, Ralf Harolde, and Kent Taylor

DIRECTED BY
Wesley Ruggles

RELEASED BY
Paramount, October 1933

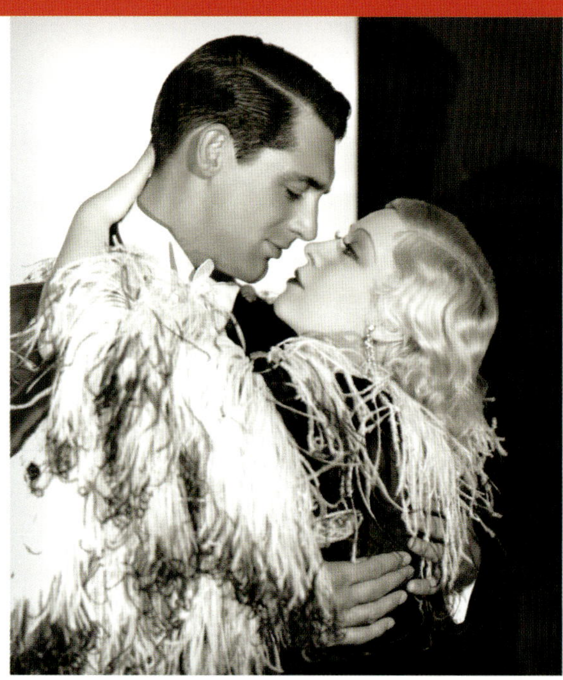

Mae West personally picked Cary Grant for *She Done Him Wrong,* and they obviously got along well enough for him to costar in *I'm No Angel* the same year.

I'm No Angel was the second starring vehicle for Mae West. When her movie career kicked off the year before, she was already infamous for staging *Sex* (1926) on Broadway—it's the name of the show, trust us—and she consequently served jail time for obscenity, making headlines around the country. In a time where many movies saw the young, sexually adventurous and svelte heroines taught the pleasures of monogamy, *I'm No Angel* has forty-year-old voracious, voluptuous Mae West getting all she can. By the end of the picture, she's beat the system at its own game—all with a knowing eye roll and smirk.

Undeniably the best West vehicle from her dozen turns in front of the camera, *I'm No Angel* is the most articulate of her (almost always) self-authored films. Here she plays lion tamer Tira, a woman with a big whip who keeps all the ravenous boys in line. Her entrance, riding an elephant into the big top, has the blue bloods of New York perked up. Tira has soon collected a suitor for each sign of the zodiac, including dapper Kirk Lawrence (Kent Taylor). Kirk's fiancée is none too pleased about it, and his cousin Jack Clayton (a young and impeccably gorgeous Cary Grant) gets involved. But as soon as Jack enters Tira's penthouse, he's smitten.

> "When I'm good, I'm very good. But when I'm bad, I'm better."
>
> **—the character's name is Tira, but it's all Mae West talking here**

Jack and Tira plan to marry, but a setup by Slick Wiley (Ralf Harolde) makes Jack think she's betrayed him. He ends their engagement, and she sues him for breach of promise. In the courtroom, Tira's old lovers are paraded out in hopes of embarrassing her. Instead, the judge and jury love her for it, and seeing the woman he adored defend herself so decisively, Jack chooses to make his way back toward Tira's bedroom.

When the SRC received the script for *I'm No Angel* a mere week before production was to begin, the tale was deemed to present real difficulties. That was just on paper, though. "Danger lies in the suggestive interpretation and portrayal which may be given to details of action, dialogue and songs," the office cautioned. Much attention was paid to that last element: the songs. Verses such as, "With a special whip" and "He can ride" from "That Dallas Man" (the title of which underwent a few alterations) raised flags and were either cut or modified, while the lyric, "I'd give myself to you for just a song" in "Give Me a Thrill" became, rather bizarrely: "I'd tell my love to you for just a song."

Upon review of the finished picture, the SRC commended Paramount "in handling what might otherwise have proved to be a difficult and embarrassing story." In a note to Will H. Hays, James Wingate affirmed that though *I'm No Angel* "contained the expected number of wise-cracks and Mae West-isms, we believe it will meet with no real difficulty." The picture also found a very strong ally in the MPPDA's Vincent Hart, who deemed it a "knockout."

Indeed, for the most part, local boards went easy on the picture. New York and Chicago lodged one cut each, while boards from Australia to Alberta deleted a handful of those West-isms, like her insisting to a man with a wink and a smile, "I ain't damaged," and grinning with a knowing look, "Am I making myself clear, boys?" The line, "She's safer in that cage than she is in bed" was also deemed too suggestive in many areas.

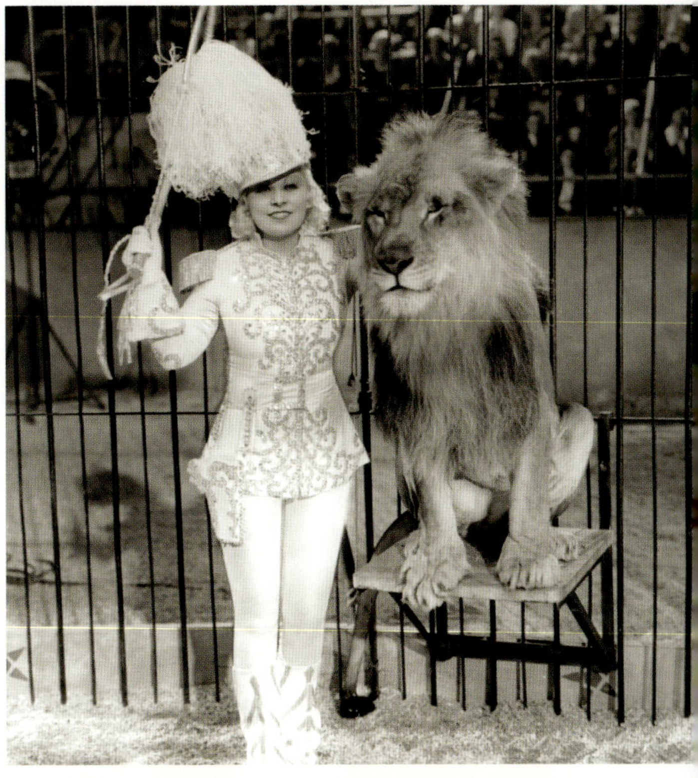

Mae West gets to use her whip in a different way in *I'm No Angel.*

Like West's *She Done Him Wrong* (1933), which premiered less than nine months earlier, *I'm No Angel* was a smash. *Variety* noted, "Mae West is today the biggest conversation-provoker, free-space grabber and all-around box office bet in the country. She's as hot an issue as Hitler." The movie won many plaudits (though not a Best Picture nomination, like West's previous outing), but it wasn't everyone's cup of tea. Martin Quigley, cowriter of the Production Code, hissed, "There is no more pretense here of romance than on a stud-farm . . . its sportive wise-cracking tends to create tolerance if not acceptance of things essentially evil."

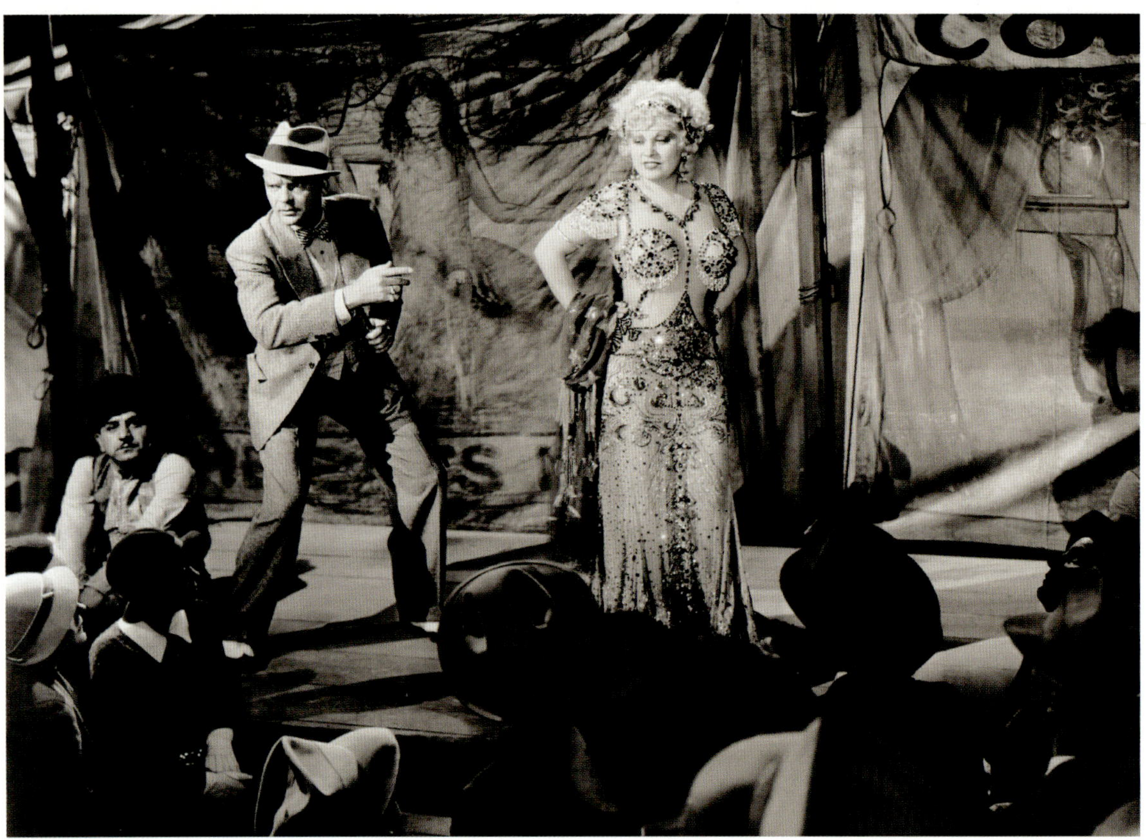

Mae West is ready for the big time!

That said, the zealously moral had the last laugh when the Code became fully enforceable. In February 1935, PCA head Joseph Breen recommended the film be pulled from circulation, and then, if it was wiped of its objectionable material, the movie could be reconsidered. According to Breen, though, *I'm No Angel* was "so thoroughly and so completely in violation" of the Code that it would be almost impossible for Paramount to alter it enough. When the subject was broached again in 1949, Breen wasted no time in sternly shutting down that idea by declaring: "No good will accrue to the industry among right-thinking people with a release of a Mae West picture."

It's easy to forget in this fervor that *I'm No Angel* is a comedy and a raucous one at that. What makes it so special—and so incendiary—is how the movie may be one of the frankest explorations of a woman's sexual freedom that you'll get out of the early 1930s. This isn't just because we get a good sense of West's unabashed love for carnal delights; even a base reading of the movie shows that her character, while adhering to the standards of the gold digger archetype, is matched against an array of societal ills that represent the problems women faced at large. Women who belittle one another out of jealousy, bosses who exploit people, and men who remove agency from women for their own

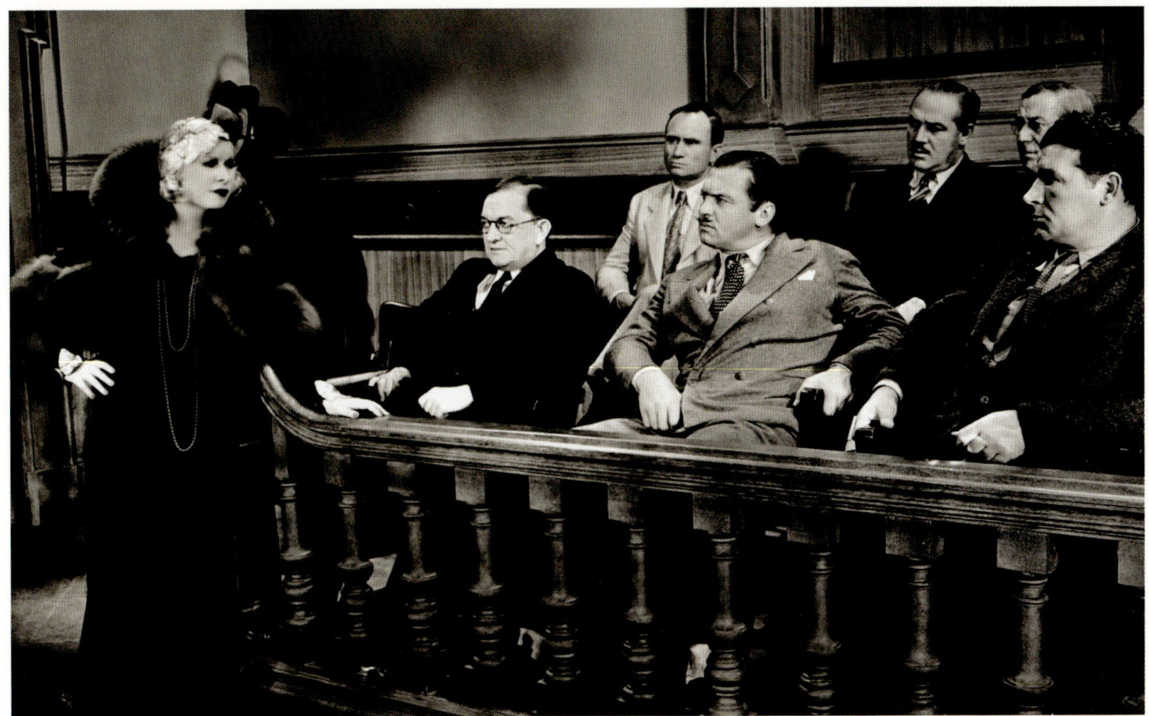

Sex is on trial, and Mae West is here for the defense.

selfish reasons are all wholly representative of the enemies feminism faced throughout the twentieth and now twenty-first centuries. West's solution, to use a modern colloquialism, was to maintain a healthy self-respect and simply forget the haters.

I'm No Angel features a few musical numbers, and while West's voice isn't exactly refined, they get the point across. West utilized singing as shorthand for sexual excitement that couldn't be shown on-screen at the time. The film's final shot, where Tira performs a reprise of the title track, noticeably cuts her off. This happens at a moment where Tira is on her back and Jack slowly comes closer to her on the couch. It's safe to say she didn't stop singing because of a burp.

I'm No Angel was among the highest-grossing movies of 1933 and, along with *She Done Him Wrong*, helped make Paramount financially solvent after they became the first major studio to declare bankruptcy in March 1933. *Picturegoer* writer Clifford Bower argued that West's reputation lies in the way she plays on the imagination of the audience and quipped that West would remain a relevant character as long as the actress wanted her to: "Why? Because it's impossible to censor the public's thoughts."

I'm No Angel is often cited as one of the films that pressured the industry to enforce the Code, making the movie a must-see for anyone who wants to understand and celebrate what the pre-Code era meant—and what American audiences subsequently lost. As a thesis statement for early-twentieth-century feminism and sexual freedom, *I'm No Angel* is a masterpiece.

WILD BOYS OF THE ROAD

STARRING
Frankie Darro, Edwin Phillips, Rochelle Hudson, and Dorothy Coonan Wellman

DIRECTED BY
William A. Wellman

RELEASED BY
Warner Bros., October 1933

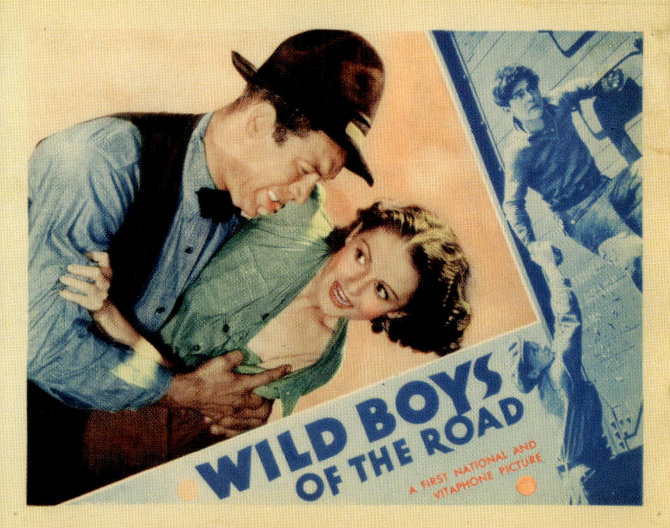

Warner Bros. put a still of Ward Bond attacking young Ann Hovey on a lobby card, and that was a *choice.*

The effects of the Depression were littered across the screen by 1933, when unemployment hit an astronomical 24.9 percent. There were plenty of films about the plight of the working man. There were also plenty of movies about women who suddenly had to carry on steady with a brave face. But, to steal an old cliché, what of the children? It was estimated that during this tumultuous period there were over two hundred thousand youths hitching their way across the country, looking for work and usually finding only heartache and grief.

Wild Boys of the Road was another Warner Bros. feature ripped from such headlines. Two teens, Eddie (Frankie Darro) and Tommy (Edwin Phillips), whose parents are struggling to make ends meet, take it on the road. They hop on a train headed toward Chicago and meet Sally (Dorothy Coonan Wellman), dressed as a boy, whose big family needed one less mouth to feed.

As they travel along the line, they meet plenty of other kids, and a multicultural gang soon accumulates with Eddie at the head to push them through the many indignities that crop up. Still, they're driven into stock pens whenever they arrive in a town and just as quickly kicked out. "We haven't got enough jobs here for men, let alone kids," one sheriff growls.

A brutal accident at a train yard costs Tommy his leg, and the gang steals a prosthesis to help him. This leads to a nasty battle with the kids, occupying a junkyard, standing up to sheriffs wielding hoses and dogs. Defeated, Eddie, Tommy, and Sally make their way to New York City. After Eddie is tricked into attempting to hold up a movie theater, a kindly judge (Robert Barrat) takes the trio under his wing and promises to help them out, an upbeat end to a downbeat tale.

Decades removed, *Wild Boys* still feels like dynamite. Imprinted with the red-blooded ethos

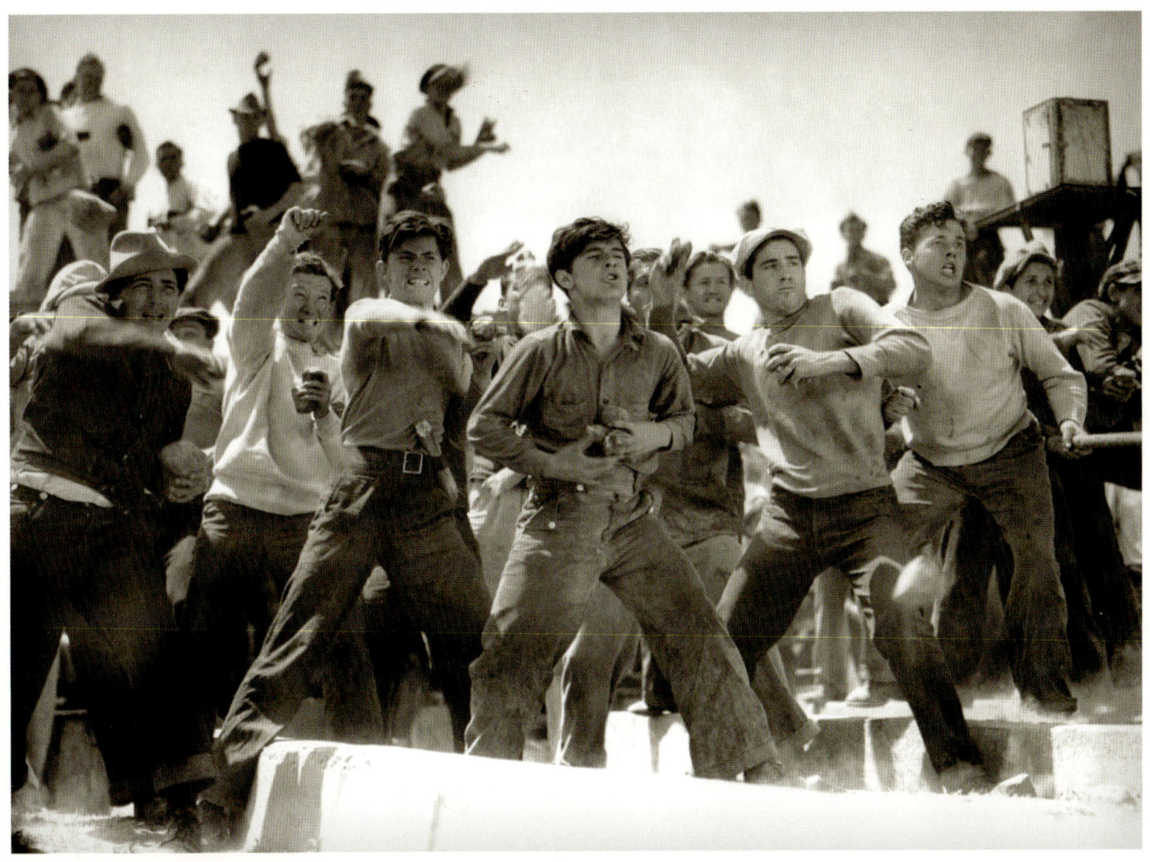

A mob of angry, desperate kids on their own trying to survive during the Depression is something you never want to incite.

of director William A. Wellman, the thrust is that these are good kids trapped in a system indifferent to their suffering. Wellman shunned putting a contemporary romance in the picture, instead filling it with a genuine male affection between Eddie and Tommy, hugging, crying, and sharing real pain running underneath.

With a cast largely made up of teens, *Wild Boys of the Road* hits a little harder; we often think of the adults who were affected by the Depression—those who lost their jobs and could no longer provide for their families—but in this film, we

"You're sending us to jail 'cause you don't want to see us. You want to forget us. Well, you can't do it 'cause I'm not the only one. There's thousands just like me. There's more hitting the road every day."

—Eddie, a youthful runaway telling a judge that he can't go home again

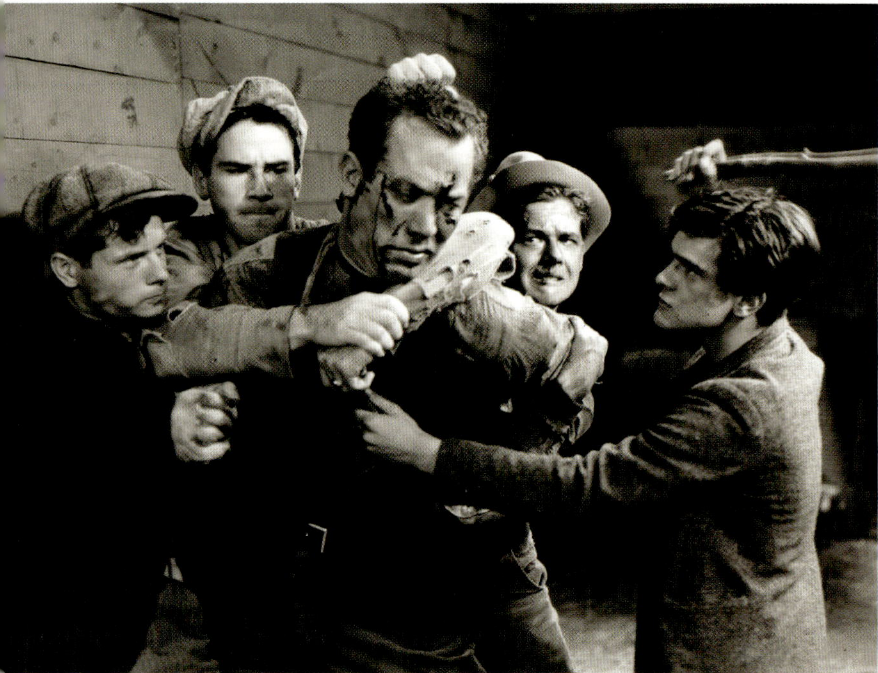

Action meet consequence: This is what one gets when they rape a young girl.

get a sense of the consequences on the youth of America. Imagine having to fend for yourself as a teen because your parents can't afford to care for you. Emotional trauma aside, the struggle these kids confront in the face of incredible adversity can ring familiar for many families—adults and children—in the fallout from the global pandemic in 2020, especially the devastating loss of familiar social structures kids endured.

Daniel Ahearn, who had spent some time as an itinerant and had seen firsthand some of the conflicts presented in the movie, wrote the short story "Desperate Youth" from which Earl Baldwin derived his screenplay. Wellman toned down and altered the source material considerably. For instance, while in the film the only robbery that occurs is Eddie's empathetic stealing of an artificial leg, the original story painted the gang as far more prolific criminals, using a toy gun in holdups. Most notably, the trio's encounter with Aunt Carrie (Minna Gombell) originally came later in the story and resulted in Sally being recruited as one of Carrie's prostitutes. Eddie's motivations for raising money become more desperate as he tries to get her out of the racket.

Shooting on location around Los Angeles, Wellman contended with pressure from several sides, including Warner's new studio production head, Hal Wallis, who felt a scene where Tommy loses a leg to a train overly brutal. "There is no doubt about it, it is effective but if we ever left this in, there would be more premature births in the theatre and more people dying than were killed in the World War," Wallis warned.

The SRC also voiced a number of concerns. In a fairly typical move, they demanded that Wellman make references to Aunt Carrie's profession more vague; in the movie, it's difficult to tell how exactly she is entertaining the customers, whether with alcohol or sex. They also protested a scene where one of the girls, Lola (Ann Hovey), is raped, calling it "bluntly explicit." There is some sign that the studio toned down this sequence, as they requested the removal of "a tear in her riding breeches and the imprint of a greasy hand . . . on her shoulder." Additionally, they expressed worry about unsympathetic portrayals of doctors and police officers, which could cause resentment and protest.

The finished film, though undoubtedly watered down, remains breathtakingly merciless. Little hope seems possible as the group seeks to unite under a common cause. Eddie, Tommy, and Sally constantly butt against a world where their identities are shattered and they are believed useless.

Wild Boys of the Road met one major complaint from critics and audiences: Its current ending with the kindly judge—wearing a pair of glasses to give him an FDR-esque profile—saving the kids from jail was simply too upbeat. The movie's original finale had Eddie getting shot during the scuffle in the theater and being sent to jail, while Tommy and Sally landed in juvenile hall. The judge in the original ending was just another unsympathetic cog of a cold, unfeeling machine.

The executives at Warner Bros. balked at that ending as "bleak" and "depressing." Wellman disagreed but was coaxed into reshooting it. While the hopeful finish may have helped audiences feel a sense of relief and even optimism, reviewers felt it portrayed the movie's core social issue as one already being solved. *The New York Times* discounted the entire film because of it, explaining, "its drama is mostly melodrama and, by endowing it with a happy ending, the producers have robbed it of its value as a social challenge."

The truth of the matter is that the SRC wanted the picture's upbeat ending. James Wingate wrote to Warner Bros., "The careful handling of the forces of established law and order as embodied in the person of the judge, will not only make it an interesting and sympathetic story, but also, we believe, save it from any great danger of censorship trouble." Warner Bros. and the SRC, still conscious of the histrionic reactions to *I Am a Fugitive from a Chain Gang*, agreed; *Wild Boys of the Road* would be a searing indictment of the problems of youth vagrancy, but, according to the new ending, not one you had to worry about on your way home.

State boards were still eager to chop the picture; the most commonly removed scene was the rape and its aftermath. (When *Wild Boys* was submitted for reissue in 1936, Joseph Breen also truncated this sequence.) Other boards were equally wary about the fight between the kids and the policeman, with New York, Ohio, and Alberta ordering large sections cut out of fear of angering police unions. Even the film's innocuous early scenes weren't safe; Pennsylvania deleted one sequence of Tommy siphoning gas out of a rival's car for fear teens would mimic it, and Australia removed another scene of Tommy and his girl necking. British Columbia added a lengthy foreword that floridly described the boys' situations, ending with a pair of urgent questions: "Shall we escape the menace that grows from such conditions? Is it nothing to you that pass by?"

Variety felt the exhaustion of the times keenly. Their critic conceded that the film's subject is of vital importance and "one of the most painful sides of the whole depression," but added, "it should never have been done at all for general commercial release." Modern critics are far more appreciative, and the movie was inducted into the National Film Registry in 2013.

The cruelty exhibited in *Wild Boys* may not have served as a wake-up call to Depression-era audiences but rather as another social ill they soon wanted to forget. Without a doubt, Wellman's direction and the film's unrelenting pace bring the immediacy of these kids' lives and travails into stunning clarity, making *Wild Boys* feel just as urgent and heartfelt as ever.

FOOTLIGHT PARADE

STARRING
James Cagney, Joan Blondell, Ruby Keeler, and Dick Powell

DIRECTED BY
Lloyd Bacon (Busby Berkeley, musical numbers)

RELEASED BY
Warner Bros., October 1933

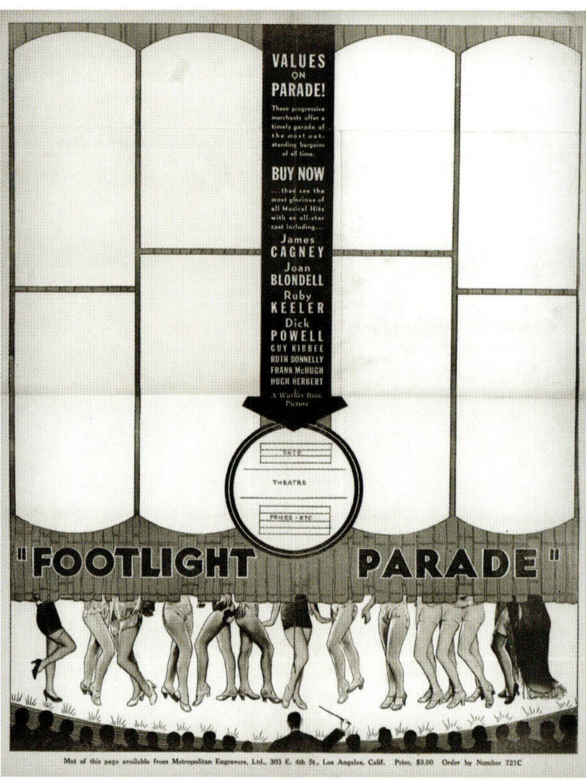

Warner Bros. sure knew how to sell a movie!

"Outside, countess. As long as they have sidewalks, you've got a job!"

—Nan, giving her "friend" Vivian the boot

Few movies were as self-reflexive of their time as *Footlight Parade*, which opens with a couple of quick jokes about the suddenness of the talkie revolution and ends with a bombastic salute to America's new president, Franklin D. Roosevelt. In between comes everything, from rousing musical numbers to brazen sexual jibes and orgiastic symbolism. That being said, the movie is a testament to self-branding, optimism, and, of course, the joys in proving your haters wrong.

Besides three show-stopping Busby Berkeley numbers that have been unceasingly parroted in pictures like *Captain America: The First Avenger* (2011), *Hail, Caesar!* (2016), and *Paddington 2* (2017), *Footlight Parade* is a cavalcade of energetic ideas. For one, it's a paean to the ingenuity of the working man and the eternal importance of adapting to change with creativity and hope. While the film conveys ideas of artistic freedom and expression, it also interrogates the all-American incentivization of white-collar crime and gold digging. It's hopeful but real, and there's also a sequence of about two dozen chorines dancing around in cat outfits, so, overall, it's pretty fun.

Footlight Parade stars James Cagney as Chester Kent, a fast-talking showman who creates rotating prologues to put in front of talking pictures. The entire retinue of Warner Bros. character actors make an appearance here, from the hard-working Joan Blondell as his secretary, Nan, who has a crush on Kent, to Frank McHugh playing "sissy" dance instructor Francis with glee. Under pressure from his opportunistic business partners and hoping to sell shows to a big circuit and undercut rivals who steal his ideas, Kent, with Nan in tow, devises three spectacular numbers starring Bea (Ruby Keeler) and Scotty (Dick Powell) to play at three different theaters across a single night. These elaborate numbers, the suggestive "Honeymoon Hotel," the magnificent "By a Waterfall," and the toe-tapping "Shanghai Lil," are saved for rapid succession at the end of the picture.

While Lloyd Bacon directed the straight sequences, former drill sergeant Berkeley brought his discipline and expansive vision with him to the dance scenes. Berkeley's previous successes at the studio, including *42nd Street* and *Gold Diggers of 1933*, gave him leeway to continue to pursue ever more elaborate production numbers.

Berkeley shot this film and the Eddie Cantor musical extravaganza *Roman Scandals* (1933) concurrently, exhausting the choreographer. Cagney's part in *Footlight Parade* could be seen to draw from Berkeley's own spate of experiences fixing misfired productions with exorbitant musical numbers. There are other in-jokes as well; early in the picture, Chester finds himself watching *The Telegraph Trail* (1933), which starred not only a young John Wayne but *Footlight Parade*'s own Frank McHugh.

Cagney, who'd been a dancer onstage but made it big in Hollywood as a tough-nosed gangster in *The Public Enemy,* fought for the lead in *Footlight Parade.* Cagney moved from New York to Hollywood in 1930 along with Joan Blondell, a longtime friend and costar, as their 1930 Broadway show *Penny Arcade* made it to the big screen. The two

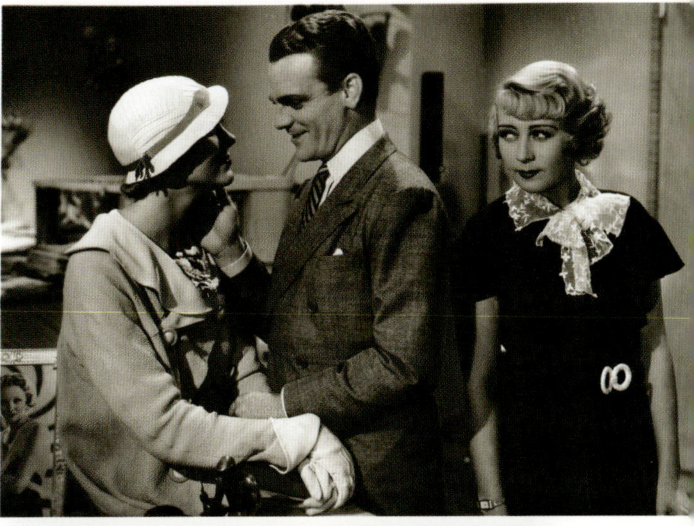

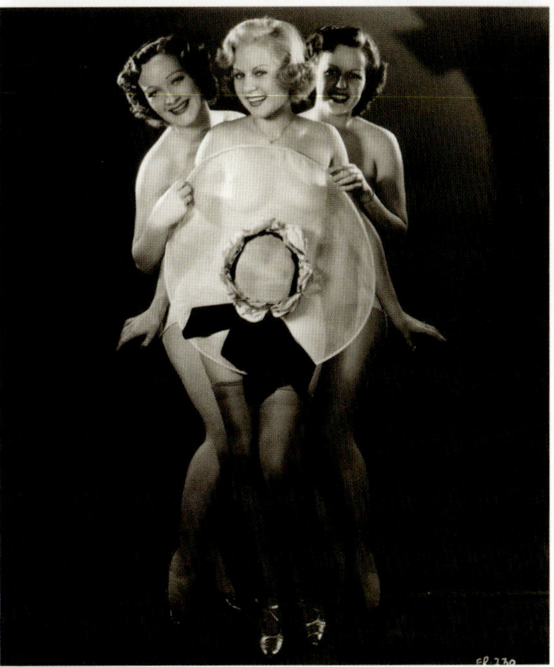

FROM TOP: Joan Blondell sizes up the competition for James Cagney, namely Claire Dodd. • Promotional images such as this one helped create audience interest in the film. For purely aesthetic reasons.

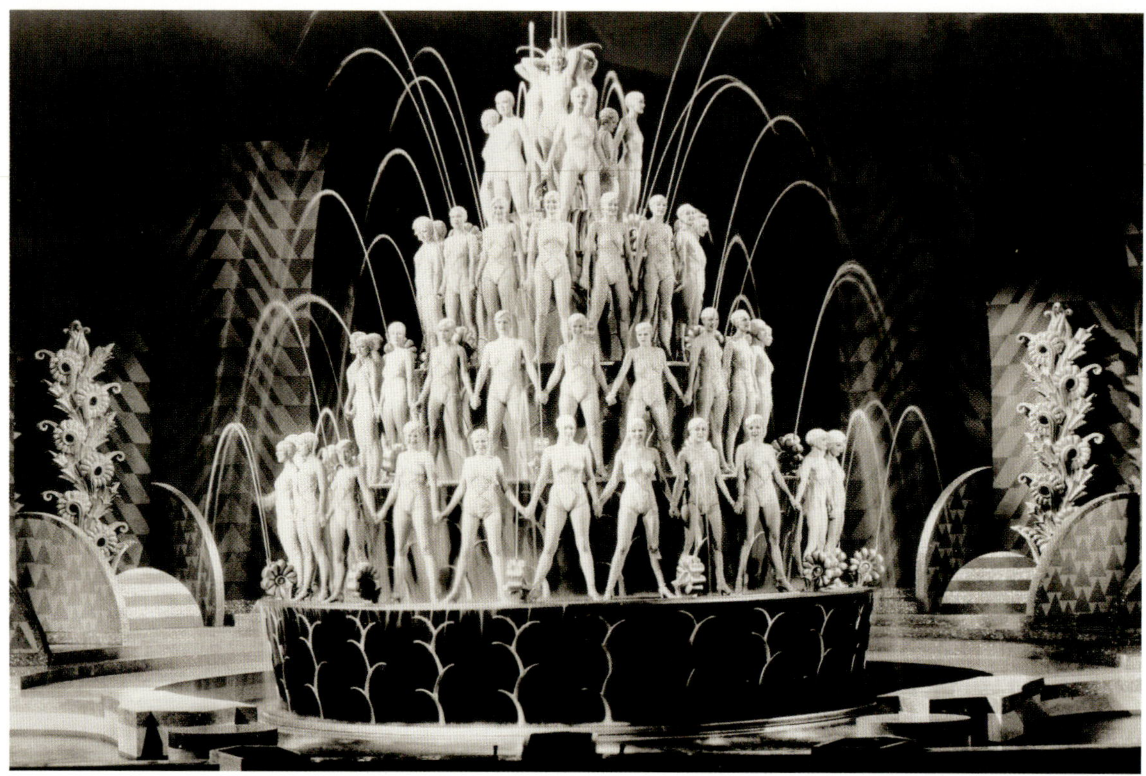

Exhibit A of choreographer Busby Berkeley creating lavish sets built on scantily clad female bodies.

actors have a delightfully comfortable chemistry throughout their many collaborations.

The most famous and widely aped musical piece of the movie, "By a Waterfall" was, at the time, Berkeley's most expensive number, clocking in at a cost of $38,000. The sequence is also one of Berkeley's least subtle, as towers of women stare in eager-eyed glee at the foot of massive fountains in scanty swimsuits. (Freud would have a field day with this.) The eighty-foot-by-forty-foot pool featured windows on the sides and bottoms to allow cameras to capture the elaborate choreography, with filming sometimes lasting for twenty-two hours straight. Amusingly, the set was designed before the song was selected.

Warner Bros. was the edgiest of the studios in the early 1930s, and the sheer amount of objectionable material packed in *Footlight Parade,* ostensibly a light comedy, may be overwhelming to audiences in the modern day. This includes little details like Claire Dodd's less-than-hardworking character, Vivian Rich, reading blue novels on the job, or when Nan almost calls Miss Rich a similar word that starts with the letter *B.*

Not surprisingly, the majority of the SRC's advice for Warner Bros. landed in sex territory. They warned against referring to Francis as a "pansy"—temperamental and fluttery would have to do, instead. The SRC also advised deleting lines like, "He hasn't seen first base in years," which remained intact.

Also notable is the muted controversy over the "Shanghai Lil" number that features Keeler in yellowface in a song centered on the town's best prostitute. The SRC was always sensitive to how American pictures played both overseas and at home, so producer Hal Wallis left the sequence out of a print shown to the Chinese Council of Los Angeles, falsely stating it was unfinished.

The film's own jabs at censorship, with Hugh Herbert's buffoonish censor, Bowers, walking around asking for closer looks at the showgirls, likely did Warner Bros. few favors. This satire continued with 1934's borderline post-Code film *Dames,* whose plot hinges on a number of righteous critics getting drunk with power and "healthy" elixirs.

Luckily, most local censor boards cut *Footlight Parade* some slack. New York approved the picture, while Australia deleted the "Shanghai Lil" number. In other locations, Nan's line to Vivian about sidewalks proved unpopular, as were shots of Bea and Scotty in bed in "Honeymoon Hotel." In 1936, Warner Bros. approached the PCA regarding rerelease, but Joseph Breen wouldn't let them off that easy. He confirmed the film would comply with the Code as long as deletions were made, including shots of Nan pulling on her stockings, Chester kissing a girl on her chest, and select Chester phrases, such as "punk" and "Stick 'em in your ear."

While everyone has their favorite of the pre-Code Warner Bros. musicals, Cagney's charms help turn *Footlight Parade* into a ready-made crowd pleaser. The film's ending is possibly one of the most ham-fisted political statements in all of the pre-Code era, with the hardworking employee rebelling against the businessmen who took advantage of him and coming out on top, and it serves as a nice counterpoint to *Gold Diggers of 1933*. Where that musical was a vehicle for the desperate, here it is the success story of everyone pitching in—and tossing the parasites out. And who doesn't love a tale of triumph like that?

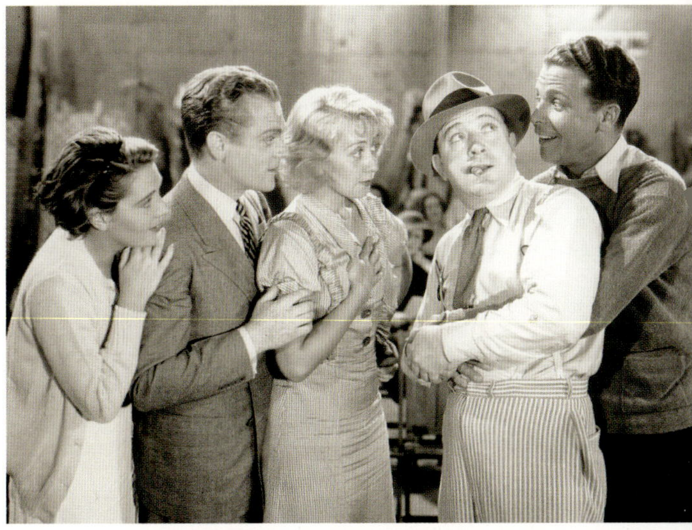

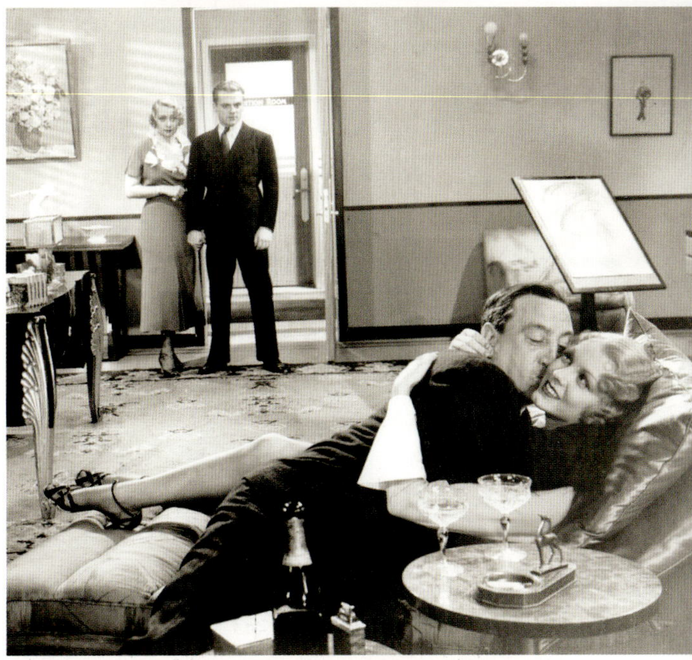

FROM TOP: Frank McHugh's "pansy" tendencies had the SRC worried. • "I'm just showing her what you can't do in Kalamazoo!"—and Ohio, Maryland, Alberta, Quebec, and all of America post-Code.

DUCK SOUP

STARRING
Groucho, Harpo, Chico, and Zeppo Marx; Margaret Dumont; Raquel Torres; and Louis Calhern

DIRECTED BY
Leo McCarey

RELEASED BY
Paramount, November 1933

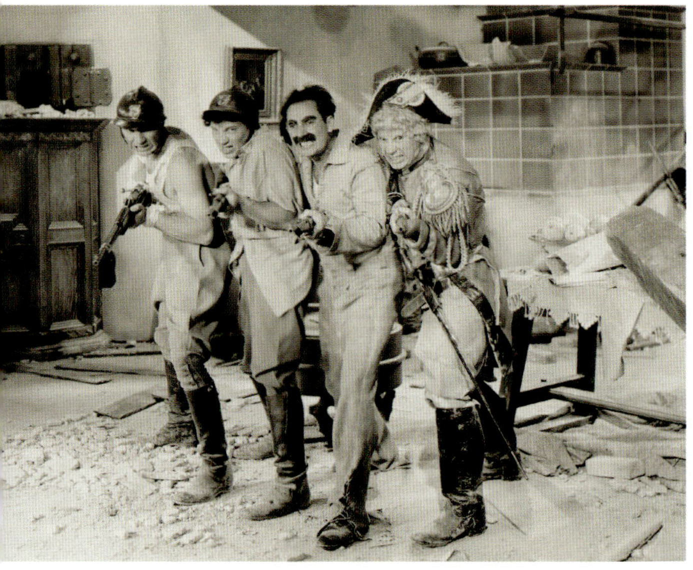

The Marx Brothers are ready and willing to fight! *What,* we have no idea—and neither did they.

"Your Excellency, haven't we seen each other somewhere before?"

"I don't think so; I'm not sure I'm seeing you now, it must be something I ate."

—Ambassador Trentino and Rufus T. Firefly, who may have eaten too many crackers in bed

Comedy in the pre-Code era was without a doubt more risqué and satirical than what would come after 1934, and for no one, save possibly Mae West and W. C. Fields, was that truer than the Marx Brothers. Comedians still had a broad mandate to mock everyone and everything before the Production Code would push comedy into the relatively harmless screwball realm for two decades, and no one was more eager to mock every aspect of propriety than the Marxes.

Duck Soup finds Mrs. Gloria Teasdale (Margaret Dumont), a wealthy widow and sole financial supporter of the government of Freedonia, insisting that Rufus T. Firefly (Groucho Marx) be installed as leader of the embattled nation. The conceited Firefly immediately starts a rivalry with Ambassador Trentino (Louis Calhern) from neighboring Sylvania. Trentino is eager to oust Firefly and recruits Chicolini (Chico Marx) and Pinky (Harpo Marx) to infiltrate as spies. Also in this hubbub is Sylvanian loyalist Vera Marcal (Raquel Torres) and Firefly's trusty secretary Bob (Bob?!) (Zeppo Marx).

A complete accounting of the film is nearly impossible given all of its absurdities. *Duck Soup* opens with a large musical number welcoming Firefly to Freedonia where he quickly lays out his plans to grift the nation, including the ever-relevant

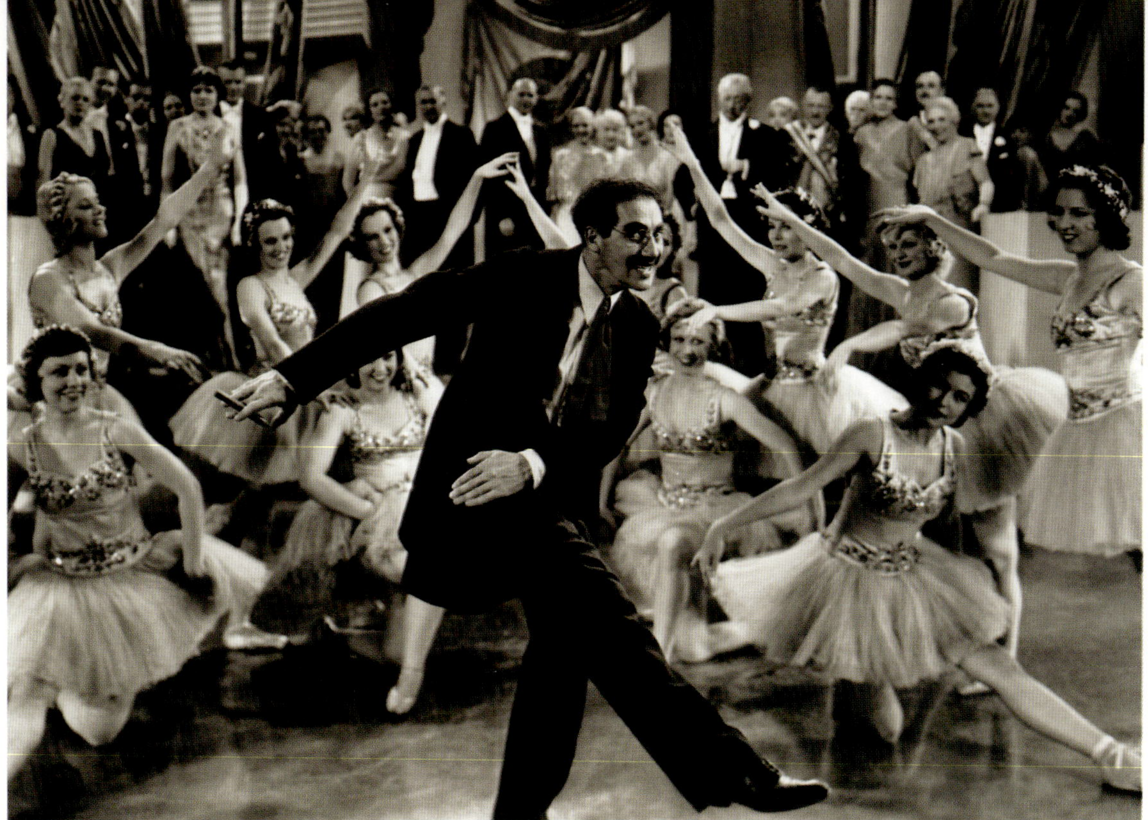

What all governments could use: another musical number.

declaration: "If you think this country's bad off now, just wait till I get through with it!" War eventually breaks out between Freedonia and Sylvania, and a series of lunatic sketches emerge, including a rousing musical number that promises: "They've got guns / We got guns / All God's children got guns!"

Firefly, Chicolini, and Bob eventually end up defending Mrs. Teasdale's home from the Sylvania onslaught. As things look bleak for the group, they send out Pinky with a hearty rejoinder from Firefly, "While you're out there risking life and limb through shot and shell, we'll be in here thinking what a sucker you are."

Duck Soup may be roughly connected and brimming with continuity errors, but its political satire remains prescient. Firefly's personality of vanity run amok echoes modern America's media-obsessed politicians, as do his questionable hiring practices and war-hungry power trips. Wars are simply escalated temper tantrums, and state protection is only afforded to the wealthy. This cynical view of the American experiment and ineffectual government, made at a time when many downtrodden Americans were looking eagerly at powerful European despots like Mussolini, can seem both downright heretical and prophetic.

Production on *Duck Soup* took time, as the comedians clashed with Paramount over money and control. While the finished picture wasn't particularly censorable, an early version of the story, back when it was first called *Cracked Ice*,

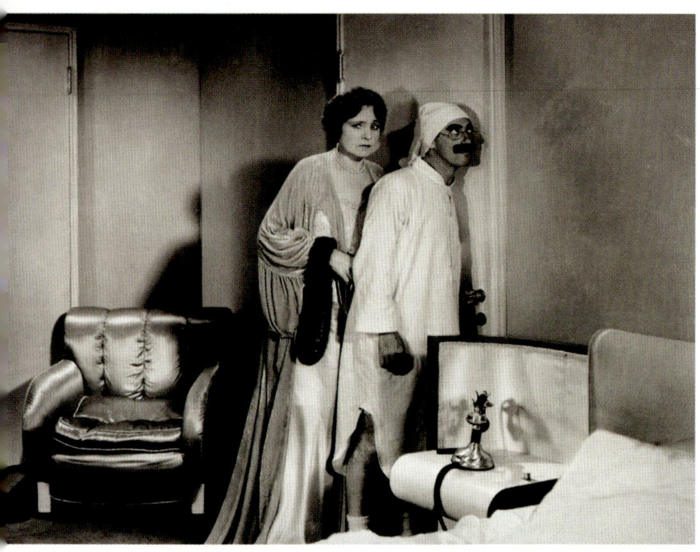

What's behind the door, Margaret Dumont and Groucho Marx? (Because this is a Marx Brothers movie, it literally could be anything.)

didn't include the gag where Harpo's chest tattoo features a barking dog. Rather, it was to be an outhouse. Groucho, after slapping Harpo on the back, would send the tattoo's door flying open, after which an animated hand would grab it and pull it closed.

That said, the Marx Brothers had always been targets for censors, even so far back as their time on Broadway in the 1920s. As a result, their first movies, near direct transplants of their stage shows, lost bits of color. This includes in *Animal Crackers* (1930) where Groucho's trimmed aside during the number "Hooray for Captain Spaulding" promises about Mrs. Rittenhouse, "I think I'll try and make her." One apocryphal story even alleges that the reason the Marxes ended up suffering during their upcoming contract negotiations at MGM stemmed from an incident where Harpo chased a stripper around Louis B. Mayer's office—while the studio head was giving a tour to censorship czar Will H. Hays. While *Duck Soup* was trimmed before release to streamline the tale, cutting down Zeppo's romantic subplot and even omitting the usual Harpo and Chico musical features, it didn't meet much resistance from local censors.

Some Marx Brothers enthusiasts decry the film for leaning too much on the slapstick style of director Leo McCarey (who helmed 1937's screwball classic *The Awful Truth*), especially in the recurring gags around a lemonade vendor. McCarey was the one who suggested the mirror scene, which had its origins in Charlie Chaplin's *The Floorwalker* (1916) and was reused in Max Linder's *Seven Years' Bad Luck* (1921). However, there's little doubt that it is now a sequence best associated with the Marx Brothers, as it was revived in 1955 when Harpo performed the same gag with Lucille Ball during his popular guest appearance on *I Love Lucy*.

Duck Soup was not the box office flop that it was later portrayed as, but neither was it the massive hit that the team's *Horse Feathers* (1932) had been. Part of the reason may be the behind-the-scenes turmoil, with Paramount and the Marx Brothers having jettisoned a completely different script before production and fighting extensively about their contract. The eventual release was so burdened with financial capital owed to the studios and stars—and lacking any harp or piano numbers that Marx Brothers fans routinely enjoyed—that many exhibitors were embittered to project such "trash." *The New York Times*, for example, declared the movie "extremely noisy." The film was eventually rediscovered and revived on college campuses in the 1960s and 1970s, with Groucho Marx, who had long dismissed the pictures the brothers made

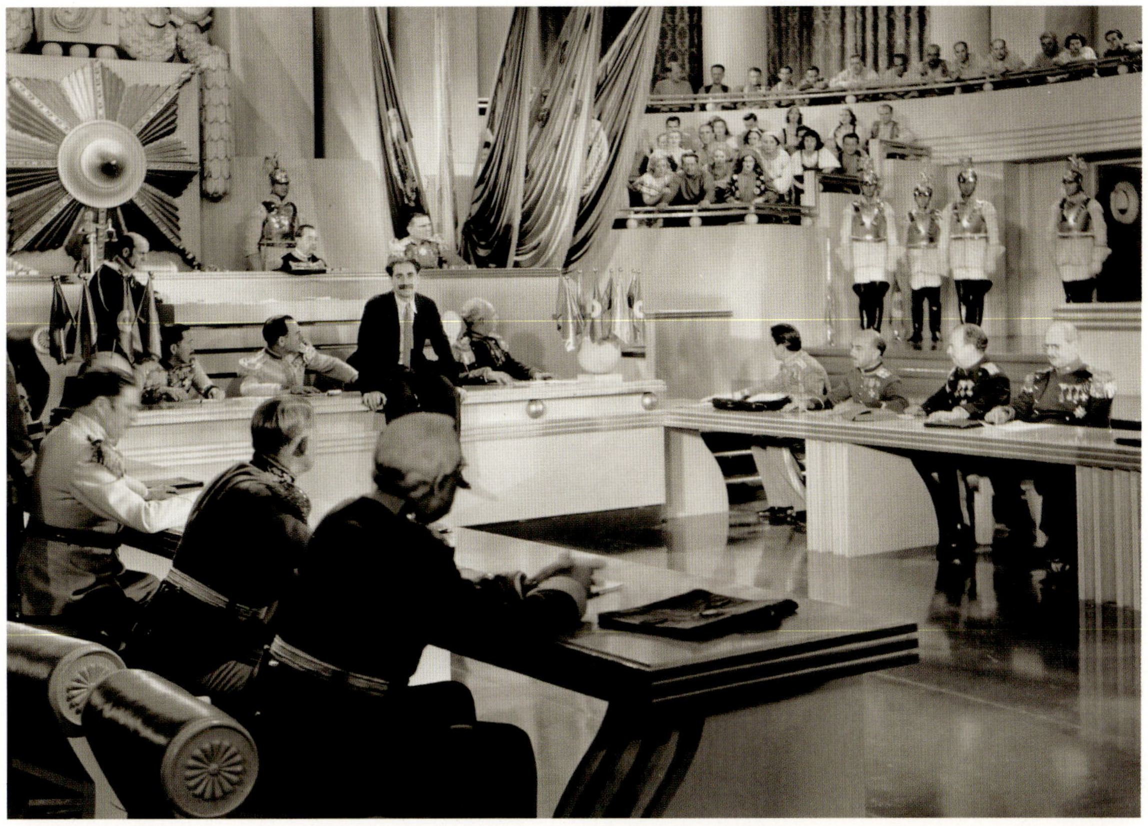

Duck Soup: Making politics incoherent again.

at Paramount, finally acceding to their superiority.

It would be two more years after *Duck Soup* before the Marx Brothers headed back to the big screen with their first (and arguably best) outing for MGM, *A Night at the Opera* (1935). That production, carefully shepherded by Irving Thalberg, sawed off the group's rough edges. (Surely, the newly enforced Production Code also had something to do with that.) No longer were they four men unleashed into an unsuspecting world, destroying friend and foe alike; at MGM they became the cutesy sidekicks for a series of progressively forgettable romantic leads. They continued to receive star billing, but they were now put in positions to usher the plot along and help keep the bland couples together, come hell or high water.

The political philosophy of the Marx Brothers films at Paramount—*The Cocoanuts* (1929), *Animal Crackers* (1930), *Monkey Business* (1931), *Horse Feathers* (1932), and this film—has long been debated, whether it can be chalked up as mere anarchy or a nuanced faith in brazen and unrelenting sabotage. *Duck Soup* is probably the closest the team ever came to making an explicit point, even if that point is to say that it's all pretty pointless, after all.

THE SIN OF NORA MORAN

STARRING
Zita Johann, John Miljan, Alan Dinehart, and Paul Cavanagh

DIRECTED BY
Phil Goldstone

RELEASED BY
Majestic Pictures, December 1933

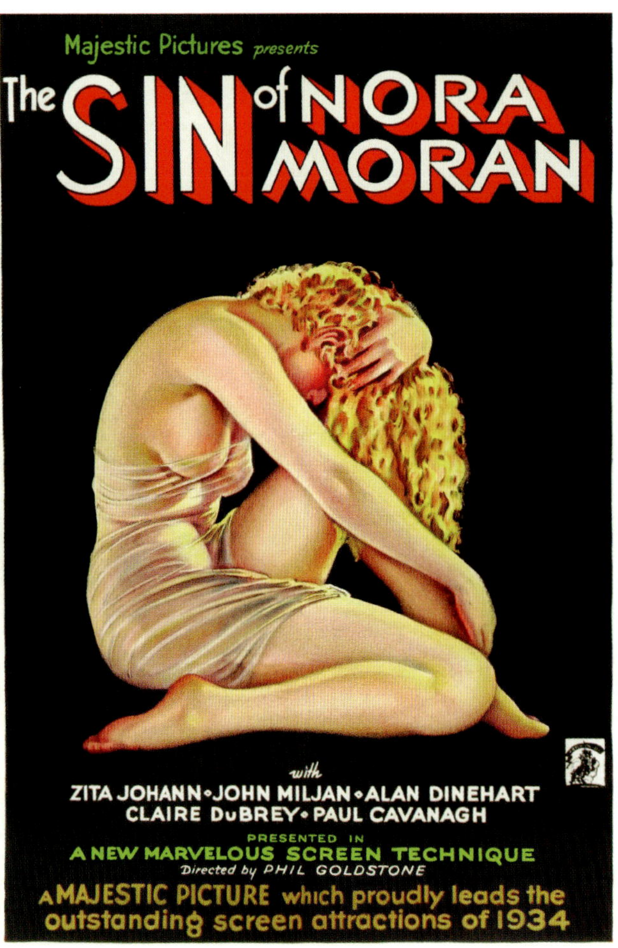

A standout Poverty Row production from Majestic Pictures, *The Sin of Nora Moran* lives up to its iniquitous title, packing a punishing pre-Code punch in a loosely confined sixty-three minutes. We're talking an illicit love affair, rape, murder, frank execution details, and a suicide evocatively conveyed through layers of flashbacks and flash-forwards, multiple narrators, and various twists that at once bewilder and elucidate the enigmatic plot. While this weight could easily overload a low-budget production, its transcendental atmosphere, hallucinatory compositions, and distorted sense of morality qualify *The Sin of Nora Moran* as one of the most exploitive and downright haunting pre-Codes, one that film historian John Cocchi termed "the best independent feature of the Thirties."

The Sin of Nora Moran begins its journey in the present day, with District Attorney John Grant (Alan Dinehart) telling his sister-in-law Mrs. Edith Crawford (Claire Du Brey) about the clandestine relationship between her husband, Governor Dick Crawford (Paul Cavanagh), and Nora Moran (Zita Johann). We're first introduced to our protagonist through her picture in the paper under the headline "Chair to Claim First Woman Victim in 20 Years." So that's where this story is headed.

John's narration both intersects with and blurs Nora's story. We watch Nora awaiting her execution, and flashbacks take us through her life:

No matter that Zita Johann didn't have blond hair! Artist Alberto Vargas knew how to catch one's eye.

Orphaned at a young age, Nora tried her luck on the New York stage before joining the circus. After her carnival boss Paulino (John Miljan) rapes her one evening, she flees to New York, lands a chorus job, and falls in love with Dick, a married man running for governor. Nora enjoys fleeting happiness in the home where she and Dick rendezvous twice a week. But once John uncovers their relationship—and Paulino, in town with the circus, finds them, too—bliss turns to tragedy as Paulino is killed in self-defense and the courts come calling for justice.

Based on W. Maxwell Goodhue's story "Burnt Offering," *The Sin of Nora Moran* was adapted by Goodhue and Frances Hyland. The latter holds the distinction of being among the first "gag women," a comedy writer, working in Hollywood. Hyland sure traveled to the complete opposite end of the spectrum for *The Sin of Nora Moran*.

Though mainly a producer, Majestic head Phil Goldstone took over as director from Howard Christy after production began on *Nora Moran*—and shooting only took one week. It certainly sounds like the chaos the story imparts extended behind the scenes, as well.

The mesmeric Zita Johann may well have contributed to the film's visceral atmosphere in more ways than one. A respected Broadway actress who only made eight movies (seven of which were pre-Codes, her best-known being 1932's *The Mummy*), Johann's own spiritual nature imbued her sensitive and sorrowful performance, and she sells intangible thoughts in an ethereal way with ease. Skating between effervescence, vulnerability, anguish, and the unearthly hauntings that come with an imminent execution, the star dexterously captured the sacrificial wrath of Nora's trauma as she traversed treacherous emotional terrain.

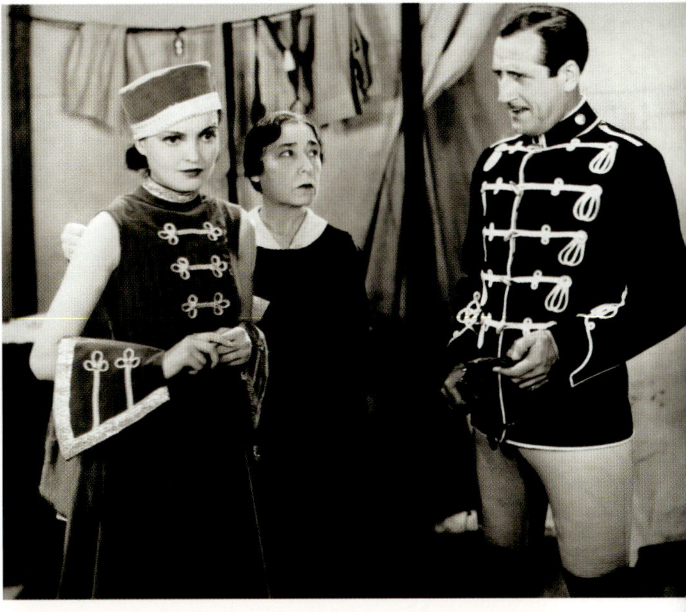

Zita Johann finds a stable job in a circus with lion tamer John Miljan, but she'd probably be safer with the lion.

"I'm not asking you to be cowardly. I'm asking you to let me keep the only happiness I've ever known."

—Nora Moran, begging to take the fall in hopes of sparing her lover's reputation

The Sin of Nora Moran conveyed provocation in bounds. Identifiable pre-Code story elements like rape and shady legal proceedings were noted in many censor board cuts. Dialogue-wise, "damn" and "my God" were cut in Massachusetts and Pennsylvania, while verbiage such as the italicized part of "He's the man *I lived with . . .*" was removed in New York. Close-ups of chorus girls' behinds, shots of liquor bottles, and a man raising a gun also faced censure in several areas.

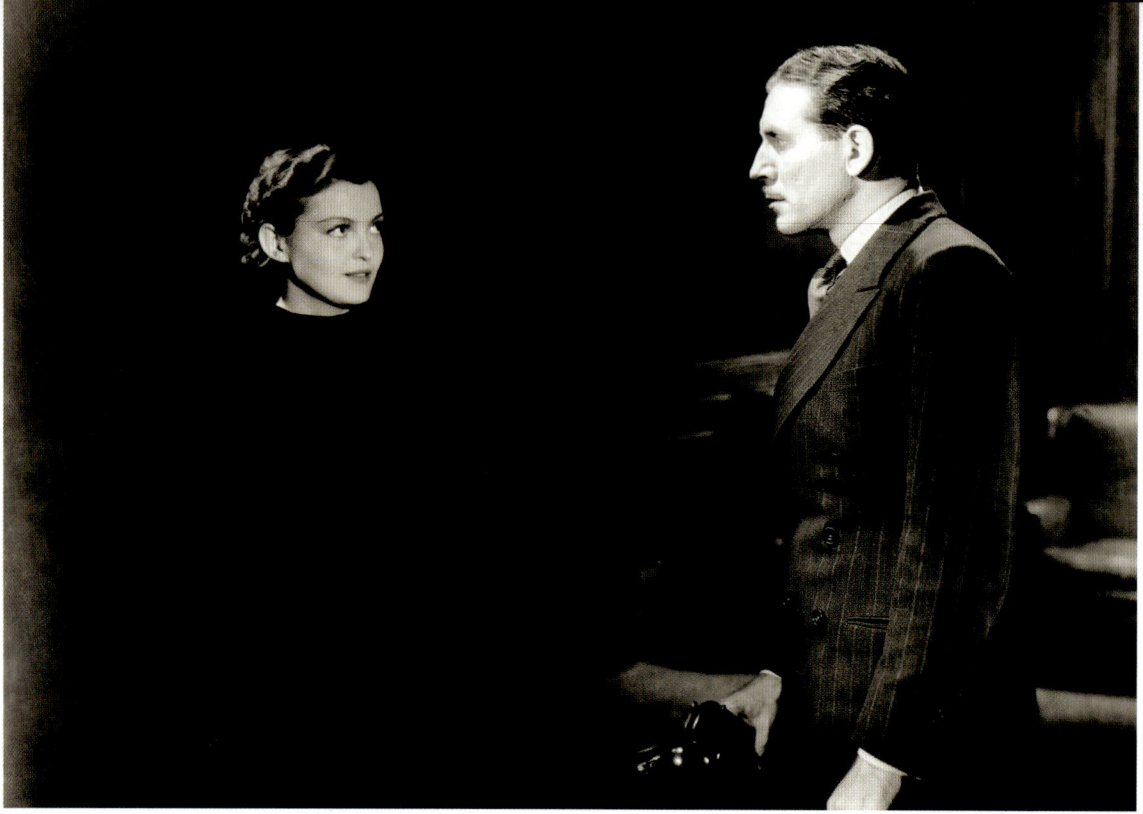

No, your eyes aren't playing tricks on you. Zita Johann's just visiting Paul Cavanagh from the afterlife.

The film was such a thematic minefield that some censor boards found banning it to be the only solution. Lithuania prohibited *The Sin of Nora Moran* because of its "ultra criminal tendencies," while Quebec initially banned it because: "Preparations electrocution [*sic*], mistress and lover story, etc." That latter rejection reminds us that part of the stimulation this movie provides hinges more on twisted psychological grounds than pre-Codes usually deliver. This includes views of an electric chair and scenes where John and Dick discuss Nora's execution while she lies in a coffin in front of them.

Nowhere is the film's provocation more apparent a century later than in its seminal pre-Code poster art. Peruvian artist Alberto Vargas, later known for his iconic World War II pinups, painted the striking central figure. Ironically, the image of a voluptuous barefoot woman curled in defeat visually stands in stark contrast to brunette star Johann.

Though many female characters enjoyed a sense of freedom during the pre-Code era, that wasn't always the case. Women could suffer greatly, as does Nora, and studios wrenched as much intrigue from such a scenario as they could. As innocent and trusting as Nora is and as much as she just wants to mind her business, her life unfolds as one tragedy after another. Her sin was falling in love with an ambitious married man and submitting her own interests to his, sealing her fate. Putting all of one's faith into a politician and getting burned is a lesson that remains difficult for some to learn.

The Sin of Nora Moran is an early example of a picture stitched together using a "narratage"

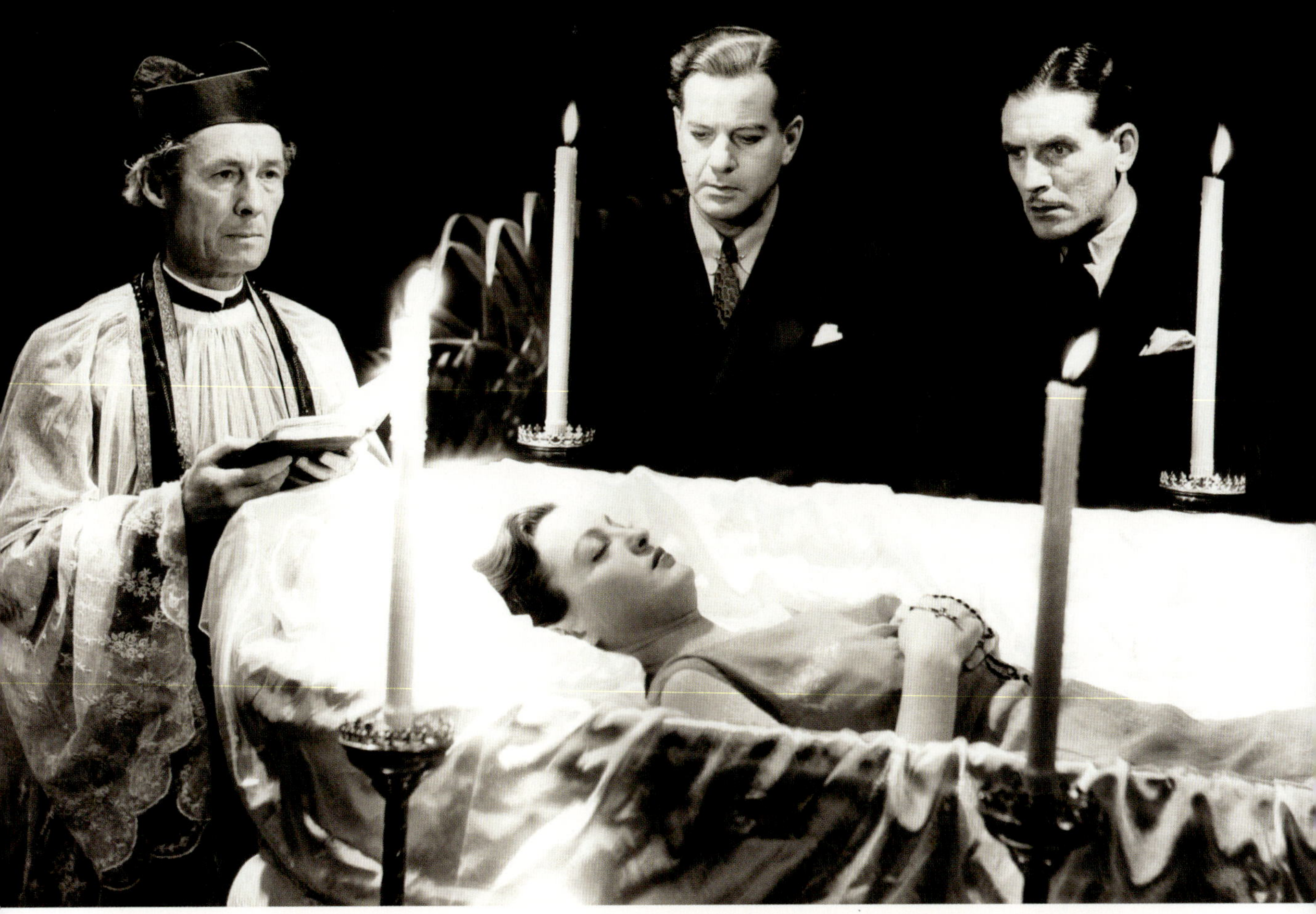

Zita Johann imagining Alan Dinehart and Paul Cavanagh ruminating on her upcoming electrocution.

assembly, a term the Fox publicity department conceived for the nonlinear structure employed in *The Power and the Glory* (1933). Unsurprisingly, that construction proved hard for some critics to untangle. The movie "might have been gripping if it weren't so confusing," the *Chicago Daily Tribune* observed. They weren't kidding: Select sequences, some dreamlike and hallucinatory in nature, take place in both the past and present, while others comment on the future and volunteer to change the narrative. The effect on the viewer is equal parts bewildering and bewitching.

The Sin of Nora Moran intrigues for its haphazard narrative structure, perhaps borne in part out of its low budget, vacillating through gauzy planes of reality, truth, and time. Anticipating more experimental and independent moviemaking to come, *The Sin of Nora Moran*'s stylistic risks and otherworldly atmosphere may have been too far ahead of its time. It's an outlier in the pre-Code canon but nonetheless one of the most uncanny and unflinching films of the era.

I AM SUZANNE!

STARRING
Lilian Harvey, Gene Raymond, and Leslie Banks

DIRECTED BY
Rowland V. Lee

RELEASED BY
Fox, December 1933

"You'll make a beautiful puppet."

—Tony, admiring Suzanne but also speaking for several other characters in the film

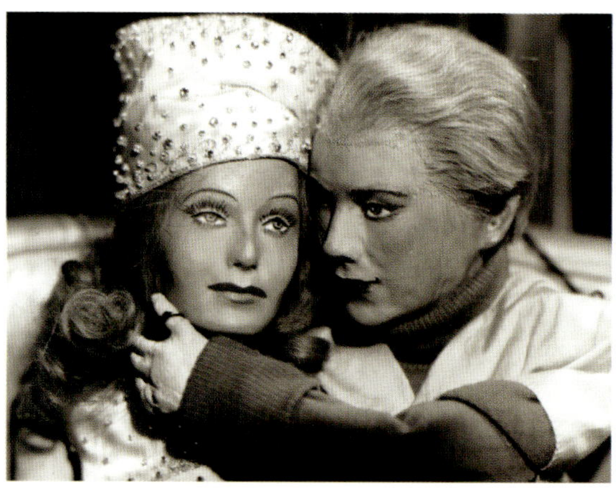

We are both incredibly disturbed and very impressed by these intricately crafted puppets of Lilian Harvey and Gene Raymond.

Rowland V. Lee's *I Am Suzanne!* is an oddball musical/body horror film that almost defies categorization. Though it wasn't pegged as horror on release, its deft combination of genres and exploration of bodily autonomy and sexual hang-ups can be seen as forebears to the works of David Lynch, David Cronenberg, and likely a few other Davids who we can't recall at the moment.

The plot of *I Am Suzanne!* sounds simple: Famous dancer Suzanne (Lilian Harvey) is the rage of Paris, but she doesn't know it. She's sheltered and exploited by her manager, the Baron (Leslie Banks), until she meets Tony (Gene Raymond), the young scion of a family of puppeteers. After Suzanne is injured, Tony re-creates her old stage show with puppets down to the last detail. Slowly, Suzanne comes to the realization that Tony isn't in love with her—he's fallen in love with the Suzanne puppet. In a fit of frustration, she grabs a pistol and shoots the puppet in the heart.

Things spiral from there, as a healed Suzanne returns to dancing and Tony seethes, "We'll see who's better—a human dancer or a puppet dancer!" While opening night of her show proceeds, an exhausted Suzanne slips into a lengthy nightmare where she faces a kangaroo court of demonic puppets. She's awoken to perform in the finale, where she is flipped and tossed for the devil's amusement. This elaborate set piece is enough for Tony to see the error of his ways—and makes the show a smashing success.

Many movies produced by Fox in the pre-Code era can be termed "unhinged," with *I Am Suzanne!* being a peak example. While some studios, like MGM and Warner Bros., kept a production head carefully monitoring their output and other studios like Paramount relied on a system that farmed out their pictures to powerful producers to

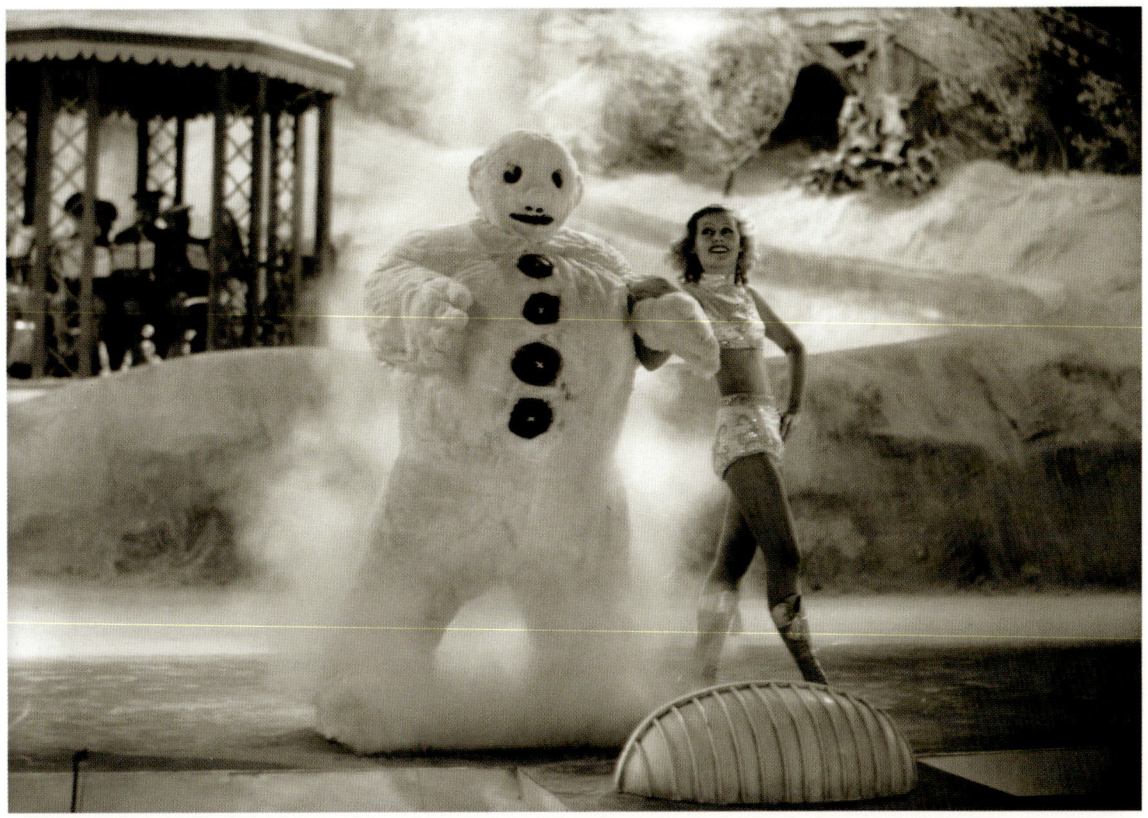

I Am Suzanne! **gets a lot weirder than this scene with Lilian Harvey dancing with a giant snowman.**

guarantee quality, Fox placed its films into the hands of directors. As directors were more commonly concerned with their own vision than financial realities, the quality of Fox's movies could vary wildly. Their films could be beautiful and touching, especially under the auspices of masters like John Ford or Frank Borzage, but just as often they could be distinctly offbeat and stupefying.

Both 1933's *Zoo in Budapest* and *I Am Suzanne!* were the brainchildren of director Roland V. Lee. *Zoo in Budapest* is a dreamy, romantic tale of a boy (also Gene Raymond) who lives in a zoo and seeks to enfold orphan Loretta Young into his luscious paradise, despite a villainous zookeeper looking to turn their fairy tale into a more conventional horror story. Both films are distinctly artistic, filled with allusions and hazy dialogue, resembling little else popular motion pictures were exhibiting at the time.

Harvey was one of many actresses lifted from Europe in the wake of Greta Garbo and Marlene Dietrich. Harvey was wooed by Fox but only made four movies in the United States. She quit during the filming of 1934's *George White's Scandals*; her vacated part helped make a star out of Alice Faye. Harvey would eventually be stripped of her German citizenship by the Nazis during World War II

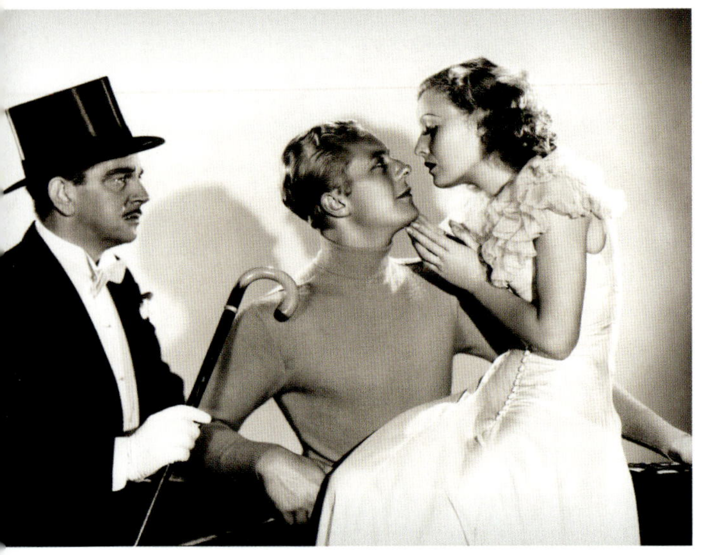

Lilian Harvey is caught in a love triangle with two of the worst men possible: puppeteer Gene Raymond, who is dangerously obsessed with her (more so in puppet form), and manipulative manager Leslie Banks.

for performing for French troops. After appearing in her last film in 1940, she retreated back to the United States during Germany's occupation of France, later returning to Paris, where she opened a souvenir shop and raised snails.

Harvey is tossed and turned frequently throughout *Suzanne*. Though her character is supposed to be a dancer, her act more closely resembles an intricate form of acrobatics as she is heedlessly flung in the air between various groups of men. The actress didn't come out of filming unscathed. It was reported that her legs and hips were bruised, one cotton snowball gave the actress a nosebleed, and she broke two toes during an attempt at a tightrope stunt, forcing the studio to film the musical sequences last.

The Yale Puppeteers built more than two hundred puppets for *I Am Suzanne!* Those puppets are exploited well in a picture that deals heavily in ideas of subsumed thoughts, deception, and sexual kink. Tony's fascination with puppets, besides showcasing the marionettes he'd crafted of ex-girlfriends, extends into his obsessive sketching of hands and legs. He sees everyone as a puppet of one kind, a Pinocchio decrying the unseen strings of society. But that freedom perverts itself in his sexual proclivities. When Suzanne is presented with an engagement present, she cries, "I think you'd really like me to bring puppets into the world instead of children—flesh and blood!"

For poor Suzanne, her identity seems beyond her control until the climactic dance number. Both the Baron and Tony take turns declaring "I am Suzanne!" with indignation, feeling that they are the clear puppet masters of the poor dancer. You don't get examples of her lack of agency more explicit than that, though the dancers who repeatedly fling Suzanne about onstage come in a close second. Strangely, it is left up to the audience to decide if Suzanne ever fully breaks free from these confines. While her frantic performance seemingly proves that humanity wins out over the imagined, she still ends the movie with a rekindled romance with Tony and continued exploitation by the Baron. Has she cut her strings or merely decided to blithefully ignore them?

The censor praise for *I Am Suzanne!* was nearly unanimous, with even the SRC's James Wingate calling the film "an interesting novelty" and Joseph Breen crowing, "It is decidedly novel and entertaining." Despite the spooky puppets and hypersexual themes, the film faced zero issues from domestic censor boards. Australia had one cut: removing a quick shot of Harvey putting on a skirt.

I Am Suzanne! flopped at the box office,

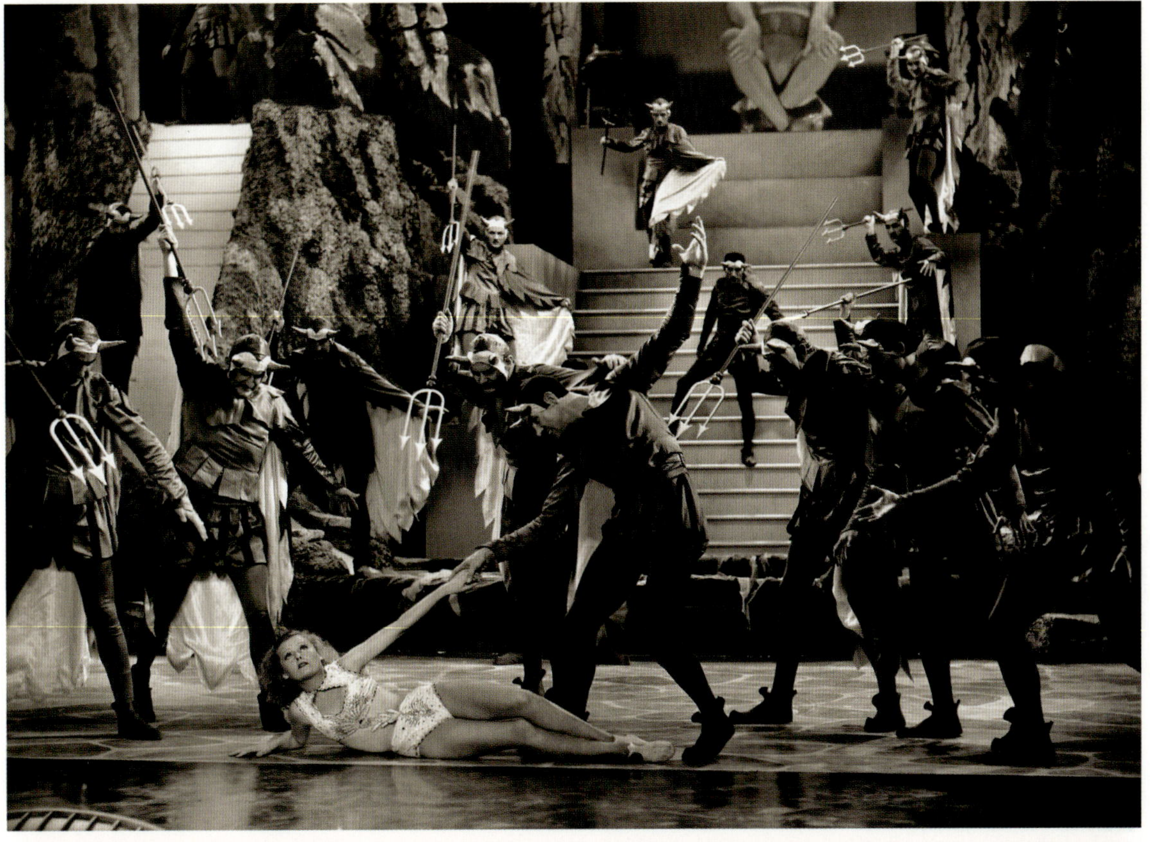

Lilian Harvey experiencing your average nightmare scenario, featuring a cadre of devils with pitchforks.

though not from a lack of praise. In a starred review, *Photoplay* trumpeted, "Here is something entirely different at last." *Modern Screen* enthused, "It's novel, it's wholesome, it's good film entertainment for the family." (Further proof that parents in the 1930s were made of sterner stuff; in a world where my child gets upset by a mildly tense episode of *PAW Patrol*, it's hard to imagine how kids would take puppets threatening to impregnate a woman.) Undoubtedly too strange for 1933 audiences, and possibly still too out-there for many twenty-first century moviegoers, *I Am Suzanne!* nonetheless earns raves when it makes brief reappearances at film festivals. In a modern world of displaced online avatars and personas, *I Am Suzanne!*'s tangled romance fits more comfortably than ever; after all, nowadays everyone has their own digital identity in cyberspace that they can choreograph exactly as they'd like. Told with music and dripping with kinky insinuations, *I Am Suzanne!* is one of the weirdest films produced for a mainstream audience, a child-friendly nightmare whose own title may be a misnomer.

FLYING DOWN TO RIO

STARRING
Dolores del Río, Gene Raymond, Raul Roulien, Ginger Rogers, and Fred Astaire

DIRECTED BY
Thornton Freeland

RELEASED BY
RKO, December 1933

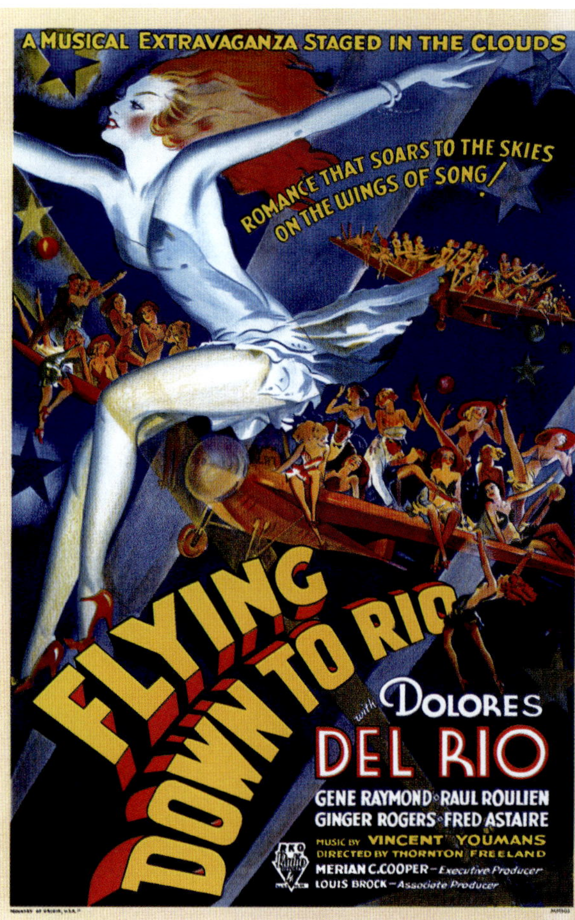

Under Warner Bros. and more specifically Busby Berkeley, the movie musical renaissance had arrived. With the addition of new technology and special effects, musical numbers could be big, loud, and over-the-top. Setting their sights on a hit, RKO decided to take a gamble on a film that would ultimately save the studio from bankruptcy and debut one of the most famous cinematic pairings of all time.

Flying Down to Rio begins in Miami with the band The Yankee Clippers. They have a problem in that their leader, Roger (Gene Raymond), has a penchant for chasing after beautiful women. His singer, Honey Hale (Ginger Rogers), and best friend Fred (Fred Astaire) commiserate and predict certain doom when Roger spots beautiful Belinha (Dolores del Río) across the hotel lobby. Roger and Belinha dance, flirt, and feud—and Roger is fired. He bounces back quickly, landing his band a gig at the grand opening of the Hotel Atlantico in Rio de Janeiro.

In Rio, they discover the hotel doesn't have an entertainment permit and desperate measures must be taken to save the venue from racketeers. Fred devises a plan that skirts the law: While the Clippers play their signature number, "The Carioca," they arrange for a daring aerial extravaganza with showgirls on biplane wings to thrill crowds just outside the hotel. The central love affair comes to its overdue conclusion, the venue is

A small part of this musical extravaganza is staged in the clouds, but there are a lot of chorus girls!

"What have these South Americans got below the equator that we haven't?"

—Belinha's innocent friend, who doesn't quite understand what she's asking

saved, and Fred and Honey toast to a job well done.

RKO, which owned the record label RCA, was a big beneficiary of music sales, and "The Carioca" helped lift the film. The snappy hit, which includes women in see-through skirts twisting and turning in tightly coordinated arrangements while rubbing foreheads with leering partners, leaves Honey blushing and moaning, "Oh, Freddy. Is my mind red!" The number features the first on-screen dance pairing of Fred Astaire and Ginger Rogers. Though they are the sidekicks here, this is the first of ten pictures that Astaire and Rogers costarred in, becoming the romantic leads in their next film, 1934's *The Gay Divorcee.*

Astaire and Rogers had dated for a short time in New York before Rogers left for Hollywood and stardom. When reunited, Rogers found Astaire, now married, a more serious and changed man, though their relationship remained cordial. At the core, however, was a fundamental difference in opinion in how the dancing was crafted. Astaire spent weeks creating and meticulously designing each step with his collaborator Hermes Pan, whom he met initially on this film. All the while, Rogers worked on a variety of other movies. Once Astaire had the composition planned out, it was Pan's job to teach Rogers her choreography in just a fraction of the time.

RKO's knack for sensational special effects, earlier showcased in *King Kong*, was again on display. The actual planes the women danced atop were only a few feet off the ground in a hangar with rear projection and wind machines to complete the illusion. Process shots helped with some of the wider angles, such as the startling sequence where one of the dancers falls off a plane and, remarkably, is caught by dancers on another aircraft. Cameramen spent a month in Rio capturing the city in every direction, fooling some audience members into thinking the whole film was made on location.

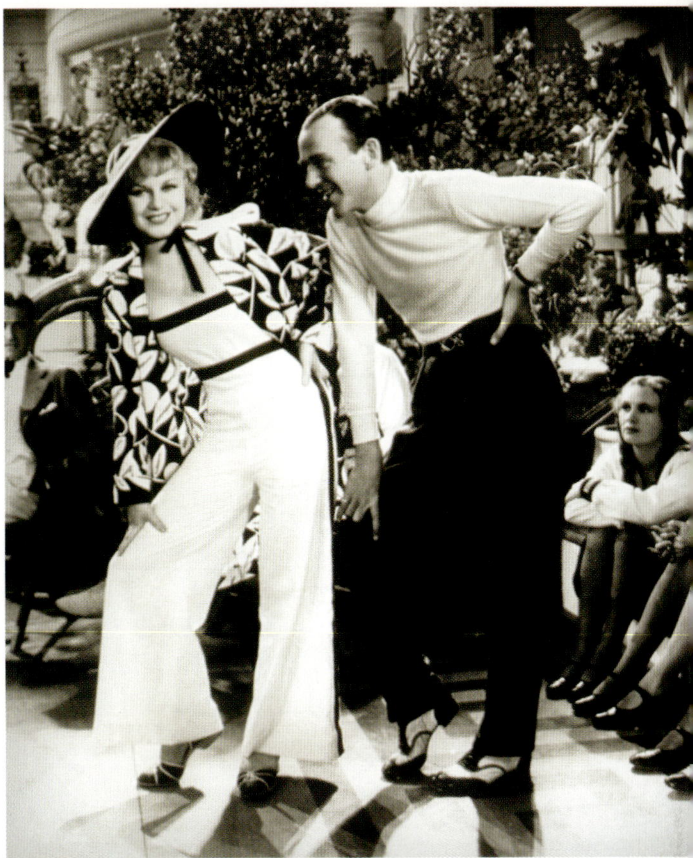

Ginger Rogers and Fred Astaire started their famed partnership during the pre-Code period.

Flying Down to Rio was a box office smash.

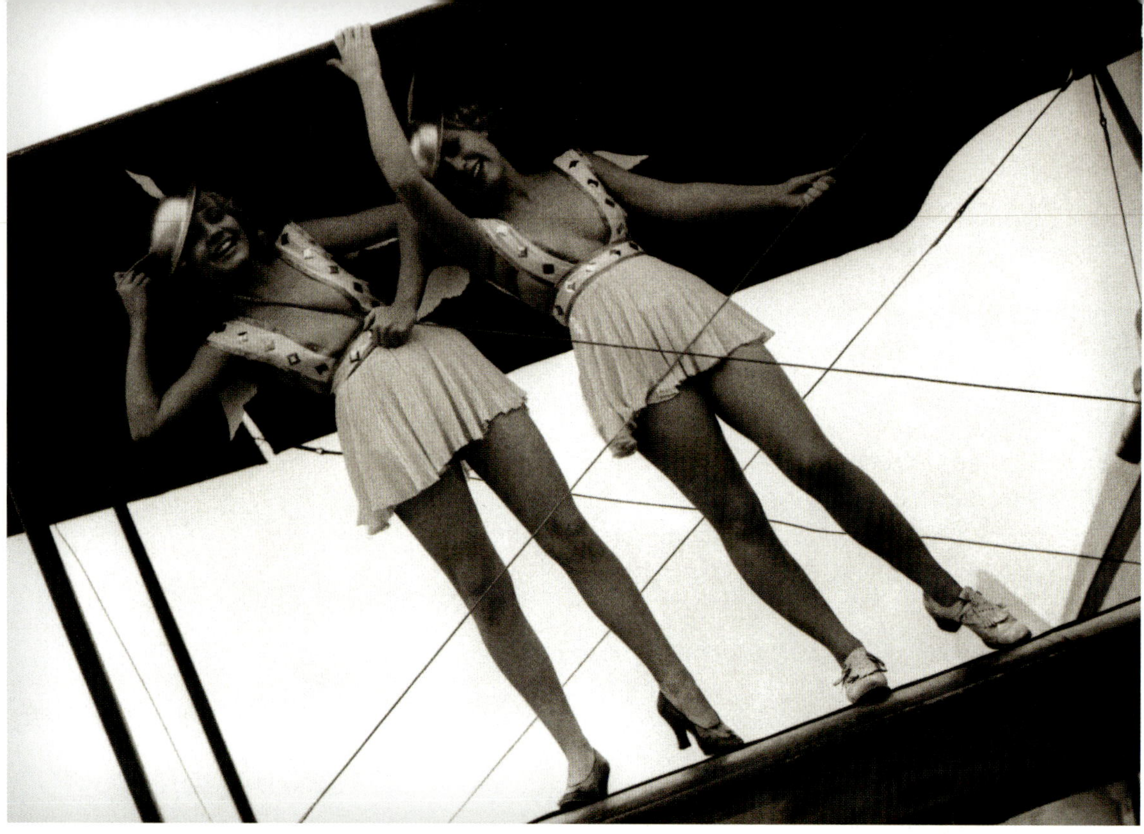

It wouldn't be a pre-Code with the word *flying* in the title if there wasn't a dance sequence atop biplanes with women whose clothes blow off midair.

Interest in flying increased nationally, much to the delight of RKO executive Merian C. Cooper, who also served on the Board of Directors for Pan Am. The film also brought such popularity to Brazil that the real-life mayor of Rio de Janeiro supposedly offered to name a town after the man who'd come up with the movie idea, producer Louis Brock.

The film's exotic flavors met some opposition. The SRC logged several suggestions following their script review, noting profanity, dialogue that could potentially offend South Americans, and the maître d's insistence that he won't tolerate "round heels" on chambermaids. (Roundheels in the 1930s was slang for a promiscuous woman. Really.) After reviewing the picture, the SRC's only advice was to remove the south-of-the-border quip quoted on the previous page, as it was "practically a thorn in a bed of roses."

The equator reference stayed in—and was subsequently excised by at least five local censor boards. The line, "I can tell what they are thinking about from up here" and suggestive shots during "The Carioca" and biplane numbers were also chopped in several locations. New York and Kansas passed the film with no cuts, while Germany rejected it on the grounds that the "picture is inartistic and immoral."

When RKO inquired about rereleasing *Flying Down to Rio* in 1935, they hit the roadblock known as the PCA. A myriad of edits was demanded to bring the movie into compliance with the Code, such as removing the "offensive sex suggestiveness" of "The Carioca," which included close-ups of a couple dancing "in an indecent manner." Additionally, "the entire colored troup [*sic*], with the exception of the finale, might well be dispensed with," they advised; we assume that's mainly due to racism. Well-known issues like the equator comment and round heel lines were also eliminated, as were many shots of the dancers on planes, as the PCA felt the cameras were focused too much on the women's posteriors and crotches.

Like much of RKO's best output in the early 1930s, *Flying Down to Rio* is sophisticated, confident, and constructed beautifully from top to bottom. While its reputation as the first pairing of Astaire and Rogers is important, the movie is also a riotous example of cross-cultural expectation bending, one that feels both art deco and decidedly modern.

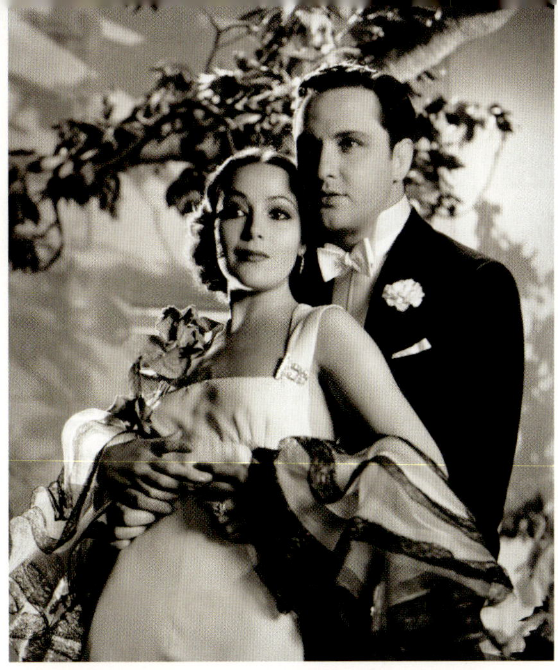

Mexican-born Dolores del Río received top billing in *Flying Down to Rio* and a plum love triangle with Raul Roulien and Gene Raymond.

Dolores del Río

While Fred Astaire and Ginger Rogers are the most recognizable cast members in *Flying Down to Rio* to modern viewers, it's easy to forget that they're fourth and fifth billed. The film's nominal star, though less well remembered in the United States, is Dolores del Río. Growing up a member of Mexican aristocracy, del Río saw famed ballerina Anna Pavlova perform and became determined to be a dancer. She was discovered by film director Edwin Carewe in 1925, and he took her and her husband back to Hollywood with the intent of capitalizing on her foreignness much in the same way Rudolph Valentino had taken the film capital by storm. Her third picture, *What Price Glory?* (1926), was one of the year's highest-grossing movies, and del Río's career took off, making her the first crossover Latina star in Hollywood.

Del Río made the transition to talkies without a bump, signing a contract with RKO and starring in pre-Code pictures like *Bird of Paradise*, where she spent most of the film wearing only a lei to cover her breasts and dancing wildly to inflame a similarly scantily clad Joel McCrea. She starred in a pair of films at Warner Bros., 1934's *Madame Du Barry* and *Wonder Bar*, both of which were heavily censored. After del Río's Hollywood stardom began a steady descent in the mid-1930s, she returned to Mexico in 1943, where she played a vital role in the emergence of the Golden Age of Mexican cinema, most notably as the lead in *María Candelaria* (1943), the first Latin American film to win the Grand Prix prize at Cannes.

DESIGN FOR LIVING

STARRING
Fredric March, Gary Cooper, Miriam Hopkins, and Edward Everett Horton

DIRECTED BY
Ernst Lubitsch

RELEASED BY
Paramount, December 1933

Would you believe in pre-Code polyamory? Watching *Design for Living* a century later, it's hard to imagine that movie theaters across America in 1933 screened a picture that so defiantly eschewed socially acceptable sexual conventions with such impunity. In *Design for Living*, not only are an unwed man and woman living together. Oh no. That was a situation actually rather commonplace during the pre-Code era. Instead, the picture one-upped the competition and threw another man into the mix.

Before cameras even rolled, Ernst Lubitsch's *Design for Living* was cast in the terrifically giant shadow of Noël Coward's celebrated stage play. Even though Ben Hecht's script retained only a few lines of Coward's original, the extremely loose adaptation could not escape comparison, most of it negative. Thankfully, time has helped the film's reputation grow on its own merits.

Design for Living starts rolling on a French train, where an amusing silent sequence introduces us to spirited Gilda (Miriam Hopkins), painter George (Gary Cooper), and playwright Tom (Fredric March). After they disembark, Gilda begins seeing both men, unbeknownst to either of them, which ruffles the feathers of her straight-edge advertising boss, Max (Edward Everett Horton). Naturally, George and Tom fall for her, but Gilda, equally enamored with both, can't choose. So, Gilda suggests all three take up residence together, with her as a "mother of the arts," and they enter into a gentleman's agreement prohibiting sex.

What can go wrong with that arrangement? Only everything. With the help of Gilda's vigorous guidance, George and Tom each achieve success, but jealousy soon surfaces. Partners are traded off, but when it comes to a head, Gilda wants none of the drama. She ditches both paramours and settles for marriage with Max, but how long could she possibly survive such convention?

Certainly, *Design for Living* benefits from Coward's foundation, Hecht's sharp script, and Lubitsch's sophisticated direction. Oh, and we can't forget to mention Hopkins, Cooper, and March, who all operate (mostly) in sync as they trek uncharted terrain as if living under normal circumstances, with few questions asked. The leads' charisma and allure advertise immorality in a radiant light despite a tendency from Lubitsch to overdramatize some of the love scenes. The SRC wasted no time scoping out this future headache,

"It's true we have a gentleman's agreement, but unfortunately, I am no gentleman."

—Gilda, a beautiful woman and, as she notes, not a gentleman

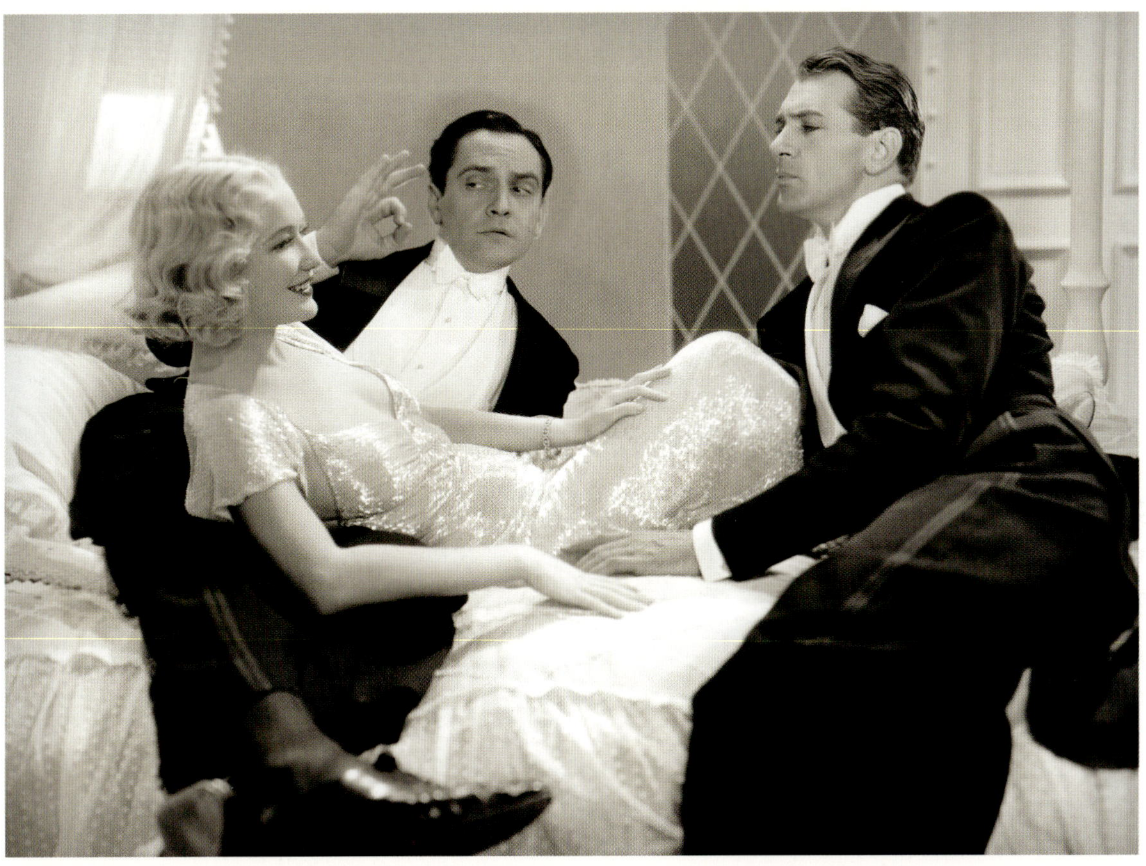

If you have a no-sex policy, maybe don't chat while sitting on a bed.

sending a representative to attend a performance one day after the play opened on Broadway in early 1933. The reviewer was "somewhat doubtful" mass audiences would share Coward's idea that his unconventional characters and their actions were excused because artists live by their own moral code. Naturally, the SRC knew they'd have to put a lid on those elements.

In reality, Hecht and Lubitsch did that themselves. James Wingate reported to Will H. Hays that the script had been significantly rewritten and admitted: "The basic story—three people who find there is something more important in life than sex—should be satisfactory under the Code, and whatever loose living is indicated, is not justified, but is shown as inimical to their happy relationship." Though Wingate understated its significance, sex plays a central role in the story, and the SRC voiced particular concern in the details. For instance, the office urged the studio to visually establish "sufficient accommodation for three to live separable," as if that was enough to hinder any implication of unsavory romantic relations.

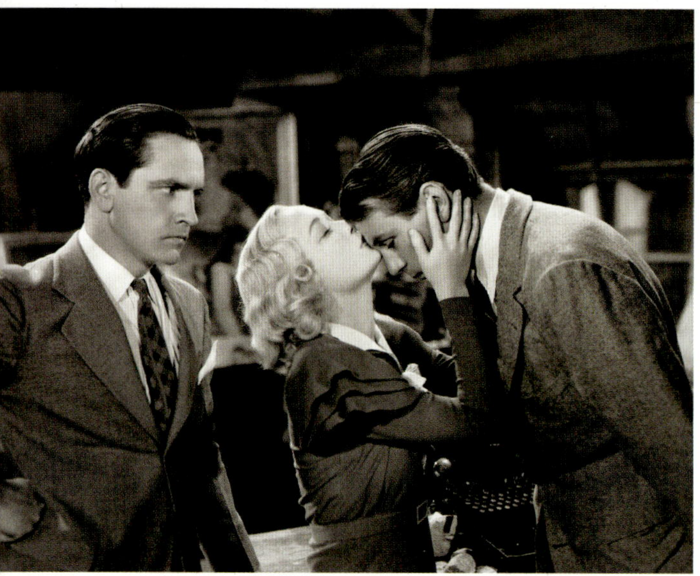

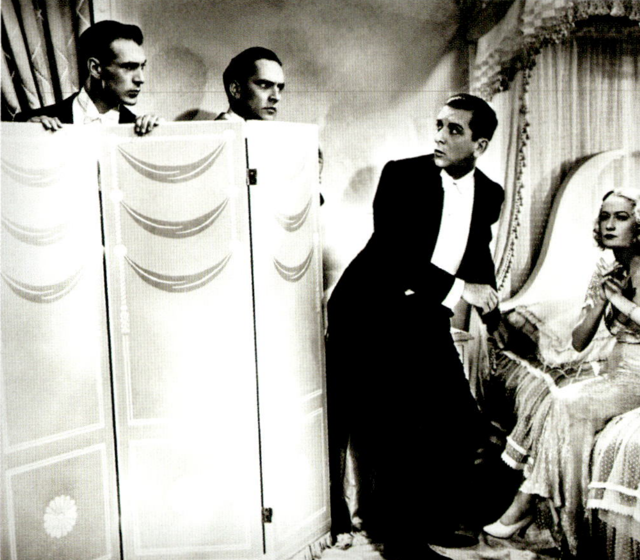

FROM LEFT: Fredric March expresses his jealousy over Miriam Hopkins's kiss on Gary Cooper's forehead. • It's clear Miriam Hopkins won't last in a conventional marriage with Edward Everett Horton as long as Fredric March and Gary Cooper are hanging around.

Eventually, Lubitsch was tasked with re-editing parts of two reels, the result of which the SRC deemed satisfactory. New York and Chicago passed the movie with zero edits, while other boards called for small cuts, including scenes where the characters are looking at a bed and the italicized part of the remark, "Two *slightly used* artists, in the ash can."

Plenty of critics highlighted (and several mourned) the differences between the play and movie, but the film also received its fair share of positive press. For instance, *The Billboard* reported the "picture should give 100 per cent satisfaction wherever shown," and *The New York Times* wrote, "It is always alert, imaginative and amusing." *Design for Living* also proved any doubters wrong at the box office, ranking among the top grossing films of 1933.

Not long after release, *Design for Living*'s sexually suggestive plot attracted the ire of the newly formed Catholic Legion of Decency, landing on the group's list of sixty-three pictures banned for Catholic viewing. In 1935, the PCA informed Paramount that the film would be withdrawn from circulation. RKO attempted a remake in 1940 and got nowhere after Breen insisted that they would have to drop inferences of illicit sexual relationships; obviously that wouldn't leave much. When Paramount dared approach Breen in 1944 regarding a rerelease, he reiterated his 1935 reply, adding that *Design for Living* "was one of the pictures which contributed much to the nation-wide public protest against motion pictures."

Many acclaim *Design for Living* for being ahead of its time, but one could argue the picture is ahead even of *our* time in certain ways. As critic Kim Morgan points out, a mainstream movie centering on a ménage à trois with such a light approach would still qualify as a rare sighting. There's also the rather atypical character portrayal, most noticeably with Gilda, described by a 1933 *Variety* reviewer as "simulating the masculine trait of amorous adventure with several before deciding on one." Test-driving love isn't socially acceptable for women, and she knows it. (Heck, though it's more common a century later, it's hardly celebrated.)

The sequence in which Gilda derides society for allowing men to play the field while the fairer sex must "decide purely on instinct" to remain "nice" still astounds for the way in which it so firmly tackles sexual inequality and social mores. Moments later, when Gilda proposes the idea of living together and proclaims, "Boys, it's the only thing we can do: Let's forget sex," we already know the declaration only serves the purpose of censorship; it's damn near impossible to put a lid on that kind of attraction.

The way in which George and Tom are portrayed also caused a stir among some critics. Most exceptionally, a *Los Angeles Times* article written by a "reasonably good feminist" asserted that "never was masculinity so shamefully belittled" and assured readers that a full-bloom matriarchy was on its way. On behalf of the female viewers, she accused the picture of "rushing emancipation upon us" and alleged the portrayal of a ménage à trois is "apt to give us ideas," particularly when Gilda dabbled in marriage and found it lacking. Surely, in the author's mind, if the status quo were to crumble anytime within the foreseeable future, *Design for Living* would undoubtedly bear some of the blame.

Design for Living freely flaunts its indiscretion and disparages the Code while staying just inside its bounds. So reform groups placing pressure on the industry wanted movies to preach morality? Okay, *Design for Living* allows Gilda to flirt with convention by hitching her with uptight Max. But it doesn't take, just like attempts to enforce the 1930 Production Code. When George and Tom swoop in to save her, we're convinced that their new "gentleman's agreement" holds as much water as the first. There are some fascinations that you can't contain.

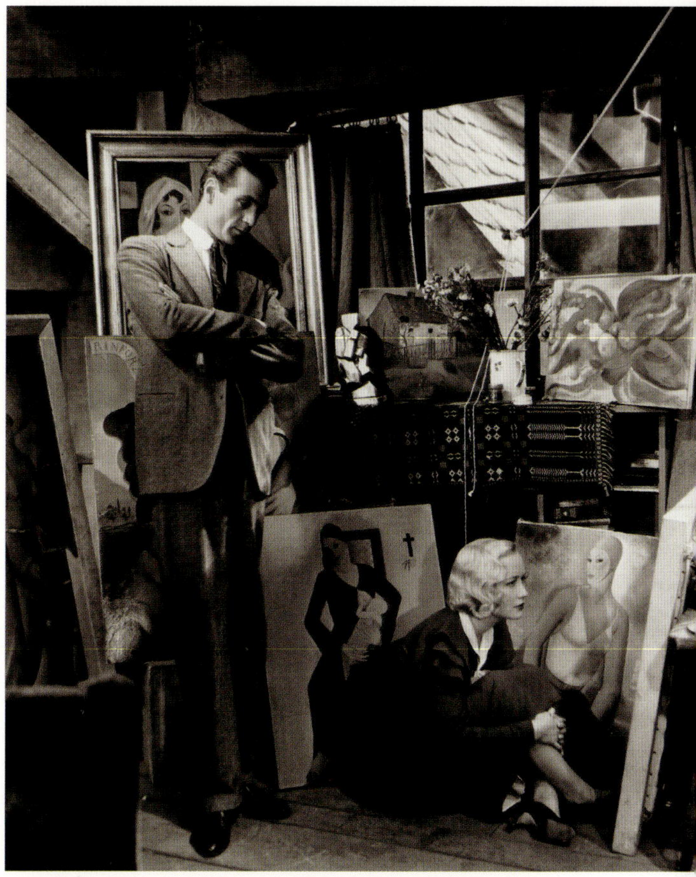

Miriam Hopkins acts as a matron of the arts to Gary Cooper (and Fredric March, not pictured), which was basically the friends with benefits of the 1930s.

QUEEN CHRISTINA

STARRING
Greta Garbo, John Gilbert, Ian Keith, Lewis Stone, Elizabeth Young, and C. Aubrey Smith

DIRECTED BY
Rouben Mamoulian

RELEASED BY
MGM, December 1933

"I have been memorizing this room. In the future, in my memory, I shall live a great deal in this room."

—Queen Christina after a night of passion, free from responsibilities; now that's the life . . .

What is it like when your sex life is the only thing other people care about? Dismaying, we assume. *Queen Christina*, MGM's big-budget take on the infamous Swedish monarch, turns her into a celebrity. While she's a capable, energetic leader with the ability to politick with ease, she suffers from innate loneliness at the top. *Queen Christina* is an exploration of what freedom really is and the sacrifices made to attain it.

The title character Christina (Greta Garbo) finds herself tired of the intricacies of war and politics after ascending the throne as a child. Though a beloved leader, Christina feels trapped. All of this changes when she encounters a Spanish envoy, Antonio (John Gilbert). The two have an intimate meet-cute, with Antonio originally believing that Christina, in her masculine clothing, is a man. When the two are pressured into sharing a room at an inn during a snowstorm, Antonio learns his error, and they spend fruitful days making love before the roaring fire.

Christina obscures her true identity until Antonio enters court and realizes he is now the queen's consort. But all of Sweden is jockeying for whom will be the next king. Christina knows it's Antonio she wants, but the demands of her position

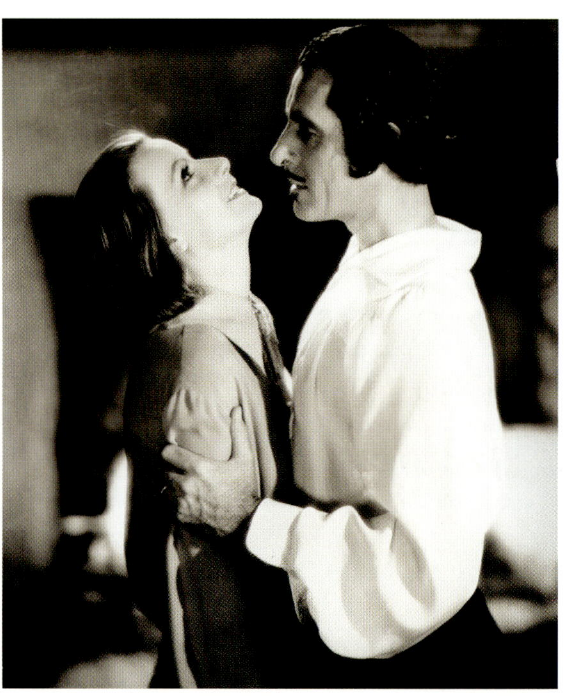

John Gilbert demonstrating that one never knows what form your true love will show up in—it could even be a queen dressed as a man.

leave her in an impossible situation, and she eventually makes the bold choice to abdicate her throne and run off with him. Mad with jealousy and anger, schemer Magnus (Ian Keith) duels Antonio, killing him in combat. Christina says her goodbyes and boards a ship toward a future unknown.

Greta Garbo was MGM's biggest moneymaker, but she was tired of working for the studio and prepared to leave the country after her contract expired in 1932. She signed a two-movie deal with MGM with unique provisions that allowed her approval of the film's script and crew, something unheard of in Hollywood at the time.

John Gilbert, who had been completely cast away from MGM after *Downstairs*, was not the first or even fifth choice for Antonio. Laurence Olivier, still a relatively unknown in Hollywood, was originally cast. After filming began, however, Garbo didn't warm up to Olivier. She then insisted on Gilbert taking the role, much to Louis B. Mayer's chagrin.

The movie's famous ending of Christina looking over the bow of the ship with her face completely emotionless came from a suggestion by producer Walter Wanger, who recalled the finale to *The Bitter Tea of General Yen* and its lengthy close-up on Barbara Stanwyck. Mamoulian, who had been fighting against the studio's impulses for a happy ending (sparing Antonio) readily agreed to this solution. To capture the shot, which moves from the distance to a close-up of Garbo's face, a new lens and shooting technique were invented. Mamoulian captured the moment in only two takes on the last day of filming.

Queen Christina is notable for its many queer undertones. Besides Christina's penchant for cross-dressing, the movie contains a same-sex kiss between Ebba (Elizabeth Young) and Christina, along with heavy-handed hints that they'd been having a love affair. The rather blatant allusions to lesbianism infuriated Joseph Breen and groups like the newly formed Catholic Legion of Decency.

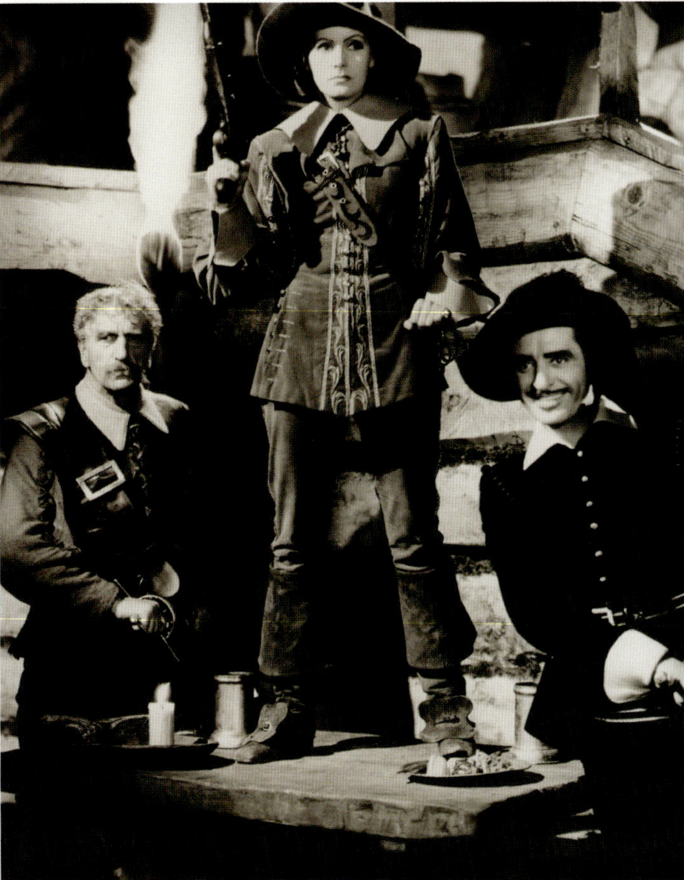

As Queen Christina, Greta Garbo feels trapped within the confines of her leadership. Solution: masquerade as a man.

From the beginning, the SRC warned that Christina and Antonio's liaison presented a major Code violation. "Perhaps it would be possible to change the sequence in such a way as to show that Antonio leaves the room after discovering that

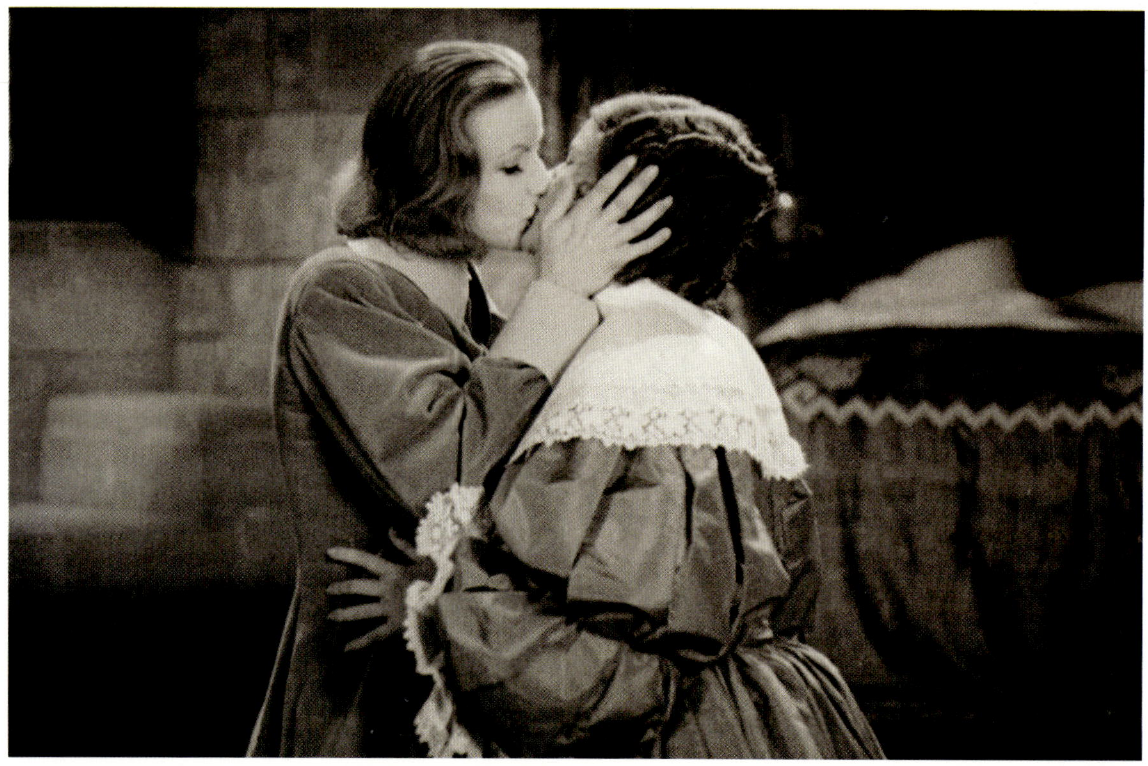

Men, women—Greta Garbo seemed open to them all in *Queen Christina*, including lady-in-waiting Elizabeth Young.

his companion is a girl," the SRC suggested. The insinuation of lesbianism was also warned to be avoided. The second issue eventually fell by the wayside, but the first remained a major sticking point, even as the studio informed the SRC they would film the sequence in several ways. Breen bluntly commented, "I think Miss Garbo should be kept away from the bed entirely."

To the SRC's chagrin, *Queen Christina* went to the New York censors without their approval; at that point, they still considered the bedroom scene unacceptable. Wanger objected to Breen's attempt to force MGM to further alter the sequence, which meant the movie, officially in violation of the Code, was sent to a jury of producers to rule on its fate. Representatives from RKO, Universal, and Fox all agreed: no further cuts to *Queen Christina*, keeping the film as it screened in New York. Once again, the studios protected one another, but across the country, the forces of censorship grew and united as never before.

Still, the bedroom scene remained a major issue for local boards, with the sequence being truncated in at least a half dozen states. Christina's line, "This is how the Lord must have felt when he first beheld the finished world" was a favorite target of many boards, too. Mamoulian had worked to compose the scene as such to resemble a tone

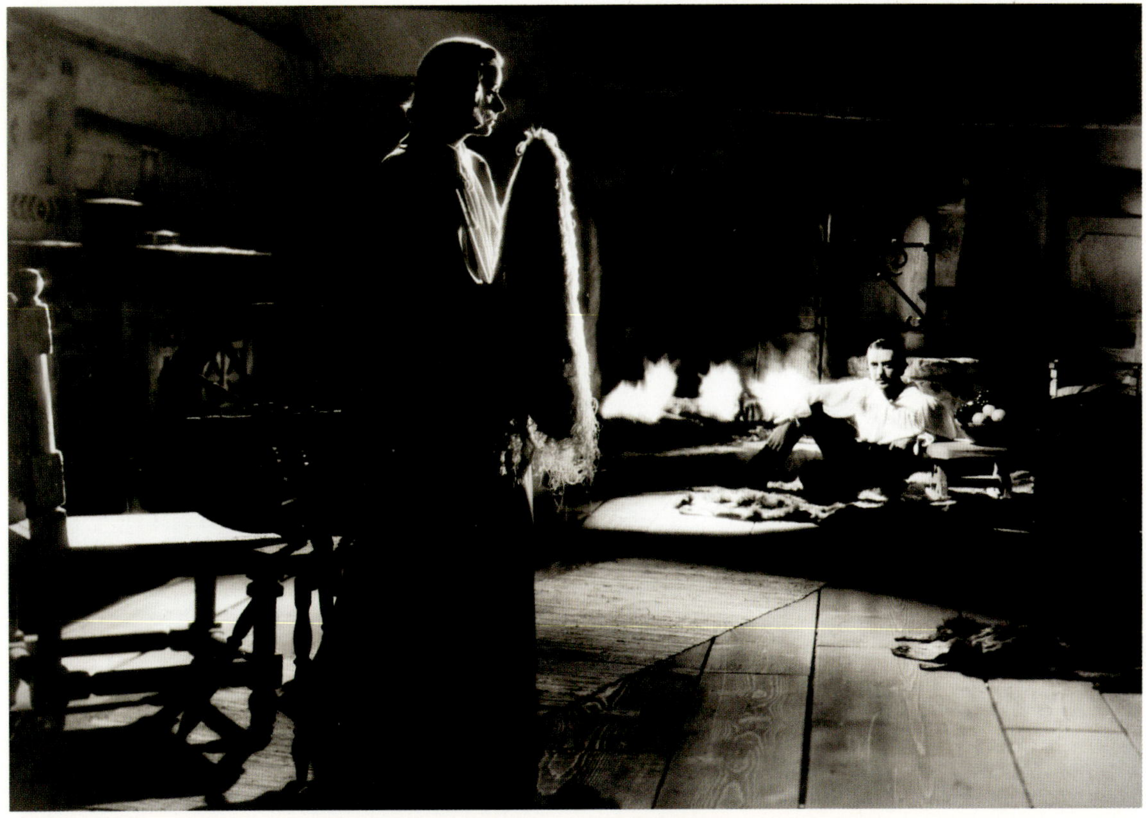

Easily one of the sexiest scenes in pre-Code cinema.

poem; censors not only eliminated subtext but an entire mood from the picture.

As a powerful female ruler, Queen Christina's love life was constantly under a microscope and up for public debate. The idea that notable figures have less privacy and personal freedom wasn't new in 1933, but it's an idea that modern audiences are so much more attuned to given the rise of social media and the invasive online scrutiny celebrities and civilians alike are subject to. Whether it's a group of men arguing over the amount of lovers Queen Christina enjoyed in the past year or her frustration at not being able to live her life as she chooses, dressing as a man so she can come and go undetected, the film reinforces the negative ways in which women's lives are perceived and regulated, themes that reverberate to this day.

Even though it stands as a flashpoint of the pre-Code era, there is nothing tawdry about *Queen Christina*, which is sophisticated and thoughtful, providing Garbo her most electric and sensuous role of the sound era. Its refreshing takes on sex and love and its faith in its main character to push her into discomfort and reflection make it among the finest American films ever crafted.

HEAT LIGHTNING

STARRING
Aline MacMahon, Ann Dvorak, Preston Foster, Lyle Talbot, Glenda Farrell, Frank McHugh, and Ruth Donnelly

DIRECTED BY
Mervyn LeRoy

RELEASED BY
Warner Bros., March 1934

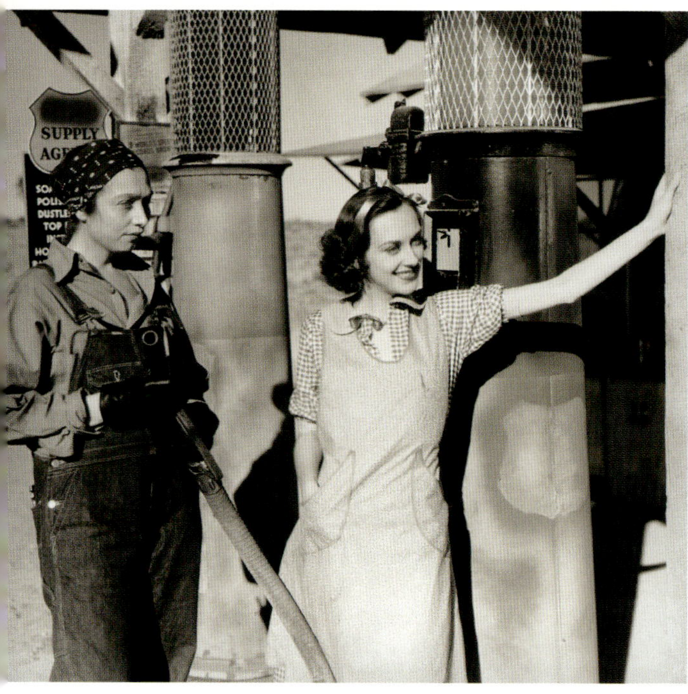

Sisters Aline MacMahon and Ann Dvorak run a gas station and restaurant in the desert in *Heat Lightning*, one of the most unique pre-Codes produced.

Audiences in the pre-Code period were no stranger to strong female characters, both at home and on the job. Representing the latter category, Ruth Chatterton starred in *Female* as a woman auto executive, while Kay Francis played authoritative doctors in *Mary Stevens, M.D.* (1933) and *Dr. Monica* (1934)—and those are just a few examples. But viewers probably weren't prepared to watch a tough-as-nails female mechanic boss it up on-screen—and neither are some of the characters in *Heat Lightning.*

Seeing women run their own business is one element that makes this picture unique—another is its desolate rural setting. *Heat Lightning*'s offbeat script called for dramatic and proto-noir flourishes that balance alongside bawdy comedy, all of which the cast and director Mervyn LeRoy executed with ease. But perhaps they did too good a job. In an already scorching setting, the film's sizzling sexual references and innuendo—three implied seductions in the course of sixty-three minutes!—unsurprisingly came under fire from the SRC and various censor entities.

In *Heat Lightning,* sisters Olga (Aline MacMahon) and Myra (Ann Dvorak) run a service station and restaurant in the middle of the desert. Olga has seen enough of life and wears her overalls with the same unadorned indifference as her unimpressed expression. Myra is still young and aches to see the world. She's met a guy in town who promises to show it to her; Olga promises to stop it.

The hot day spirals out of control from there. The small sheds the sisters keep in the back fill up with guests unexpectedly, like Ms. Tifton (Glenda Farrell), Ms. Ashton-Ashley (Ruth Donnelly), and their chauffeur Frank (Frank McHugh). There's also Everett (Willard Robertson), a local crushing on Olga. And then arrives a pair of criminals on the lam, led by George (Preston Foster), who has a rocky history with Olga, one of manipulation and aggression. Their reunion turns south by the end of the night, resulting in an explosion of violence.

Atmosphere is king in *Heat Lightning*. The picture is infused with it, a mix of lackadaisical waiting and sinister yearning on an endless night. Distant storms line the horizon, entrapping the characters. Sex permeates the air as something forbidden but limiting; any escape it offers comes at a price.

The picture began life as a Broadway play penned by Leon Abrams and George Abbott, briefly mounted on the Great White Way just before production on the film began. Warner Bros. chose to produce *Heat Lightning* mostly on location in central California. LeRoy remembered it as being "probably the most uncomfortable film I ever made" due to the intense heat and a hurried schedule.

Bottled up in different ways—Olga emotionally restrained, Myra frustrated with her dead-end situation—MacMahon and Dvorak possessed an uncanny sisterly resemblance and created a convincing dynamic on-screen. *Heat Lightning* marked MacMahon's first (and one of her few) leading roles, while Dvorak was on her way down at the studio, mostly the result of her skipping out on her contract in favor of a yearlong honeymoon in 1932.

As far as censorship goes, *Heat Lightning*'s main objection from the SRC was the suggested sexual relationships. In a letter from James Wingate to Will H. Hays, he reported that the screenplay "indicated three seductions, only one of which seemed to be legitimate plot material." The SRC also fixated on specific language that implied illicit relations; they even advised changing one of Myra's lines with the addition of a single word, from: "What if I was with a man?" to: "What if I was *out* with a man?" To the SRC, one term could make all the difference.

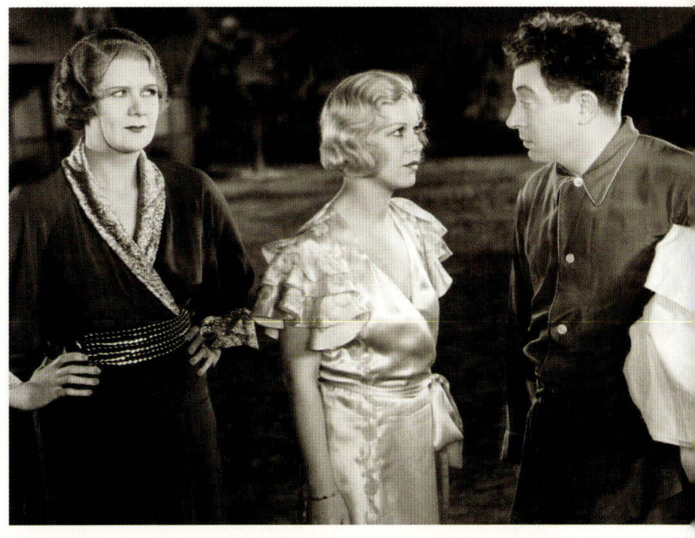

Rich divorcées Ruth Donnelly and Glenda Farrell give chauffeur Frank McHugh plenty of grief—and provide some laughs while they're at it.

In May 1934, Detroit Catholic publications were running their first list of films banned for members of the Catholic Legion of Decency, and *Heat Lightning* was among the titles. The picture

"Must be a big help sometimes, being like you, Olga. Not having any feeling."

—Everett to Olga, after she took out a rat who once meant something to her—and we're not talking about the animal

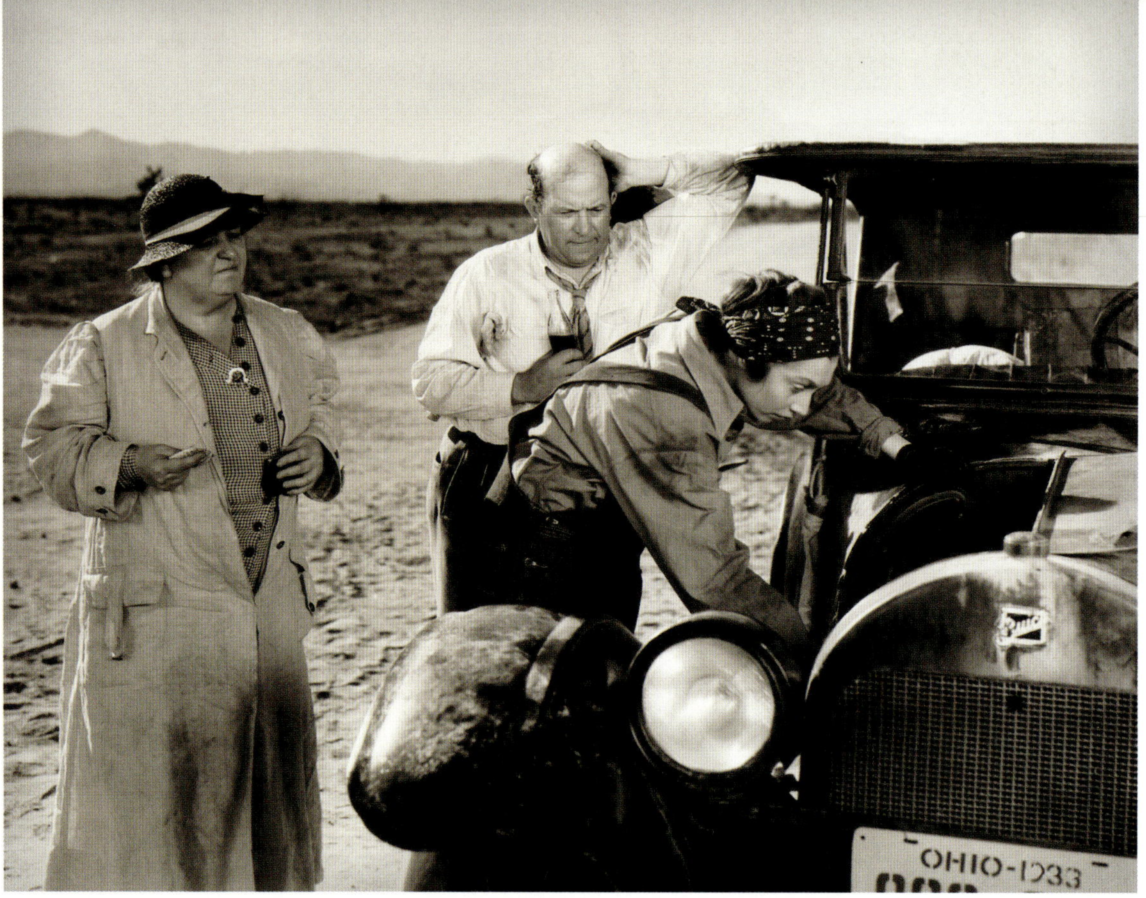

Aline MacMahon proving two more doubters wrong.

also faced considerable censorship in the United States, where sex and violence topped the complaints. (Save for one outlier, the Chicago board, which astonishingly passed the movie with no eliminations.) Many boards took issue with the italicized portion of George's dialogue: "You get that safe open. *I didn't spend all that time with that dame for nothing*," and his lack of feeling for the men he murdered during a robbery: "Those two guys were born to be drilled at two o'clock Tuesday and that's when they got it." Several entities also butchered Myra and Olga's fiery confrontation, including the phrase: "I'll tell you, because you were with a man yourself!"

When Warner Bros. attempted to secure a PCA certificate to rerelease *Heat Lightning* in 1936, it did not go well. Grouped with other questionable movies, the PCA argued the films' correspondence proved the pictures contained so much unacceptable material that it would be near impossible to edit them to pass the Code. What a difference two years makes.

Censorship aside, *Heat Lightning* is unique in several ways. At the top of the list is the way the movie upends gender roles and presents a tough woman—a middle-aged one, at that!—undertaking a traditionally male job without reservations. Olga embodies an independent spirit, forging her own

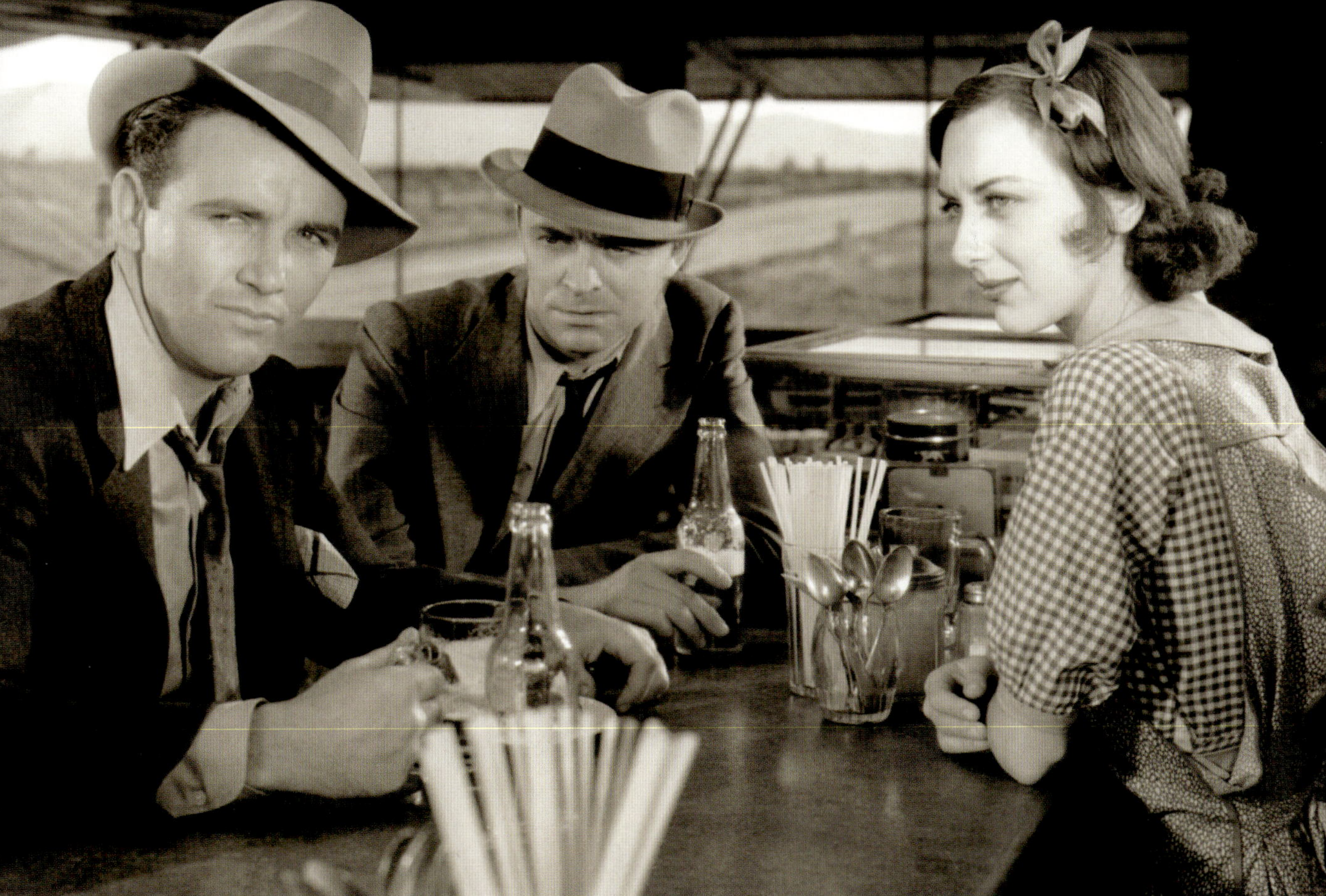

Preston Foster and Lyle Talbot, criminals on the lam, bring suspense, drama, and even more heat to the quiet desert life Ann Dvorak leads with her sister.

life and identity in a way that certainly did not align with expected female roles in the 1930s. The sisters make it patently clear that they don't need men to get the job(s) done; in fact, Myra seems to thoroughly enjoy telling customers her *sister* will be the one to fix their car. Surely, modern-day girl bosses can't help but recognize how powerfully noteworthy these portrayals are.

Many reviewers touted the elements that make *Heat Lightning* exemplary. *The New Movie Magazine* commended how comedy and tragedy "flourish side by side," while *The Hollywood Reporter* noted that the movie is a "poignant, simple thing with a style that is artfully artless," offering "a new atmosphere and background to audiences weary of seeing the same sets."

Heat Lightning radiates a distinct style; a modern, fierce spirit; and a brazen female-centered storyline that sets it apart from other pre-Code entries. Right in line with the period, though, the film possesses a lot of tantalizing innuendo—and a few sexual encounters—that caused enough of a stir to suppress it from the public a mere two years after its initial release.

TARZAN AND HIS MATE

STARRING
Johnny Weissmuller, Maureen O'Sullivan, Neil Hamilton, and Paul Cavanagh

DIRECTED BY
Cedric Gibbons, James C. McKay, and Jack Conway

RELEASED BY
MGM, April 1934

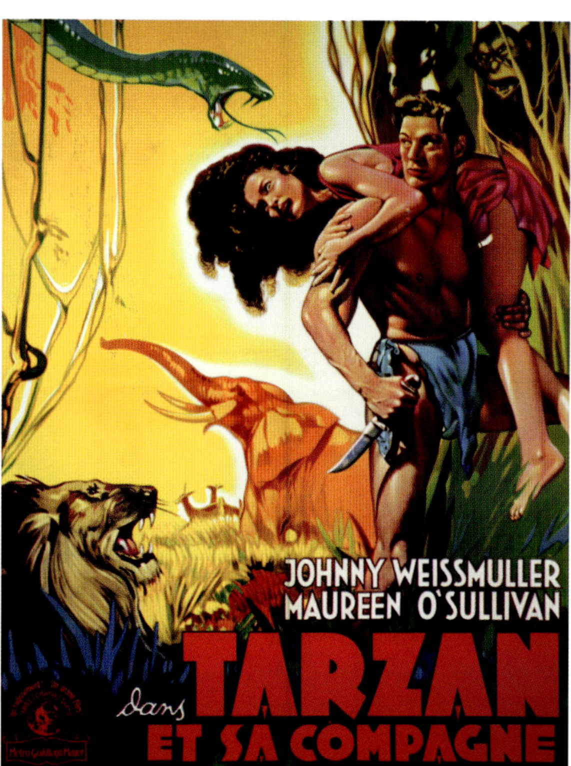

How many potential dangers can you find in this French *Tarzan and His Mate* poster?

Where was Hollywood headed by early 1934? There was little doubt even among the general public that the wheels were coming off the wagon. While horror and gangster movies had been reined in, comedies and adventure films were filled with ribald humor and an unrestrained eroticism. At the same time, the release of *Little Women* and the ascension of Shirley Temple showed a different path for profit-hungry studios. Would sin and sex be the future, or would it be books and the good ship Lollipop?

These eccentric impulses came to a head in MGM's second Tarzan film, a fantasy for boys as well as a risqué sexual odyssey for discerning adults. By 1934, Tarzan mania was far and wide. Tarzan books and comics sold in huge numbers to audiences wanting to fantasize over attaining a sort of savage glory. The relationship between Tarzan and Jane was laced with sexual yearning, while the violence kept audiences enraptured. (Jane, it should be noted, never does get around to marrying Tarzan in any of the series' numerous installments.)

Tarzan the Ape Man (1932) was filled with lurid sensuality as it featured Johnny Weissmuller posed dramatically in the moody jungle, wearing perhaps the flimsiest loincloth allowable. Tarzan in the original picture was a creature imbued with primitive sex and longing, framed with more than enough lingering shots of his lithe, sweaty body for its female audience to take home with them for later.

Having domesticated Tarzan in the first film, *Tarzan and His Mate* picks up with Tarzan and Jane (Maureen O'Sullivan) in a state of Eden-esque

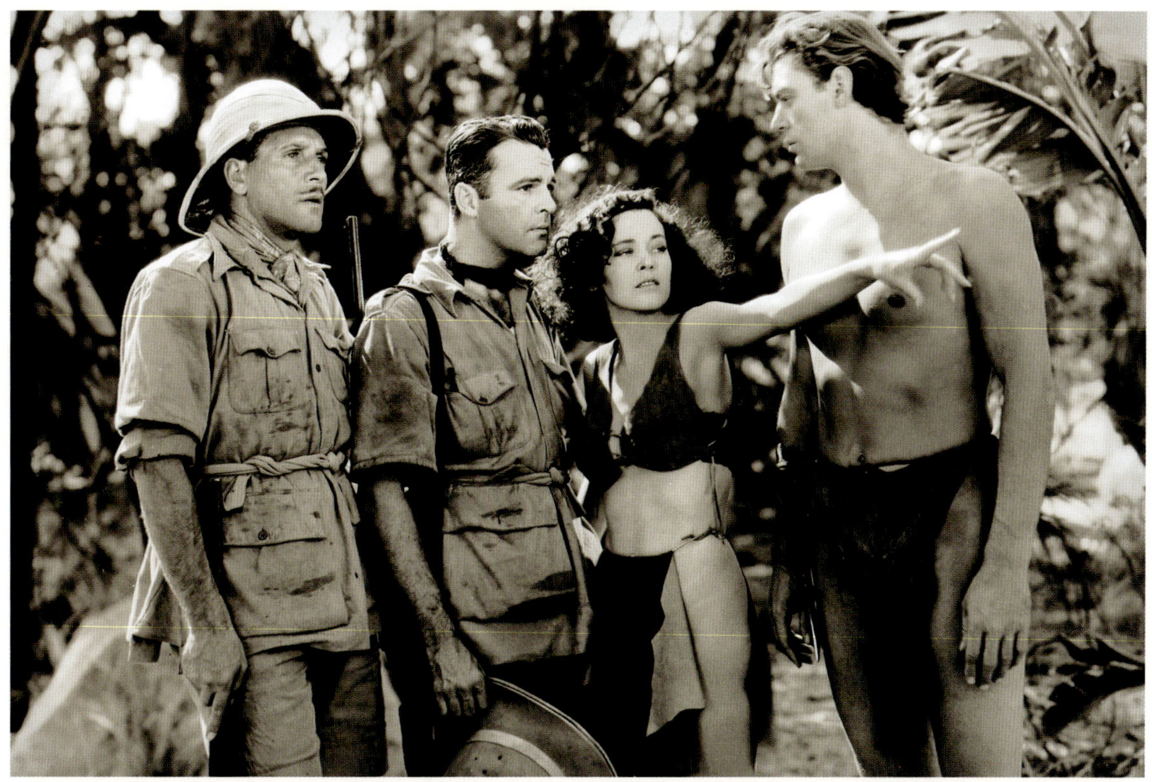

Maureen O'Sullivan diverting attention away from her infamously skimpy costume.

domestic bliss, even if their chimpanzee friend, Cheeta, is a bit of an asshole. Into this stumble a pair of explorers, the calculating Martin (Paul Cavanagh) and Jane's prior romantic interest, Harry (Neil Hamilton). They're searching for the mythical elephant graveyard filled with a fortune of ivory. Once they find their burial ground, they betray Tarzan and leave him for dead. In between, the King of the Jungle battles crocodiles and lions before finally triumphing and rescuing Jane.

Still regarded as one of the greatest swimmers of all time, statuesque Weissmuller won a half dozen Olympic medals—five gold and one bronze—and broke more than sixty world records before Hollywood came calling. Weissmuller followed the money and the fame, and while his stiff acting could be successfully masked by the monotone role, there's no doubt that his physical beauty made up for it. He would go on to play Tarzan in a dozen movies before moving on to the role of Jungle Jim for sixteen films at Columbia.

Even though the sequel entered production shortly after the original, it became impossible for filmmakers to get a handle on, and production eventually stretched for an incredibly long six months. Rotating through screenwriters and filled with state-of-the-art special effects and a zoo full of animal costars, *Tarzan and His Mate*

"A woman's greatest weapon is man's imagination."

—Jane, just saying it like it is

was to be a spectacular, big-budget actioner that led to spectacular, big-budget overruns.

Chaos reigned behind the scenes. The original plan was for W. S. Van Dyke and Cedric Gibbons, MGM's chief art director from the 1930s to '50s, to codirect the picture, with Van Dyke handling the actors and Gibbons overseeing the special effects. Van Dyke left before filming started and Gibbons, who would retain the final solo directing credit, began production. A month later, director Jack Conway was tapped to film additional scenes and soon MGM shut down Gibbons's unit entirely due to cost overruns. For reshoots and wild animal scenes, James C. McKay was called in to direct. While reshoots were not unusual, these were extensive enough that they necessitated the replacement of several supporting actors, including Rod La Rocque being swapped for Paul Cavanagh. This makes the entire movie difficult to successfully attribute to any one vision.

The film's title—an evocative double entendre mixing the idea of Jane as Tarzan's mate as well as denoting their act of mating—was just one of the picture's many risqué components. The SRC noted that a few scenes played up the sex element "rather strongly"; they also objected to the indication that Jane "will be shown as nearly nude as possible." (Not subtle, those scriptwriters.) The SRC also opposed stage direction instructing Jane to express "contented laughter" upon being spanked and dragged inside their shared hut.

These comments dance around the film's most infamous scene. Jane, having challenged Tarzan's masculinity, is thrown into the water. In a single, smooth motion, he also rips off her evening dress. Olympic swimmer Josephine McKim doubles for O'Sullivan for this lengthy sequence as Tarzan and a nude Jane swim around each other in delicate harmony.

Unsurprisingly, the SRC immediately rejected this sequence. The general feeling was that the "appearance" of full nudity was just as bad as complete nudity. When the movie was previewed, the swimming sequence was noted as "very daring and almost took away audiences' breath."

With that controversial scene, the SRC officially rejected the picture as violating the Code. Thus, it went to a jury of producers, where MGM argued their case for releasing the movie with the swimming sequence. In a rare occurrence, the producers sided with the SRC; MGM countered, pointing out that RKO's *Bird of Paradise* had likewise featured a skinny-dipping scene. The jury was unmoved. Irving Thalberg tried again, charging that MGM's 1928 feature *White Shadows in the South Seas* had "fifty naked women." The jury, apparently feeling threatened with a good time by Thalberg, again dismissed MGM's claims. The swimming scene had to go.

Thalberg dwelled on the jury's decision and made one of his own: He double-crossed the SRC. With reshoots on *Tarzan and His Mate* underway, he ordered the underwater sequence be filmed two other ways: one with Jane wearing a loincloth but topless, and another, family-friendly version of Jane not losing her clothing at all. All that was left was to distribute the scenes to the correct territories.

This sequence was reported on breathlessly. *Variety*'s review noted that "the lady is brassiere-less, but photographed from the side only." Reviews could hardly contain their own lusting. *Variety*

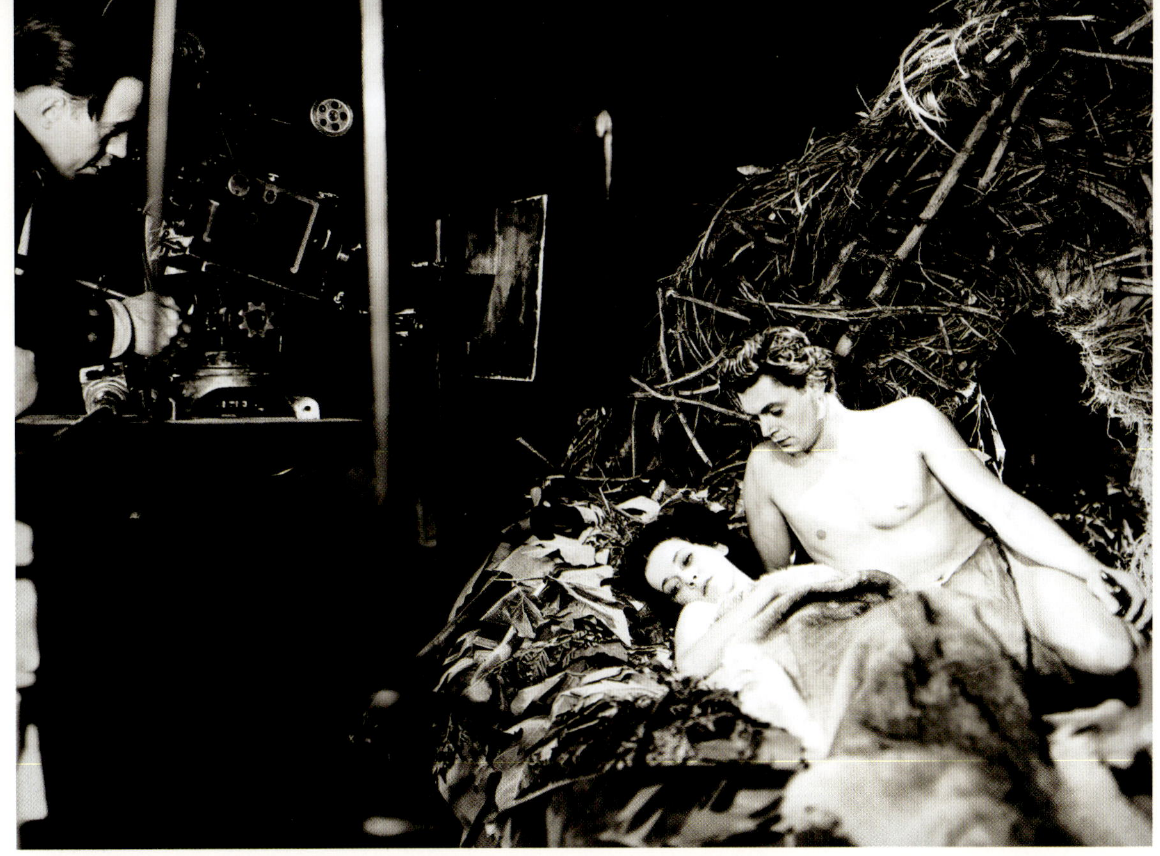

The magic of movies! Behind the scenes filming *Tarzan and His Mate* with Maureen O'Sullivan and Johnny Weissmuller.

again observed that "the girls will go strong for him [Weissmuller] again," adding that "Miss O'Sullivan, never wearing much in the way of clothes, isn't bad to look at from the masculine viewpoint." *Motion Picture Herald* did not comment on the sex appeal but did suggest that exhibitors had a rare opportunity "to go the limit."

Most censor boards took issue with the nude swimming scene, the native killings, and lions eating people. Maryland removed Jane's line, "Can't you see I have nothing on?" while Pennsylvania left the swim in but removed Jane changing her clothes in silhouette. The SRC, upon discovering that prints of *Tarzan and His Mate* still circulated with the forbidden scene, was given more ammunition by a surprised public to push back against MGM's cavalier attitude.

After Code enforcement in July 1934, the film was reissued to theaters but in truncated form. The swimming sequence on every print featured Jane fully clothed and her nude silhouette early in the movie was excised to spare young, impressionable boys in the Midwest. Joseph Breen tamed the ape man, sending the jungle adventure yarns into their bargain basement corner.

The battle over *Tarzan* would also be one of MGM's last great fights of the pre-Code era. The SRC's aim at the nubile body of Jane made one thing clear: Violence was ancillary to the censors. The future of film was platonic—and bloody.

THE BLACK CAT

STARRING
Boris Karloff, Bela Lugosi, and David Manners

DIRECTED BY
Edgar G. Ulmer

RELEASED BY
Universal, May 1934

"Did you ever hear of Satanism, the worship of the devil, of evil? Herr Poelzig is the great modern priest of this ancient cult, and tonight, the dark of the moon, the rites of Lucifer are celebrated. And if I am not mistaken, he intends you to play a part in that ritual! A very important part."

—Dr. Vitus Werdegast warning a nubile bride, Joan, that she's in serious danger—and yeah, she should bounce

The pre-Code period undoubtedly produced some of the most memorable horror movies of the classic film era, such as *Dracula* (1931), *Frankenstein* (1931), *The Mummy* (1932), and *The Invisible Man* (1933). It's even awash in lesser-known cult films like *Murders in the Zoo* (1933), which features a man with his mouth sewn shut, and *Island of Lost Souls* (1932), where a corpulent scientist vivisects screaming animals into obscene human figures. But none compare with the long-awaited matchup of horror titans Bela Lugosi and Boris Karloff in *The Black Cat*. Directly evoking war crimes, incest, rape, necrophilia, and a host of other proclivities, *The Black Cat* showcases many themes that later horror films, like *Night of the Living Dead* (1968) and *Carnival of Souls* (1962), would mercilessly expand upon.

The movie starts innocently enough: American mystery writer Peter Alison (David Manners) is traveling through Eastern Europe with his new bride, Joan Alison (Julie Bishop). Due to a mix-up with the cabins, they find Dr. Vitus Werdegast (Lugosi) joining them for the journey. A storm and car accident force Peter and Joan to accompany Werdegast in his meeting with Hjalmar Poelzig (Karloff), his old military commander, in Poelzig's expansive mansion built on the old fortifications of one of the deadliest battles of the war.

Werdegast has come back seeking revenge on Poelzig, both for betraying the men under his command and for stealing Werdegast's wife and young daughter from him. A battle of the wits, manifested in a chess match, reaches a climax as Poelzig prepares to preside over a dark mass of Satanists with Joan as the sacrifice. An unseen horror derails the proceedings, allowing Werdegast the opportunity to save Joan and finally exact retribution on Poelzig by skinning his nemesis alive.

The Black Cat, as it stands to modern viewers, is a movie of odd ellipses, unrelated moments of chilling horror that unsettle the audience by cultivating dread and mysteries at the edge of the reasoning mind. The film's choppy editing, the result of forced reshoots, plus frequent slips into different characters' viewpoints and close-ups, disjoint its reality, creating an oppressive, mournful world clawing its way back from the darkness.

Director Edgar G. Ulmer pitched the team up of Karloff and Lugosi as a surefire box office hit to his friend, Universal's production head Carl Laemmle Jr. He also proposed taking Edgar Allan Poe's poem "The Black Cat" and turning it into something unrecognizable but thrilling. Working with screenwriter Peter Ruric, they crafted a story with a host of historical and European influences. The "rivers of blood" battle that led to the Werdegast-Poelzig rift was based on a real incident during the Battle of Verdun in France. Poelzig's personality was inspired by Aleister Crowley, a flamboyant British Satanist. Besides Crowley's outsize influence as an occult expert and counterculture icon due to his advocacy for drugs and sex at the turn of the twentieth century, he also lived in the United States during World War I as a double agent for the British. This dichotomy fascinated Ulmer.

When Universal submitted the script to the SRC, Joseph Breen patiently noted it complied with the Code overall—but then suggested over a dozen items to cut. The most strenuously considered scene was the finale, where Poelzig is skinned alive. "This entire sequence is a very dangerous one and it would be advisable for us to discuss them thoroughly before any further preparation is made," Breen relayed.

Production began in earnest while Carl Laemmle Sr. was on a trip abroad and concluded in a brisk fifteen days. The returning studio head screened the picture and was aghast at the result. Laemmle ordered reshoots, which are notable for the fact that they underline the film's perversity rather than lessen it. Added were scenes of Poelzig leering at the splayed, glass-encased corpses of women and suggestively petting the black cat, along with the somber classical music score. Possible scenes slated for removal included more shots of the skinning, detailed mentions of what sacrificial acts would be performed upon Joan, and an explanation for the woman screaming during the mass—orgiastic delight—rendering yet another sequence open to viewers' interpretations.

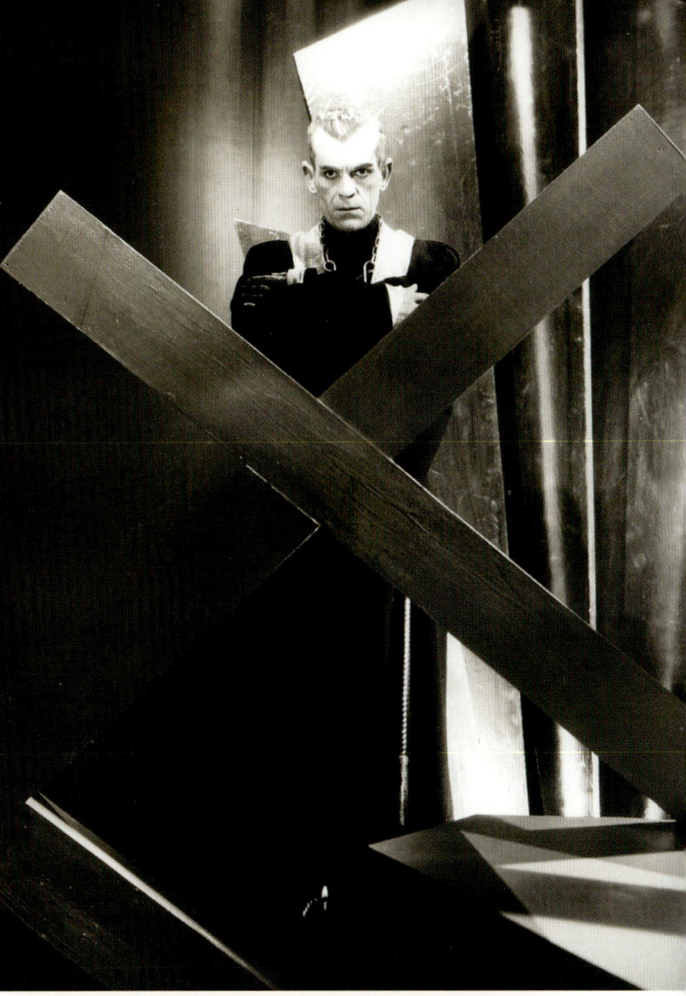

Boris Karloff in his most terrifying role yet: a cult leader.

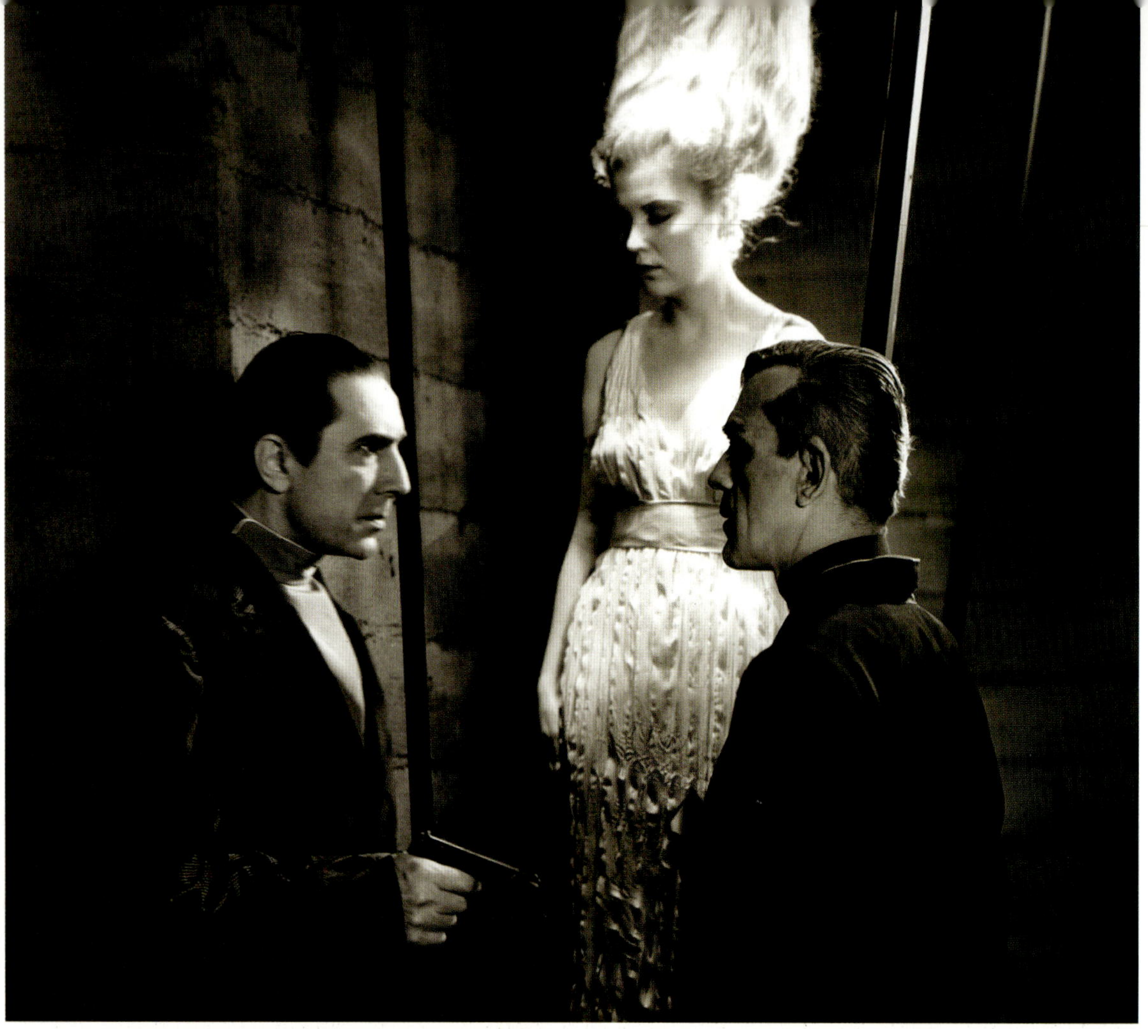

Bela Lugosi and Boris Karloff chatting in front of a preserved dead woman. Perfectly normal.

But the most emphatic change to the film's tone was eliminating the more sexual nature of Werdegast's obsession with Joan; as originally written, he is just as fixated on the woman as Poelzig and is not playing their game of chess to save her but rather to have her as his own. The resulting editing and reshoots softened this into a paternal interest.

While Karloff intimated later that the two actors were friendly after Lugosi was assured that Karloff wasn't trying to upstage him, Lugosi's lower billing and lesser pay irked the star. The two made seven pictures together, with only 1939's *Son of Frankenstein* achieving any other artistic merit. While Karloff found it easier to move into dramatic pictures, Lugosi struggled. That said, Ulmer later noted that Karloff had trouble taking the role seriously; filming Poelzig's entrance, Karloff ended the first take by shouting "BOO!" into the camera.

The Black Cat's undertones set it apart from its contemporaries. It's as much a film of the lost generation between the World Wars as any of Ernest Hemingway's works, a tale of bravery and cowardice, about military men who've seen slaughter and how that has hollowed out their souls. As the daffy American who barely understands the history of the town he's decided to honeymoon in and, at a crucial moment, blunders and kills the wrong man, Peter rings with symbolic futility. If Americans have been accused of not knowing their own history, it may be also believed that their ignorance of the rest of the world's can be lethal.

Breen eventually praised the final product, but even handled with delicacy, the film didn't escape censor boards unscathed. Maryland removed all references to Poelzig being flayed, including the silhouette of the doctor holding the knife. Chicago, Quebec, Ontario, and Ohio trimmed the scene and dialogue further, while the British board was more brutal, excising the scenes of mummified women and any mention of the devil or Lucifer, as well as much of the blasphemous ceremony. (The cult became "sun worshippers" instead, as much sense as that makes among the mansion's haunting interiors.) Singapore and Finland banned the film as did Italy, whose censors explained their reason with underwhelming bluntness: "Because it may create horror."

These boards were not alone in their feelings. One Universal executive went so far as to dub *The Black Cat* "too vile for public consumption." Contemporary critics were just about as effusive, with *Variety* scoffing, "Skinning alive is not new, a truly horrible and nauseating bit of extreme sadism. Its inclusion in a motion picture is dubious showmanship."

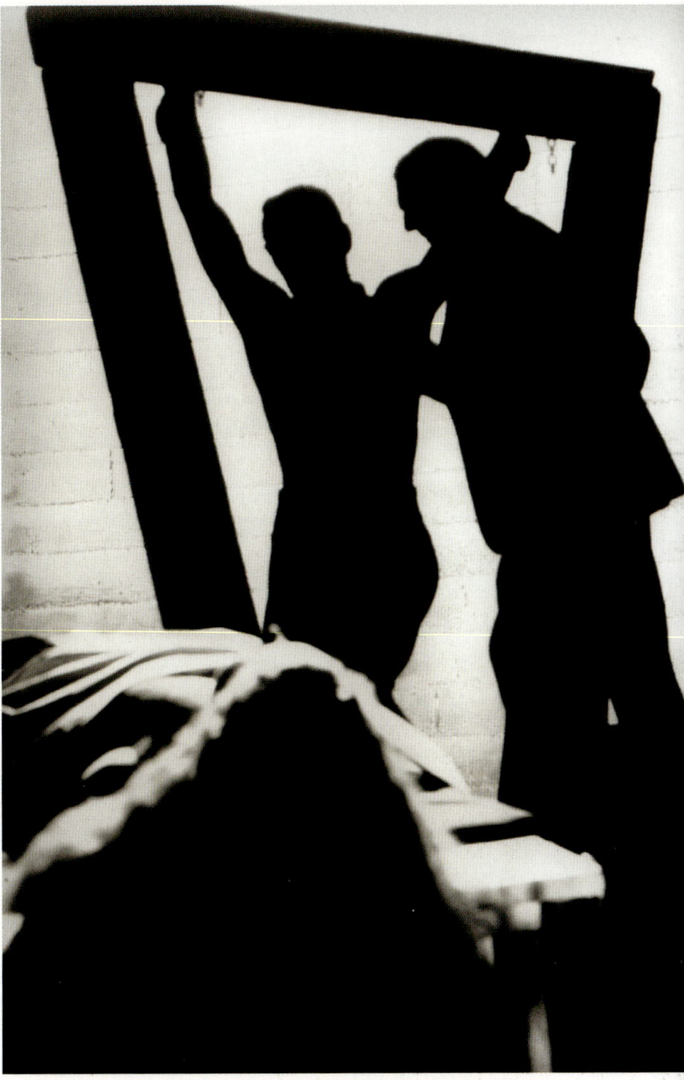

Universal obviously couldn't show one character skinning another alive, but you certainly get the point.

Besides its legendary team up of Lugosi and Karloff, *The Black Cat* remains an important stepping stone in the evolution of the horror genre. It's one of the last great chillers of not just the pre-Code era but of the entire studio era, as Universal would soon relegate its monster movies to cheaper budgets and lesser scripts.

SMARTY

STARRING
Joan Blondell, Warren William, Edward Everett Horton, Frank McHugh, and Claire Dodd

DIRECTED BY
Robert Florey

RELEASED BY
Warner Bros., May 1934

"If he really loved me, he'd have hit me long ago."

—Vicki, expressing some uncomfortable thoughts about her marriage

There are a lot of great, smart, well-made, and well-intentioned movies contained in this book. *Smarty* is none of those. It is a raucous sex comedy that, due to the nature of public discourse at the time, could not mention sex. It is everything a Lubitsch film strives *not* to be, with its uses of metaphors confusing the audience and its attempts to romanticize domestic violence atrocious. That this movie was released by a major studio and not greeted with a gigantic controversy was perhaps a sign of how far things had gone by the spring of 1934.

Smarty tells the story of Tony Wallace (Warren William) and his wife, Vicki Wallace (Joan Blondell), a married couple who have run into a problem: Tony spends his days and nights listening to Vicki's giggling allusions to his fear of "diced carrots," a barren euphemism for impotence. She mercilessly teases Tony, emasculating him in front of their friends, including colossal bore George (Frank McHugh), gossipy Anita (Claire Dodd), and fussbudget Vernon (Edward Everett Horton).

Tony's patience finally snaps, and he slaps Vicki. She divorces him and marries Vernon in an attempt to further boil her now-ex-husband's blood. Vicki parades about in scanty dresses and uses every trick to infuriate the men in her life to provoke them into hitting her. When they refuse to resort to violence, she escalates her rhetoric and sheds even more clothing.

Vicki's desire could be code for rough sex, but the film is told through so many half implications that the intention is almost indecipherable. Vernon and Vicki soon split, and she retreats back to Tony. After taunting him with a jar of diced carrots, he lets her have it, to which Vicki coos, "Hit me again."

If the metaphor of domestic violence for sexual satisfaction was distasteful at the time, more than ninety years later it's downright appalling and basically unthinkable. It's hard not to marvel at the vulgarity of the picture that was originally titled, if you can believe it, *Hit Me Again*. Filmed in usual Warner Bros. fashion—a fourteen-day shooting schedule pushing the actors as hard as they could to get the most bang for their buck—the movie became a jagged bone of contention with the SRC, which certainly had its hands full.

There was a great deal of dispute about the portrayal of marriage, though surprisingly little remarks made about the physical violence depicted or encouraged. Joseph Breen's script conferences listed numerous suggestions to tone

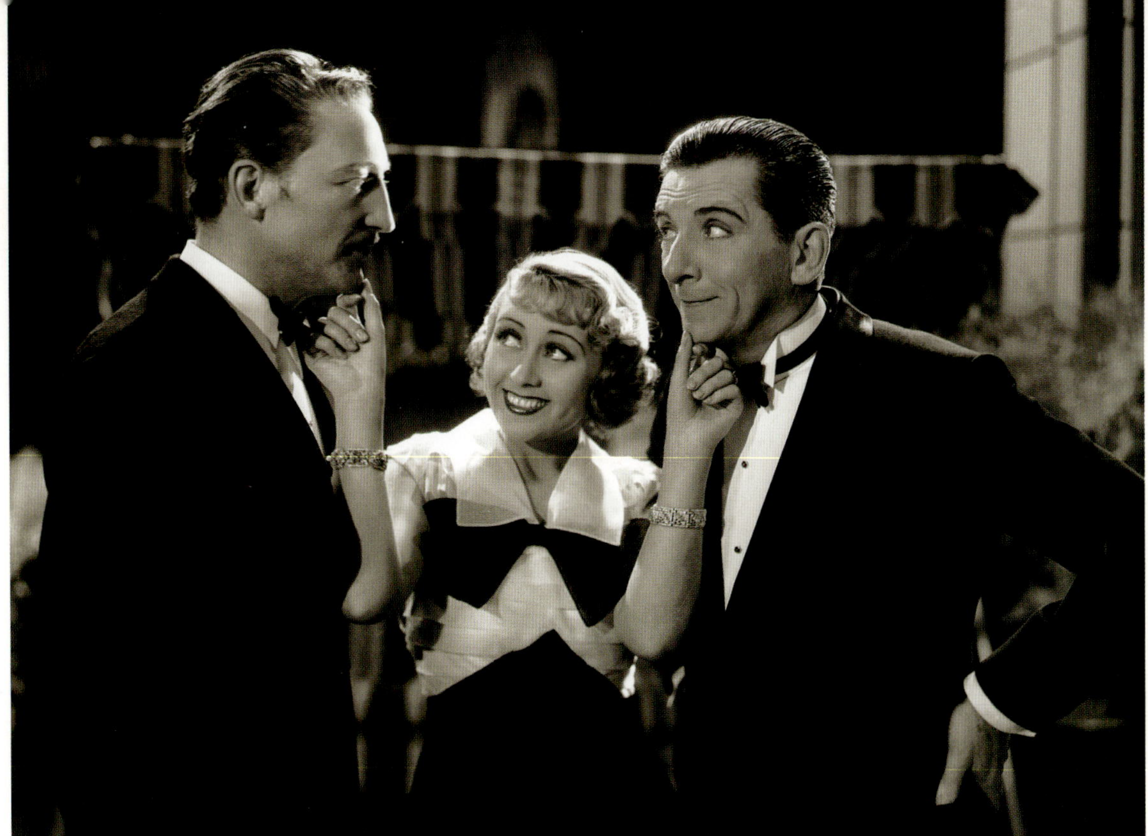

Joan Blondell drives Warren William and Edward Everett Horton thoroughly wild in *Smarty*.

down the sex, from Tony ripping off Vicki's dress at the film's end (it stayed) to downplaying the appearance of unmarried people spending the night together. (Lines like "You're not going to stay here all night" would see the last few words chopped off to add a sense of ambiguity.)

Even with that advice, Breen's report was not a condemnation but rather a focused sense of pity: "[*Smarty* is] somewhat lacking in comedy values. It too is based on the divorce and remarriage theme. [The movie is] below par, not only from the standpoint of moral values, but also of entertainment." One censor noted: "I think it is reasonable to expect that Warners themselves have seen the error of their way and are not likely to attempt such atrocities in the near future." The studio would, but not on their own accord; the strict enforcement of the Production Code in July 1934 took care of that for them.

Smarty met with mixed reviews. For instance, *Screenland* lamented, "If there was ever more fun in a picture, this reviewer had the misfortune to miss it." The same went for the cast. Blondell almost had a nervous breakdown and required a recuperation after filming finished, while William felt completely disconnected from the movie, dubbing it "the most embarrassing moment of my life." His biographer called attention to one unique promotional tool as "despicable insanity": a standee of William with a motorized arm that would slap a standee of Blondell over and over again.

Smarty got a relatively light sentence in the States. While it passed in both New York and Chicago without any edits, many lines were mutilated

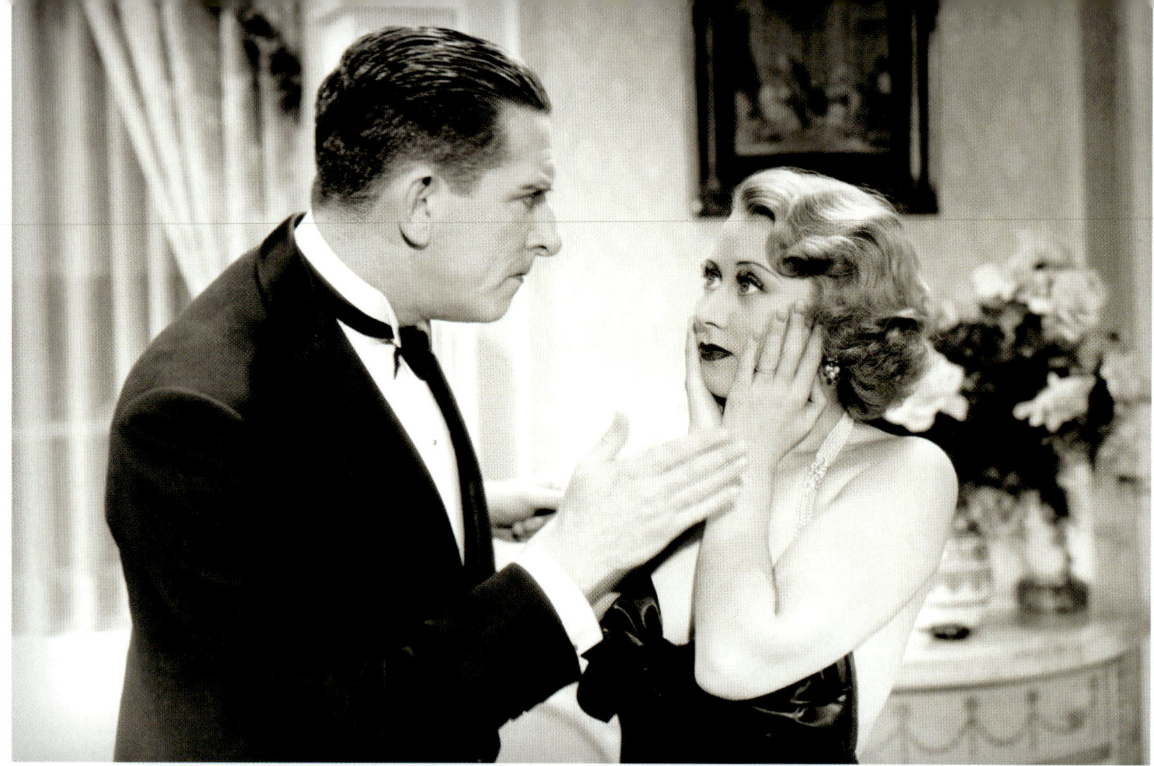

Joan Blondell

If you've been reading this book from the beginning, you should be familiar with the name Joan Blondell. (And if you've just started here, you picked a hell of an entry to begin with!)

Viewers of a certain age probably first saw Blondell as Vi the waitress in the hit *Grease* (1978). But that was just one of over 150 credits in a career that lasted five decades—and it all started during the pre-Code era.

Born to a vaudeville family, Blondell made her stage debut at four months old. Talk about an auspicious beginning! Warner Bros. bought the rights to a Broadway play she and future icon James Cagney starred in, whisking them away to Hollywood for the movie adaptation, *Sinner's Holiday*. The rest is history—and Blondell and Cagney went on to make seven films together from 1930–1934.

A feisty, wisecracking stalwart in the stable of pre-Code Warner Bros. stars, Blondell appeared in over thirty movies during this period. Her sassy persona fit Warner's fast-paced, ripped-from-the-headlines pictures perfectly, no matter the genre, and her expressive eyes and trim figure made her a favorite of photographers. There's obviously too many of her pre-Codes to mention them all here, but in addition to her films that we've featured in this book, we suggest you check out *Blonde Crazy* (1931), in which she and Cagney fleece the rich; *Union Depot* (1932), a grittier version of *Grand Hotel* (1932); *Blondie Johnson* (1933), where she plays a crime boss; and *Havana Widows* (1933), one of her seven pictures with fellow fast-talking dame Glenda Farrell.

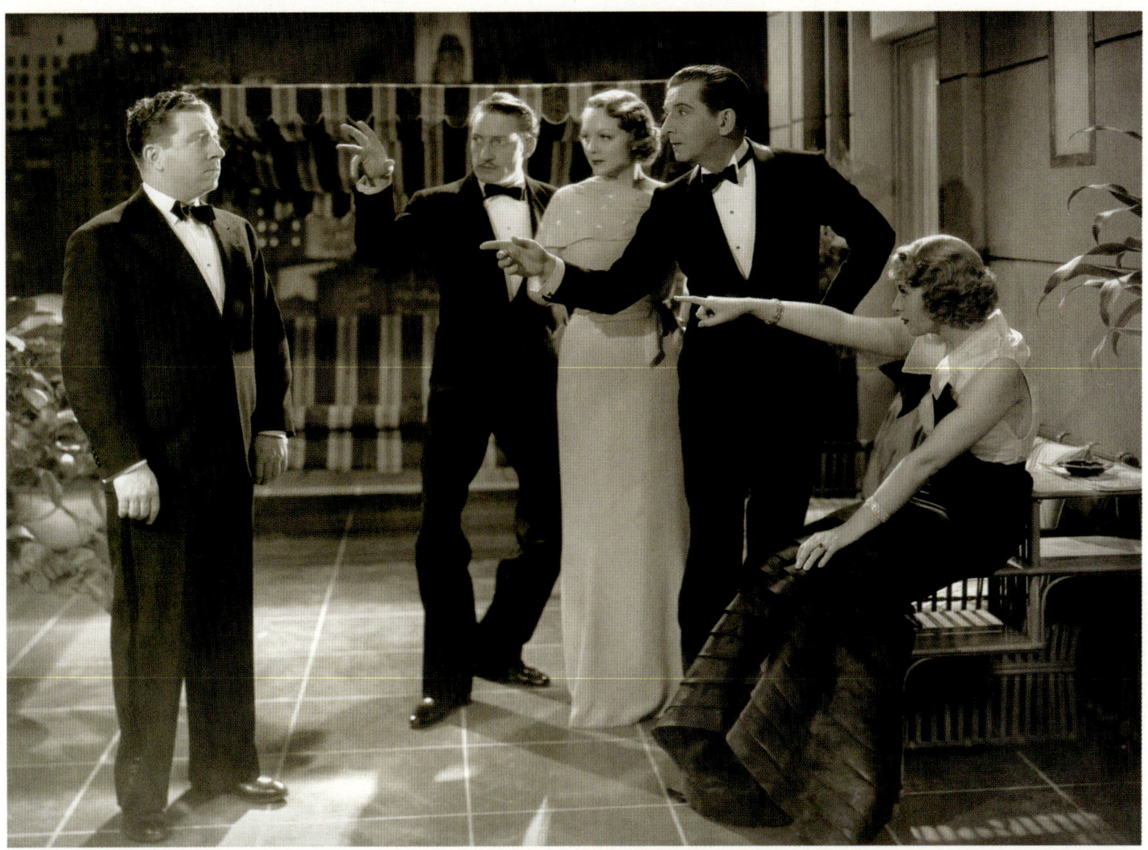

OPPOSITE: Joan Blondell dishes it out—and takes it—in *Smarty*. **ABOVE:** We're not sure why everyone is pointing at Frank McHugh, but he probably deserved it.

in Pennsylvania, Ohio, and Maryland. Pennsylvania and Australia also demanded that the opening shot, a carefully composed swoop up the curvature of Blondell's legs, be cut entirely, while Maryland and Ontario requested the removal of a scene where a bare back is delicately kissed. In 1936, when Warner Bros. inquired about reissuing the film, their request was summarily denied; *Smarty* contained so many objectionable elements that it would be almost impossible to edit the picture enough to bring it within the confines of the Code.

Why list *Smarty* as essential if it's so utterly vile? Placed together with a number of other 1934 releases, *Smarty* is a fascinating indication of where the industry was headed without the creation of the PCA and enforcement of the Code. While *Smarty* doesn't quite stake out the same territory as a film like 2002's kinky sub/dom comedy *Secretary*, its focus on sexual foibles was something that classic Hollywood filmmaking was simply unequipped to portray at this point. The result is a deeply distasteful film that continues to appall modern viewers.

MURDER AT THE VANITIES

STARRING
Victor McLaglen, Jack Oakie, Kitty Carlisle, and Carl Brisson

DIRECTED BY
Mitchell Leisen

RELEASED BY
Paramount, May 1934

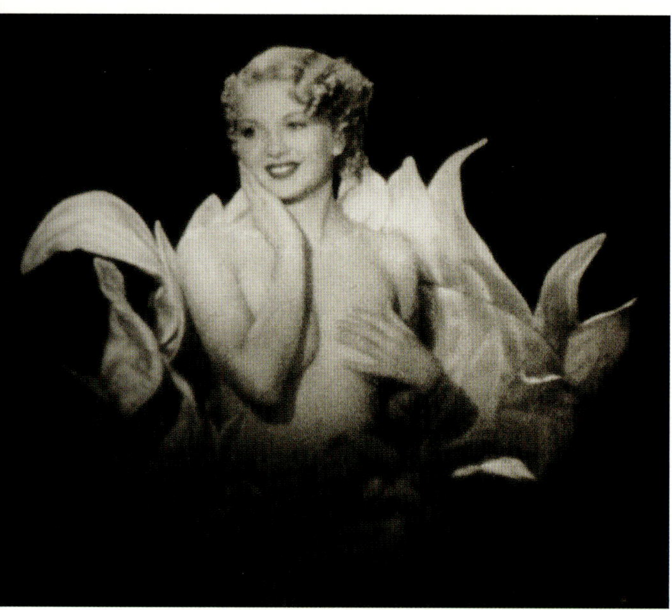

One of the most scandalous outfits, or lack thereof, in *Murder at the Vanities*.

Which pre-Code movie incited ire from the Opium Advisory Committee and the US Department of State more than a year *after* its initial release in America? That would be *Murder at the Vanities.* The censorship battle that would rage focused on the "Sweet Marijuana" musical number; really, you can't get much more pre-Code than an entire song devoted to drugs.

Premiering mere weeks before Joseph Breen took full control of Hollywood's moral compass in July 1934, *Murder at the Vanities* went all out with murder, nudity, and overt drug references, hitting hot spot after hot spot conveniently as the censorship controversy reached a tipping point. Not to mention that it did all that with a flippant grin, keeping the proceedings light and reality at bay. With a censorship history as dramatic and incendiary as the film itself, *Murder at the Vanities* provides a unique look at pre- and post-Code attitudes and enforcements.

And scantily clad women. Lots of that.

Murder at the Vanities turns tongue-in-cheek musical revue *Earl Carroll's Vanities* on its ear with a bit of homicide thrown into the mix. It begins on opening night with stage manager Jack (Jack Oakie) shooing away detective Bill (Victor McLaglen) and making sure leads Ann (Kitty Carlisle) and Eric (Carl Brisson) show up in time. They do, but—surprise!—they're getting married after the show. The gossip spreads like wildfire, agitating, among others, callous bosses, jealous costars, secret mothers, and blackmailers. Clearly, someone's not happy with the impending wedding bells, because multiple attempts are made to kill Ann before the curtain even goes up. Jack brushes it off—the people paid to be entertained, so the show must go on—and even when blood starts dripping from the rafters, the play continues until the killer is unmasked.

Speaking of the show, one of the numbers is "The Rape of the Rhapsody," in which a classical ensemble is overtaken by Duke Ellington's orchestra and Black dancers. The latter group is soon machine-gunned down by the disgruntled classical leader in a scene played for comedy to the theater audience, which adds even more to unpack.

Paramount seemed intent on courting potential censorship danger from the get-go. The studio threw early notes from the SRC about scantily clad showgirls out the window and took a page from Carroll to apparently invest in the skimpiest, most translucent costume material they could find. (Indeed, *Variety* starkly called out that the "girls are costumed sparingly for eye appeal and in the press book this is stressed for exploitation.")

The tantalizing "Sweet Marijuana" number took the aforementioned nudity note and one-upped the situation with drugs; in addition to the lyrics Rita (Gertrude Michael) croons, you have a visual of a giant cactus centerpiece budding with topless chorus girls strategically covering their chests with their hands. The lines for "Marahuana" [*sic*] as submitted to the SRC after production started, read: "Soothe me with your caress / Sweet Marahuana, Marahuana / Help me in my distress / Sweet Marahuana / Please do / You alone can bring my lover back to me / Even tho I know it's all a fantasy / And then / Put me to sleep."

"Why don't you take your lamps off those dames and do a little police work, huh?"

—stage manager Jack, who cozies up to those same dames, reminding policeman Bill that he's got a murder to solve

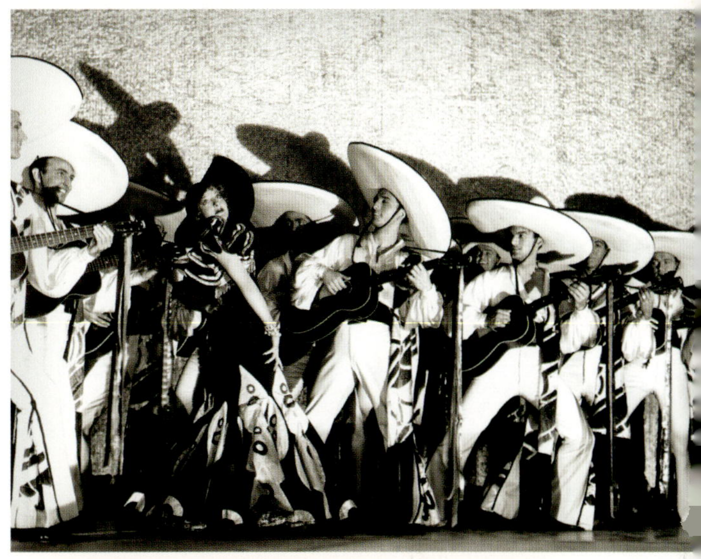

Gertrude Michael leads the infamous "Sweet Marijuana" number.

Unsurprisingly, these lyrics agitated Breen and company. But Paramount assured the SRC there was no cause for concern, especially since there would be no visual indications of marijuana use in the sequence. A month later, Breen also had to deal with, and eventually approve, the studio using the word *rape* in a theater program for "The Rape of the Rhapsody" number.

When the SRC finally previewed *Murder at the Vanities*, they begrudgingly admitted that, *officially*, it conformed to the Production Code. Breen, however, was dubious when it came to local boards. For an organization that supposedly had a finger on the pulse of how the censor boards would react, the SRC got it really wrong, because in addition to an encouraging reception in New York, *Murder at the Vanities* got off scot-free in Chicago, Kansas, Maryland, Singapore, Norway, and Denmark. Other boards, like Massachusetts,

Paramount Productions Inc.,
5451 Marathon St.,
Hollywood, Calif.,

COPY Sept. 14, 1935.

Mr. Joseph I. Breen,
5504 Hollywood Blvd.,
Hollywood, Calif.,

Dear Mr. Breen:

Yesterday, Friday, Sept. 13th, the Paramount Pictures Studio issued orders to the Paramount New York office to inform all Exchanges to eliminate the song "Marahauna" in all prints of MURDER AT THE VANITIES.

The same elimination will be made in the original negative.

This elimination is done under protest, as a matter of friendship and policy. It is not to be taken to indicate that anyone at Paramount agrees in any part with the thought that the song, as used in the picture, either deliberately or unconsciously conveys any effect whatsoever in connection with narcotics.

Best regards.

Sincerely,

A. M. Botsford

AMB:M

Paramount made sure their objection to cutting "Sweet Marijuana" was known.

made two or three edits, such as deleting the title of that music program featuring the word *rape*, and Quebec turned out to be one of the only entities to take issue with all the near-nude ladies.

So Paramount won, right? Not so fast. As much as we hate to say it, Breen's forewarning of problems proved correct. It's just that the largest clash came over a year after the picture's domestic release, thousands of miles away from Hollywood.

As the story goes, in July 1935, one year after the establishment of the PCA, Geoffrey Shurlock, Breen's eventual successor, was notified that the US Department of State was greatly distressed by the "Sweet Marijuana" number. An Italian delegate in Geneva for an Opium Advisory Committee saw the movie, erroneously noting that it featured "a chorus of cigarette smoking girls to emphasize the affects [*sic*] of this drug." Is this blasphemy what America was doing to stop marijuana propaganda? (At the time, the drug was truly thought to be more perilous than opium or morphine.)

To cover their bases, Shurlock explained that Paramount "sold" them on the idea that the interlude was harmless. Shurlock seemingly relished the thought of throwing this late-game victory in Paramount's face, writing to the US Department of State contact: "As I recall, the studio took quite a top-lofty attitude at the time, insisting that we were being frightened by shadows, and I should like to show them that once again we were both wrong—they in their contention and we in being persuaded by them."

The PCA had to act fast, because the US Department of State fervently maintained that if nothing was done regarding the scene, it would be devastating publicity for America's stance on drugs. But Paramount wouldn't fold so easily, replying that many people would have no clue the song had anything to do with drugs. The studio even tried to claim that the tune would be as effective if another word, like *manuella*, was used

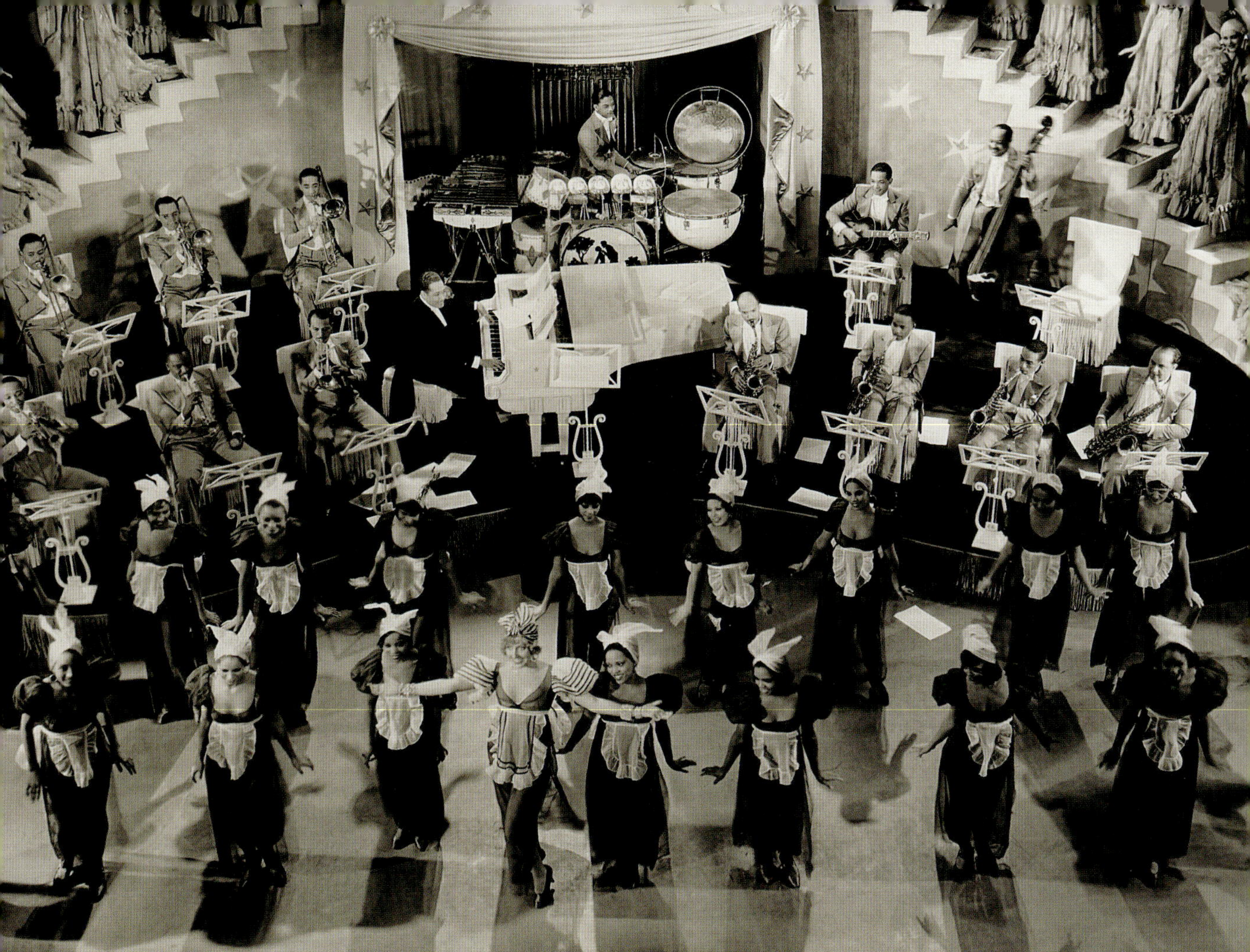

instead of *marijuana*. Nice try, but the lyrics, well, fittingly describe marijuana use. With more pressure from the US Department of State and the PCA, Paramount buckled, and in mid-September 1935, the studio removed the song from all circulating prints. (The tune remains intact in the version of the film available for home viewing, so the scene wasn't wholly destroyed.)

Murder at the Vanities' unique censorship situation differentiates Breen and company in operation pre- and post-Code. Whereas the SRC only had the power to suggest edits and forewarn studios of potential censorship difficulties before July 1934, after that, the PCA held more authority to force studios' hands. (And in this case, they had additional weight from the government behind them!) Nevertheless, Paramount's boldness demonstrated how far studios were willing to go in those days and weeks right before Breen was knighted head of the PCA.

"The Rape of the Rhapsody" features several Black performers, with an orchestra led by Duke Ellington . . . but it ends in a startlingly horrid way.

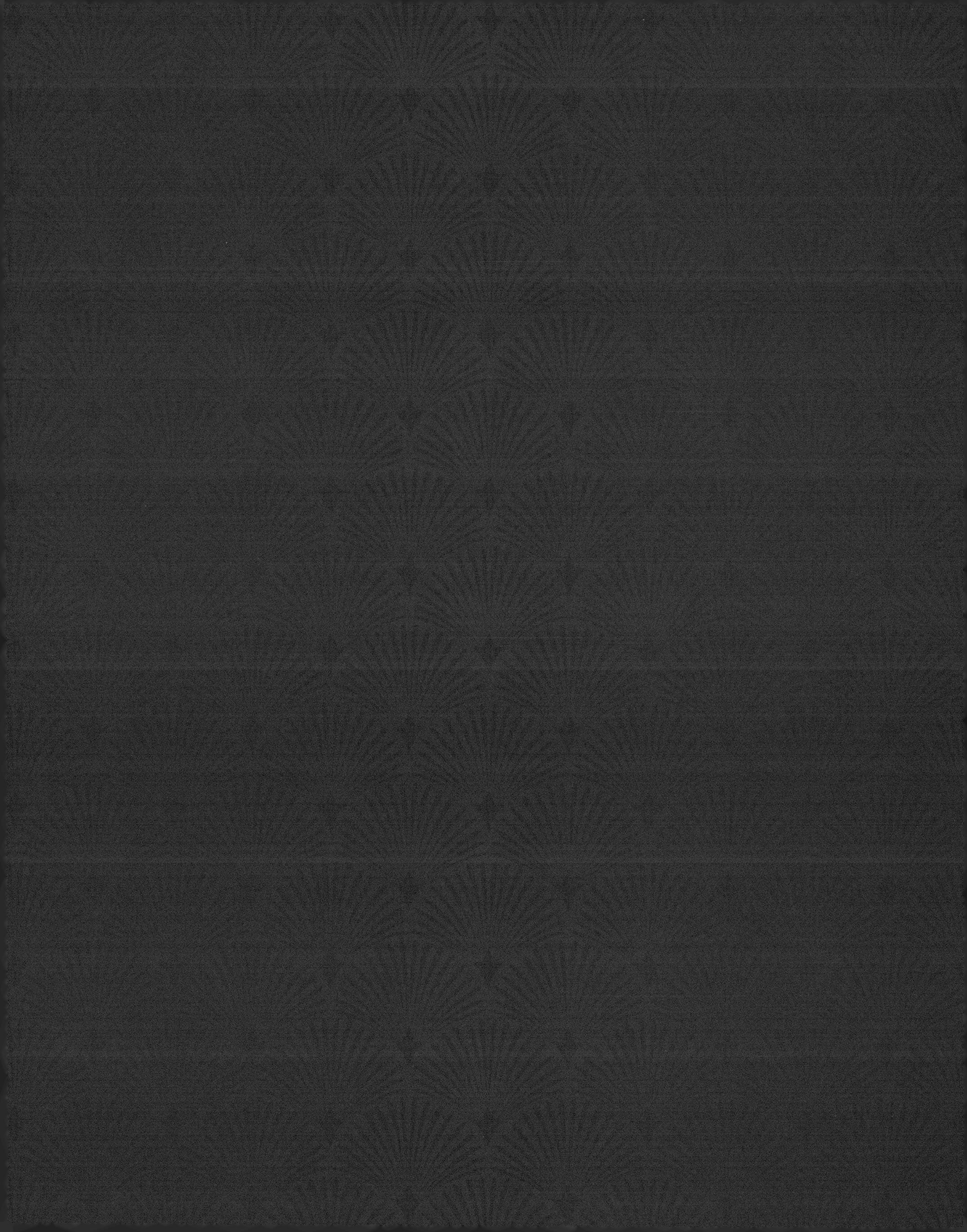

Epilogue

July 1934 was the messy end for pre-Code Hollywood. While some films in late 1934 would still be scandalous or unpopular with local censors, theirs would be a mitigated problem. Like America's fight against the Great Depression, Breen and the studios were assuring the country that happy days would be here again. "The Movies Clean Up . . ." announced a headline in *Motion Picture Daily*, a proclamation as tentative as the mood around Hollywood.

All films produced by the major studios would now be subject to review by the PCA. This went from script reviews to screenings; reshoots or cuts they demanded were now mandatory. With Breen's takeover complete, audiences were treated to a new sight enshrined in credits: the Production Code seal, marked with a number, a symbol not of quality but rather compliance. At least one audience reportedly booed the seal after seeing it for the first time.

The transition wouldn't be an easy one. Filmmakers still sought to push boundaries. The PCA's complete neutering of the MGM comedy *Forsaking All Others* (1934), after forcing reshoots and rewrites, ended with Breen punching the film's director, W. S. Van Dyke, in the nose. Other moves were more subtle but nonetheless noticed: Mae West's next screen outing, originally called *It Ain't No Sin*, became the less-provocatively titled *Belle of the Nineties* (1934) after the PCA objected. When Delmer Daves wrote *Dames*, the first post-Code film to boast Busby Berkeley's signature extravagant musical numbers, he added a self-important censor (Hugh Herbert) whose own foibles were front and center—leaving him in the theater, drunk, hooting and hollering along with the rest of the audience.

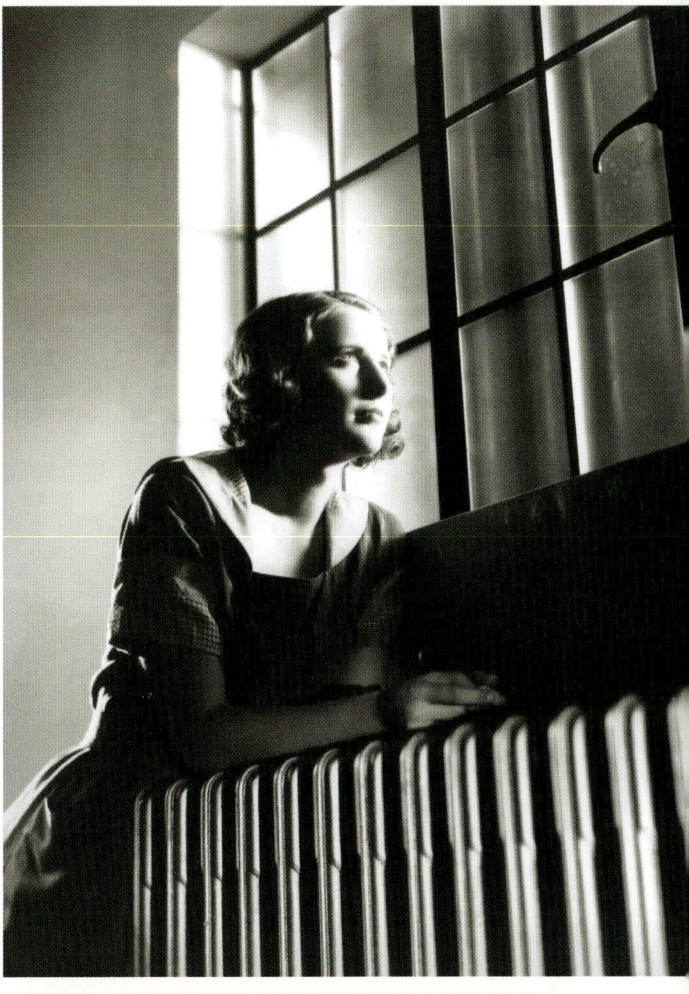

Barbara Stanwyck ponders life post-Code enforcement. (Just kidding, this is from 1933's *Ladies They Talk About*.)

But Breen persisted, and cementing who got the final say in matters clarified the process for

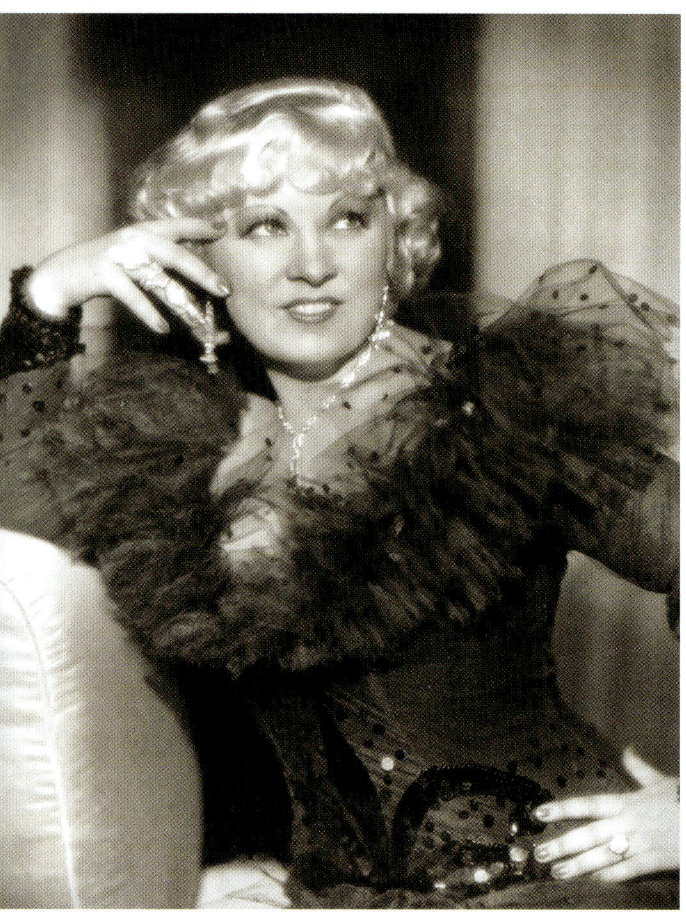

Code enforcement put a lid on Mae West's raucous brand of comedy.

all involved. Movies in the late 1930s would shed many of their scandalous trappings as Breen made good on his promises. Shirley Temple, whose stardom skyrocketed in 1934, became the poster child of the family-friendly movie business of the late 1930s. Ginger Rogers and Fred Astaire, first paired together in *Flying Down to Rio*, would settle into their formula with *The Gay Divorcee* and waltz through the rest of the decade. Adaptations of respectable literary works, touched off by the box office success of *Little Women*, would flourish, peaking in 1939 with works based on *The Hunchback of Notre Dame*, *Gone with the Wind*, and *Wuthering Heights*.

But also under Breen's watch, Hollywood films were steered away from criticizing Nazi Germany or the deteriorating situation in Europe. Comedies, robbed of sex, went screwball, skewering class differences while steadfastly refusing to comment on them with any sting. While social commentaries like *I Am a Fugitive from a Chain Gang* had led to real reform (and threats of violence), later polemics drifted toward moralizing. Movies like *The Ox-Bow Incident* (1943) and *Fury* (1936) no doubt criticize mob mentality, but they avoid hard looks at the sociological conditions that underlie why the incidents they portray come to pass. As guided by Breen, social films could only condemn the act, not the causes.

Under Breen's authority, Hollywood movies became more formulaic. Sex was minimized while violence was more condoned, especially the cartoonish kind. Some stars—Kay Francis, Warren William, Miriam Hopkins—would see their personas decline and vanish in the late 1930s and move into supporting roles or B pictures. Other stars flourished, like Barbara Stanwyck, Clark Gable, and Bette Davis. Breen and the PCA would slowly loosen their grip after World War II, when the postwar boom left a country craving complex and international tastes, but until the late 1960s the PCA still held considerable power over what American audiences could see on the silver screen. The story of the unwinding of the PCA in the 1960s is a wacky one, full of hubris, denial, breasts, and a stunning lack of imagination—but that's a story for a different day.

May 16, 1934

J.I.B.

The Motion Picture Daily of May 14, 1934, carried an item from Detroit dated May thirteenth to the effect that local Catholic publications were currently carrying the first list of films which are banned for members of the Legion of Decency, the Detroit organization of which was initiated the previous Sunday by Bishop Michael J. Gallagher.

For your ready reference the 63 pictures named were as follows:

ALL OF ME
A MAN'S CASTLE
BLOOD MONEY
BOMBAY MAIL
BOLERO
CATHERINE THE GREAT
COME ON MARINES
CONVENTION CITY ✓
CROSS COUNTRY CRUISE
COMING OUT PARTY
DARK HAZARD
DESIGN FOR LIVING
DAYS OF RECKONING
EAST OF FIFTH AVENUE
EASY TO LOVE
EIGHT GIRLS IN A BOAT
ESKIMO
FASHIONS OF 1934
FEMALE
FOUR FRIGHTENED PEOPLE
FINISHING SCHOOL
GAMBLING LADY
GEORGE WHITE'S SCANDALS
GOODBYE LOVE
GOOD DAME
GUILTY PARENTS
GLAMOR
HIPS, HIPS, HOORAY
HOLD THE PRESS
HEAT LIGHTNING
JIMMY THE GENT
JOURNAL OF A CRIME
LAZY RIVER
LET'S BE RITZY
LOVE BIRDS
MEN IN WHITE
MANDALAY
MANHATTAN LOVE SONG
MARRIAGE ON APPROVAL
MIDNIGHT
NANA
NO MORE WOMEN
PALOOKA
POWER AND GLORY
SEARCH FOR BEAUTY
SLEEPERS EASY
SUCCESS AT ANY PRICE
SING AND LIKE IT
THE BIG SHAKEDOWN
THE TRUMPET BLOWS
THE MEANEST GAL IN TOWN
THE WORST WOMAN IN PARIS
THE SONG YOU GAVE ME
THE STORY OF TEMPLE DRAKE
THIS MAN IS MINE
TWO ALONE
UNKNOWN BLONDE
WEST OF THE DIVIDE
WHARF ANGEL
WOMEN IN HIS LIFE
WONDER BAR
WHIRLPOOL
WHEN STRANGERS MEET

On the basis of the information which we have been able to gather, it seems that pledge cards for the Legion of Decency are being circulated for signature in every Catholic church in Detroit, and that this list of pictures is receiving much attention among local Catholics, but that the newspapers have ignored the list so far. Apparently it was published only in "St. Leo", a local weekly religious magazine published in the Detroit Diocese and a semi-official organ of that Diocese.

The actual list seems to have been compiled by Mons. Hunt. pastor of the Cathedral in Detroit, who is quite bitter against motion pictures. He is said to have stated recently that 90% of the movies were unfit to be shown to the public. Bishop Gallagher

The Catholic Legion of Decency banned sixty-three pictures for its members in May 1934. How many of these movies have you seen?

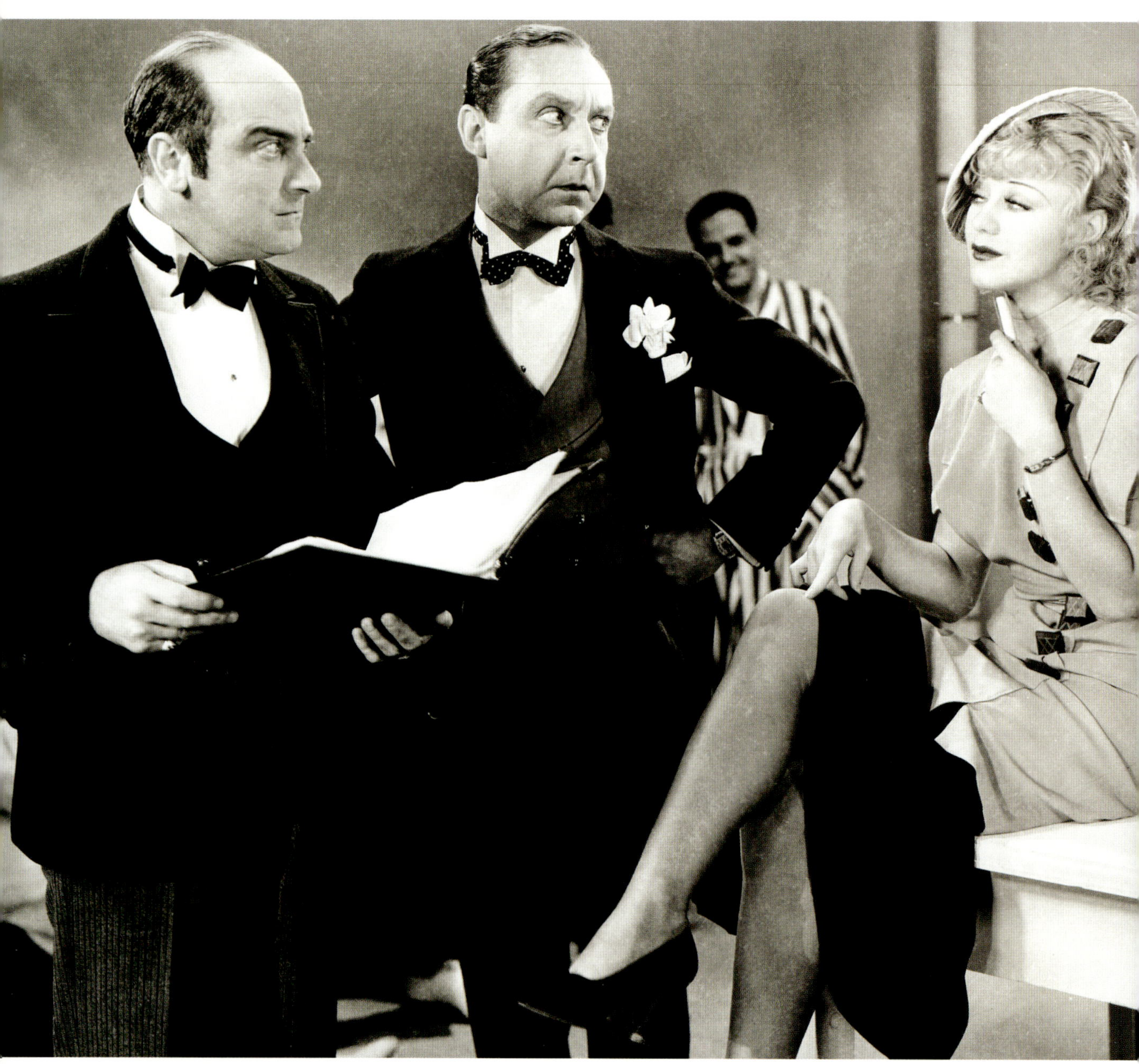

Ginger Rogers in *Flying Down to Rio* (1933): pre-Code mentality.
Eric Blore and Franklin Pangborn: post-Code mentality.

The Code's enforcement should not be chalked up as simply the Catholic Legion of Decency's triumph, or Breen's, or the government's. The Code's stranglehold on Hollywood required not just the threat of government censorship by moral and religious groups, but a large, silent majority in the industry standing by, willing to accept stricter limitations on cinema without considering how this trade-off could affect American filmmaking for decades to come. And while several timeless and undoubtedly influential movies were produced during the post-Code era, it makes you wonder how much further some of those pictures could have gone if the Code was never enforced.

The framework that Breen imprinted on the movies never truly went away; in every superhero CGI blockbuster we see the minimization of romance and a cynical reliance on violence. Social message pictures routinely continue to exonerate the root causes over encouraging change. War films mumble about being anti-war amid their explosions and stylish cinematography. And crime barely pays—at least in the movies.

The brief yet unique period of pre-Code Hollywood continues to entice and reveal—both cinematically and for our broader collective history. While the American experience has never been a straight line of ignorance to sophistication, the pre-Code era fought, in its own small way, to broaden the scope of the tales Hollywood told. It wove a bold tapestry, one that pushed the boundaries while staying true to the realities of the time—censorship, infidelity, racism, war, death, and more. If there is a lesson to be derived, then we learn that we can fold ourselves into the stories of our ancestors and see our problems for what they truly are. Difficult, yes, but not forever, and certainly made all the better with a dash of wit and style.

Acknowledgments

FUN FACT: WE ALWAYS READ THE ACKNOWLEDGMENTS in books. It's fun, plus, hey, you may even be mentioned. You never know.

FROM BOTH OF US:

Thank you to those who have provided invaluable knowledge, guidance, and feedback on all aspects of this book and the pre-Code era, from general advice to giving notes on our manuscript: Christina Rice, Darin Barnes, Jeremy Arnold, Galen Booth, Raquel Stecher, Steve Voccola, Anne Kloss, David Pierce, David Stenn, Sean Savage, and Christy Putnam.

The pre-Code writings of Mark A. Vieira, Tom Doherty, and Mick LaSalle incited our curiosity and passion for the period and paved the way for this book. The curatorial work of Turner Classic Movies, Warner Home Media, and Warner Archive have also made a profound difference in highlighting the popularity and vitality of this era, so a big cheer to that.

We also owe tremendous thanks to the classic film fans and scholars we've met and interacted with—in person and online—who have fascinated, delighted, educated, and inspired us. Some names we would like to give a shoutout to include: Cliff Aliperti, Laura Boyes, Farran Nehme Smith, Emily Rauber Rodriguez, Kellee Pratt, Jessica Pickens, Kristen Lopez, Megan Hesketh, Marya E. Gates, Jill Blake, Angela Petteys, Karen Burroughs Hannsberry, Laura Grieve, Alan K. Rode, and Aurora Bugallo.

None of this would have been possible without the vast resources used for our research, including Turner Classic Movies, the Internet Archive, the Media History Digital Library, and the Los Angeles Public Library.

Staff at the Academy of Motion Picture Arts and Sciences' Margaret Herrick Library have always been so knowledgeable and helpful; special thanks to Louise Hilton, Ben Friday, Caroline Jorgenson, Mona Huntzing, Cole McCabe, Ben Del Vecchio, Tori De Santiago, Andrea Battiste, Bijan S., and everyone who assisted with Special Collections files, research, and questions over the years. Thanks also go out to the Warner Bros. Archives at the School of Cinematic Arts at the University of Southern California, Los Angeles, for their aid in viewing various Warner Bros. film files and the Academy Film Archive for assisting with select frame scans.

From Turner Classic Movies, we'd like to thank Lindsey Griffin, Aaron Spiegeland, Mathew Ownby, Charles Tabesh, Taryn Jacobs, and Diana Bosch. We are also grateful for the help and support we've received from the team at Running Press, including Susan Van Horn, Seta Zink, Amy Cianfrone, Elizabeth Parks, Betsy Hulsebosch, Kristin Kiser, Leah Gordon, and Lindsay Ricketts. Last but certainly not least, thank you to our editor, Cindy Sipala, who championed this book and idea for many years and provided immense guidance, insight, and advice along the way.

KIM WOULD LIKE TO THANK:

First, thank you to my family. My grandmothers, Frances and Alma, nurtured my love of classic films at different times in my life. My parents, Barbara and Bob, indulged in teenage Kim's obsession with old Hollywood and didn't seem too worried when I became overly interested in the pre-Code era. My brother, Chris, faithfully taped my detailed list of movies off TCM and even labeled the VHS tapes for me while I was away at college! Their support fostered my curiosity and engagement with classic Hollywood, leading me on the path I am on today.

My professor and advisor at Allegheny College, Lloyd Michaels, encouraged me to apply for a grant to conduct archival research in the Production Code Administration files for my thesis on *Baby Face*. Without this introduction to the PCA files, which greatly informed this book, I probably wouldn't have developed my full-fledged fascination with the era.

A big thank-you to my friends—those who are in the classic film world and those who aren't—who have always cheered me on and didn't run away when I'd bring up the topic of old movies.

And finally, thanks to my partner, Sean Savage, who has lived the highs and lows of this experience by my side, read everything I wrote, watched countless pre-Codes with me, and provided phenomenal analysis, even when I sometimes didn't want to hear it. He has been my sounding board and my biggest supporter every step of the way, and for that, I am forever grateful.

I also want to thank my kids, Ruby and Jay, who both love me but probably love Scooby-Doo more. On that note, I also thank my dogs, Harpo, Dipper, and Mabel, who all often smell very bad but are very, very good pups. (Don't worry, they won't read the part about being smelly.)

I also want to thank my parents, Joe and Carol, as well as my sisters, Katie and Laurenn. When I was sixteen and working in a video store, my dad insisted I watch *Animal Crackers*, telling me that, sixty-plus years later, everyone still wishes they were as funny as the Marx Brothers—and it's still true. My mother is an avid reader and did something approaching a metaphysical judo roll into getting me to be a librarian just like her. She taught me the joys of losing yourself to research and the importance of the First Amendment in absolutely everything.

Lastly, thank you, the reader, for reading the acknowledgments. Remember that part at the beginning of the acknowledgments? It was foreshadowing. That's how you know this was written well.

DANNY WOULD LIKE TO THANK:

Primarily, I would like to dedicate this book to my wife, Aubrey, who has always been supportive of my niche hobby and fascination even when she occasionally has the misfortune of walking in on me watching a Conrad Nagel film.

Availability

INFORMATION IN THIS INDEX IS ACCURATE as of late 2024. Rights for films can fluctuate wildly from year to year, but patience rewards all diligent hunters.

One other thing to remember: It is in many ways easier to see most of these films in complete and uncensored cuts now than it was in the time of their original release. *Be thankful!*

- *All Quiet on the Western Front* is owned by Universal Pictures. It is available on DVD, Blu-ray, and for digital purchase or rent.
- *Ann Vickers* was produced by RKO but is now owned by Warner Bros. It is available on DVD.
- *Baby Face* is owned by Warner Bros. It is available on DVD as part of the first *Forbidden Hollywood* DVD collection. It is also available for digital rent or purchase and occasionally appears on various streaming services.
- *The Bitter Tea of General Yen* was produced by Columbia Pictures and is now owned by Sony. It is available on DVD, Blu-ray, and for digital rent or purchase.
- *The Black Cat* was produced by Universal and is available on DVD and Blu-ray, usually paired with other Boris Karloff/Bela Lugosi joints.
- *Call Her Savage* was produced by the Fox Film Corporation. The Fox Film library is currently owned by Disney. *Call Her Savage* has been released on DVD.
- *Design for Living* was produced by Paramount and is now owned by Universal Pictures. It is available on DVD and Blu-ray via the Criterion Collection.
- *The Divorcee* was produced by MGM and is now owned by Warner Bros. It is available on DVD as part of the second *Forbidden Hollywood* DVD collection, as well as being available for digital rental or purchase.
- *Downstairs* was produced by MGM and is now owned by Warner Bros. It is available on DVD in the sixth volume of *Forbidden Hollywood.*
- *Dr. Jekyll and Mr. Hyde* was produced by Paramount Pictures. The rights to the film were purchased by MGM for their 1941 remake starring Spencer Tracy (avoid), so the movie is now owned by Warner Bros. It is available on DVD and for digital rental and purchase.
- *Duck Soup* was produced by Paramount but is now owned by Universal Pictures. It is available on DVD and Blu-ray and occasionally pops up on various digital streaming platforms.
- *The Emperor Jones* was an independent production and is now in the public domain. It is available on many streaming platforms, as well as on DVD from the Criterion Collection. A Blu-ray release from Film Masters has been announced for 2025.
- *Employees' Entrance* was produced by Warner Bros. It is available on DVD as part of the seventh *Forbidden Hollywood* collection.
- *Flying Down to Rio* was produced by RKO and is now owned by Warner Bros. It is available on DVD and for digital rental and purchase.
- *Footlight Parade* was produced by Warner Bros. It is available on DVD, Blu-ray, and for digital rental or purchase.

- *Frankenstein* is owned by Universal. It is available on DVD, Blu-ray, and for digital rental or purchase. Like, if you can find any movie in this book, you can find this one.
- *Freaks* was produced by MGM and is now owned by Warner Bros. It is available on DVD as well as for digital rental or purchase.
- *Gabriel Over the White House* was produced by MGM and is now owned by Warner Bros. It is available on DVD.
- *Gold Diggers of 1933* was produced by Warner Bros. It is available on DVD and for digital rental or purchase.
- *Grand Hotel* was produced by MGM and is now owned by Warner Bros. It is available on DVD, Blu-ray, and for digital rental or purchase.
- *Heat Lightning* was produced by Warner Bros. It is available on DVD and for digital rental or purchase.
- *Heroes for Sale* was produced by Warner Bros. It is available on DVD in the third volume of *Forbidden Hollywood* and can be found available digitally.
- *I Am a Fugitive from a Chain Gang* is owned by Warner Bros. It is available on DVD and for digital rental or purchase.
- *I Am Suzanne!* was produced by the Fox Film Corporation and is now owned by Disney. It is unavailable on home video, but there is a copy at the Museum of Modern Art in New York that is shown at repertory film houses every so often.
- *I'm No Angel* was produced by Paramount and is now owned by Universal. It is available on DVD and Blu-ray.
- *Jewel Robbery* was released by Warner Bros. and is available on DVD in the fourth volume of *Forbidden Hollywood*, as well as being available for digital rental or purchase.
- *King Kong* was produced by RKO, but its copyright history is a long and thrilling one with multiple lawsuits involved. No matter: It's available on DVD, Blu-ray, LaserDisc, and for digital rental or purchase.
- *Ladies They Talk About* was released by Warner Bros. It is available on DVD in the fifth volume of *Forbidden Hollywood*. It is also available for digital rental or purchase.
- *Love Me Tonight* was produced by Paramount and is now owned by Universal. It is available on DVD and Blu-ray.
- *Madam Satan* was produced by MGM and is now owned by Warner Bros. It is available on DVD.
- *Merrily We Go to Hell* was produced by Paramount and is now owned by Universal. It is available on DVD and Blu-ray.
- *The Most Dangerous Game* was produced by RKO and is in the public domain, which means you can find it just about anywhere. There is nothing stopping you. (But also, it's available on DVD and Blu-ray if you'd like to support physical media.)
- *Murder at the Vanities* was produced by Paramount and is now owned by Universal. It is available on DVD and Blu-ray.
- *Night Nurse* was released by Warner Bros. and is available in the second volume of *Forbidden Hollywood*; plus it is available for digital rental or purchase.
- *The Public Enemy* was released by Warner Bros. It is currently available on DVD, Blu-ray, and for digital rental or purchase.

- *Queen Christina* was produced by MGM and is now owned by Warner Bros. It is available on DVD and Blu-ray.
- *Red Dust* was produced by MGM and is now owned by Warner Bros. It is available on DVD and, Amazon is telling me, VHS tape, so good for it.
- *Red-Headed Woman* was produced by MGM and is now owned by Warner Bros. It is available in the first *Forbidden Hollywood* DVD collection and for digital rental or purchase.
- *Safe in Hell* was released by Warner Bros. and is available on DVD and for digital rental or purchase.
- *Scarface* was an original Howard Hughes production released by United Artists. It has rights issues surrounding it that have led to numerous times where it's been unavailable, but right now Universal has a DVD of it circulating.
- *Shanghai Express* was produced by Paramount and is now owned by Universal. It's on DVD, Blu-ray, you name it.
- *The Sign of the Cross* was produced by Paramount and is now owned by Universal. It's in a bunch of Cecil B. DeMille box sets and is available on Blu-ray.
- *The Sin of Nora Moran* was produced by Majestic Pictures and is in the public domain, but there is a beautiful Blu-ray transfer out there from The Film Detective worth checking out.
- *Smarty* was released by Warner Bros. It's available on DVD.
- *So This Is Africa* was produced by Columbia Pictures and is now owned by Sony. Sony has shown absolutely no interest in releasing this on home video. There are copies of the film floating around on the internet.
- *The Story of Temple Drake* was produced by Paramount and is now owned by Universal. It is available on DVD and Blu-ray.
- *Tarzan and His Mate* was produced by MGM and is now owned by Warner Bros. You can find it on DVD packaged up neatly with other *Tarzan* outings, though none of them are quite as good.
- *Three On a Match* was released by Warner Bros. It is available in the third *Forbidden Hollywood* collection but can also be found online for digital rental or purchase.
- *Trouble in Paradise* was produced by Paramount and is now owned by Universal. It was released on DVD by the Criterion Collection.
- *Wild Boys of the Road* was released by Warner Bros. It is available in the third *Forbidden Hollywood* collection but can also be found online for digital rental or purchase.

The Motion Picture Production Code of 1930

Reprinted below is the Motion Picture Production Code of 1930 as it appeared in *Exhibitors Herald World* on April 5, 1930. While this version was published in a popular trade magazine right at the beginning of the "pre-Code" era, in reality, it appears no definitive version of the Code publicly circulated. Even the version printed here may differ from other contemporaneous accounts due to how editors could have chosen to print it, how it was distributed, or miscommunications caused by the effort and care needed to transmit data in the early 1930s. The Code would be augmented in July of 1934 as it came into full enforcement and would evolve, either through amendment or revision, through the 1960s. Other books and materials covering the Production Code may contain different texts because of these circumstances.

A CODE REGULATING PRODUCTION OF MOTION PICTURES

Formulated by the Association of Motion Picture Producers, Inc., and the Motion Picture Producers & Distributors of America, Inc.

Motion picture producers recognize the high trust and confidence which have been placed in them by the people of the world and which have made motion pictures a universal form of entertainment.

They recognize their responsibility to the public because of this trust and because entertainment and art are important influences in the life of a nation.

Hence, though regarding motion pictures primarily as entertainment without any explicit purpose of teaching or propaganda, they know that the motion picture within its own field of entertainment may be directly responsible for spiritual or moral progress, for higher types of social life, and for much correct thinking.

During the rapid transition from silent to talking pictures they have realized the necessity and the opportunity of subscribing to a Code to govern the production of talking pictures and of reacknowledging this responsibility.

On their part, they ask from the public and from public leaders a sympathetic understanding of their purposes and problems and a spirit of cooperation that will allow them the freedom and opportunity necessary to bring the motion picture to a still higher level of wholesome entertainment for all the people.

General Principles

1. No picture shall be produced which will lower the moral standards of those who see it. Hence the sympathy of the audience shall never be thrown to the side of crime, wrongdoing, evil or sin.

2. Correct standards of life, subject only to the requirements of drama and entertainment, shall be presented.

3. Law, natural or human, shall not be ridiculed, nor shall sympathy be created for its violation.

Particular Applications

I. Crimes against the Law

These shall never be presented in such a way as to throw sympathy with the crime as against law and justice or to inspire others with a desire for imitation.

1. *Murder*
   a. The technique of murder must be presented in a way that will not inspire imitation.
   b. Brutal killings are not to be presented in detail.
   c. Revenge in modern times shall not be justified.

2. *Methods of Crime* shall not be explicitly presented:
   a. Theft, robbery, safe-cracking, and dynamiting of trains, mines, buildings, etc., should not be detailed in method.
   b. Arson must be subject to the same safeguards.
   c. The use of firearms should be restricted to essentials.
   d. Methods of smuggling should not be presented.

3. *Illegal drug traffic* must never be presented.

4. *The use of liquor* in American life, when not required by the plot or for proper characterization, should not be shown.

II. Sex

The sanctity of the institution of marriage and the home shall be upheld. Pictures shall not infer that low forms of sex relationships are the accepted or common thing.

1. *Adultery*, sometimes necessary plot material, must not be explicitly treated, or justified, or presented attractively.

2. *Scenes of Passion*
   a. They should not be introduced when not essential to the plot.
   b. Excessive and lustful kissing, lustful embraces, suggestive postures and gestures, are not to be shown.
   c. In general, passion should so be treated that these scenes do not stimulate the lower and baser element.

3. *Seduction or Rape*
   a. They should never be more than suggested, and only when essential for the plot, and even then never shown by explicit method.
   b. They are never the proper subject for comedy.

4. *Sex perversion* or any inference to it is forbidden.

5. *White slavery* shall not be treated.

6. *Miscegenation* (sex relationships between the white and black races) is forbidden.

7. *Sex hygiene* and venereal diseases are not subjects for motion pictures.

8. Scenes of *actual child birth*, in fact or in silhouette, are never to be presented.

9. *Children's sex organs* are never to be exposed.

III. Vulgarity

The treatment of low, disgusting, unpleasant, though not necessarily evil, subjects should be subject always to the dictate of good taste and a regard for the sensibilities of the audience.

IV. Obscenity

Obscenity in word, gesture, reference, song, joke, or by suggestion (even when likely to be understood only by part of the audience) is forbidden.

V. Profanity

Pointed profanity (this includes the words God, Lord, Jesus, Christ—unless used reverently—Hell, S.O.B., damn, Gawd), or every other profane or vulgar expression however used, is forbidden.

VI. Costume

1. *Complete nudity* is never permitted. This includes nudity in fact or in silhouette, or any lecherous or licentious notice thereof by other characters in the picture.

2. *Undressing scenes* should be avoided, and never used save where essential to the plot.

3. *Indecent* or undue exposure is forbidden.

4. *Dancing costumes* intended to permit undue exposure of indecent movements in the dance are forbidden.

VII. Dances

1. Dances suggesting or representing sexual actions or indecent passion are forbidden.

2. Dances which emphasize indecent movements are to be regarded as obscene.

VIII. Religion

1. No film or episode may throw *ridicule* on any religious faith.

2. *Ministers of religion* in their character as ministers of religion should not be used as comic characters or as villains.

3. *Ceremonies* of any definite religion should be carefully and respectfully handled.

IX. Locations

The treatment of bedrooms must be governed by good taste and delicacy.

X. National Feelings

1. *The use of the Flag* shall be consistently respectful.

2. *The history,* institutions, prominent people and citizenry of all nations shall be represented fairly.

XI. Titles

Salacious, indecent, or obscene titles shall not be used.

XII. Repellent Subjects

The following subjects must be treated within the careful limits of good taste:

1. *Actual hangings* or electrocutions as legal punishments for crime.

2. *Third Degree* methods.

3. *Brutality and possible gruesomeness.*

4. *Branding* of people or animals.

5. *Apparent cruelty* to children or animals.

6. *The sale of women,* or a woman selling her virtue.

7. *Surgical operations.*

Bibliography

Aaronson, Charles S. "Heat Lightning." *Motion Picture Herald,* March 17, 1934.

Abramovitch, Seth, and Ray Morton. "Origin of 'Kong': The Unbelievable True Backstory of Hollywood's Favorite Giant Ape." *The Hollywood Reporter,* April 17, 2023. https://www.hollywoodreporter.com/heat-vision/king-kong-unbelievable-true-story-hollywoods-favorite-giant-ape-984785.

"Actress Alice White Dead at 76." UPI, February 25, 1983. https://www.upi.com/Archives/1983/02/25/Actress-Alice-Whitedead-at-76/3556414997200/.

Adamson, Joe. *Groucho, Harpo, Chico, and Sometimes Zeppo: A History of the Marx Brothers and a Satire on the Rest of the World.* New York: Simon and Schuster, 1973.

"AFI Catalog of Feature Films: Employees' Entrance." AFI, Accessed August 26, 2024. https://catalog.afi.com/Catalog/moviedetails/4468.

"AFI Catalog of Feature Films: Love Me Tonight." AFI. Accessed August 27, 2024. https://catalog.afi.com/Film/4125-LOVE-ME-TONIGHT.

Aliperti, Cliff. "Employees' Entrance (1933) Starring Warren William and the Franklin-Monroe Department Store." Immortal Ephemera, September 21, 2014. https://immortalephemera.com/8792/employees-entrance-1933-starring-warren-william/.

Aliperti, Cliff. "Lew Ayres—A Brief Biography of the Dr. Kildare Star." Immortal Ephemera, March 28, 2015. https://immortalephemera.com/134/lew-ayres-dr-kildare-star/.

Aliperti, Cliff. "Louis Wolheim—Biography of the All Quiet on the Western Front Star." Immortal Ephemera, March 28, 2014. https://immortalephemera.com/13093/louis-wolheim-biography/.

Aliperti, Cliff. "Wild Boys of the Road (1933) Meets 'Boy and Girl Tramps of America.'" Immortal Ephemera, September 14, 2015. https://immortalephemera.com/63442/wild-boys-of-the-road-1933/.

Als, Hilton. "Master of Disguise: Paul Robeson and the Emperor Jones." The Criterion Collection, November 11, 2009. https://www.criterion.com/current/posts/1269-master-of-disguise-paul-robeson-and-the-emperor-jones.

Arnold, Jeremy. "Heroes For Sale—Richard Barthelmess Stars in William Wellman's HEROES FOR SALE on DVD." Turner Classic Movies, April 3, 2009. https://www.tcm.com/tcmdb/title/1125/heroes-for-sale#articles-reviews?articleId=237605.

Axmaker, Sean. "Ladies of Leisure." Turner Classic Movies, October 21, 2009. https://www.tcm.com/tcmdb/title/3792/ladies-of-leisure#articles-reviews?articleId=274271.

Axmaker, Sean. "The Most Dangerous Game." Turner Classic Movies, July 10, 2012. https://www.tcm.com/tcmdb/title/84006/the-most-dangerous-game#articles-reviews?articleId=498925.

"Baby Face (1933)." *The New York Times,* June 24, 1933.

Bailey, John, and Matt Severson. "Video essay." In *The Story of Temple Drake,* dir. by Dorothy Arzner. Criterion, 2019.

Balio, Tino. *Grand Design: Hollywood as a Modern Business Enterprise, 1930–1939.* Berkeley, CA: University of California Press, 1996.

Balio, Tino, and Arthur Hove, eds. *Gold Diggers of 1933.* Madison, WI: University of Wisconsin Press, 1980.

Barrios, Richard. *Dangerous Rhythm: Why Movie Musicals Matter.* New York: Oxford University Press, 2015.

Bartlett, Donald L., and James B. Steele. *Howard Hughes: His Life and Madness.* New York: W. W. Norton, 2004.

Basinger, Jeanine. *A Woman's View: How Hollywood Spoke to Women 1930–1960.* New York: Knopf, 1993.

Beauchamp, Cari. "Video essay." In *Merrily We Go to Hell,* dir. by Dorothy Arzner. Criterion, 2021.

Beauchamp, Cari, and Mary Anita Loos, eds. *Anita Loos Rediscovered: Film Treatments and Fiction.* Berkeley, CA: University of California Press, 2003.

Bernstein, Matthew, and Robert Wise. *Walter Wanger, Hollywood Independent.* Minneapolis: University of Minnesota Press, 2000.

"'The Best Friend I Ever Had.'" Frankensteinia, February 2, 2014. https://frankensteinia.blogspot.com/2014/02/the-best-friend-i-ever-had.html.

Biery, Ruth. "Dumb Like a Fox." *Modern Screen,* September 1934.

Bigelow, Joe. "Baby Face." *Variety,* June 27, 1933.

Bigelow, Joe. "Tarzan and His Mate." *Variety,* April 24, 1934.

Birchard, Robert S. *Cecil B. DeMille's Hollywood.* Lexington, KY: University Press of Kentucky, 2021.

"The Black Cat and the Queer String of Films It Inspired." Medium, January 13, 2022. https://36toesproductions.medium.com/the-black-cat-and-the-queer-string-of-films-it-inspired-f778e3a3c36.

Black, Gregory D. *Hollywood Censored: Morality Codes, Catholics, and the Movies.* New York: Cambridge University Press, 1994.

Bogdanovich, Peter. *Who the Devil Made It: Conversations with Legendary Film Directors.* New York: Alfred A. Knopf, 1997.

"Bow Pulls 'Em In." *The Film Daily,* December 14, 1932.

Bower, Clifford T. "Are Mae West's Films Indecent?" *Picturegoer,* August 4, 1934.

Boyes, Laura. "All Quiet on the Western Front." Moviediva, 2001. https://moviediva.com/reviewpages/MDAllQuietWesternFront/.

Boyes, Laura. "The Black Cat." Moviediva, January 25, 2022. https://moviediva.com/reviewpages/mdblackcat/.

Boyes, Laura. "Employees' Entrance." Moviediva, January 27, 2022. https://moviediva.com/reviewpages/mdemployeesentrance/.

Boyes, Laura. "Flying Down to Rio." Moviediva, January 27, 2022. https://moviediva.com/reviewpages/mdflyingdowntorio/.

Boyes, Laura. "Red Dust." Moviediva, March 21, 2022. https://moviediva.com/reviewpages/MDRedDust/.

Brown, Peter Harry, and Pat H. Broeske. *Howard Hughes: The Untold Story.* Cambridge, MA: Da Capo Press, 2004.

Bryant, Roger. *William Powell: The Life and Films.* Jefferson, NC: McFarland & Company, 2006.

Cady, Brian. "Employees' Entrance." Turner Classic Movies, April 29, 2003. https://www.tcm.com/tcmdb/title/1770/employees-entrance/#articles-reviews?articleId=25806.

Cagney, James. *Cagney by Cagney.* London: New English Library, 1976.

"Cal York Announcing the Monthly Broadcast of Hollywood Goings Ons." *Photoplay* XLV, no. 2, January 1934.

Callahan, Dan. *Barbara Stanwyck.* Jackson, MS: University Press of Mississippi, 2012.

Calvert, Bruce. "Raymond Griffith—The Silk Hat Comedian." May 28, 2024. http://www.silentfilmstillarchive.com/raymond.htm.

Campbell, Duncan. "The Unknown Soldier." *The Guardian,* November 3, 2003. https://www.theguardian.com/film/2003/nov/03/1.

Capra, Frank. *Frank Capra: The Name Above the Title: An Autobiography.* New York: Macmillan Co., 1971.

Carey, Gary. *Anita Loos: A Biography.* New York: Knopf, 1988.

Carr, Jay. "Heroes for Sale." Turner Classic Movies, September 12, 2007. https://www.tcm.com/tcmdb/title/1125/heroes-for-sale#articles-reviews?articleId=182329.

Chartier, Roy. "Murder at the Vanities." *Variety,* May 22, 1934.

Cheatham, Maude. "Kay Francis and Bill Powell Talk About Each Other." *Screenland,* August 1934.

Chrisman, J. Eugene. "Please Scare Us, Mr. Karloff!" *Hollywood,* July 1934.

"Clara Bow's OK Film Comeback." *Variety,* November 15, 1932.

"Clara Bow Sets Roxy High." *The Film Daily,* November 26, 1932.

Clarke, Mae, and James Curtis. *Featured Player: An Oral Autobiography of Mae Clarke.* Santa Barbara, CA: Santa Teresa Press; in association with the Scarecrow Press, 1996.

Collier, Lionel. "On the Screens Now: Heat Lightning." *Picturegoer Weekly,* August 18, 1934.

Collier, Lionel. "On the Screens Now: Murder at the Vanities." *Picturegoer,* October 13, 1934.

Colwell, Katie. "SCARFACE: The Effects of Its Censorship." Screen Culture Journal, May 8, 2019. https://screenculturejournal.com/2019/05/scarface-the-effects-of-its-censorship/.

Conway, Michael, and Mark Ricci. *The Films of Jean Harlow.* New York: Citadel Press, 1965.

"Court Decides Movie Role of Miss Stanwyck." *Chicago Daily Tribune.*

Cowan, Wm. G. "What Do You Think?: Letters from our Readers: Prosperous 'Down and Outs.'" *Picturegoer,* August 26, 1933.

Czitrom, Daniel. "The Politics of Performance: Theater Licensing and the Origins of Movie Censorship in New York." *Movie Censorship and American Culture.* Edited by Francis G. Couvares. Washington: Smithsonian Institution Press, 1996.

Delson, Susan. *Dudley Murphy: Hollywood Wild Card.* Minneapolis: University of Minnesota Press, 2006.

DeMille, Cecil B., and Donald Hayne. *The Autobiography of Cecil B. DeMille.* New York: Garland Pub, 1985.

DeMille, Cecilia, and Mark A. Vieira. *Cecil B. DeMille: The Art of the Hollywood Epic.* Philadelphia: Running Press, 2014.

Despres, Louie. "'So This Is Africa' (1933)—Gentlemen, Sharpen Your Scissors!" "Give me the good old days!," April 16, 2009. https://web.archive.org/web/20111018222227/http://www.elbrendel.com/2009/04/so-this-is-africa.html.

Dick, Bernard F. *Claudette Colbert: She Walked in Beauty.* Jackson: University of Mississippi Press, 2009.

Dirks, Tim. "I Am a Fugitive from a Chain Gang (1932)." Filmsite. Accessed August 26, 2024. https://www.filmsite.org/iama.html.

Dixon, Wheeler Winston. "Kicking over the Traces: Dorothy Arzner's Merrily We Go to Hell (1932)." Senses of Cinema, February 15, 2017. https://www.sensesofcinema.com/2017/cteq/merrily-we-go-to-hell/.

Doherty, Thomas Patrick. *Pre-Code Hollywood: Sex, Immorality, and Insurrection in American Cinema, 1930–1934.* New York: Columbia University Press, 1999.

Doll, Susan. "Merrily We Go to Hell." Turner Classic Movies, August 18, 2020. https://www.tcm.com/tcmdb/title/83340/merrily-we-go-to-hell#articles-reviews?articleId=1582843.

Druxman, Michael B. *Paul Muni: His Life and His Films.* South Brunswick, NJ: Barnes, 1974.

"Duck Soup." Turner Classic Movies, March 21, 2006. https://www.tcm.com/tcmdb/title/73717/duck-soup#articles-reviews?articleId=122429.

Eberwein, Robert T. *The Hollywood War Film.* Hoboken, NJ: John Wiley & Sons, Inc., 2009.

Eder, Bruce. "Audio commentary." In *The Most Dangerous Game,* dir. by Ernest B. Schoedsack and Irving Pichel. Criterion, 2001.

Eder, Bruce. "The Emperor Jones." The Criterion Collection, September 2, 1993. https://www.criterion.com/current/posts/950-the-emperor-jones.

Eells, George. *Ginger, Loretta, and Irene Who?* New York: Putnam, 1976.

"The Emperor Jones AFI Notes." Turner Classic Movies. Accessed August 29, 2024. https://www.tcm.com/tcmdb/title/74043/the-emperor-jones#notes.

Erickson, Glenn. "The Bela Lugosi Collection." DVD Talk, September 8, 2005. https://www.dvdtalk.com/dvdsavant/s1728bela.html.

Erickson, Glenn. "Blu-ray Review: The Most Dangerous Game / Gow, The Headhunter." DVD Savant, July 1, 2012. http://www.dvdtalk.com/dvdsavant/s3922game.html.

Evans, Delight. "Reviews of the Best Pictures: I Am Suzanne!" *Screenland,* April 1934.

Evans, Delight. "Tagging the Talkies: Smarty." *Screenland,* August 1934.

Eyman, Scott. "Audio commentary." In *Trouble in Paradise,* dir. by Ernst Lubitsch. Criterion, 2003.

Eyman, Scott. *Empire of Dreams: The Epic Life of Cecil B. DeMille.* New York: Simon & Schuster, 2014.

Eyman, Scott. *Ernst Lubitsch: Laughter in Paradise.* Baltimore: Johns Hopkins University Press, 2000.

Feaster, Felicia. "Frankenstein." Turner Classic Movies, September 25, 2003. https://www.tcm.com/tcmdb/title/75587/frankenstein#articles-reviews?articleId=18617.

Ferrier, Aimee. "Al Pacino Discusses the Cultural Importance of 'Scarface.'" *Far Out Magazine UK*, February 25, 2023. https://faroutmagazine.co.uk/al-pacino-cultural-importance-scarface/.

Files #679 (special), #1745, and #2769, Warner Bros. Archives, School of Cinematic Arts, University of Southern California, Los Angeles.

"Flying Down to Rio." Turner Classic Movies. Accessed August 26, 2024. https://www.tcm.com/tcmdb/title/75236/flying-down-to-rio#notes.

"Fort Douaumont." Wikipedia, June 18, 2024. https://en.wikipedia.org/wiki/Fort_Douaumont.

Foster, G. A. "Wild Boys of the Road." Library of Congress, 2003. https://www.loc.gov/static/programs/national-film-preservation-board/documents/wild_boys.pdf.

"Gabriel Over the White House." *Variety,* January 1, 1933. https://variety.com/1932/film/reviews/gabriel-over-the-white-house-1200410757/.

Galbraith, Stuart. "Forbidden Hollywood Three." DVD talk, March 24, 2009. https://www.dvdtalk.com/reviews/36899/forbidden-hollywood-three-other-mens-women-purchase-price-frisco-jenny-midnight-mary-heroes-for-sale-wild-boys-of-the-road/.

Gallagher, John. "Audio commentary." In *Heroes for Sale,* dir. by William Wellman. Warner Bros., 2009.

Gammie, John. "Why They 'Call Her Savage.'" *Film Weekly,* January 6, 1933.

"Gold Diggers of 1933." Warner Bros. Pressbook, 1933.

Goldblatt, Burt, and Paul D. Zimmerman. *The Marx Brothers at the Movies.* New York: Putnam, 1968.

Greason, Alfred. "Wild Boys of [the] Road." *Variety,* September 26, 1933.

Greason, Alfred Rushford. "Frankenstein." *Variety,* December 7, 1931. https://variety.com/1931/film/reviews/frankenstein-2-1200410509/.

Greenfield, Jeff. "Gabriel Over the White House." YouTube, April 3, 2018. https://www.youtube.com/watch?v=apCLCjK2ArA.

Grost, Mike. "Edgar G. Ulmer." The Films of Edgar G. Ulmer. Accessed August 29, 2024. http://mikegrost.com/ulmer.htm.

H. R. "Call Her Savage." *The Manchester Guardian,* January 4, 1933.

Hall, Mordaunt. "'I, Jerry, Take Thee, Joan.'" *The New York Times,* June 11, 1932. https://www.nytimes.com/1932/06/11/archives/i-jerry-take-thee-joan.html.

Hall, Mordaunt. "Marlene Dietrich in a Brilliantly Directed Melodrama Set Aboard a Train Running from Peiping to Shanghai." *The New York Times,* February 18, 1932. https://www.nytimes.com/1932/02/18/archives/marlene-dietrich-in-a-brilliantly-directed-melodrama-set-aboard-a.html.

Hall, Mordaunt. "Mr. Lubitsch's 'Design for Living.'" *The New York Times,* December 3, 1933.

Hall, Mordaunt. "The Screen; a Man-Made Monster in Grand Guignol Film Story." *The New York Times,* December 5, 1931. https://www.nytimes.com/1931/12/05/archives/the-screen-a-manmade-monster-in-grand-guignol-film-story-lawrence.html.

Hall, Mordaunt. "A Tale of Woe." *The New York Times,* December 13, 1933.

Harris. "Gabriel Over the White House." *The Billboard,* April 3, 1933.

Hart, Dorothy, and Robert Kimball, eds. *The Complete Lyrics of Lorenz Hart.* New York: Da Capo Press, 1995.

Harvey, James. *Romantic Comedy in Hollywood from Lubitsch to Sturges.* New York: Knopf, 1987.

"Heat Lightning." *The Film Daily,* March 7, 1934.

"'Heat Lightning' with Aline MacMahon and Ann Dvorak." *Harrison's Reports,* March 10, 1934.

Hillier, Jim, and Peter Wollen, eds. *Howard Hawks: American Artist.* London: BFI Publishing, 1996.

Homer, Dickens. *The Films of Gary Cooper.* New York: Citadel Press, 1970.

"I Am a Fugitive from a Chain Gang." Turner Classic Movies. Accessed August 26, 2024. https://www.tcm.com/tcmdb/title/782/i-am-a-fugitive-from-a-chain-gang#articles-reviews.

Jewell, Richard B. *The Golden Age of Cinema: Hollywood, 1929–1945.* Malden, MA: Blackwell, 2007.

"Joan Blondell, Actress, Dies at 70; Often Played Wisecracking Blonde." *The New York Times,* December 26, 1979.

"Johnny Weissmuller." Olympics.com. Accessed August 28, 2024. https://olympics.com/en/athletes/johnny-weissmuller.

"Josef von Sternberg." Britannica. https://www.britannica.com/biography/Josef-von-Sternberg.

Kael, Pauline. "Shanghai Express." http://www.geocities.ws/paulinekaelreviews/s3.html.

Karloff, Sara Jane, and Scott Allen Nollen. *Boris Karloff: A Gentleman's Life: The Authorized Biography.* Baltimore: Midnight Marquee Press, 1999.

Kawin, Bruce. "The Most Dangerous Game." The Criterion Collection, June 7, 1999. https://www.criterion.com/current/posts/52-the-most-dangerous-game.

Kear, Lynn, and John Rossman. *Kay Francis: A Passionate Life and Career.* Jefferson, NC: McFarland, 2006.

Kehr, Dave. "A Wanton Woman's Ways Revealed, 71 Years Later." *The New York Times,* January 9, 2005. https://www.nytimes.com/2005/01/09/movies/a-wanton-womans-ways-revealed-71-years-later.html.

Kelly, Andrew. *Filming All Quiet on the Western Front.* London: I.B. Tauris, 1998.

Kennedy, Matthew. *Joan Blondell: A Life Between Takes.* Jackson, MS: University Press of Mississippi, 2014.

Khoshbakht, Ehsan. "Architecture of the Black Cat." Notes On Cinematograph, July 24, 2009. https://notesoncinematograph.blogspot.com/2009/07/architectures-of-black-cat.html.

"King Kong." Turner Classic Movies. Accessed August 27, 2024. https://www.tcm.com/tcmdb/title/2690/king-kong#articles-reviews.

Kobal, John, and Robert Dance. *The Lost World of DeMille.* Jackson, MS: University Press of Mississippi, 2019.

Kreuger, Miles. "Audio Commentary." In *Love Me Tonight,* dir. by Rouben Mamoulian. Kino Lorber, 2020.

Kuersten, Erich. "Wild Boys and Midnight Maries: Social Realism and Pre-Code in Forbidden Hollywood (Vol. 3)—Bright Lights Film Journal." *Bright Lights Film Journal,* April 30, 2009. https://brightlightsfilm.com/wild-boys-and-midnight-marie-ssocial-realism-and-pre-code-in-forbidden-hollywood-vol-3/.

Landazuri, Margarita. "Shanghai Express—Shanghai Express." TCM, July 28, 2003. https://www.tcm.com/tcmdb/title/89803/shanghai-express#articles-reviews?articleId=18558.

Landazuri, Margarita. "The Sign of the Cross." Turner Classic Movies, March 25, 2004. https://www.tcm.com/tcmdb/title/90102/the-sign-of-the-cross#articles-reviews?articleId=72483.

LaSalle, Mick. *Complicated Women: Sex and Power in Pre-Code Hollywood.* New York: St. Martin's Press, 2000.

LaSalle, Mick. "Video essay." In *The Story of Temple Drake,* dir. by Dorothy Arzner. Criterion, 2019.

"The Latest Films Reviewed: Three on a Match." *Film Weekly,* December 2, 1932.

Laurence, Rebecca. "Why Frankenstein Is the Story That Defines Our Fears." *BBC News,* August 16, 2022. https://www.bbc.com/culture/article/20180611-why-frankenstein-is-the-story-that-defined-our-fears.

Lawrence, Jerome. *Actor: The Life and Times of Paul Muni.* New York: Putnam, 1974.

Leff, Leonard J., and Jerold Simmons. *The Dame in the Kimono: Hollywood, Censorship, and the Production Code.* Lexington, KY: University Press of Kentucky, 2001.

LeMay, John. *Kong Unmade: The Lost Films of Skull Island.* Roswell, NM: Bicep Books, 2019.

LeRoy, Mervyn, and Richard Kleiner. *Mervyn LeRoy: Take One.* New York: Hawthorn Books, 1974.

Levine, Debra. *Theodore Kosloff & Cecil B. DeMille Meet Madam Satan.* The Egyptian Theatre in Hollywood, 2014.

Lopez, Kristen. "Seminar: Freaks | Lecture | Coolidge Corner Theatre." YouTube, February 17, 2021. https://www.youtube.com/watch?v=dl-6VG2LO0c.

Louvish, Simon. *Cecil B. DeMille: A Life in Art.* New York: Thomas Dunne Books/St. Martin's Press, 2008.

"Love Me Tonight." Turner Classic Movies. Accessed August 27, 2024. https://www.tcm.com/tcmdb/title/82022/love-me-tonight#articles-reviews.

Luhrssen, David. *Mamoulian: Life on Stage and Screen.* Lexington, KY: University Press of Kentucky, 2013.

Lusk, Norbert. "Bow Comeback Voted Success." *Los Angeles Times,* December 4, 1932.

Lusk, Norbert. "The Screen in Review: Heroes for Sale." *Picture Play Magazine* XXXIX, no. 2, October 1933.

Madsen, Axel. *Stanwyck.* New York: HarperCollins Publishers, 1994.

Maietta, Tony, and Jeffrey Vance. "Audio commentary for *The Divorcee.*" In *TCM Archives—Forbidden Hollywood Collection, Vol. 2.* Warner Bros., 2008.

Mank, Gregory William. *Hollywood Cauldron: Thirteen Horror Films from the Genre's Golden Age.* Jefferson, NC: McFarland, 2001.

Mason, Fran. *American Gangster Cinema: From Little Caesar to Pulp Fiction.* London: Palgrave Macmillan UK, 2002.

Mast, Gerald. *Howard Hawks: Storyteller.* New York: Oxford University Press, 1982.

McBride, Joseph, ed. *Hawks on Hawks.* Berkeley: University of California Press, 1982.

McCarthy, Todd. *Howard Hawks: The Grey Fox of Hollywood.* New York: Grove Press, 1997.

McElwee, John. "Favorites List—Warren William and Employees' Entrance." Greenbriar Picture Shows, September 24, 2011. https://greenbriarpictureshows.blogspot.com/2011/09/favorites-list-warren-william-and.html.

McElwee, John. *Showmen, Sell It Hot!: Movies as Merchandise in Golden Era Hollywood.* GoodKnight Books, 2013.

Meehan, Leo. "Hollywood Openings." *Motion Picture Herald,* July 30, 1932.

"Merrily We Go to Hell." *Photoplay* XLII, no. 2, July 1932. https://lantern.mediahist.org/catalog/photo43chic_0012.

"Merrily We Go to Hell—Notes." Turner Classic Movies. Accessed August 28, 2024. https://www.tcm.com/tcmdb/title/83340/merrily-we-go-to-hell#notes.

Miller, Frank. "All Quiet on the Western Front." Turner Classic Movies, November 10, 2010. https://www.tcm.com/tcmdb/title/67079/all-quiet-on-the-western-front#articles-reviews?articleId=357365.

Miller, Frank. *Censored Hollywood: Sex, Sin, and Violence on Screen.* Atlanta: Turner Publishing, 1994.

Miller, Frank. "The Divorcee." Turner Classic Movies, February 12, 2008. https://www.tcm.com/tcmdb/title/114/the-divorcee#articles-reviews?articleId=25799.

Miller, Frank. "Footlight Parade." Turner Classic Movies, July 28, 2003. https://www.tcm.com/tcmdb/title/3122/footlight-parade#articles-reviews?articleId=12783.

Miller, Frank. "Freaks." Turner Classic Movies, February 20, 2013. https://www.tcm.com/tcmdb/title/163/freaks#articles-reviews?articleId=581451.

Miller, Frank. "Gold Diggers of 1933—Gold Diggers of 1933." Turner Classic Movies, April 23, 2004. Retrieved from http://www.tcm.com/tcmdb/title/3463/Gold-Diggers-of-1933/articles.html.

Miller, Frank. "Queen Christina." Turner Classic Movies, June 26, 2003. https://www.tcm.com/tcmdb/title/385/queen-christina#articles-reviews?articleId=29966.

Milne, Tom. *Mamoulian.* Bloomington, IN: Indiana University Press, 1970.

Mitchell, Glenn. *The Marx Brothers Encyclopedia: Revised and Expanded New Edition.* London: Titan Books, 2012.

Morgan. "From the Box-Office Point of View: Design for Living." *The Billboard,* December 2, 1933.

Morgan, Kim. *"Design for Living: It Takes Three."* The Criterion Collection, December 6, 2011. https://www.criterion.com/current/posts/2084-design-for-living-it-takes-three.

Morris, Ruth. "Uncommon Chatter." *Variety,* December 22, 1931.

Motion Picture Association of America. Production Code Administration records, Margaret Herrick Library, Academy of Motion Picture Arts and Sciences.

N. L. "The Circus Side Show." *The New York Times,* July 9, 1932. https://www.nytimes.com/1932/07/09/archives/the-circus-side-show.html.

Nehme, Farran S. "Get Thee to MoMA's To Save and Project Festival." Self-Styled Siren, October 2013. http://selfstyledsiren.blogspot.com/2013/10/get-thee-to-momas-to-save-and-project.html.

Neibaur, James. *James Cagney: Films of the 1930s.* Lanham, MD: Rowman & Littlefield Publishers, 2014.

New York State Archives series A1418, NYS Motion Picture Division License Application Case Files, Box 223, Casefile #25491, Baby Face.

New York State Archives series A1418, NYS Motion Picture Division License Application Case Files, Box 235, Casefile #25806, Baby Face (Revised).

Nixon, Rob. "Behind The Camera—Gold Diggers of 1933." Turner Classic Movies, February 27, 2013. https://www.tcm.com/tcmdb/title/3463/gold-diggers-of-1933#articles-reviews?articleId=582520.

Nixon, Rob. "Trivia—Gold Diggers of 1933—Trivia & Fun Facts About GOLD DIGGERS OF 1933." Turner Classic Movies, February 27, 2013. https://www.tcm.com/tcmdb/title/3463/gold-diggers-of-1933#articles-reviews?articleId=582523.

Nixon, Rob. "Trouble In Paradise." Turner Classic Movies, January 23, 2003. https://www.tcm.com/tcmdb/title/93978/trouble-in-paradise#articles-reviews?articleId=17865.

"Notes—Grand Hotel." Turner Classic Movies. https://www.tcm.com/tcmdb/title/183/grand-hotel#notes.

Nugent, Frank S. "America's Juvenile Hoboes." *The New York Times,* September 22, 1933. https://www.nytimes.com/1933/09/22/archives/americas-juvenile-hoboes.html.

Nugent, Franklin S. "Pity the Hero." *The New York Times,* July 22, 1933. https://www.nytimes.com/1933/07/22/archives/pity-the-hero.html.

O'Brien, Geoffrey. "The Story of Temple Drake: Notorious." The Criterion Collection, December 3, 2019. https://www.criterion.com/current/posts/6716-the-story-of-temple-drake-notorious.

O'Connor, John E., and Peter C. Rollins, eds. *Why We Fought: America's Wars in Film and History.* Lexington, KY: University Press of Kentucky, 2008.

O'Hanlon, Michael. "Box Office Information." Kay Francis' Life & Career, November 26, 2014. http://kayfrancisfilms.com/box-office-information/.

O'Malley, Sheila. "Heroes for Sale (1933); Dir. William Wellman." The Sheila Variations, April 18, 2018. https://www.sheilaomalley.com/?p=10041.

O'Malley, Sheila. "Merrily We Go to Hell (1932); Dir. Dorothy Arzner." The Sheila Variations, April 28, 2009. https://www.sheilaomalley.com/?p=9308.

Pedelty, Donovan. "Here's HUSTLE for YOU!" *Film Weekly,* October 3, 1931.

Pelswick, Rose. "Baby Face." *New York Evening Journal,* June 26, 1933.

Phillips, Malcolm D. "Can Clara Bow Come Back?" *Picturegoer,* November 26, 1932.

Phillips, Michael. "A Curio for the Trump Era: 'Gabriel Over the White House.'" *Chicago Tribune,* June 6, 2018. https://www.chicagotribune.com/2017/02/02/a-curio-for-the-trump-era-gabriel-over-the-white-house/.

Phillips, Michael. "'Trouble in Paradise' Review: The Lubitsch Touch, Newly Polished." *Chicago Tribune,* June 2, 2018. https://www.chicagotribune.com/entertainment/movies/ct-mov-trouble-in-paradise-1005-story.html.

"Pictures: First WB Slash Drops Average Cost Per Picture to $225,000; Second Cut Now to $200,000." *Variety,* December 8, 1931.

"Pictures: Wanted—Male Lead." *Variety,* July 26, 1932.

Pitts, Michael R. *Poverty Row Studios, 1929–1940: An Illustrated History of 55 Independent Film Companies, with a Filmography for Each.* Jefferson, NC: McFarland, 2005.

Pizzitola, Louis. *Hearst Over Hollywood: Power, Passion, and Propaganda in the Movies.* New York: Columbia University Press, 2002.

Procter, Ben H. *William Randolph Hearst: Final Edition, 1911–1951.* New York: Oxford University Press, 2007.

Quirk, Lawrence J. *The Complete Films of William Powell.* Secaucus, NJ: The Citadel Press, 1986.

Quirk, Lawrence J. *The Films of Fredric March.* New York: Citadel Press, 1971.

"A Racy film! Not for the Sunday School class!" *Mirror,* June 24, 1933.

Randall, Richard S. *Censorship of the Movies: The Social and Political Control of a Mass Medium.* Madison: University of Wisconsin Press, 1968.

Rice, Christina. *Ann Dvorak: Hollywood's Forgotten Rebel.* Lexington, KY: The University Press of Kentucky, 2013.

Rice, Jonah. "40 Years Later—The Cultural Impact of Scarface." Movieweb, September 10, 2023. https://movieweb.com/scarface-cultural-impact-40-years-later/.

Ringgold, Gene, and DeWitt Bodeen. *Films of Cecil B. DeMille.* New York: Citadel Publishing, 1974.

Roche, Adam. *A Universe of Horrors,* 2016.

Rooney, Darrell. *Harlow in Hollywood: The Blonde Bombshell in the Glamour Capital, 1928–1937.* Santa Monica, CA: Angel City Press, 2022.

"Round Table Club." *Motion Picture Herald,* July 28, 1934.

"Safe in Hell." Warner Bros. Pressbook, 1931.

Schatz, Thomas. *The Genius of the System: Hollywood Filmmaking in the Studio Era.* New York: Henry Holt and Co., 1996.

Scott, John. "Clara Bow Back on Screen." *Los Angeles Times,* December 2, 1932.

Senn, Bryan. *Golden Horrors: An Illustrated Critical Filmography of Terror Cinema, 1931–1939.* Jefferson, NC: McFarland, 1996.

Sennwald, Andre. "From the Viennese: Jewel Robbery." *The New York Times,* July 23, 1932.

"The Shadow Stage: Employees' Entrance." *Photoplay* XLIII, no. 3, February 1933.

"The Shadow Stage: Frankenstein." *Photoplay* XLI, no. 2, January 1932.

"The Shadow Stage: Heroes for Sale." *Photoplay* XLIV, August 1933.

"The Shadow Stage: Merrily We Go to Hell." *Photoplay* XLII, no. 3, August 1932.

"The Shadow Stage: Queen Christina." *Photoplay* XLV, no. 4, March 1934.

Shaffer, Rosalind. "Sordid Themes Come to Front in Film World." *Chicago Daily Tribune.*

Shallert, Edwin. "Foreign Star Gets New Chance at Cinema Brightness; Stage and Studio News, Gossip." *Los Angeles Times,* October 30, 1933.

"Shoddy!" *The Billboard,* October 7, 1933.

"Showmen's Reviews: Tarzan and His Mate." *Motion Picture Herald,* April 28, 1934.

"The Sin of Nora Moran." *Chicago Daily Tribune,* March 6, 1934.

Slide, Anthony. *Silent Players.* Lexington: University Press of Kentucky, 2002.

Smith, Farran Nehme. "Self-Styled Siren: Wild Boys of the Road (1933)." The Self-Styled Siren, January 14, 2008. https://selfstyledsiren.substack.com/p/wild-boys-of-road-1933.

Smith, Imogen Sara. "Video essay." In *The Story of Temple Drake,* dir. by Dorothy Arzner. Criterion, 2019.

Sova, Dawn B., and Marjorie Heins. *Forbidden Films: Censorship Histories of 125 Motion Pictures.* New York: Facts on File, 2001.

Spicer, Chrystopher J. *Clark Gable: Biography, Filmography, Bibliography.* Jefferson, NC: McFarland, 2002.

Spivak, Jeffrey. *Buzz: The Life and Art of Busby Berkeley.* Lexington, KY: University Press of Kentucky, 2010.

Stafford, J. "Wild Boys of the Road." Turner Classic Movies, March 4, 2009. https://www.tcm.com/tcmdb/title/3430/wild-boys-of-the-road#articles-reviews?articleId=91129.

Stafford, Jeff. "The Most Dangerous Game." Turner Classic Movies, June 25, 2007. https://www.tcm.com/tcmdb/title/84006/the-most-dangerous-game#articles-reviews?articleId=176198.

Stafford, Jeff. "Night Nurse." Turner Classic Movies, October 27, 2004. https://www.tcm.com/tcmdb/title/3158/night-nurse#articles-reviews?articleId=83980.

Stangeland, John. *Warren William: Magnificent Scoundrel of Pre-Code Hollywood.* Jefferson, NC: McFarland & Co., Publishers, 2011.

"Stanwyck Takes Role as Col. Seeks Writ." *Variety,* September 8, 1931.

Steffen, James. "Downstairs." Turner Classic Movies, March 15, 2007. https://www.tcm.com/tcmdb/title/119/downstairs#articles-reviews?articleId=87836.

Stenn, David. *Bombshell: The Life and Death of Jean Harlow.* New York: Doubleday, 1993.

Stenn, David. *Clara Bow: Runnin' Wild.* New York: Cooper Square Press, 2000.

Sterritt, David. "The Bitter Tea of General Yen." Turner Classic Movies, March 20, 2008. https://www.tcm.com/tcmdb/title/68828/the-bitter-tea-of-general-yen#articles-reviews?articleId=196843.

Stevens, George Jr. *Conversations with the Great Moviemakers of Hollywood's Golden Age at the American Film Institute.* New York: A. A. Knopf, 2006.

Stewart, Jeffrey C. "Audio commentary for *The Emperor Jones.*" In *Paul Robeson: Icon.* Criterion, 2007.

Stewart, Justin. "TCM Diary: The Wild Boys of Wellman." Film Comment, August 31, 2018. https://www.filmcomment.com/blog/tcm-diary-wild-boys-of-wellman/.

Sweeney, R. Emmet. "Rep Diary: I Am Suzanne!" *Film Comment*, October 22, 2013. https://www.filmcomment.com/blog/to-save-and-project-moma-i-am-suzanne/.

"Tarzan & His Mate (1934)." AFI. Accessed August 28, 2024. https://catalog.afi.com/Film/5873-TARZAN-ANDHISMATE?sid=60abb0ba-33c8-48b2-b727-d21752fd24aa&sr=14.518494&cp=1&pos=0.

Tatara, Paul. "Tarzan and His Mate." Turner Classic Movies, May 24, 2004. https://www.tcm.com/tcmdb/title/2958/tarzan-and-his-mate#articles-reviews?articleId=76281.

"Teatro Dei Piccoli." *World Encyclopedia of Puppetry Arts*, May 22, 2016. https://wepa.unima.org/en/teatro-dei-piccoli/.

Tinee, Mae. "'Safe in Hell' Well Acted as Talkie Thriller." *Chicago Daily Tribune.*

Tinee, Mae. "Three Use One Match—Result a Melodrama." *Chicago Daily Tribune,* November 22, 1932.

Valinoti, Raymond, Jr. *Hollywood's Pre-Code Horrors 1931–1934.* Orlando: BearManor Media, 2017.

Van de Water, Frederic F. "First Nights on Broadway with the New Pictures." *The New Movie Magazine,* June 1934.

Vieira, Mark A. *Forbidden Hollywood: The Pre-Code Era (1930–1934): When Sin Ruled the Movies.* Philadelphia: Running Press, 2019.

Vieira, Mark A. *Greta Garbo: A Cinematic Legacy.* New York: Harry N. Abrams, 2005.

Vieira, Mark A. *Irving Thalberg: Boy Wonder to Producer Prince.* Berkeley, CA: University of California Press, 2010.

Vieira, Mark A. *Sin in Soft Focus: Pre-Code Hollywood.* New York: Harry N. Abrams, 1999.

"VIRGINIA BRUCE, 72, ACTRESS PORTRAYED ZIEGFELD SHOWGIRL." *The New York Times,* February 26, 1982.

"Warners Has First 3 in Action Since June." *Variety,* September 15, 1931.

"Warners' 'Heat Lightning' Enjoyable Entertainment." *The Hollywood Reporter,* February 16, 1934.

Watz, Edward. *Wheeler & Woolsey: The Vaudeville Comic Duo and Their Films, 1929–1937.* Jefferson, NC: McFarland & Co., 2001.

"Way Out West." The Yale Puppeteers. The Turnabout Theatre. Accessed August 26, 2024. https://exhibits.lapl.org/lifeonastring/section-2/.

"WB Shutting Down 1st." *Variety,* June 9, 1931.

Weber, Eric. "Ladies They Talk About." Turner Classic Movies, June 19, 2006. https://www.tcm.com/tcmdb/title/2800/ladies-they-talk-about#articles-reviews?articleId=139173.

Weld, John. *September Song: An Intimate Biography of Walter Huston.* Lanham, MD: Scarecrow Press, 1998.

Wellman, William, Jr. *Wild Bill Wellman: Hollywood Rebel.* New York: Pantheon Books, 2015.

"What the Picture Did for Me." *Motion Picture Herald,* May 19, 1934.

"What to Do with 'Freaks'?" *Harrison's Reports,* April 9, 1932.

Whitaker, Alma. "'Emancipation' for Women Achieved by Films—And How!" *Los Angeles Times,* December 3, 1933.

White, Armond. *"Trouble in Paradise: Lovers, On the Money."* The Criterion Collection, January 6, 2003. https://www.criterion.com/current/posts/1073-trouble-in-paradise-lovers-on-the-money.

Williams, Whitney. "Three Girls Play Leads in Picture." *Los Angeles Times,* November 25, 1932.

Willis, Donald C. *The Films of Howard Hawks.* Metuchen, NJ: Scarecrow Press, 1975.

Wilson, Victoria. *A Life of Barbara Stanwyck: Steel-True 1907–1940.* New York: Simon & Schuster, 2013.

Wood, Bret. "Yea or Nay (Freaks)." Turner Classic Movies, October 26, 2006. https://www.tcm.com/tcmdb/title/163/freaks#articles-reviews?articleId=149028.

Wood, Bret. "In the Know (Freaks)." Turner Classic Movies, October 26, 2006. https://www.tcm.com/tcmdb/title/163/freaks#articles-reviews?articleId=149025.

Wood, Bret. "Insider Info (Freaks)." Turner Classic Movies, October 26, 2006. https://www.tcm.com/tcmdb/title/163/freaks#articles-reviews?articleId=149026.

Wood, Bret. "The Black Cat." Turner Classic Movies, September 26, 2003. https://www.tcm.com/tcmdb/title/68854/the-black-cat#articles-reviews?articleId=17869.

"Works on Adaptation." *Los Angeles Times,* August 30, 1926.

Wray, Fay. *On the Other Hand: A Life Story.* London: Weidenfeld & Nicolson, 1990.

"Yale Puppeteers." *World Encyclopedia of Puppetry Arts*, September 2, 2016. https://wepa.unima.org/en/yale-puppeteers/.

Index

Page numbers in italics indicate photographs.